INTERNATIONAL CONVEN'
THE ELIMINATION OF ALL
OF RACIAL DISCRIMINA'

# SELECTED DECISIONS OF THE COMMITTEE ON THE ELIMINATION OF RACIAL DISCRIMINATION

## Volume I

Thirty-sixth to seventy-fifth sessions
(August 1988 – August 2011)

**UNITED NATIONS**
**New York and Geneva, 2012**

**NOTE**

The designations employed and the presentation of the material in this publication do not imply the expression of any opinion whatsoever on the part of the Secretariat of the United Nations concerning the legal status of any country, territory, city or area, or of its authorities, or concerning the delimitation of its frontiers or boundaries.

\*

\* \*

Symbols of United Nations documents are composed of capital letters combined with figures. Mention of such a symbol indicates a reference to a United Nations document.

HR/CERD/PUB/1

| UNITED NATIONS PUBLICATION |
| --- |
| *Sales N° E.12.XIV.2* |
| ISBN-13: 978-92-1-154195-3 |
| e-ISBN-13: 978-92-1-055245-5 |

# Contents

# Introduction

Promoting and encouraging universal respect for and observance of human rights and fundamental freedoms for all, without distinction, exclusion, restriction or preference based on race, colour, descent, or national or ethnic origin is one of the main purposes of the United Nations. The adoption of the International Convention on the Elimination of All Forms of Racial Discrimination was an important step in the codification process to combat such discrimination. It constitutes the normative basis upon which international efforts to eliminate it should be built.

As at 20 January 2012, there were 175 State parties to the Convention, which was adopted by the General Assembly in resolution 2106 (XX) of 21 December 1965 and opened for signature and ratification in New York on 7 March 1966. The Convention entered into force on 4 January 1969 in accordance with the provisions of its article 19.

In accordance with its article 8, the Committee on the Elimination of Racial Discrimination was established to ensure that the Convention is observed and implemented. The Committee is composed of 18 independent experts of high moral standing and acknowledged impartiality. Members are elected for a term of four years and serve in their personal capacity. They may be re-elected if nominated.

The Committee convenes twice a year for three-week sessions. It elects a Chair, three Vice-Chairs and a Rapporteur from among its own members for a term of two years. These officers are eligible for re-election. The Committee's main activity is to monitor the implementation of the Convention by its State parties through periodic reporting. In addition to the reporting procedure, there are two other mechanisms through which the Committee performs its monitoring functions: the examination of inter-State communications and the examination of individual communications under article 14 of the Convention.

Under the individual communications procedure, individuals can, under certain circumstances, lodge complaints claiming that any of the rights set forth in the Convention have been violated. No communication can be received by the Committee if it concerns a State party to the Convention that has not recognized the competence of the Committee to receive and consider communications from individuals or group of individuals, under article 14. Such communications are considered in closed meetings and all documents pertaining to the work of the Committee under article 14 are confidential until a final decision has been made.

By 20 January 2012, the following 54 States had made the declaration under article 14:

Algeria, Andorra, Argentina, Australia, Austria, Azerbaijan, Belgium, Bolivia (Plurinational State of), Brazil, Bulgaria, Chile, Costa Rica, Cyprus, Czech Republic, Denmark, Ecuador, Estonia, Finland, France, Georgia, Germany, Hungary, Iceland, Ireland, Italy, Kazakhstan, Liechtenstein, Luxembourg, Malta, Mexico, Monaco, Montenegro, Morocco, Netherlands, Norway, Peru, Poland, Portugal, Republic of Korea, Romania, Russian Federation, San Marino, Senegal, Serbia, Slovakia, Slovenia, South Africa, Spain, Sweden, Switzerland, the former Yugoslav Republic of Macedonia, Ukraine, Uruguay, and Venezuela (Bolivarian Republic of).

Upon receiving a communication, the Committee transmits it to the State party concerned for observations relevant to the question of admissibility of the communication. Conditions for admissibility are specified in the Convention and in the Committee's rules of procedure (HRI/GEN/3/Rev.3), pursuant to which the Committee ascertains:

- That the communication is not anonymous and that it comes from an individual or group of individuals subject to the jurisdiction of a State party recognizing the competence of the Committee under article 14;

- That the individual claims to be a victim of a violation by the State party concerned of any of the rights set forth in the Convention. As a general rule, the communication should be submitted by the individual himself or by his relatives or designated representatives;

- That the communication is submitted to the Committee within six months after the exhaustion of domestic remedies;

- That the communication is compatible with the provisions of the Convention;

- That the communication is not an abuse of the right to submit a communication in conformity with article 14;
- That the individual has exhausted all available domestic remedies. However, this shall not be the rule where the application of the remedies is unreasonably prolonged.

The Committee may request the State party concerned or the author of the communication to submit additional written information or clarification relevant to the question of admissibility of the communication.

The Committee's usual course of action is to consider the admissibility and merits of the case simultaneously.

However, the Committee may examine the admissibility of the communication separately from its merits. If, in its decision on admissibility, the Committee decides that a communication is inadmissible, it will inform the State party concerned and the petitioner of its decision, setting out the reasons for declaring the communication inadmissible. An inadmissibility decision taken by the Committee in conformity with article 14, paragraph 7 (a), of the Convention (exhaustion of domestic remedies) may be reviewed at a later date by the Committee upon written request by the petitioner. If the Committee decides that a communication is admissible, the Committee will inform the State party and the petitioner of the communication of its decision. The State party concerned shall submit written observations regarding the merits of the communication to the Committee within three months. The petitioner will later be given the opportunity to comment on such observations.

In the course of its consideration, the Committee, pursuant to rule 94 of its rules of procedure, may inform the State party of its views on the desirability, because of urgency, of taking interim measures to prevent possible irreparable damage to the person or persons who claim to be victim(s) of the alleged violation. Such expression of its views on interim measures does not prejudge its final opinion on the merits of the communication or its eventual suggestions and recommendations.

In the light of all the information made available to it by the complainant and the State party concerned, the Committee considers the communication and formulates its opinion. The opinion is forwarded to the petitioner and to the State party, together with any suggestion and recommendations the Committee may wish to make. The State party concerned is invited to inform the Committee within six months of the action it takes in conformity with the Committee's suggestions and recommendations.

The Committee includes the communications examined and its suggestions and recommendations in its annual report.

By the end of its 79th session, the Committee had adopted 44 decisions. Since 1984 up to the end of its 79th session, the Committee had registered a total of 48 complaints. Of those, 1 complaint was discontinued and 17 were declared inadmissible. The Committee adopted opinions (decisions on the merits) on 27 complaints and found violations of the Convention in 11 of them. Three complaints were pending for consideration and decision.

This first volume of selected decisions of the Committee on the Elimination of Racial Discrimination presents 32 of the most significant decisions on admissibility only, as well as on both admissibility and merits, addressing the issue of racial discrimination in relation to civil and political rights and to economic, social and cultural rights.

Throughout its existence, the Committee has established and developed its own jurisprudence on the admissibility criteria under the Convention, including the notion of exhaustion of domestic remedies, the six-month rule under article 14, paragraph 5, of the Convention, the issue of victim status and the Committee's competence *ratione materiae*. In its opinions, the Committee has addressed a variety of issues such as the use of offensive and discriminatory statements or demonstrations in public or in the media, access to any place or service intended for use by the general public, indirect discrimination or access to education.

The indexes by article of the Convention, by subject, and by author and victim aim at facilitating the reader's access to the relevant jurisprudence.

# I. Opinions under article 14 of the Convention

## Communication No. 1/1984

*Submitted by*: A. Yilmaz-Dogan (represented by counsel, H.F. Doeleman).
*Alleged victim*: The petitioner.
*State party*: Netherlands.
*Date of adoption of Opinion:* 10 August 1988.
*Subject matter:* Termination of employment contract during pregnancy; statements of discriminatory character made by employer; access to effective mechanisms of protection; discrimination based on national origin.
*Procedural issues:* Inadmissibility *ratione materiae.*
*Substantive issues:* Right to work, to free choice of employment, to just and favourable conditions of work, to protection against unemployment, to equal pay for equal work, to just and favourable remuneration; right to an effective remedy against acts of racial discrimination.
*Articles of the Convention:* 4 (a), 5 (e) (i) and 6.
*Finding*: Violation (art. 5 (e) (i)).

*Opinion*

1. The communication (initial letter dated 28 May 1984, further letters dated 23 October 1984, 5 February 1986 and 14 September 1987) placed before the Committee on the Elimination of Racial Discrimination by H.F. Doeleman, a Netherlands lawyer practising in Amsterdam. He submits the communication on behalf of Mrs. A. Yilmaz-Dogan, a Turkish national residing in the Netherlands, who claims to be the victim of a violation of articles 4 (a), 5 (e) (i) and 6 of the International Convention on the Elimination of All Forms of Racial Discrimination by the Netherlands.

2.1 The petitioner states that she had been employed, since 1979, by a firm operating in the textile sector. On 3 April 1981, she was injured in a traffic accident and placed on sick leave. Allegedly as a result of the accident, she was unable to carry out her work for a long time; it was not until 1982 that she resumed part-time duty of her own accord. Meanwhile, in August 1981, she married Mr. Yilmaz.

2.2 By a letter dated 22 June 1982, her employer requested permission from the District Labour Exchange in Apeldoorn to terminate her contract. Mrs. Yilmaz was pregnant at that time. On 14 July 1982, the Director of the Labour Exchange refused to terminate the contract on the basis of article 1639h (4) of the Civil Code, which stipulates that employment contracts may not be terminated during the pregnancy of the employee. He pointed, however, to the possibility of submitting a request to the competent Cantonal Court. On 19 July 1982, the employer addressed the request for termination of the contract to the Cantonal Court in Apeldoorn. The request included the following passage: [...]

> "When a Netherlands girl marries and has a baby, she stops working. Our foreign women workers, on the other hand, take the child to neighbours or family and at the slightest setback disappear on sick leave under the terms of the Sickness Act. They repeat that endlessly. Since we all must do our utmost to avoid going under, we cannot afford such goings-on."

After hearing the request on 10 August and 15 September 1982, the Cantonal Court agreed, by a decision of 29 September 1982, to terminate the employment contract with effect from 1 December 1982. Article 1639w (former numbering) of the Civil Code excludes the possibility of an appeal against a decision of the Cantonal Court.

2.3 On 21 October 1982, Mrs. Yilmaz requested the Prosecutor at the Supreme Court to seek annulment of the decision of the Cantonal Court in the interest of the law. By a letter of 26 October, she was informed that the Prosecutor saw no justification for proceeding in that way. Convinced that the employer's observations of 19 July 1982 constituted offences under the Netherlands Penal Code, Mrs. Yilmaz, on 21 October 1982, requested the Prosecutor at the District Court at Zutphen to prosecute her employer. On 16 February 1983, the Prosecutor replied that he did not consider the initiation of penal proceedings to be opportune. The petitioner further applied to the Minister of Justice, asking him to order the Prosecutor at Zutphen to initiate such proceedings. The Minister, however, replied on 9 June 1983 that he saw no reason to intervene, since recourse had not yet been had to the complaint procedure pursuant to article 12 of the Code of Penal Procedure, which provided for the possibility of submitting a request to the Court of Appeal to order prosecution of a criminal offence. In conformity with the Minister's advice, Mrs. Yilmaz, on 13 July 1983, requested the Court of Appeal at Arnhem, under article 12 of the Code of Penal Procedure, to order the prosecution of her employer. On 30 November 1983, the Court of Appeal rejected the petition, stating, inter alia, that it could not be determined that the defendant, by raising the issue of differences in absenteeism owing to childbirth and illness between foreign and Netherlands women workers, intended to discriminate by race, or that his actions resulted in race discrimination. While dismissing the employer's remarks in the letter of 19 July 1982 as "unfortunate and objectionable", the Court considered "that the institution of criminal proceedings [was] not in the public interest or in the interest of the petitioner". The Court's decision taken pursuant to article 12 of the Code of Penal Procedure cannot be appealed before the Supreme Court.

2.4 Petitioner's counsel concludes that the Netherlands violated article 5 (e) (i) of the Convention, because the alleged victim was not guaranteed the right to gainful work and protection against unemployment, which is said to be reflected in the fact that both the Director of the Labour Exchange and the Cantonal Court endorsed the termination of her employment contract on the basis of reasons which must be considered as racially discriminatory. Secondly, he claims that the Netherlands violated article 6 of the Convention since it failed to provide adequate protection as well as legal remedies because Mrs. Yilmaz was unable to have the discriminatory termination of her contract reviewed by a higher court. Thirdly, it is alleged that the Netherlands violated article 4 of the Convention because it did not order the Prosecutor to proceed against the employer on the basis of either article 429 quater or article 137c to article 137e of the Netherlands Penal Code, provisions incorporated in that Code in the light of the undertaking, under article 4 of the Convention, to take action to eliminate manifestations of racial discrimination. Finally, it is argued that article 6 of the Convention was violated because the State party denied the petitioner due process by virtue of article 12 of the Code of Penal Procedure, when she unsuccessfully petitioned for penal prosecution of the discrimination of which she claims to have been the victim.

3. At its thirty-first session in March 1985, the Committee on the Elimination of Racial Discrimination decided to transmit the communication, under rule 92, paragraphs 1 and 3, of its rules of procedure, to the State party, requesting information and observations relevant to the question of the admissibility of the communication.

4.1 By submissions dated 17 June and 19 November 1985, the State party objects to the admissibility of the communication. It affirms that the Committee is entitled, under its rules of procedure, to examine whether a prima facie consideration of the facts and the relevant legislation reveals that the communication is incompatible with the Convention. For the reasons set out below, it considers the communication to be incompatible *ratione materiae* with the Convention and therefore inadmissible.

4.2 The State party denies that either the Director of the Labour Exchange or the Cantonal Court in Apeldoorn violated any of the rights guaranteed by article 5 (e) (i) of the Convention and argues that it met its obligation under that provision to guarantee equality before the law in the enjoyment of the right to employment by providing non-discriminatory remedies. With respect to the content of the letter of Mrs. Yilmaz's employer dated 19 July 1982, the State party points out that the decision of the Cantonal Court does not, in any way, justify the conclusion that the court accepted the reasons put forth by the employer. In reaching its decision to dissolve the contract between the petitioner and her employer, the Court merely considered the case in the light of the relevant rules of civil law and civil procedure; it refrained from referring to the petitioner's national or ethnic origin.

4.3 With respect to the petitioner's argument that the State party should have provided for a more adequate mechanism of judicial review and appeal against Cantonal Court judgements related to the termination of employment contracts, the State party points out that the relevant domestic procedures, which were followed in the present case, provide adequate protection and legal remedies within the meaning of article 6 of the Convention. Article 6 does not include an obligation for States parties to institute appeal or other review mechanisms against judgements of the competent judicial authority.

4.4 With respect to the allegation that the State party violated articles 4 and 6 of the Convention by failing to order the Prosecutor to prosecute the employer, the State party argues that the obligation arising from article 4 of the Convention was met by incorporating in the Penal Code articles 137c to e and articles 429 ter and quater and penalizing any of the actions referred to in these provisions. Article 4 cannot be read as obligating States parties to institute criminal proceedings under all circumstances with respect to actions which appear to be covered by the terms of the article. Concerning the alleged violation of article 6, it is indicated that there is a remedy against a decision not to prosecute: the procedure pursuant to article 12 of the Code of Criminal Procedure. The State party recalls that the petitioner indeed availed herself of this remedy, although the Court of Appeal did not find in her favour. It further observes that the assessment made by the Court of Appeal before deciding to dismiss her petition was a thorough one. Thus, the discretion of the court was not confined to determining whether the Prosecutor's decision not to institute criminal proceedings against the employer was a justifiable one; it was also able to weigh the fact that it is the Minister of Justice's policy to ensure that criminal proceedings are brought in as many cases as possible where racial discrimination appears to be at issue.

5.1 Commenting on the State party's submission, petitioner's counsel, in a submission dated 5 February 1986, denies that the communication should be declared inadmissible as incompatible *ratione materiae* with the provisions of the Convention and maintains that his allegations are well founded.

5.2 In substantiation of his initial claim, it is argued, in particular, that the Netherlands did not meet its obligations under the Convention by merely incorporating into its Penal Code provisions such as articles 137c to e and 429 ter and quater. He affirms that, by ratifying the Convention, the State party curtailed its freedom of action. In his opinion, this means that a State cannot simply invoke the expediency principle which, under domestic law, leaves it free to prosecute or not; rather, it requires the Netherlands actively to prosecute offenders against sections 137c and e and 429 ter and quater unless there are grave objections to doing so.

5.3 Furthermore, petitioner's counsel maintains that in the decision of the Court of Appeal of 30 November 1983, the causal relationship between the alleged victim's dismissal and the different rate of absenteeism among foreign and Netherlands women workers, as alleged by the employer, is clear. On the basis of the Convention, it is argued, the Court should have dissociated itself from the discriminatory reasons for termination of the employment contract put forth by the employer.

6. On 19 March 1987, the Committee, noting that the State party's observations concerning the admissibility of the communication essentially concerned the interpretation of the meaning and scope of the provisions of the Convention and having further ascertained that the communication met the admissibility criteria set out in article 14 of the Convention, declared the communication admissible. It further requested the State party to inform the Committee as early as possible, should it not intend to make a further submission on the merits, so as to allow it to deal expeditiously with the matter.

7. In a further submission dated 7 July 1987, the State party maintains that no violation of the Convention can be deemed to have taken place in the case of Mrs. Yilmaz. It argues that the alleged victim's claim that, in cases involving alleged racial discrimination, the

weighing by the judge of the parties' submissions has to meet especially severe criteria, rests on personal convictions rather than legal requirements. The requirement in civil law disputes are simply that the judge has to pronounce himself on the parties' submissions inasmuch as they are relevant to the dispute. The State party further refutes the allegation that the terms of the Convention require the establishment of appeal procedures. In this respect, it emphasizes that criminal law, by its nature, is mainly concerned with the protection of the public interest. Article 12 of the Code of Criminal Procedure gives individuals who have a legitimate interest in prosecution of an offence the right to lodge a complaint with the Court of Appeal against the failure of the authorities to prosecute. This procedure guarantees the proper administration of criminal law, but it does not offer the victims an enforceable right to see alleged offenders prosecuted. This, however, cannot be said to constitute a violation of the Convention.

8.1 Commenting on the State party's submission, petitioner's counsel, in a submission dated 14 September 1987, reiterates that the State party violated article 5 (e) (i) in that the cantonal judge failed to protect the petitioner against unemployment, although the request for her dismissal was, allegedly, based on racially discriminatory grounds. He asserts that, even if the correspondence between the Director of the Labour Exchange and the employer did not refer to the national or ethnic origin of the alleged victim, her own family name and that of her husband must have made it clear to all the authorities involved that she was of Turkish origin.

8.2 With respect to the State party's argument that its legislation provides for adequate protection—procedural and substantive—in cases of alleged racial discrimination, it is claimed that domestic law cannot serve as a guideline in this matter. The expediency principle, i.e., the freedom to prosecute, as laid down in Netherlands law, has to be applied in the light of the provisions of the Convention with regard to legal protection in cases of alleged racial discrimination.

9.1 The Committee on the Elimination of Racial Discrimination has considered the present communication in the light of all the information made available to it by the parties, as required under article 14, paragraph 7 (a),

of the Convention and rule 95 of its rules of procedure, and bases its opinion on the following considerations.

9.2 The main issues before the Committee are (a) whether the State party failed to meet its obligation, under article 5 (e) (i), to guarantee equality before the law in respect of the right to work and protection against unemployment, and (b) whether articles 4 and 6 impose on States parties an obligation to initiate criminal proceedings in cases of alleged racial discrimination and to provide for an appeal mechanism in cases of such discrimination.

9.3 With respect to the alleged violation of article 5 (e) (i), the Committee notes that the final decision as to the dismissal of the petitioner was the decision of the Sub-District Court of 29 September 1982, which was based on article 1639w (2) of the Netherlands Civil Code. The Committee notes that this decision does not address the alleged discrimination in the employer's letter of 19 July 1982, which requested the termination of the petitioner's employment contract. After careful examination, the Committee considers that the petitioner's dismissal was the result of a failure to take into account all the circumstances of the case. Consequently, her right to work under article 5 (e) (i) was not protected.

9.4 Concerning the alleged violation of articles 4 and 6, the Committee has noted the petitioner's claim that these provisions require the State party actively to prosecute cases of alleged racial discrimination and to provide victims of such discrimination with the opportunity of judicial review of a judgement in their case. The Committee observes that the freedom to prosecute criminal offences— commonly known as the expediency principle—is governed by considerations of public policy and notes that the Convention cannot be interpreted as challenging the raison d'être of that principle. Notwithstanding, it should be applied in each case of alleged racial discrimination, in the light of the guarantees laid down in the Convention. In the case of Mrs. Yilmaz-Dogan, the Committee concludes that the prosecutor acted in accordance with these criteria. Furthermore, the State party has shown that the application of the expediency principle is subject to, and has indeed in the present case been subjected to, judicial review, since a decision *not* to prosecute may be, and was reviewed in this case, by the Court of Appeal, pursuant to article 12 of the Netherlands Code of Criminal

Procedure. In the Committee's opinion, this mechanism of judicial review is compatible with article 4 of the Convention; contrary to the petitioner's affirmation, it does not render meaningless the protection afforded by sections 137c to e and 429 ter and quater of the Netherlands Penal Code. Concerning the petitioner's inability to have the Sub-District Court's decision pronouncing the termination of her employment contract reviewed by a higher tribunal, the Committee observes that the terms of article 6 do not impose upon States parties the duty to institute a mechanism of sequential remedies, up to and including the Supreme Court level, in cases of alleged racial discrimination.

10. The Committee on the Elimination of Racial Discrimination, acting under article 14, paragraph 7, of the Convention, is of the opinion that the information as submitted by the parties sustains the claim that the petitioner was not afforded protection in respect of her right to work. The Committee suggests that the State party take this into account and recommends that it ascertain whether Mrs. Yilmaz-Dogan is now gainfully employed and, if not, that it use its good offices to secure alternative employment for her and/or to provide her with such other relief as may be considered equitable.

# Communication No. 2/1989

*Submitted by*: G.A.C. Enkelaar (counsel).
*Alleged victim*: Demba Talibe Diop.
*State party*: France.
*Date of adoption of Opinion:* 18 March 1991.
*Subject matter:* Rejection of the author's application for membership in the Bar Association; discrimination based on national origin.
*Procedural issues:* Exhaustion of domestic remedies; inadmissibility *ratione materiae*.
*Substantive issues:* Right to work, to free choice of employment, to just and favourable conditions of work, to protection against unemployment, to equal pay for equal work, to just and favourable remuneration.
*Articles of the Convention:* 1 (1), 5 (e) (i) and 14 (7) (a).
*Finding*: No violation.

*Opinion*

1.    The author of the communication (initial submission dated 15 March 1989 and subsequent correspondence) is Demba Talibe Diop, a Senegalese citizen born in 1950, currently residing in Monaco. He claims to be the victim of a violation by France of article 5 of the International Convention on the Elimination of All Forms of Racial Discrimination. He is represented by counsel, who has provided a copy of his power of attorney.

*The facts as submitted*

2.1  The author, who is married to a French citizen and has one child, has been domiciled in Monaco since December 1985. From July 1982 to December 1985, he practised law in

Dakar. On 30 January 1986, the author formally applied for membership in the Bar of Nice, submitting all the documentary evidence required. On 5 May 1986, the Bar Council of Nice rejected his application; on 8 May 1986, the competent authorities in Nice delivered his resident's permit (*visa d'établissement*). On 30 May 1986, Mr. Diop appealed the decision of the Bar Council to the Court of Appeal of Aix-en-Province. By judgement of 27 October 1986, the Court of Appeal dismissed the appeal; a subsequent appeal to the Court of Cassation was dismissed on 4 October 1988.

2.2  The decision of the Bar Council of Nice was based on the fact that Mr. Diop did not hold the Certificate of Aptitude for the Exercise of the Legal Profession (CAPA), as required by article 11 of Act No. 71.1130 of 31 December 1971; the Court of Appeal upheld the decision on the same grounds. The Court of Cassation, however, found that the Court of Appeal had erroneously interpreted the text on waiver of the CAPA requirement, and that it had "substituted purely juridical considerations for those that were justifiably criticized in the first of the grounds of appeal". The Court of Cassation found that the author met all the statutory requirements for the exercise of the lawyers' profession except one: the French nationality. The author points out that the Bar Council of Nice had not referred to his Senegalese nationality as an obstacle to his exercising the legal profession in France.

2.3 Article 11, paragraph 1, of Act No. 71.1130 of 31 December 1971 stipulates that "no one may enter the legal profession if he is not French, except as provided for in international Conventions". The author argues that his case falls within the scope of application of the Franco-Senegalese Convention on Establishment (*Convention d'établissement franco-sénégalaise*) of 29 March 1974, article 1 of which prohibits discrimination between French and Senegalese citizens in the enjoyment of civil liberties to which they are entitled on the same terms (including the right to work, set forth in the preamble of the French Constitution of 4 October 1958). In the light of this provision, according to the author, the Court of Cassation should not have considered Senegalese citizenship as an impediment to the exercise of the legal profession in France. He further indicates that the legal profession does not fall within the occupational categories to which the restrictions of article 5 of the Convention apply, and no other Convention provision expressly prohibits the free exercise of the legal profession.

2.4 Article 9 of the Franco-Senegalese Convention on Movement of Persons (*Convention franco-sénégalaise relative à la circulation des personnes*) of 29 March 1974 stipulates that "French nationals wishing to *establish themselves in Senegal and Senegalese nationals wishing to establish themselves in France for the purpose of engaging in self-employed activities*, or without engaging in any gainful occupation, must ... produce the required evidence of the means of subsistence available to them" (emphasis added). The author states that the legal profession is considered in France to be the epitome of self-employed activity; this is confirmed by article 7, paragraph 1, of Act No. 71.1130.

2.5 Article 23 of the Franco-Senegalese Tax Convention (*Convention fiscale franco-sénégalaise*) of 29 March 1974 provides that "[T]he income that a person domiciled in a Contracting State draws from a liberal profession or similar independent activity shall be subject to tax in that State alone, unless that person is regularly possessed of a fixed base for the exercise of his profession in the other Contracting State ... For the purposes of the present article, scientific, artistic, literary, educational and pedagogical activities, inter alia, as well as the activities of doctors, *advocates*, architects and engineers, are considered liberal professions" (emphasis added).

2.6 The author further notes that, on 12 February 1990, he requested that his name be added to the list of legal counsel (*conseils juridiques*), as French nationality is no prerequisite for the practice as legal counsel. By letter dated 24 April 1990, he was informed that his inscription was imminent. On 26 June 1990, however, he was told that his request could not be complied with, as he had not demonstrated that he had fulfilled the requirement of a three-year apprenticeship (*stage*); the author affirms that his application had been complete and included, in particular, proof of such an apprenticeship.

*The complaint*

3.1 The author considers that he was denied the right to work on the ground of national origin, and alleges that the French judicial authorities violated the principle of equality, enshrined in article 5 of the International Convention on the Elimination of All Forms of Racial Discrimination. Allegedly, his right to equal treatment before the tribunals was violated in two respects: First, whereas he was denied to practise law in Nice, six lawyers of Senegalese nationality are members of the Paris Bar. According to the author, his application would have been granted had he submitted it in Paris; he considers it unacceptable that the State party should allow such differences within the national territory. Secondly, it is submitted that the principle of equality and reciprocity at the international level is also affected by virtue of the fact that on the basis of the above-mentioned bilateral instruments, all French lawyers have the right to exercise their profession in Senegal and vice versa.

3.2 Distinctions, exclusions, restrictions or preferences established in the application of the International Convention on the Elimination of All Forms of Racial Discrimination must be spelled out in legislative provisions which, the author claims, do not exist in his case. Such distinctions would contravene article 34 of the French Constitution. Furthermore, even if there were pertinent domestic legislation, the bilateral Franco-Senegalese Conventions of 29 March 1974 prevail over domestic legislation and authorize French and Senegalese citizens to exercise a liberal profession, including the legal one, on the territory of the State of which they do not have the citizenship.

3.3 The author claims that existing Senegalese legislation (Law on the Exercise of the Legal Profession of 1984) does not prohibit legal practice by French citizens in Senegal. In this context, he notes that on 8 January 1985, Ms. Geneviève Lenoble, a French citizen and member of the Paris Bar, was admitted to the Bar of Senegal; so was, on 7 January 1987, another French citizen, Ms. Dominique Picard. On the other hand, the Governing Body of the Bar Council of Nice required, for Mr. Diop's inscription on the roll, the Certificate of Aptitude for the Exercise of the Legal Profession (CAPA), although article 44 of the decree of 9 June 1972, concerning the application of article 11, paragraph 3, of the Law of 31 December 1971 stipulates that this Certificate is not necessary for individuals who already are qualified to practise law in a country with which France concluded an agreement of judicial cooperation.

3.4 It is submitted that the State party violated the author's right to a family life because, in the light of the impossibility to practise law in Nice, the author was forced to temporarily leave his home and take up residence and practise law in Dakar, so as to be able to provide for his family.

3.5 The author claims that the decision of the Bar Council of Nice of 5 May 1986, confirmed by the Court of Appeal on 27 October 1986, is irreconcilable with the judgement of the Court of Cassation of 4 October 1988. The Court of Cassation did not annul the decision of the Bar Council as contrary to the law in criticizing its motivation; it simply substituted its own motives in dismissing the appeal. In the author's opinion, the irreconcilability of the judicial decisions in the case is equivalent, in law, to a refusal to adjudicate his request for admission to the bar altogether, thus denying him an effective remedy before domestic courts. In this way, it is submitted, he was denied the exercise of a fundamental public freedom, that is, his right to work in France.

*The State party's observations*

4.1 The State party contends that the author has failed to raise, before the domestic courts, the issue of discriminatory treatment of which he claims to have been the victim; accordingly, his communication should be declared inadmissible because of non-exhaustion of domestic remedies, under article 14, paragraph 7 (a), of the Convention.

4.2 The State party further observes that the communication is inadmissible as incompatible with the provisions of the Convention in accordance with article 1, paragraph 2, which stipulates that the "Convention shall not apply to distinctions, exclusions, restrictions or preferences made by a State party to this Convention between citizens and non-citizens". In Mr. Diop's case, the rejection of his application by the Bar Council of Nice was exclusively based on his nationality, not because he was Senegalese but because he was *not* French within the meaning of article 1, paragraph 2. The State party adds that the *ratio legis* of article 11, paragraph 1, of Act No. 71.1130 of 31 December 1971 is to protect French lawyers from foreign competition. In so doing, France exercises her sovereign prerogatives expressly recognized by article 1, paragraph 2, of the Convention.

4.3 With respect to the contention that the author meets all the requirements for the exercise of the legal profession in France, the State party claims that, for the Court of Cassation, the fact that the author was not of French nationality was in itself sufficient to dismiss the appeal, thus making it superfluous to consider whether other conditions for the exercise of the legal profession in France had or had not been met. The State party endorses the interpretation of article 1 of the Franco-Senegalese Convention on Establishment by the Court of Cassation, according to which this provision merely concerns the enjoyment of civil liberties and cannot be construed as encompassing a right to exercise the legal profession. For the State party, the author's argument that the right to work is a civil liberty and that, since the legal profession is gainful occupation it is a civil liberty, is a mere "sophism" and must be rejected.

4.4 The State party further explains the organization and the functions of the system of Bar Councils attached to each regional court (*Tribunal de Grande Instance*). These Bar Councils are administered by a Governing Board (*Conseil de l'Ordre*), enjoy legal personality and operate independently of one another. It is the duty of the Governing Board of each Bar Council to decide on applications for admission to the Bar; decisions on such matters by the Board may only be appealed by the applicant and the Public Prosecutor (*Procureur général*) of the competent Court of Appeal, within two months of the notification of the decision. The State party adds that each Governing Body decides independently on applications for admission to the Bar and may, in the process, err in its interpretation of applicable legal provisions.

4.5 Inasmuch as the admission of six Senegalese lawyers to the Bar of Paris is concerned, the State party submits that the Governing Body of the Bar of Paris erroneously interpreted applicable regulations by admitting these Senegalese citizens. The State party affirms that this situation does not create any rights for the author, nor a legal basis on which the inscription of every Senegalese lawyer on the Bar Roll could be justified, as any such act would violate the applicable rules and regulations. Furthermore, these lawyers were admitted prior to the Court of Cassation's judgement in the author's case; if this jurisprudence were to be invoked before the ordinary tribunals, it is likely, according to the State party, that these lawyers would have to be stripped of membership.

4.6 With respect to the treatment of French lawyers by the Senegalese judicial authorities, the State party explains that article 16 of a Senegalese Law on the Exercise of the Legal Profession of 1984 stipulates that no one may be admitted to the Bar in Senegal if he is not Senegalese or the citizen of a State that grants reciprocity. In application of this provision, the Bar Council of Dakar rejected, on 14 March 1988, the application of a French lawyer admitted to the Bar of Senegal on a probationary basis in 1984. The decision of the Bar Council of Dakar was based on the fact that the applicant was not Senegalese and that no international Convention or other applicable provision provided for reciprocity in the matter. The Court of Appeal of Dakar confirmed this decision by judgement of 15 April 1989. During the appeal proceedings, it was submitted on behalf of the Bar Council that the Franco-

Senegalese Convention on Establishment of 1974 did *not* provide for reciprocity with respect to liberal professions. In his pleadings, the Public Prosecutor, who had himself participated in the elaboration of the 1974 Convention, contended that the omission of liberal professions had been deliberate; the State party notes that one of the Convention's aims purportedly was to forestall the admission of French lawyers to the Bar of Senegal. The State party concludes that Mr. Diop's situation in France is similar to that of French lawyers wishing to practise in Senegal and that, accordingly, the principle of equality of treatment and of reciprocity invoked by him may be applied to his disadvantage.

*Issues and proceedings before the Committee*

5.1 Before considering any claims contained in a communication, the Committee on the Elimination of Racial Discrimination must, in accordance with rule 91 of its rules of procedure, determine whether or not it is admissible under the International Convention on the Elimination of All Forms of Racial Discrimination.

5.2 The Committee took note of the State party's observation that the communication was inadmissible on the ground of non-exhaustion of domestic remedies, since the author had not invoked discriminatory treatment based on national origin before the domestic courts. The Committee noted, however, that on the basis of the information before it, the issue of the author's national origin was first addressed by the court of last instance, the Court of Cassation, in its decision of 4 October 1988. Furthermore, the State party had not indicated the availability of any other remedies to the author. In the circumstances, the Committee concluded that the requirements of article 14, paragraph 7 (a), of the Convention and of rule 91 (e) of the Committee's rules of procedure, had been met.

5.3 In respect of the State party's observation "that the communication should be declared inadmissible as not falling within the scope of the Convention in the light of article 1, paragraph 2", the Committee observed that the question of the application of this article was one of substance which should be examined at a later stage, in conformity with rule 95 of the rules of procedure. The Committee further observed that rule 91 (c) of the rules of procedure enjoined it to ascertain whether any communication is compatible with the provisions of the Convention, and that "compatibility" within the meaning of rule 91 (c) must be understood in procedural, not substantive, terms. In the Committee's opinion, the communication did not suffer from procedural incompatibility.

5.4 On 22 August 1990, therefore, the Committee on the Elimination of Racial Discrimination declared the communication admissible.

6.1 The Committee on the Elimination of Racial Discrimination has examined the present communication in the light of all the information made available by the parties, as provided for in rule 95, paragraph 1, of its rules of procedure.

6.2 The Committee has noted the author's claims (a) that he was discriminated against on one of the grounds defined in article 1, paragraph 1, of the Convention on the Elimination of All Forms of Racial Discrimination, (b) that the rejection of his application for admission to the Bar of Nice constituted a violation of his right to work (art. 5 (e) of the Convention) and his right to a family life, and (c) that the rejection of his application violated the Franco-Senegalese Convention on Movement of Persons. After careful examination of the material placed before it, the Committee bases its decision on the following considerations.

6.3 In respect of the alleged violations of the Franco-Senegalese Convention on Freedom of Movement of 29 March 1974, the Committee observes that it is not within its mandate to interpret or monitor the application of bilateral conventions concluded between States parties to the Convention, unless it can be ascertained that the application of these conventions result in manifestly discriminatory or arbitrary treatment of individuals under the jurisdiction of States parties to the International Convention on the Elimination of All Forms of Racial Discrimination, which have made the declaration under article 14. The Committee has no evidence that the application or non-application of the Franco-Senegalese Conventions of March 1974 has resulted in manifest discrimination.

6.4 As to the alleged violation of article 5 (e) of the Convention and of the right to a family life, the Committee notes that the rights protected by article 5 (e) are of programmatic character, subject to progressive implementation. It is not within the Committee's mandate to see to it that these rights are established; rather, it is the Committee's task to monitor the implementation of these rights, once they have been granted on equal terms. Insofar as the author's complaint is based on article 5 (e) of the Convention, the Committee considers it to be ill-founded.

6.5 Finally, inasmuch as the allegation of racial discrimination within the meaning of article 1, paragraph 1, of the Convention is concerned, the Committee notes that article 11, paragraph 1, of the French Act No. 71.1130 of 31 December 1971 stipulates that no one may accede to the legal profession if he is not French, except as provided for in international conventions.

6.6 This provision operates as a preference or distinction between citizens and non-citizens within the meaning of article 1, paragraph 2, of the Convention: the refusal to admit Mr. Diop to the Bar was based on the fact that he was not of French nationality, not on any of the grounds enumerated in article 1, paragraph 1. The author's allegation relates to a situation in which the right to practise law exists only for French nationals, not to a situation in which this right has been granted in principle and may be generally invoked; accordingly, the Committee concludes that article 1, paragraph 1, has not been violated.

7. The Committee on the Elimination of Racial Discrimination, acting under article 14, paragraph 7 (a), of the International Convention on the Elimination of All Forms of Racial Discrimination, is of the opinion that the facts as submitted do not disclose a violation of any of the provisions of the Convention.

# Communication No. 3/1991

*Submitted by*: Michel L.N. Narrainen (represented by counsel).
*Alleged victim*: The petitioner.
*State party*: Norway.
*Date of adoption of Opinion:* 15 March 1994.
*Subject matter:* Discrimination at court; partial investigation and partial judgement; discrimination based on national origin.
*Procedural issues:* Substantiation for purposes of admissibility.
*Substantive issues:* Right to equal treatment before the tribunals and all other organs administering justice.
*Article of the Convention:* 5 (a).
*Finding*: No violation.

*Opinion*

1.    The author of the communication (initial submission dated 15 August 1991) is Michel L.N. Narrainen, a Norwegian citizen born in 1942, currently detained in a penitentiary in Oslo. He claims to be a victim of violations by Norway of his rights under the International Convention on the Elimination of All Forms of Racial Discrimination, but does not invoke specific provisions of the Convention.

*The facts as found by the Committee*

2.1   The author is of Tamil origin and was born in Mauritius; in 1972, he was naturalized and became a Norwegian citizen. On 25 January 1990, he was arrested in connection with a drug-related offence. On 8 February 1991, before the Eidsivating High Court (Court of Appeal—"Lagmannsretten"), a jury of 10 found him guilty of offences against section 162 of the Criminal Code (drug trafficking), and the author was sentenced to six and a half years of imprisonment. The author appealed to the Supreme Court, but leave to appeal was denied in early March 1991. On 17 February 1992, the author filed a petition for re-opening of the case. By order of 8 July 1992, the Court of Appeal refused the request. The author again appealed the order to the Supreme Court which, on 24 September 1992, ruled that the case was not to be reopened.

2.2   The author contends that there was no case against him, except for the evidence given by another individual, S.B., already convicted of drug-related offences, who allegedly had been promised a reduction of his sentence in exchange for providing incriminating evidence against the author. In

court, S.B. withdrew these allegations. In the same context, the author complains about the allegedly "racist" attitude of the investigating police officer, S.A., who reportedly made it clear that he "wished that people like me had never set foot in his country" (author's quote).

2.3   The author contends that under the terms of the initial indictment, he was accused of having travelled to the Netherlands in the early summer of 1989 to buy amphetamines. When he was able to produce evidence that, at the time in question, he was in Mauritius, the initial indictment allegedly was changed in court, after his own legal representative had contacted the prosecution and asked for the indictment to be changed. The author adds that it was impossible for him to have had any contacts with S.B. or his friends prior to or during the trial.

2.4   The author further contends that two jurors in the Court of Appeal were biased against him and that they openly stated that individuals such as the author, who lived on taxpayers' money, should be sent back to where they had come from. The remarks allegedly included slurs on the colour of the author's skin. Yet these jurors, although challenged, were not disqualified by the Court and participated in the deliberations of the verdict.

2.5   The State party gives the following version of the incident referred to by the author (see para. 2.4):

   "The Court record shows that during a break in the court proceedings, a law student, Ms. S.R.H., overheard a private conversation between two members of the jury, Ms. A.M.J. and Ms. S.M.M. This conversation was referred to defence counsel, who requested that one of the jurors be dismissed. The court called the law student and the two jurors to testify. [They] agreed on the facts: Ms. J. had expressed dismay at the defendant receiving NKr 9,000 a month without having to work for it, and had also said that he ought to be sent back to where he came from. Ms. M. had said that the purpose of a case like this was to get more information about the drug trafficking. The law student, Ms. H., had at this point entered the conversation, saying that the purpose of a case like this was to determine whether the defendant was guilty. According to the three witnesses, the question of guilt had otherwise not been mentioned by any of them.

Defence counsel requested that Ms. J. be dismissed from the jury because, according to section 108 of the Courts' Act, a juror could be disqualified if there are circumstances ... apt to impair confidence in his or her impartiality. The Prosecutor claimed that nothing had been said that could influence the members of the jury, and that everyone was entitled to have opinions. Discussing private opinions during a break [was] no ground for disqualification, and the case itself had not been discussed by the three persons.

The Court unanimously decided that Ms. J. should not be disqualified because she had not discussed the question of guilt in the present case, and the views she had expressed were not uncommon in Norwegian society."

*The complaint*

3.1 The author claims that racist considerations played a significant part in his conviction, as the evidence against him would not have supported a guilty verdict. He adds that he could not have expected to obtain a fair and impartial trial, as "all members of the jury came from a certain part of Oslo where racism is at its peak". He asserts that this situation violated his rights under the International Convention on the Elimination of All Forms of Racial Discrimination.

3.2 The author claims that other factors should be taken into consideration in assessing whether he was the victim of racial discrimination. In this context he mentions the amount of time spent in custody prior to the

trial (381 days), out of which a total of nine months were allegedly spent in isolation, and the quality of his legal representation: thus, although he was assigned legal counsel free of charge, his representative "was more of a prosecutor than a lawyer of the defence". Finally, the author considers that a previous drug-related conviction, in 1983, was disproportionably and unreasonably used as character evidence against him during the trial in February 1991.

*The State party's information and observations and author's comments*

4.1 The State party considers that the communication should be declared inadmissible as manifestly ill-founded, "in accordance with the established practice in similar international human rights monitoring bodies".

4.2 As to the author's claim that he was denied his right to equal treatment before the courts because the jurors were selected from a part of Oslo known for a prevalence of racist opinions, the State party notes that no documentation has been adduced in support of this contention. Author's counsel only requested that one juror be disqualified; for the rest of the jurors, it is submitted that the matter should have been raised in court, and domestic remedies cannot be deemed exhausted in their respect.

4.3 After explaining the operation of section 108 of the Courts' Act (governing the disqualification of jurors), the State party points out that it is not uncommon for jurors to have negative feelings towards the defendant in a criminal case, but that this does not imply that they are incapable of giving the defendant a fair hearing. In the instant case, the views expressed by the jurors were of a general nature, and the court's decision not to disqualify the juror was unanimous.

4.4 As to the author's claim of unfairly expeditious dismissal of his appeal to the Supreme Court, the State party notes that under section 335, subsection 2, of the Code of Criminal Procedure, no appeal may be filed with the Supreme Court if it merely concerns the evaluation of evidence in the case. In the author's case, the appeal was based on two grounds: the issue of the jury's impartiality (as a procedural error) and the severity of the prison term imposed on the author. The State party notes that under section 349 of the Code of Criminal Procedure, leave to appeal should not be granted if the Appeals Board is unanimous that an appeal would not succeed. Under section 360, procedural errors shall only be taken into consideration if they are deemed to have affected the substance of the judgement. In the author's case, the issue of the length of the prison term was considered, but as the answer to whether the Supreme Court should hear the appeal was negative, it was deemed unlikely that the sentence would be reduced. Concluding on this issue, the State party insists that there is no indication that the author was not given the same opportunities to defend his case before the courts as other individuals, in connection both with the appeal and the request for a re-opening of the case, regardless of race, colour of skin, ethnic origin, etc.

4.5 As to the length of the pretrial detention, the State party explains that a little over one year of pretrial custody is not unusual in cases involving drug-related offences. According to the State party, the delay of nine months from arrest to the dispatch of the indictment to the Court of Appeal was partly attributable to the author himself, since he changed his lawyer several times while in custody, which in turn delayed the preparations for the main hearing. The State party submits that nothing indicates that the author was kept in custody longer than other suspects merely because of his origin; this part of the complaint therefore is also said to be inadmissible as manifestly ill-founded.

4.6 Finally, the State party dismisses as manifestly ill-founded the author's complaint about the quality of his legal representation. Under section 107 of the Code of Criminal Procedure, a court-appointed lawyer is remunerated by the State; the author had the opportunity to choose his own counsel throughout the judicial proceedings, and it cannot be said that he was subjected to racial discrimination in this respect.

5.1 In his comments, the author challenges the State party's submission on various procedural and factual grounds. He claims that the State party's version of the judicial proceedings is one-sided, because it is adapted from the Court Book, which according to him reveals little of substance. He further asserts that in a letter to the Registry of the Supreme Court, the prosecutor himself admitted that the only prosecution witness against Mr. Narrainen acknowledged in court to have been pressed by the investigating officer to make a false and incriminating statement. As this virtually destroyed the probative value of the prosecution's case, the author concludes that he was convicted on the basis of racist ideas and serious errors committed by the investigating authorities.

5.2 The author reiterates that several factors in his case, including the gathering and the evaluation of evidence, the omission of important statements in the court book, the absence of serious preparation of his defence by the court-appointed lawyers, the handling of his appeal, all underline that he was denied a fair and impartial hearing, and that his conviction was based on racist considerations.

*The Committee's admissibility decision*

6.1 During its forty-second session in March 1993, the Committee examined the admissibility of the case. It duly considered the State party's contention that the author's complaint was inadmissible as his allegations were either unsubstantiated or unfounded but concluded that the communication satisfied the conditions for admissibility laid down in rule 91 of the Committee's rules of procedure.

6.2 On 16 March 1993, therefore, the Committee declared the communication admissible insofar as it may raise issues under article 5 (a) of the Convention.

*The State party's observations on the merits and counsel's comments*

7.1 The State party dismisses as incorrect the author's allegation that the members of the jury in his trial came from those parts of Oslo where racism is rampant and that they had neo-Nazi affiliations. It notes that the list of jurors in the case was drawn up in accordance with Chapter 5 of the Courts Act, that neither prosecutor nor counsel for the defence objected to the way the list was drawn up, and that counsel challenged two jurors whose names appeared on the initial list. Six of the jurors came from areas outside Oslo, and four from different parts of Oslo. The State party notes that no part of Oslo can be described as particularly racist, and that neither the courts nor the Government have any knowledge about the affiliation of jurors with political parties. However, the procedure for jury selection makes it unlikely that jurors from fringe parties will be chosen, as jurors are drawn by lot from lists that are provided by municipal politicians.

7.2 As to the impartiality of the jurors, the State party reiterates its earlier observation (see para. 2.5). It adds that the person who had made the inimical remarks during court recess, Ms. J., is a salaried worker who, in 1990, earned less income than the author received in terms of social benefits during the same year. In these circumstances, the State party submits, the rather general remarks of Ms. J. were "a not very surprising reaction to a matter that must have seemed unjust to her".

7.3 The State party recalls that the issue of whether the fact that the remark *was* made meant that Mr. Narrainen did not receive a fair trial was examined in detail by the Interlocutory Appeals Committee of the Supreme Court since, under section 360, paragraph 2 *lit.* 3, of the Norwegian Code of Criminal Procedure, a judgement is declared null and void by the Supreme Court if it is found that one of the jurors was disqualified. According to the State party, the fact that the Interlocutory Appeals Committee denied leave to appeal to the Supreme Court implies that the Board considered it obvious that there were no circumstances in the case likely to impair confidence in the impartiality of Ms. J. It is noted that in deciding whether leave to appeal to the Supreme Court shall be granted or not, the Interlocutory Appeals Committee also relies on international instruments such as [the International Convention on the Elimination of Racial Discrimination] as relevant sources of law.

7.4 In respect of the assessment of evidence in the case, the State party explains the rationale for trying cases involving crimes punishable with imprisonment of six years or more at first instance before the High Court. In such cases, the court is constituted of three professional judges and a jury of 10; the jury decides on the question of guilt. A judgement of the High Court may be appealed to the Supreme Court, but errors in the evaluation of evidence in relation to the question of guilt are not permissible grounds of appeal (sect. 335, para. 2, of the Code of Criminal Procedure). The State party explains that "it is important that serious criminal cases are dealt with in a reassuring manner from the beginning. This is why such cases are dealt with in the High Court, with a jury, at first instance. The jury decides on the guilt. This is common practice, based on the principle that a defendant shall be judged by equals ... This principle would be of little value if the jury's assessment of

evidence ... could be overruled by the professional judges in the Supreme Court".

7.5 As to the admissibility of the evidence placed before the High Court and the alleged pressure exerted by the police on witness S.B. to make a false statement, the State party recalls that Norwegian courts assess evidence freely. That Mr. Narrainen was convicted indicates that in the case, the jurors did not believe S.B. when he retracted his earlier statement and claimed that the author was innocent. In this context, the State party submits that the most likely explanation for S.B.'s attitude in court was his fear of reprisals if he upheld his earlier statement; it notes that S.B., himself a detainee at the prison of Bergen, was placed under pressure to withdraw his initial statement at around the time the author himself arrived at the prison, and that he was afraid of reprisals. Still in the same context, the State party dismisses as incorrect or misleading parts of the author's statements reproduced in paragraph 5.1 above.

7.6 The State rejects as incorrect the author's claim that S.B. was promised a reduced sentence in exchange for providing incriminating evidence against the author, as neither the police nor the public prosecutor are competent to engage in any plea bargaining with the accused. The State party similarly rejects as unfounded the author's claim that S.B. was "promised a cosy place to serve his sentence" in exchange for information on the author: in fact, S.B. was confined to the main prison for the Rogaland area where, according to his own statement, he was subjected to considerable pressure from other prisoners, including the author.

7.7 Concerning the use of a previous conviction as evidence against Mr. Narrainen, the State party submits that it is normal under Norwegian criminal law to admit such evidence, and that there is absolutely no evidence that the admission of the evidence had any connection with the author's ethnic origin.

7.8 With regard to the alleged illegal change in the author's indictment, the State party refers to section 38, paragraph 2, of the Code of Criminal Procedure, which stipulates that "with regard to the penal provision applicable to the matter, the Court is not bound by the indictment ... The same applies with regard to punishment and other sanctions applicable". A change in the determination of which provision is applicable to the same offence can also be made by the prosecutor's office (sect. 254, para. 3, of the Code of Criminal Procedure); this is what occurred in the author's case. The State party explains that the reason why the applicable provision may be changed, after indictment but before start of the trial, is that the defendant is *not* being charged with a new offence; it is simply a question of choosing the appropriate provision applicable to the same facts.

7.9 Finally, as to the duration of Mr. Narrainen's pretrial detention the State party reiterates its comments detailed in paragraph 4.5 above. As to the quality of his counsel, it recalls that since the author "was imprisoned in Oslo, he had the opportunity to choose between many highly qualified lawyers". It explains that when the court has appointed a legal aid representative, it will not appoint another one unless asked to do so by the defendant: therefore, any lawyer assisting Mr. Narrainen must have been chosen pursuant to his requests. The State party concludes that there is no reason to believe that Mr. Narrainen did not receive the same legal services as any other accused. Rather, he was given every opportunity to request a new representative every time he was dissatisfied with his previous one, thereby using the "safeguard provisions" of the criminal procedure system to the full.

8.1 In his comments on the State party's submission, counsel provides detailed information about the composition of juries under the criminal justice system. According to recent statistics, 43 per cent of foreign nationals residing in Norway live in Oslo or neighbouring boroughs. Of the foreign-born Norwegian citizens some 60,516, of [whom] half come from Latin America, Asia and Africa, lived in Oslo. Between 10 and 15 per cent of all persons living in Oslo have cultural and ethnic backgrounds that differ from the rest of the population.

8.2 Counsel observes that few if any foreigners or foreign-born Norwegians figure in lists from which jury members are selected. Eidsivating High Court was unwilling to provide him with a copy of the jury lists from the Oslo area, on the ground that the lists, comprising some 4,000 names, contain private data that should not be made public. According to counsel, Norwegian court practice clearly shows that Norwegian juries are all white—in interviews with prosecutors, lawyers and convicted prisoners, no one remembered ever

having met a coloured member of a jury. This information is corroborated by a newspaper report, dated 24 February 1994, which screens the lists of jurors provided by the city of Oslo. It states that out of 2,306 individuals, no more than 25 have a foreign background, and most of the foreign names are English, German or American ones. It further notes that according to official statistics, 38,000 foreign nationals aged 20 or more live in Oslo; another 67,000 persons were either born abroad or have foreign parents.

8.3 Counsel notes that the reason for the lack of equal representation of ethnic groups in juries may be explained by the fact that local political parties appear reluctant to nominate members of such groups and the fact that five years of residence in Norway and proficiency in Norwegian are prerequisites for jury duty. Counsel opines that this situation should prompt the Norwegian high courts to give special attention to ensuring a fair trial for coloured defendants.

8.4 As to the alleged impartiality of the jurors, counsel subscribes to the analysis of the allegedly racist remark of Ms. J. made by the lawyer who appealed on the author's behalf to the Supreme Court. In his brief to the Interlocutory Appeals Committee, this lawyer argued, by reference to section 135 (a) of the Criminal Code which prohibits public expressions of racism, that remarks such as Ms. J.'s aimed at an accused person are particularly reprehensible if made during the proceedings in front of a member of the audience, and if made in a case such as the author's, who was foreign-born. To this lawyer, Ms. J., when repeating her statement from the witness stand, gave the clear impression of harbouring racial prejudices against persons of foreign origin.

8.5 Counsel further doubts that, given the extremely heavy workload of the Interlocutory Appeals Committee which handles an average of 16 cases per day, the Appeals Committee really had the time to take into consideration all the relevant factors of the author's case, including those concerning racial discrimination under international law. He further notes that the parties are not represented before the Interlocutory Appeals Committee which, moreover, does not give any reasons for its decision(s).

8.6 Concerning the evaluation of evidence in the case, counsel notes that Mr. Narrainen was convicted on the basis of one police report and the testimonies of the police officers who had taken the statement of S.B. That this lack of other substantial evidence against Mr. Narrainen raised doubts about his guilt was demonstrated by the fact that one of the three judges in the case found that the guilt of the accused had *not* been proven beyond reasonable doubt. Counsel argues that it cannot be excluded that some of the jurors had similar doubts; in the circumstances, the presence in the jury of a person who had displayed-evidence of bias against the author may easily have tipped the balance.

8.7 In the light of the above, counsel claims that the Norwegian courts violated article 5 (a) of the Convention through the judgement of the High Court of 6 February 1991 and the decision of the Interlocutory Appeals Committee of 7 March 1991. While the juror's remark may not in itself have amounted to a violation of the Convention, the fact that Ms. J was not removed from the jury constituted a violation of article 5 (a). In this context, counsel refers to the Committee's Opinion in the case of *L.K.* v. *Netherlands*,[1] where it was held that the enactment of legislation making racial discrimination a criminal offence does not in itself represent full compliance with the obligations of States parties under the Convention.

8.8 Counsel concludes that the way in which Norwegian juries are constituted does not ensure racial equality, that the remark made by Ms. J. to another juror was evidence of bias against the author because of his origin and colour, and that neither the High Court nor the Interlocutory Appeals Committee devoted appropriate attention to counsel's claim of racial discrimination or properly evaluated the possibility of a violation of Norway's obligations under the Convention.

*Examination of the merits*

9.1 The Committee has considered the author's case in the light of all the submissions and documentary evidence produced by the parties. It bases its findings on the following considerations.

9.2 The Committee considers that in the present case the principal issue before it is whether the proceedings against Mr. Narrainen respected his right, under

article 5 (a) of the Convention, to equal treatment before the tribunals, without distinction as to race, colour or national or ethnic origin. The Committee notes that the rule laid down in article 5 (a) applies to all types of judicial proceedings, including trial by jury. Other allegations put forward by the author of the communication are in the Committee's view outside the scope of the Convention.

9.3 If members of a jury are suspected of displaying or voicing racial bias against the accused, it is incumbent upon national judicial authorities to investigate the issue and to disqualify the juror if there is a suspicion that the juror might be biased.

9.4 In the present case, the inimical remarks made by juror Ms. J. were brought to the attention of the Eidsivating High Court, which duly suspended the proceedings, investigated the issue and heard testimony about the allegedly inimical statement of Ms. J. In the view of the Committee, the statement of Ms. J. may be seen as an indication of racial prejudice and, in the light of the provision of article 5 (a) of the Convention, the Committee is of the opinion that this remark might have been regarded as sufficient to disqualify the juror. However, the competent judicial bodies of Norway examined the nature of the contested remarks, and their potential implications for the course of the trial.

9.5 Taking into account that it is neither the function of the Committee to interpret the Norwegian rules on criminal procedure concerning the disqualification of jurors, nor to decide as to whether the juror had to be disqualified on that basis, the Committee is unable to conclude, on the basis of the information before it, that a breach of the Convention has occurred. However, in the light of the observations made in paragraph 9.4, the Committee makes the following recommendations pursuant to article 14, paragraph 7, of the Convention.

10. The Committee recommends to the State party that every effort should be made to prevent any form of racial bias from entering into judicial proceedings which might result in adversely affecting the administration of justice on the basis of equality and non-discrimination. Consequently, the Committee recommends that in criminal cases like the one it has examined, due attention be given to the impartiality of juries, in line with the principles underlying article 5 (a) of the Convention.

---

[1] Communication No. 4/1991, Opinion of 16 March 1993, para. 6.4.

# Communication No. 4/1991

*Submitted by*: L.K. * (represented by counsel).
*Alleged victim*: The petitioner.
*State party*: Netherlands.
*Date of adoption of Opinion:* 16 March 1993.
*Subject matter:* Protests against the author's settling into a neighbourhood; access to effective mechanisms of protection; effective investigation; legal aid; unduly delay on court proceedings.
*Procedural issues:* None
*Substantive issues:* Right to an effective remedy against acts of racial discrimination; right to an effective investigation; State parties are required to prohibit and bring to an end, by all appropriate means, racial discrimination; prohibition of disseminating ideas based on racial superiority or hatred, incitement to racial discrimination, as well as all acts of violence or incitement to such acts against any race or group of persons; right to freedom of movement and residence within the border of the State.
*Articles of the Convention:* 2 (1) (d), 4 (a) and (c), 5 (d) (i) and (iii), and 6.
*Finding:* Violation (arts. 4 (a) and 6).

* At his request, the name of the author is not disclosed.

---

*Opinion*

1.    The author of the communication (dated 6 December 1991) is L.K., a Moroccan citizen currently residing in Utrecht, the Netherlands. He claims to be a victim of violations by the Netherlands of articles 2, paragraph (1) (d), 4 *litera* (c), 5 *litera* (d) (i) and *litera* (e) (iii), and 6 of the International Convention on the Elimination of All Forms of Racial Discrimination. The author is represented by counsel.

*The facts as found by the Committee*

2.1   On 9 August 1989, the author, who is partially disabled, visited a house for which a lease had been offered to him and his family, in the Nicolaes Ruychaverstraat, a street with municipal subsidized housing in Utrecht. He was accompanied by a friend, A.B. When they arrived, some 20 people had gathered outside the house. During the visit, the author heard several of them both say and shout: "No more foreigners". Others intimated to him that if he were to accept the house, they would set fire to it and damage his car. The author and A.B. then returned to the Municipal Housing Office and asked the official responsible for the file to accompany them to the street. There, several local inhabitants told the official that they could not accept the author as their neighbour, due to a presumed rule that no more than 5 per cent of the street's inhabitants should be

foreigners. Told that no such rule existed, street residents drafted a petition, which noted that the author could not be accepted and recommended that another house be allocated to his family.

2.2   On the same day, the author filed a complaint with the municipal police of Utrecht, on the ground that he had been the victim of racial discrimination under article 137 (*literae* (c) and (d)) of the Criminal Code (*Wetboek van Strafrecht*). The complaint was directed against all those who had signed the petition and those who had gathered outside the house. He submits that initially, the police officer refused to register the complaint, and that it took mediation by a local anti-discrimination group before the police agreed to prepare a report.

2.3   The State party's version of the facts coincides to a large extent with that given by the author, with some differences. According to the State party, the author visited the house allocated to him by the Municipality of Utrecht twice, once on 8 August 1989, together with an official of the Utrecht Municipal Housing Department, and again on 9 August 1989 with a friend. During the first visit, the official started a conversation with a local resident, a woman, who objected to the author as a future tenant and neighbour. During the conversation, several other residents approached and made remarks such as "We've got enough foreigners in this street" and "They wave knives about and you don't even feel safe in your own street". While the author was no longer present when these remarks were made, the Housing Department official was told that the house would be set on fire as soon as the prior tenant's lease had expired. As to the second visit, it is submitted that when the author arrived at the house with a friend. A.B., a group of local residents had already gathered to protest against the potential arrival of another foreigner. When the author remained reluctant to reject the Housing Department's offer, the residents collected signatures on a petition. Signed by a total of 28 local residents, it bore the inscription "Not accepted because of poverty? Another house for the family please?", and was forwarded to the Housing Department official.

2.4 In response to the complaint of 9 August 1989, the police prepared a report on the incident (Proces-Verbal No. 4239/89) on 25 September 1989; according to the State party, 17 out of the 28 residents who had signed the petition had been questioned by the police, and 11 could not be contacted before the police report was finalized.

2.5 In the meantime, the author's lawyer had apprised the prosecutor at the District Court of Utrecht of the matter and requested access to all the documents in the file. On 2 October 1989, the prosecutor forwarded these documents, but on 23 November 1989 he informed the author that the matter had not been registered as a criminal case with his office, because it was not certain that a criminal offence had taken place. On 4 January 1990, therefore, counsel requested the Court of Appeal of Amsterdam (*Gerechtshof*) to order the prosecution of the "group of residents of the Nicolaes Ruychaverstraat in Utrecht" for racial discrimination, pursuant to article 12 of the Code of Criminal Procedure.

2.6 Counsel submits that after several months, he was informed that the Registry of the Court of Appeal had indeed received the case file on 15 January 1990. On an unspecified date but shortly thereafter, the Prosecutor-General at the Court of Appeal had requested further information from the District Court Prosecutor, which was supplied rapidly. However, it was not until 10 April 1991 that counsel was able to consult the supplementary information, although he had sought to obtain it on several occasions between 15 February 1990 and 15 February 1991. It was only after he threatened to apply for an immediate judgement in tort proceedings against the prosecutor at the Court of Appeal that the case was put on the Court agenda for 10 April 1991. On 5 March 1991, the Prosecutor-General at the Court of Appeal asked the Court to declare the complaint unfounded or to refuse to hear it on public interest grounds.

2.7 Before the Court of Appeal, it transpired that only two of the street's inhabitants had actually been summoned to appear; they did not appear personally but were represented. By judgement of 10 June 1991, the Court of Appeal dismissed the author's request. It held inter alia that the petition was not a document of deliberately insulting nature, nor a document that was inciting to racial discrimination within the meaning of article 137, *literae* (c) and (e), of the Criminal Code. In this context, the Court of Appeal held that the heading to the petition—which, taking into account statements made during the hearing and to the police, should be interpreted as meaning "Not accepted because of a fight? Another house for the family please?"—could not be considered to be insulting or as an incitement to racial discrimination, however regrettable and undesirable it might have been.

2.8 Under article 12 of the Code of Criminal Procedure, counsel requested the Prosecutor-General at the Supreme Court to seek the annulment of the decision of the Court of Appeal, in the interest of law. On 9 July 1991, the request was rejected. As a last resort, counsel wrote to the Minister of Justice, asking him to order the prosecutor to initiate proceedings in the case. The Minister replied that he could not grant the request, as the Court of Appeal had fully reviewed the case and there was no scope for further proceedings under article 12 of the Code of Criminal Procedure. However, the Minister asked the Chief Public Prosecutor in Utrecht to raise the problems encountered by the author in tripartite consultations between the Chief Public Prosecutor, the Mayor and the Chief of the Municipal Police of Utrecht. At such tripartite consultations on 21 January 1992, it was agreed that anti-discrimination policy would receive priority attention.

*The complaint*

3.1 The author submits that the remarks and statements of the residents of the street constitute acts of racial discrimination within the meaning of article 1, paragraph 1, of the Convention, as well as of article 137, *literae* (c), (d) and (e), of the Dutch Criminal

Code; the latter provisions prohibit public insults of a group of people solely on the basis of their race, public incitement of hatred against people on account of their race, and the publication of documents containing racial insults of a group of people.

3.2 The author contends that the judicial authorities and the public prosecutor did not properly examine all the relevant facts of the case or at least did not formulate a motivated decision in respect of his complaint. In particular, he submits that the police investigation was neither thorough nor complete. Thus, A.B. was not questioned; and street residents were only questioned in connection with the petition, not with the events outside the house visited by the author on 8/9 August 1989. Secondly, the author contends that the decision of the prosecutor not to institute criminal proceedings remained unmotivated. Thirdly, the prosecutor is said to have made misleading statements in an interview to a local newspaper in December 1989, in respect of the purported intentions of the street residents vis-à-vis the author. Fourthly, the Prosecutor-General at the Court of Appeal is said to have unjustifiably prolonged the proceedings by remaining inactive for over one year. Finally, the Court of Appeal itself is said to have relied on incomplete evidence.

3.3 Author's counsel asserts that the above reveals violations of articles 2, paragraph 1 (d), *juncto* 4 and 6; he observes that articles 4 and 6 must be read together with the first sentence and paragraph 1, *litera* (d) of article 2, which leads to the conclusion that the obligations of States parties to the Convention are not met if racial discrimination is merely criminalized. Counsel submits that although the freedom to prosecute or not to prosecute, known as the expediency principle, is not set aside by the Convention, the State party, by ratifying the Convention, accepted to treat instances of racial discrimination with particular attention, inter alia, by ensuring the speedy disposal of such cases by domestic judicial instances.

*The State party's information and observations and counsel's comments*

4.1 The State party does not formulate objections to the admissibility of the communication and concedes that the author has exhausted available domestic remedies. It also acknowledges that article 137, *literae* (c), (d), and (e), of the Criminal Code are in

principle applicable to the behaviour of the street's residents.

4.2 In respect of the contention that the police investigations of the case were incomplete, the State party argues that it is incorrect to claim that the residents of the street were questioned only about the petition. A number of residents made statements about the remark that a fire would be set if the author moved into the house. The State party also contends that although lapse of time makes it impossible to establish why A.B. was not called to give evidence before the Court of Appeal, it is "doubtful ... whether a statement from him would have shed a different light on the case. After all, no one disputes that the remarks objected to were made".

4.3 The State party similarly rejects the contention that the prosecutor did not sufficiently motivate the decision not to prosecute and that the interview given by the press officer of the prosecutor's office to an Utrecht newspaper on 6 December 1989 was incomplete and erroneous. Firstly, it observes that the decision not to prosecute was explained at length in the letter dated 25 June 1990 from the public prosecutor in Utrecht to the Prosecutor-General at the Amsterdam Court of Appeal, in the context of the author's complaint filed under article 12 of the Code of Criminal Procedure. Secondly, the interview of 6 December 1989 did not purport to reflect the opinion of the public prosecutor's office but that of the residents of the street.

4.4 In respect of the contention that the proceedings before the Court of Appeal were unduly delayed, the State party considers that although the completion of the report by the Prosecutor-General took longer than anticipated and might be desirable, a delay of 15 months between lodging of the complaint and its hearing by the Court of Appeal did not reduce the effectiveness of the remedy; accordingly, the delay cannot be considered to constitute a violation of the Convention.

4.5 The State party observes that Dutch legislation meets the requirements of article 2, paragraph 1 (d), of the Convention, by making racial discrimination a criminal offence under articles 137, *literae* (c) et seq. of the Criminal Code. For any criminal offence to be prosecuted, however, there must be sufficient evidence to warrant prosecution. In the Government's opinion, there can be no question of a violation of articles 4 and 6 of the Convention because, as set out in the public prosecutor's letter of 25 June 1990, it had not been sufficiently established that any criminal offence had been committed on 8 and 9 August 1989, or who had been involved.

4.6   In the State party's opinion, the fact that racial discrimination has been criminalized under the Criminal Code is sufficient to establish compliance with the obligation in article 4 of the Convention, since this provision cannot be read to mean that proceedings are instituted in respect of every type of conduct to which the provision may apply. In this context, the State party notes that decisions to prosecute are taken in accordance with the expediency principle, and refers to the Committee's opinion on communication 1/1984 addressing the meaning of this very principle.[1] The author was able to avail himself of an effective remedy, in accordance with article 6 of the Convention, because he could and did file a complaint pursuant to article 12 of the Code of Criminal Procedure, against the prosecutor's refusal to prosecute. The State party emphasizes that the review of the case by the Court of Appeal was comprehensive and not limited in scope.

4.7   Finally, the State party denies that it violated article 5 (d) (i) and (e) (iii) of the Convention vis-à-vis the author; the author's right to freely choose his place of residence was never impaired, either before or after the events of August 1989. In this context, the State party refers to the Committee's Opinion on communication No. 2/1989, where it was held that the rights enshrined in article 5 (e) of the Convention are subject to progressive implementation, and that it was "not within the Committee's mandate to see to it that these rights are established" but rather to monitor the implementation of these rights, once they have been granted on equal terms.[2] The State party points out that "appropriate rules have been drawn up to ensure an equitable distribution of housing ...", and that these rules were applied to the author's case.

5.1   In his comments, counsel challenges several of the State party's observations. Thus, he denies that the police inquiry was methodical and asserts that A.B. could and indeed would have pointed out those who made threatening and discriminatory remarks on 9 August 1989, had he been called to give

_____

[1] *Yilmaz-Dogan* v. *Netherlands*, Opinion of 10 August 1988. para. 9.4.
[2] *D.T. Diop* v. *France*, Opinion of 18 March 1991, para. 6.4.

evidence. Counsel further submits that he was not able to consult the public prosecutor's decision of 25 June 1990 not to institute criminal proceedings until 10 April 1991, the date of the hearing before the Court of Appeal.

5.2   Counsel takes issue with the State party's version of the prosecutor's interview of 6 December 1989 and asserts that if the press officer related the version of the street residents without any comment whatsoever, she thereby suggested that their account corresponded to what had in fact occurred. Finally, counsel reaffirms that the judicial authorities made no effort to handle the case expeditiously. He notes that criminal proceedings in the Netherlands should duly take into account the principles enshrined in article 6 of the European Convention on the Protection of Human Rights, of which the obligation to avoid undue delays in proceedings is one.

*Issues and proceedings before the Committee*

6.1   Before considering any claims contained in a communication, the Committee on the Elimination of Racial Discrimination must, in accordance with rule 91 of its rules of procedure, decide whether or not it is admissible under the Convention. Under rule 94, paragraph 7, the Committee may, in appropriate cases and with the consent of the parties concerned, join consideration of the admissibility and of the merits of a communication. The Committee notes that the State party does not raise objections to the admissibility of the communication, and that it has formulated detailed observations in respect of the substance of the matter under consideration. In the circumstances, the Committee decides to join consideration of admissibility and consideration of the merits of the communication.

6.2   The Committee has ascertained, as it is required to do under rule 91, that the communication meets the admissibility criteria set out therein. It is, therefore, declared admissible.

6.3   The Committee finds on the basis of the information before it that the remarks and threats made on 8 and 9 August 1989 to L.K. constituted incitement to racial discrimination and to acts of violence against persons of another colour or ethnic origin, contrary to article 4 (a) of the International Convention on the Elimination of All Forms of Racial

Discrimination, and that the investigation into these incidents by the police and prosecution authorities was incomplete.

6.4 The Committee cannot accept any claim that the enactment of law making racial discrimination a criminal act in itself represents full compliance with the obligations of States parties under the Convention.

6.5 The Committee reaffirms its view as stated in its Opinion on Communication No. 1/1984 of 10 August 1987 (*Yilmaz-Dogan* v. *Netherlands*) that "the freedom to prosecute criminal offences—commonly known as the expediency principle—is governed by considerations of public policy and notes that the Convention cannot be interpreted as challenging the raison d'être of that principle. Notwithstanding, it should be applied in each case of alleged racial discrimination in the light of the guarantees laid down in the Convention".

6.6 When threats of racial violence are made, and especially when they are made in public and by a group, it is incumbent upon the State to investigate with due diligence and expedition. In the instant case, the State party failed to do this.

6.7 The Committee finds that in view of the inadequate response to the incidents, the police and judicial proceedings in this case did not afford the applicant effective protection and remedies within the meaning of article 6 of the Convention.

6.8 The Committee recommends that the State party review its policy and procedures concerning the decision to prosecute in cases of alleged racial discrimination, in the light of its obligations under article 4 of the Convention.

6.9 The Committee further recommends that the State party provide the applicant with relief commensurate with the moral damage he has suffered.

7. Pursuant to rule 95, paragraph 5, of its rules of procedure, the Committee invites the State party, in its next periodic report under article 9, paragraph 1, of the Convention, to inform the Committee about any action it has taken with respect to the recommendations set out in paragraphs 6.8 and 6.9 above.

# Communication No. 6/1995

*Submitted by*: Z.U.B.S.
*Alleged victim*: The petitioner.
*State party*: Australia.
*Date of adoption of Opinion:* 26 August 1999.
*Subject matter:* Discrimination on job selection process, on employment conditions and in relation to termination of contract; harassment and unfair treatment at work; access to effective mechanisms of protection; effective investigation; legal aid.
*Procedural issues:* Exhaustion of domestic remedies; inadmissibility *ratione materiae*; substantiation for purposes of admissibility.
*Substantive issues:* Right to an effective remedy against acts of racial discrimination; right to an effective investigation; right to work, to free choice of employment, to just and favourable conditions of work, to protection against unemployment, to equal pay for equal work, to just and favourable remuneration; right to equal treatment before the tribunals and all other organs administering justice; State parties undertake to prevent, prohibit and eradicate all practices of racial segregation and apartheid in territories under their jurisdiction.
*Articles of the Convention:* 2, 3, 5 (a), (c) and (e) (i), 6, and 14 (7) (a).
*Finding*: No violation.

*Opinion*

1. The author of the communication is Mr. Z.U.B.S., an Australian citizen of Pakistani origin born in 1955, currently residing in Eastwood, New South Wales, Australia. He claims to be a victim of violations by Australia of several provisions of the International

Convention on the Elimination of All Forms of Racial Discrimination.

*The facts as submitted by the author*

2.1   In February 1993 the author, who had by then been residing for approximately two years in Australia, was hired as an engineering officer by the New South Wales Fire Brigade (NSWFB), which is part of the Public Service. Before being hired, he had applied for two higher-level positions which he claims were commensurate with his qualifications, experience and skills. He was, however, interviewed and hired for a lower-level position for which he had not applied and for which he contends that he was not provided with a job description. He says he was adversely treated in appointment because he lacked (so-called) local knowledge, a requirement that was not mentioned in the position description or the list of desirable criteria and had no relevance to the job performance. He claims that local experience was a requirement created by the selection committee after receiving his personal details, which reflected his past professional experience of 13 years in Pakistan and Saudi Arabia.

2.2   According to the author, his position was identical to that of two other engineering officers. One of them was Australian born Anglo-origin and the other was a Buddhist Malaysian-Chinese. The three were hired almost at the same time. He claims that the difference in treatment between himself (an experienced professional engineer) and the other two officers (sub-technicians) was racially motivated. Such differentiation allegedly included that the author's qualifications exceeded those of his colleagues, that his salary was inferior to that of one of the officers and that he was placed on six months' probation, unlike one of the officers. In each case, he was treated the same as the other colleague, although he argues that he was not informed of the probationary requirement.

2.3   The author contends that he was given a heavier workload compared to his colleagues, that his participation in business trips was limited, and that his access to workplace information was curtailed. He alleges harassment and unfair treatment in the performance of his duties; he notes, for example, that one day he was ridiculed for refusing to drink beer with colleagues towards the end of one day's duties, although he had pointed out that his origin and religion did not allow him to drink alcoholic beverages. He says that he was continuously reminded of his background (professional and social) from Pakistan and Saudi Arabia through racially motivated comments.

2.4   After he had filed two complains with the relevant department under the Fire Brigade's grievance policy, the management prepared a report on his "poor performance". On 30 July 1993, he lodged a complaint of racial discrimination in employment with the New South Wales Anti-Discrimination Board (ADB), indicating that the matter was "urgent". On 6 August 1993 his employment was terminated, allegedly without written notice. The author informed the ADB of this development by fax of 9 August 1993. After his dismissal the three positions were upgraded and the other two officers were re-employed in two of the three vacant positions without competition.

2.5   The author alleges that the handling of his claim by the ADB was biased and discriminatory, and that the bias was racially motivated. He bases this assessment on the delay in the handling of his case which, in his opinion, led to his being dismissed. He contends that in a telephone conversation with a senior conciliation officer of the ADB on 12 August 1993, the ADB had taken part of his former employer, as ADB agreed with the employer's suggestion that he should appeal to the Government and Related Employees Appeal Tribunal (GREAT). GREAT examines cases of wrongful dismissal, whereas ADB processes cases of racial discrimination. The author was therefore reluctant to file his grievances with GREAT, and took ADB's suggestion to mean that ADB did not believe that it was faced with a case of racial discrimination.

2.6   The author consulted with the NSW Legal Aid Commission (LAC) with a view to obtaining legal aid for proceedings before GREAT. However, in accordance with the Legal Aid Commission Act, legal aid is not provided in respect of matters before the GREAT. On 30 August 1993, the author addressed a letter to the ADB, confirming his decision not to proceed with an appeal before GREAT and asking ADB to give priority to his complaint.

2.7   The author also contacted the New South Wales Council for civil Liberties (NSWCCL) which informed him, on 1 July 1994, that his complaint had been forwarded to the Council's Complaints Sub-Committee for further consideration. After that, the NSWCCL never contacted him again.

2.8 On 19 December 1994, ADB informed the author that its investigation had been completed, and that the complaint had been found without merit. No reasons for this evaluation were provided. At the same time he was informed of his right to appeal the decision within 21 days to the Equal Opportunity Tribunal (EOT). However, the procedure before the EOT is long and expensive, and the author could not pay the costs for representation since he remained unemployed after his dismissal. He claims that the LAC again refused to provide him with legal assistance on the basis of biased criteria. He further complains about the manner in which the EOT and the NSW Ombudsman handled his case subsequently.

2.9 Finally, the author claims that the conduct and practices of the State party's organs, including the EOT, had a discriminatory effect on his professional career and that he has not been able to find a suitable employment since his dismissal in 1993.

*The complaint*

3. It is submitted by the author that the facts stated above amount to violations of the following provisions of the Convention:

— Articles 3, 5 (c), 5 (e) (i) and 6 by the NSWFB, in that he was discriminated on racial grounds in the terms of his appointment, in his employment conditions and in the termination of his employment. He also alleged race-based harassment and offensive behaviour on the part of colleagues.

— Articles 5 (a) and 6 by the ADB, the EOT, the Ombudsman and the LAC. He contends that the ADB did not handle his urgent complaint impartially, that it victimized and disadvantaged him and that by delaying the case for 22 months it protected the personnel of the NSWFB. He also complains about the way in which EOT evaluated the facts and the evidence presented during the hearings held from 11 to 15 September 1995 as well as the conduct of the Ombudsman who, without contacting him, accepted the ADB's version of the dispute. He was particularly disappointed in view of the fact that the NSW Ombudsman in office served as

Race Discrimination Commissioner in the Federal Human Rights and Equal Opportunities Commission for several years and was fully aware of racism in Australia, including the ADB's general attitude in handling complaints of race discrimination.

— Article 2, in connection with the above-mentioned provisions.

*State party's observations on admissibility and author's comments thereon*

4.1 In a submission dated March 1996, the State party noted that when the author initially submitted his case to the Committee, it was clearly inadmissible for non-exhaustion of domestic remedies, as the author had then instituted proceedings before the EOT. On 30 October 1995, however, the EOT handed down a judgement in the author's favour by which it awarded him $A 40,000 of damages and ordered his former employer to address a written apology (within 14 days) to him. While the EOT dismissed the author's claims of racial discrimination, it did find that the author's dismissal as a result of his complaint amounted to victimization. Victimization of an individual who has initiated a complaint of racial discriminations is unlawful under section 50 of the New South Wales Anti-Discrimination Act of 1977.

4.2 The State party considered that with the judgement of the EOT, the author's case should be considered closed. It added that the author could have appealed the judgement on a point of law, but that no notification of appeal had been received.

4.3 In June 1997, the State party transmitted further admissibility observations to the Committee. It argued that the claim under article 2 of the Convention should be considered inadmissible as incompatible with the provisions of the Convention, pursuant to rule 91 (c) of the rules of procedure. It pointed out that the Committee had no jurisdiction to review the laws of Australia *in abstracto*, and that, in addition, no *specific* allegations had been made by the author in relation to article 2. If the Committee were to consider itself competent to review the allegation, then it should be rejected as inadmissible *ratione materiae*. It argued that the author's rights under article 2 were accessory in nature, and that if no violation under articles 3, 5 or 6 of the Convention was established in relation to the conduct of the NSWFB, the ADB, the EOT, the Ombudsman's Office or the LAC, then no violation of article 2 could be established either. Subsidiarily, the State party contended that if the Committee were to hold that article 2 was not accessory in nature, it remained the case that the author did not provide prima facie evidence that the above bodies engage in acts or practices of racial discrimination against him.

4.4 The State party also rejected the author's claims of a violation of article 3 of the Convention in that he "was segregated ... from English-speaking background personnel during a trip to Melbourne and in an external training course". That was deemed inadmissible as incompatible *ratione materiae* with the Convention. For the State party, the author had failed to raise an issue in relation to article 3. Subsidiarily, it was argued that the claim under article 3 had been insufficiently substantiated for the purposes of admissibility: there was no system of racial segregation or apartheid in Australia.

4.5 The State party submitted that the claim of a violation of article 5 (c) and (e) (i) of the Convention by the NSWFB, the EOT, the ADB, the Ombudsman and the LAC was inadmissible *ratione materiae*. In relation to the allegations against the conduct of the case by the EOT and the LAC it further argued that the author had failed to exhaust available and effective domestic remedies.

4.6 As to the author's claim that the NSWFB violated his rights under subparagraph 5 (c), to inter alia have equal access to public service and subparagraph 5 (e) (i), to work, to free choice of employment, to just and favourable conditions of work and just remuneration, the State party argued that:

– These allegations were reviewed by Australian tribunals in good faith and in accordance with established procedures. It would be incompatible with the role of the Committee to act as a further court of appeal in these circumstances;

– Subsidiarily, the State party submitted that alleged racial discrimination in employment had been insufficiently substantiated, for purposes of admissibility, as the author had not provided prima facie evidence which might give rise to a finding of racial discrimination.

4.7 As to the claim that the author's right to equal treatment before the ADB, the EOT, the Ombudsman and the LAC were violated, the State party argued that:

– These allegations (with the exception of the one against the LAC) were incompatible with the provisions of the Convention, on the ground that the Committee was not mandated to review the determination of facts and law of domestic tribunals, in particular in cases in which the complainant failed to exhaust available and effective domestic remedies;

– The claims related to the unfair and unequal treatment of the author by EOT and LAC were inadmissible, as the author failed to exhaust available domestic remedies. They could have been reviewed, respectively, by the New South Wales Supreme Court and the Legal Aid Review Committee. Neither avenue was pursued by the author.

4.8 With respect to the author's contention that the NSWFB, the ADB, the EOT, the Ombudsman and the LAC violated his rights under article 6 of the Convention, the State party submitted that:

– This allegation was inadmissible *ratione materiae*, as the alleged violations of the author's rights by the NSWFB and the ADB were properly reviewed by the domestic courts, "in a reasonable manner and in accordance with the law". The State party emphasizes that it was incompatible with the role of the Committee under the Convention to act as a further court of appeal in these circumstances. Australia had a domestic system which provided effective protection and remedies against any acts of racial discrimination. The mere fact that the author's allegations were dismissed did not mean that they were ineffective;

– Subsidiarily, the State party argued that the rights under article 6 of the Convention were similar to those enshrined in article 2 of the International Covenant on Civil and Political Rights. These are general rights which are accessory in nature and linked to the specific rights enshrined in the Convention. As no independent violation of articles 2, 3 and 5 of the Convention had been made out by the author, no violation of article 6 could be established;

– Still subsidiarily, the State party submitted that the allegations under article 6 had been insufficiently substantiated, for purposes of admissibility, as the author did not submit any prima facie evidence that he did not have the opportunity to seek effective protection and remedies against alleged acts of racial discrimination in his employment, in a manner similar to every individual in New South Wales.

5. In comments the author reiterated his allegations, claiming inter alia that:

– "Six Anglo-Celtic officials" of the NSWFB "maliciously employed" him, treated him unfairly during his employment and victimized him when he complained about their attitude;

– He had exhausted all available domestic remedies under Australian anti-discrimination legislation, "although the remedies were unfair, extensively exhaustive and prolonged";

– He did not file an appeal against the decision of the LAC because the LAC's advice to appeal for a review of its decision "was not in good faith and was misleading";

– As for the proceedings before the EOT, the case was conducted "in a biased environment". A NSWFB barrister "tampered with subpoena documents" and removed files from the record. Moreover, EOT "planted" a document in his personnel file "in order to dismiss the case of racial discrimination against the members of the dominant race".

*The Committee's admissibility decision*

6.1 At its fifty-first session, in August 1997, the Committee examined the admissibility of the communication. The Committee noted that the author had alleged violations of articles 2 and 6 of the Convention by all the instances seized of his grievances, and of article 3 by the New South Wales Fire Brigade. The Committee did not agree with the State party's assessment that the author had failed to substantiate these allegations for purposes of admissibility and considered that only the examination on the merits would enable it to consider the substance of the author's claim.

6.2 The Committee noted that the author's claims under article 5 (c) and (e) (i) against his former employers, the New South Wales Fire Brigade, which were reviewed by the Equal Opportunities Tribunal, dismissed the author's claims as far as they were related to racial discrimination. The Committee did not agree with the State party's argument that to admit the author's claim would amount to a review, on appeal, of all the facts and the evidence in his case. At the admissibility stage, the Committee was satisfied that the author's claims were compatible with the rights protected by the Convention, under rule 91 (c) of the rules of procedure.

6.3 The author had alleged a violation of article 5 (a) of the Convention by those administrative and judicial organs seized of his case. The Committee did not share the State party's argument that this claim was incompatible with the provisions of the Convention, since to declare it admissible would amount to a review of the determination of facts and law by Australian tribunals. Only an examination on the merits would allow the Committee to determine whether the author was treated by these organs in any way different from any other individual subject to their jurisdiction. The same consideration as in paragraph 6.2 above in fine applied.

6.4 Finally, the State party had claimed that the author could have appealed the judgement of the EOT of 30 October 1995 to the Supreme Court of New South Wales, and could have availed himself of the opportunity to have the decisions of the LAC to deny him legal aid by the Legal Aid Review Committee. The Committee considers that even if this possibility still remained open to the author, it would be necessary to take into account the length of the appeal process; as the consideration of the author's grievances took in excess of two years before the ADB and the EOT, the circumstances of the present cased justified the conclusion that the application of domestic remedies would be unreasonably prolonged, within the meaning of article 14, paragraph 7 (a), of the Convention.

6.5 Accordingly, on 19 August 1997 the Committee declared the communication admissible.

*State party's observations on the merits*

*A. Observations concerning author's claims under article 2 of the Convention*

7.1 In a submission dated 3 August 1998 the State party argues, with respect to the author's claims under article 2 of the Convention, that article 2 deals with the general observations of State parties to condemn racial discrimination and to pursue policies of eliminating all forms of racial discrimination and promoting interracial understanding. Any rights which may arise under article 2 of the Convention are also general rights which are accessory in nature and linked to the specific rights enshrined in the Convention. Accordingly, a violation of article 2 may only be found once a violation of another right has been established. Since no other violation of the Convention has been established, as submitted below, the author's allegations with respect to article 2 are without merit. Furthermore, the allegation that the State party has violated the rights of the author under article 2 of the Convention is incompatible with the role of the Committee on the ground that the Committee has no jurisdiction to review the laws of Australia in the abstract.

7.2  If the Committee is of the view that the rights under article 2 of the Convention are not accessory in nature, then the State party submits, in the alternative, that the allegations lack merit. The laws and policies of the Australian Government are designed to eliminate direct and indirect racial discrimination and to actively promote racial equality. Anti-discrimination legislation, policies and programmes exist at both the federal and the State and Territory level to ensure that all individuals are treated on the basis of racial equality and to ensure an effective means of redress if racial discrimination occurs. The laws, practices and policies in relation to the NSWFB, the ADB, the EOT, the Ombudsman and the LAC fully conform with Australia's obligations under the Convention. The author has provided no evidence that the NSWFB, the ADB, the EOT, the Ombudsman and the LAC engaged in acts or practices of racial discrimination against him.

*B. Observations concerning alleged violations of the Convention by the New South Wales Fire Brigade*

7.3  The author's allegations that his rights under the Convention were violated by the NSWFB concern three different issues: his appointment, conditions during his employment and the termination of his employment.

7.4  The author alleges that he was discriminated against by not being appointed to the position of Facilities Management Officer or Service Manager, for which he had applied, because his overseas qualifications and experience were not taken into consideration. The State party describes the process leading to the fulfilment of those posts and states that the author's academic qualifications were not at any stage disregarded nor devalued; however, he lacked the experience required, in particular local experience. He was granted an interview for the position of Service Manager, during which he did not demonstrate that he had sufficient relevant experience or sufficient knowledge and understanding of the duties and requirements of the position.

7.5  The unsuccessful applications were destroyed in December 1993, in accordance with the NSWFB policy to retain applications for 12 months only. The author first raised a complaint over the selection process when he made his complaints to the EOT in 1995. Prior to this, his complaints had been restricted to work-related issues.

7.6  The author did not apply initially for the three vacant positions of Engineering Officer. However, the selection committee contained some common membership with the selection committee for the service manager communications position. Recognizing that the author met all the requirements for one of the three positions, he was invited to submit a late application. He submitted an application on 21 December 1992 and on 28 January 1993 he was recommended for appointment on probation.

7.7  Regarding the claim that one of the other two engineering officers was getting more salary than the author the State party indicates that the reason was that the said officer had already been in the Public Service for some time.

7.8  As to probation, the usual practice is to appoint persons on probation when first joining the public service. The author had not been advised that his appointment was on probation due to a "systemic error"; the restructure of the NSWFB and subsequent recruitment action had created heavy demands on the personnel area. A number of letters of appointment were sent out around the same time as that of the author's which neglected to mention appointment on probation.

7.9  The EOT judgement, a copy of which was provided by the State party, indicates, in particular: "There is no doubt that Mr. S. was treated differently to his colleagues in relation to his appointment to the position of Engineering Officer, both with respect to his salary and other terms of his employment. The issue is whether this amounts to discrimination on the ground of race. We are of the view, after a careful consideration of all the evidence, that the reason that Mr. S. was treated differently was that Mr. S. did not have sufficient local experience. In our view this does not amount to discrimination on the ground of race. The failure of the Respondent to inform Mr. S. that he was only appointed for a probationary period was unfortunate. Without doubt Mr. S. had ground for complaint in relation to his appointment. His contract was breached at the outset. That is not a matter for us to redress. He was probably exploited. But he was not discriminated against unlawfully. Whilst he has been treated adversely, it was not on the ground concerning his race or a characteristic of his race or a characteristic imputed to his race."

7.10 The EOT found that, while the author's supervisor had a "robust approach" to the work to be done by those within his section, he did not treat the author differently to anyone else in the section, nor was the author treated differently from his colleagues to any marked degree with reference to the tasks assigned to him.

7.11 The author had access to workplace information in the same manner as other officers. All files were available to him and he was provided with all information relevant to the projects for which he was responsible. In relation to business trips he was treated in the same manner as the other engineering officers. The author was not segregated from his colleagues on a trip to Melbourne. He did not participate in that trip because his presence was not required. As for his exclusion from the external training course on Fleet Mobile Communication in June 1993, it was due to financial constraints and his lack of seniority. As to training opportunities, the allegation appears to relate to a course for MS Projects/Windows that the other engineering officers attended while the author did not. However, the author attended an Excel computer training course. Further, the EOT found that the NSWFB was justified in excluding the author from both the business trip to Melbourne and the Fleet Mobile Communication course, due to his lack of seniority and the need to avoid unnecessary expenditure of public funds.

7.12 When the author complained that his workload was too high, this was reviewed but not considered to be the case by his supervisors. He was granted an extension to complete a project on at least one occasion in response to his request. The EOT found it correct that at one stage the author had five projects assigned to him while his colleagues had two each. However, an analysis of the tasks assigned to the latter showed that they were of substantially greater complexity and scope that those assigned to the author. Moreover, the EOT did not accept the author's case that he was required to attend to duties of contract administration that were of higher accountability than those of his colleagues. Material tendered by the NSWFB indicated that at various times throughout their employment all three were required to attend to duties of contract administration and consideration of vendor submissions.

7.13 Several comments alleged to have been made by the author's colleagues were carefully evaluated by the EOT, which concluded that they were isolated remarks made on purely social occasions and did not reflect any vilification or a basis for finding of racial discrimination.

7.14 Regarding the termination of the author's employment the State party submits that it was primarily due to the fact that he refused to do certain work, was unable to maintain good work relationships and created disruptive tension in the workplace by accusations against staff members. Furthermore, all three engineering officer positions were re-described and re-advertised in December 1993. The process commenced in May 1993, i.e., before the author made his complaints of 13 and 19 July 1993. His two colleagues were appointed to two of the re-described positions. The author did not apply.

7.15 The author alleges that he lodged two complaints of discrimination which were not investigated by the NSWFB according to their grievance policy. Although it is clear that the complaints were not investigated strictly according to the NSWFB grievance policy, this does not, of itself, indicate that the author was victimized. However, it appears to have contributed to the finding by the EOT that the author had been victimized. It was the author's continued insistence that he would not carry out certain duties unless he was paid engineers' rates which was the primary factor which led to the Director General's decision to annul his probationary appointment. Another factor was that, although his annulment depleted the resources of the communications unit at a time of great activity and change, the Director General was aware that the author's continued presence was creating disharmony and adversely affecting the work performance of all involved. All officers in the Unit had become increasingly concerned that their every action and conversation was being scrutinized by him and recorded in a manner not consistent with workplace harmony.

7.16 The EOT considered that the author's complaints of racial discrimination significantly hardened his superior's views of him and were "a substantial and operative factor" upon the NSWFB adopting the view that he should be dismissed rather than seeking to resolve the issue by resorting to a grievance procedure. It also considered that although the NSWFB had stated, in a letter to the President of the ADB, that the author was dismissed because he refused to do certain work, the NSWFB had "subjected" the author "to a detriment, namely to termination of his employment without notice" because of his disciplinary allegations: this, in the tribunal's opinion, was contrary to section 50 of the Anti-Discrimination Act 1977.

7.17 The State party concludes that the author has not provided any evidence that could justify his claims that the NSWFB violated articles 5 (c) and 5 (e) (i) in his appointment, during the course of his employment and the termination of his employment. As noted above and consistent with the evidence before the EOT, the selection committee concerned with the author's appointment to the NSWFB placed an emphasis on relevant local experience. This was on the basis that the engineering conditions and practices in Australia in relation to which the author was employed are significantly different to those conditions and practices in which the author had previously operated. For this reason the author's starting salary was $A 2,578.00 less than that of his colleagues. The EOT also found that there was no racial discrimination in relation to any aspect of the author's employment.

7.18 In the NSWFB and throughout every jurisdiction in Australia there are no restrictions to access to public service on the basis of race, colour, descent or national or ethnic origin. The New South Wales Government—like all jurisdictions throughout Australia—has a policy of Equal Employment Opportunity which actively encourages the recruitment of,

inter alia, people from other than English-speaking backgrounds into the public service.

7.19 The State party submits that the communication does not raise an issue under article 3 of the Convention in relation to any aspect of his employment with the NSWFB, since there is no system of racial segregation or apartheid in Australia. It also submits, in relation to the author's allegations that the NSWFB failed to investigate his complaints according to the official grievance policy, that the author has not provided any evidence that the investigation of his grievance by his superiors at the NSWFB was an ineffective way to provide him with protection and remedies.

7.20 The State party reiterates that it is not the function of the Committee to review the findings of the EOT. That submission is based on jurisprudence of the Human Rights Committee in deciding cases under the Optional Protocol to the International Covenant on Civil and Political Rights. It is also analogous to the well-established "fourth instance (*quatrième instance*)" doctrine of the European Court of Human Rights, that an application that merely claims that a national court has made an error of fact or law will be declared inadmissible *ratione materiae*. The evidence provided in the transcript of the hearing before the EOT and the EOT's judgement shows that the author's allegations were carefully considered within the meaning of racial discrimination under the Anti-Discrimination Act, which in turn reflects the terms of the Convention, and were found to be unsubstantiated.

*C. Observations concerning alleged violations of the Convention by the Anti-Discrimination Board, the Equal Opportunity Tribunal, the Ombudsman and the Legal Aid Commission*

7.21 Regarding the author's complaint vis-à-vis ADB the State party submits that the author has failed to provide any evidence to demonstrate a casual connection between the ADB's acts and the alleged discrimination he suffered at work. When he lodged a complaint with ADB on 30 July 1993 he was already aware that he was about to lose his job. Accordingly, it could not have been "as a result" of the ADB's behaviour that the author allegedly suffered discrimination, hostile behaviour and lost his job. As for the complaint that ADB did not apply for an interim order to preserve his rights the State party contends that the power in section 112 (1) (a) to preserve the status quo between the parties does not extend to preserving a complainant's employment.

7.22 As to the allegation that the ADB did not act promptly, it is submitted that an ADB officer spoke with NSWFB on 10 August 1993 and asked if the NSWFB would delay the decision to dismiss the author until the ADB had investigated his complaint. The ADB had no power under the Anti-Discrimination Act to compel the NSWFB to reinstate the author. After the author advised the ADB that he was not proceeding with an appeal to GREAT because he did not want reinstatement, the matter was no longer considered by the ADB to be urgent, in accordance with the ADB's usual policy. Furthermore, there is no evidence that the ADB did not act impartially in considering the author's complaints. Indeed, it is clear from correspondence from the ADB and the Ombudsman that the conciliation officer complied with the ADB's usual procedures.

7.23 The author twice complained about the conduct of the ADB in investigating his complaint to the New South Wales Ombudsman. Each of the author's complaints was declined. The Ombudsman informed the author that he was declining to investigate the author's urgent complaint about the alleged delay of the ADB because he considered that the ADB had adhered to its usual procedure for dealing with urgent complaints. The State party submits that the author's claim against the ADB is manifestly ill-founded and lacking in merit.

7.24 As for the author's allegations concerning the EOT's handling of the hearing, the State party submits that it would appear from the transcript that, as is often the case with proceedings involving unrepresented persons and all the more so where the particular tribunal's raison d'être is the elimination of discrimination, the EOT went to great lengths to be fair to the author. The author obtained a fair and relatively long hearing (the proceedings took five days). In particular, the transcript indicates that the EOT:

— Was very polite at all times to the author and assisted him with questions;

— Granted the author leave to be assisted by a friend;

— Invited him "not to hurry, there was plenty of time";

— Protected him when giving evidence and allowed a witness to be recalled at the author's request;

— Allowed the author to cross-examine one of the NSWFB's witnesses for almost a whole day;

— On many occasions tried to assist the author to explain why events and actions were or were not based on race.

7.25 The author has failed to provide any evidence that the proceedings were unfair, or motivated or tainted in any way by racial discrimination, or that the EOT judgement was unjust. Accordingly, the proceedings before the EOT were neither in violation of article 5 (a) nor ineffective within the meaning of article 6.

7.26 Regarding the author's claim with respect to the Ombudsman, the State party explains that the author made two complaints in writing to the Ombudsman about the handling of his case by the ADB. The Ombudsman's Office declined to investigate because the author had alternative means of redress before the EOT. As explained to the author, because of the high number of complaints and the limited resources available to the Ombudsman to investigate them, priority is given to those matters which identify systemic and procedural deficiencies in public administration, where complainants have no alternative and satisfactory means of redress. The author's allegation that a government department "can get away with it" if there is an alternative means of redress available to the victim is illogical. If there is an alternative means available then the government department "cannot get away with it".

7.27 Furthermore, there is absolutely no evidence to support the allegation that the Ombudsman "colluded" with ADB officials. The preliminary inquiries undertaken by the Ombudsman disclosed that the conduct of the relevant ADB officer complied with the usual ADB procedure. In the absence of prima facie evidence of misconduct on the part of the ADB, the Ombudsman had no alternative but to decline to investigate the author's complaint. No amount of consultation with the author would have altered this fact.

7.28 In a letter dated 26 April 1995 the author wrote to the Ombudsman seeking a review of the decision. In that letter he had the opportunity to raise his specific objections to the decision to decline his complaint. He did not do so and merely reiterated his earlier complaint and outlined developments in the hearing of this matter by the EOT.

7.29 There has been no evidence submitted by the author that the decision of the Ombudsman was motivated or tainted by racial discrimination in violation of article 5 (a), or that this remedy was ineffective within the meaning of article 6.

7.30 As for the author's claims regarding the decision of the LAC to refuse his application for legal aid, the State party argues that the decision was made in accordance with the Legal Aid Commission Act and the Legal Aid Policy Manual, in a manner which treated the author no differently to any other person making an application for legal aid. The author was advised by the LAC that legal aid was not available for any person in respect of matters before the GREAT. The refusal of legal aid did not preclude the author from accessing and effectively conducting proceedings before GREAT. This body is designed to be used by unrepresented persons. Finally, it was the author's choice to pursue his complaint through the ADB and withdraw his proceedings before the GREAT, since he was not interested in reinstatement. Accordingly, the author has failed to provide any evidence that he was treated unfairly by the LAC in relation to his application for aid for legal representation before GREAT, or that lack of legal aid was the determinative factor in his decision to pursue a remedy through the ADB.

7.31 If the matter is one for which legal aid is available and the means test is satisfied, but there is some doubt concerning the merit, then, in accordance with the Legal Aid Commission Act, the LAC may cover the cost of obtaining an opinion from junior counsel on whether the applicant has reasonable prospects for success. On 28 March 1995, the LAC authorized the author to seek an opinion from junior counsel as to whether the proceedings before the EOT had reasonable prospects for success and the likely quantum of damages that might be awarded to the author. The solicitor's expenses were paid by the LAC. However, it was finally found that the author's application did not satisfy the LAC's merit test. The author has failed to demonstrate how the LAC's decision to refuse him legal aid on the basis that his claim lacked merit was unfair or amounted to unequal treatment.

7.32 The author was advised in writing in respect of the refusal of his application for legal aid to appear before the GREAT and of his application for legal aid to appear before the EOT that he could lodge an application to have each of these decisions reviewed by a Legal Aid Review Committee within 28 days. The author states that it was impossible for him "to comply with the EOT hearing dates and complete the LAC's appeal process. The LAC explicitly informed the author of section 57 of the Legal Aid Commission Act which provides for the adjournment of proceedings by a court of tribunal pending the determination of an appeal by the Legal Aid Review Committee. The author did not lodge an appeal to the Legal Aid Review Committee in respect of either decision to refuse his applications for legal aid. The fact that the LAC advised the author of his right of appeal is further evidence that he was treated fairly.

7.33 The author's claim against the LAC is manifestly ill-founded and lacking in merit. The author has failed to provide any evidence that the LAC decisions to refuse the author legal aid for representation before GREAT or EOT were unfair or motivated or tainted in any way by racial discrimination, and therefore in violation of article 5 (a), or that this remedy was ineffective within the meaning of article 6.

*Author's comments*

*A. Allegations concerning violations of the Convention by the New South Wales Fire Brigade*

8.1 With respect to the fact that the author was not appointed to two positions for which he had applied he disagrees with the State party's argument that understanding of the local market was an essential criterion advertised or mentioned in the description for the position of Service Manager and states that during his employment he was given several tasks of local contract market and purchase. His application showed his skills and experience to carry out all the accountabilities mentioned in the job description for the two positions. Furthermore, he was more suitable than the person appointed as Service Manager, as he had a postgraduate training course in maintenance management and six years of experience in the management of emergency services communication. During his employment the author was assigned with one task of the Service Manager's position, i.e., the purchase of Test Analyser. He was less favourably treated on the ground of his racial background in that he was not even granted interview for both positions. Furthermore, it is not correct that he only complained over the selection process when he filed a complaint with the EOT in 1995. He did raise the matter with his submission of 15 December 1993 to the ADB.

8.2 The author does not fully agree with the State party's statement regarding the steps that led to his appointment as an engineering officer. As for his remuneration, he says it is not true that one of his two colleagues received the same salary as him. The EOT found that the colleague also received allowances by reason of being placed on a special "on-call" roster which gave him additional salary and permanent access to a car.

8.3 As for the probation issue the author argues that under section 28 (2) of the Public Sector Management Act, a person may be appointed to a position in the Public Service without being required to serve a probation period. Given his qualifications, skills and experience he could have been exempted from probation. The reason for not being exempted was based on racial considerations.

8.4 Concerning the workload he says that he had to work during the Easter holidays in order to complete a project that, given its complexity, took longer than what his supervisors suggested. He also says that his supervisor treated the migrant staff as second-class citizens and that his regret and denial of discriminatory intent is untrue.

8.5 The author insists that he was segregated from the white officers on a trip to Melbourne in connection with a project he was working on and, for which, he had previously been sent to Sydney. As for training, the Fleet Mobile Communications course dealt with the latest technologies in mobile radio communication. He was the most deserving employee of the NSWFB for his course, as he was made responsible for the radio communications projects. The cost of the course was not very high.

8.6 As for the State party's statement that the author did not apply when the position was re-advertised he states that, by then, he had already been dismissed. Applying would have meant that he had to compete, as an external candidate, with hundreds of other applicants. Furthermore it would have been useless. As

the EOT found, the NSWFB was unwilling to employ him.

8.7 As for the State party's claim that the author had refused to carry out work assigned to him the author refers to the EOT judgement in which the tribunal was of the view that the incidents referred to by his superiors did not amount to clear refusal by the author. He also states that he did not refuse the lawful order or requested engineer's pay; the State party's allegations that he refused duties for money are baseless. With regard to the workplace harmony and productivity, there was no complaint against the author from any staff member, neither did EOT find that there was any evidence that he created disruptive tension in the workplace.

*B. Allegations concerning violations of the Convention by the Anti-Discrimination Board, the Equal Opportunity Tribunal, the Ombudsman and the Legal Aid Commission*

8.8 The author states that when he requested the ADB to deal with his case on an urgent basis, as he feared he would be dismissed, the ADB limited itself to inform the NSWFB that a complaint had been lodged. ADB did not act promptly and deliberately delayed action until the dismissal took place. The author also argues that the ADB was unwilling to investigate his claims regarding "discrimination in appointment", in an attempt to minimize his prospects of success in the EOT and in seeking legal aid; indeed, the ADB's baseless findings that the author's complaint was lacking in substance undermined his prospects of success with other organs.

8.9 The author complains about the manner in which the EOT handled his case. He says, for instance, that it did not order the ADB to provide an officer to assist the inquiry, despite the fact that it could have done so under the provisions of the Anti-Discrimination Act; during the conduct of the inquiry the EOT gave advantage to the NSWFB; it further disadvantaged the author by conducting the hearing in public, reporting to the media and publishing the judgement; enormous amounts of duplicated documentation was given to him to read during the hearing, however, he was not given extra time to read it, except for a few minutes adjournment; the transcripts of the five-day hearing show that he did not have sufficient time to cross-examine the six NSWFB witnesses; two of the witnesses brought by the NSWFB were migrants whose testimony in the witness box did not fully coincide with their affidavits; the EOT allows the NSWFB to be represented by the Crown Solicitor against the unrepresented author without witnesses.

8.10 In its judgement the EOT justified the treatment of the author by the authorities as "unfair", "unfortunate", "exploitation", "adverse", etc., but failed to acknowledge the discriminatory impact and outcome on the author due to his different race to others in similar circumstances. The EOT failed to recognize the continuous pattern of unequal treatment between the author and the other two officers in the same circumstances and considered that the race based harassment in the workplace during duty hours were simple jokes on social occasions.

8.11 The author claims that his personnel file with the NSWFB was taken over by the EOT and he was not allowed to inspect it. The EOT judgement indicates that his personnel file contained a letter dated 4 May 1993 according to which he should be considered for further promotion at the end of his first year of employment. The author expressed doubts as to the authenticity of that letter and considers that it was "planted" by the EOT to justify its judgement that the NSWFB did not discriminate against him on racial grounds.

8.12 The author states that the Ombudsman abused her discretionary powers by declining to investigate his complaints and deliberately misinterpreting section 13 of the Ombudsman Act, despite the fact that the author had identified systemic and procedural deficiencies in the ADB. She did not answer as to why she did not investigate the wrongdoings of the ADB officials. The Ombudsman was deliberately not understanding that in one instance the ADB "got away" by colluding with the NSWFB and declaring that the author's claim of victimization lacked substance. The victimization claim was later substantiated and NSWFB paid the damages, not the ADB. After receiving two complaints against a public administration, it is unfair that the Ombudsman was relying on the information or advice supplied by the same public administration and reporting it back to the author. The author sent a letter to the Ombudsman, dated 26 April 1995, in which he explained in detail the types of improper conduct by the ADB official. Furthermore, the Ombudsman failed to advise the author as to the kind of additional information she needed to reopen the case.

8.13 The author states that the report of the LAC's sponsored counsel and the LAC's decision to refuse legal aid were unfair, as the author was successful in establishing his case of victimization in the EOT. It is incorrect to say that the author had to choose ADB instead of GREAT because he was not interested in reinstatement. If he was not interested in reinstatement, why did he seek reinstatement through EOT? The real reason for his withdrawal from the GREAT appeal was the denial of legal assistance.

8.14 Finally, the author disagrees with the State party's observations regarding non-violation of article 2 of the Convention. He refers to the Committee's opinion on communication No. 4/1991, in which it is stated that "the Committee cannot accept any claim that the enactment of law making racial discrimination a criminal act in itself represents full compliance with the obligations of States parties under the Convention".[1]

*Examination on the merits*

9.1 The Committee has considered the author's case in the light of all the submissions and documentary evidence produced by the parties, as required under article 14, paragraph 7 (a), of the Convention and rule 95 of its rules of procedure. It bases its findings on the following considerations.

9.2 The Committee notes that the author's claims were examined in accordance with the law and procedures set up by the State party to deal with cases of racial discrimination. It notes, in particular, that the complaint was examined by the New South Wales Anti-Discrimination Board (ADB) first and by the Equal Opportunity Tribunal (EOT) on appeal. The EOT examined the author's claims regarding racial discrimination and victimization concerning his appointment, employment and dismissal. On the basis of the information at its disposal, in particular the text of the EOT's judgement, the Committee is of the opinion that the EOT examined the case in a thorough and equitable manner.

9.3 The Committee considers that, as a general rule, it is for the domestic courts of State parties to the Convention to review and evaluate the facts and evidence in a particular case. After reviewing the case before it, the

---

[1] *L.K.* v. *Netherlands*, para. 6.4.

Committee concludes that there is no obvious defect in the judgement of the EOT.

10. In the circumstances the Committee on the Elimination of Racial Discrimination, acting under article 14, paragraph 7 (a) of the International Convention on the Elimination of All Forms of Racial Discrimination, is of the opinion that the facts as submitted do not disclose a violation of the Convention by the State party.

11. Pursuant to article 14, paragraph 7 (b), of the Convention, the Committee suggests that the State party simplify the procedures to deal with complaints of racial discrimination, in particular those in which more than one recourse measure is available, and avoid any delay in the consideration of such complaints.

# Communication No. 8/1996

*Submitted by*: B.M.S. (represented by counsel).
*Alleged victim*: The petitioner.
*State party*: Australia.
*Date of adoption of Opinion:* 12 March 1999.
*Subject matter:* Discriminatory medical examination system for overseas doctors applying for medical registration; access to effective mechanisms of protection; effective investigation; legal aid.
*Procedural issues:* Exhaustion of domestic remedies.
*Substantive issues:* Right to an effective remedy against acts of racial discrimination; right to an effective investigation; discrimination based on national origin; right to work, to free choice of employment, to just and favourable conditions of work, to protection against unemployment, to equal pay for equal work, to just and favourable remuneration; right to equal treatment before the tribunals and all other organs administering justice.
*Articles of the Convention:* 5 (a), (b) and (e) (i), and 14 (7) (a).
*Finding*: No violation.

*Opinion*

1. The author of the communication is B.M.S., an Australian citizen since 1992 of Indian origin and a medical doctor. He claims to be a victim of violations of the Convention by Australia. He is represented by counsel.

*The facts as submitted by the author*

2.1 The author graduated from Osmania University (India). He holds a diploma in Clinical Neurology (DCN) from the University of London. He has practised medicine in England, India, Ireland and the United States. For 10 years he has worked as a medical practitioner under temporary registration in Australian public hospitals.

2.2 The author states that doctors trained overseas who have sought medical registration in Australia have to undergo and pass an examination involving two stages, a multiple choice examination (MCQ) and a clinical examination. The whole process is conducted by the Australian Medical Council (AMC), a non-governmental organization partly funded by the Government.

2.3 In 1992, the Australian Minister of Health imposed a quota on the number of doctors trained overseas who pass the first stage of this examination. As a result, doctors who were trained abroad and who are Australian residents and Australian citizens may not be registered precisely because they fall outside the quota. On the other hand, quota places may be allocated to persons without any immigration status in Australia.

2.4 Following the imposition of the quota system the author sat the MCQ examination on three occasions. He satisfied the minimum requirements but was always prevented, by the quota system, from proceeding to the clinical examination.

2.5 In March 1993, the author filed a formal discrimination complaint with the Australian Human Rights and Equal Opportunity Commission (HREOC) against the quota and the examination system. In August 1995, the Commission found the quota policy unlawful under the Australian Racial Discrimination Act, considering it "grossly unfair, resulting in unnecessary trauma, frustration and a deep sense of injustice". As regards the examination system, the Commission held that the decision to require the author to sit for and pass examinations was not based on his national origin or on the consideration that he was a person not of Australian or New Zealand origin.

2.6 The Australian Government and the AMC appealed the decision of the HREOC. On 17 July 1996, the Federal Court of Australia ruled in their favour, finding that the quota and the examination system were reasonable.

2.7 The author did not appeal this decision to the High Court of Australia. According to counsel the appeal to the High Court is not an effective remedy within the meaning of article 14, paragraph 7 (a), of the Convention. On the one hand, there is no automatic right of appeal to the High Court, since the Court must first grant special leave to appeal. On the other hand, the High Court has consistently stated that a prima facie case of error will not of itself warrant the granting of an application for leave to appeal. There must be some special feature which warrants the attention of the Court, with its public role in developing and clarifying the law and in maintaining procedural regularity in the lower courts, outweighing the private rights of litigants.

2.8 Furthermore, the author did not have the means to pursue the appeal without being awarded legal aid, and a cost order would be imposed on him if the appeal was unsuccessful. In fact, on 28 October 1996 Legal Aid advised that it would not fund the author's appeal to the High Court.

2.9 In subsequent submissions counsel indicates that following HREOC's decision and notwithstanding that an appeal had been lodged, the AMC decided to abandon the quota. As a result all overseas-trained doctors (OTDs) who, like the author, have met the minimum requirements of the MCQ examination but have been prevented from doing so by the quota, are now allowed to undertake the clinical examination. The author has attempted the clinical examination on several occasions. The examination has three components and it is necessary to pass all the components at the one sitting. The author has passed each component at least once but not all three at the same sitting.

2.10 The standard of the AMC examination is supposedly that of an Australian-trained medical student who is about to commence an intern year. Counsel states that it is objectively preposterous that a person of the author's experience, with 13 years working as a doctor and 8 years in the Australian health system, is not at least of the standard of a newly graduated medical student.

2.11 Studies on Australian medical graduates show serious deficiencies in clinical skills. For example, a University of Queensland study published in 1995 indicates that at the commencement of the intern year, medical staff did not consider all graduates competent even in history-taking and clinical-examination skills and most graduates were not considered competent in such areas as diagnosis, interpreting investigations, treatment procedures and emergency procedures. At the conclusion of the intern year, only 45 per cent of medical staff considered all interns competent at history-taking and only 36 per cent of medical staff considered all interns competent at physical examination. In view of such studies, it is clear that overseas-trained doctors are examined at a higher standard than Australian graduates. In the author's case, the fact that the AMC persistently fails him raises the additional question of whether he is being penalized for taking his case to the HREOC.

*The complaint*

3.1 Counsel claims that both the AMC examination system for overseas doctors as a whole and the quota itself are unlawful and constitute racial discrimination. In this respect the judgement of the Federal Court of Australia condones the discriminatory acts of the Australian Government and the AMC and thereby reduces the protection accorded to Australians under the Racial Discrimination Act. At the same time, it eliminates any chance of reform of this discriminatory legislation.

3.2 Counsel contends that the restrictions to practise their profession imposed on overseas-trained doctors before they can be registered aim at limiting the number of doctors to preserve the more lucrative areas of medical practice for domestically trained doctors.

4.1 In a submission dated 7 January 1997 the State party informs the Committee that in October 1995 the AMC decided to discontinue the quota system following the HREOC's conclusion that the system was racially discriminatory. That decision was taken in spite of the Federal Court's ruling that the quota system was reasonable and not racially discriminatory. As a result, the 281 candidates who had fallen outside the quota, including the author, were informed that they were eligible to undertake the clinical examinations.

4.2 The State party notes that the author has sat the AMC clinical examination and failed it three times. As a result of the HREOC's decision in the author's case an independent observer appointed by the author was present during his first two attempts. Under the current AMC regulations, he may resit the clinical examination in the next two years, without having to resit the MCQ examination. Currently, there is no restriction, other than satisfactory performance, on the author's progress through the AMC examinations.

4.3 With respect to counsel's allegation that the Federal Court ordered the author to pay the legal costs of the AMC, the State party informs the Committee that in November 1996 the AMC agreed to discontinue pursuit of costs against the author. The Federal Court had made no order for costs in respect of the Commonwealth of Australia, which agreed to bear its own costs.

4.4 In the light of the above the State party considers the author's complaint to be moot.

5.1 In his comments, counsel informs the Committee that the author does not wish to withdraw his communication. He notes that although the quota system was discontinued it may be reintroduced at any time in the light of the Federal Court's ruling which overturned the HREOC's decision. According to counsel the State party authorities have indeed contemplated the possibility of reintroducing it.

5.2 Counsel reiterates that the discontinuation of the quota has not solved the problem of discrimination, since the AMC has simply increased the pass criteria to compensate for the absence of the restrictive effects of the quota. He further claims that although the author has been allowed to proceed to the clinical examination he was failed on each occasion, in circumstances which suggest that he is being penalized for having originally complained to the HREOC. He has lodged a further complaint with the Commission about this issue.

5.3 Furthermore, the fact that a discriminatory practice has been discontinued does not change its previous discriminatory nature or render void complaints concerning its application and operation when it was still in force. Consequently, it is argued that the author's rights were violated from 1992 to 1995, causing him a detriment which has not been redressed by the discontinuation of the quota system.

*The Committee's admissibility decision and State party's comments thereon*

6.1 During its fifty-first session the Committee examined the communication and noted that the main issues before it were: (a) whether the State party had failed to meet its obligation under article 5 (e) (i) to guarantee the author's right to work and free choice of employment; and (b) whether the order of costs against the author by the Federal Court violated the author's rights under article 5 (a) to equal treatment before the courts.

6.2 On 19 August 1997 the Committee adopted a decision by which it considered the communication admissible with respect to the claim relating to the discriminatory nature of both the AMC examination and its quota system. The Committee noted, inter alia, that the Federal Court's decision provided a legal basis for the reintroduction of the quota system at any time. The Committee did not share the State party's reasoning that since the quota system had been discontinued, the author's complaint for the discrimination alleged to have taken place between 1992 and 1995 had become moot. In respect of the fact that the author did not appeal the Federal Court's decision to the High Court of Australia, the Committee considered that even if this possibility were still open to the author, and taking into account the length of the appeal process, the circumstances of the case justified the conclusion that the application of domestic remedies had been unreasonably prolonged.

6.3 The Committee declared the case inadmissible as to the author's complaint that he was discriminated against because the pass criteria had been raised, since that matter had been submitted to the HREOC and therefore domestic remedies had not been exhausted. It also considered the case inadmissible as to the author's claim that costs ordered by the Court against him constituted discrimination, in view of the State party's information that the AMC would not be pursuing further the costs imposed by the Court.

6.4 By letter dated 24 December 1997 the State party informed the Committee that its submission of 17 January 1997 contained a request for advice on whether the communication was ongoing. This request was made because the alleged victim had effectively received a remedy as a result of the Government's decision to lift the quota. This request did not constitute the State party's pleadings on admissibility and was not submitted under rule 92 of the Committee's rules of procedure. The submission clearly indicated that if the Committee decided to proceed with its consideration of the author's complaint the State party would like to be given the opportunity to make submissions on the admissibility and merits of the communication. The State party also indicated that it had never been advised that the author had declined to withdraw his complaint.

6.5 By letter dated 11 March 1998 the Committee informed the State party that rule 94, paragraph 6, of the Committee's rules of procedure provides for the possibility of reviewing an admissibility decision when the merits of a communication are examined. Accordingly, the Committee would revisit its earlier decision on admissibility upon receipt of relevant information from the State party.

*State party's observations on admissibility and merits*

7.1 The State party submits that the author's interpretation of the requirement imposed on overseas-trained doctors such as himself to sit written and clinical examinations to demonstrate competence is incorrect. The author is not subject to the system of examinations because of his (Indian) national origin, but because he has trained at an overseas institution. All OTDs, regardless of national origin, are required to sit the examinations. The objective of the examination process is to establish that medical practitioners trained in medical institutions not accredited formally by the AMC have the necessary medical knowledge and clinical competence for the practice of

medicine with safety within the Australian community. Its standard is the level of attainment of medical knowledge and clinical skills corresponding to that required of newly qualified graduates of Australian medical schools who are about to commence intern training. The author has sat the MCQ examinations on a total of six occasions. His first three attempts predated the introduction of the quota in 1992. On each occasion, he failed to reach the "pass mark". After the introduction of the quota in 1992, the author sat the MCQ examination a further three times. Whilst succeeding in obtaining a "pass", he did not come within the top 200 candidates passing the MCQ and so was unable to proceed to the clinical examination. When the quota was discontinued, the author was permitted to sit for the clinical examination in March 1996, August 1996, October 1996 and March 1997. On each occasion he failed to demonstrate sufficient proficiency in each of the subject areas to be granted registration. He currently is on the waiting list to sit the clinical examination again.

7.2 The State party submits that the scheme, in general and in its application to the author, does not represent a breach of Australia's obligations under article 5 (e) (i). The underlying basis of the author's complaint is that OTDs, particularly those who have "proven competence" through practice in Australian public hospitals, should be similarly placed to doctors trained in AMC-accredited schools. In the view of the Australian Government, however, graduates of overseas universities and those from Australian and New Zealand universities cannot be accepted as having equal medical competence without further investigation. Educational standards vary across the globe and the Australian Government is justified in taking account of this difference in devising schemes to test the comparability of standards. To accept the author's complaint would be to engage in a circular argument which prejudges the question of equivalence of standards, a matter which the Australian Government is entitled to question. The scheme in fact ensures equality of treatment.

7.3 Furthermore, the State party does not accept that working in Australian hospitals under temporary registration is necessarily sufficient proof of competence to justify the waiving of examination requirements. When working under temporary registration, overseas-trained doctors are subject to strict supervision and practice requirements and may not be exposed to the broad range of medical conditions which exist in the Australian community. Satisfactory performance under such restricted conditions does not equate with sufficient knowledge and competence over the range of areas of permitted practice under general registration.

7.4 The requirement that OTDs sit for and pass AMC examinations is not based on national origin. The distinction made is on the basis of the identity of the medical school, regardless of the national origin (or any other personal characteristic) of the candidate seeking registration. In practice, no matter the race or national origin of a candidate, that candidate must fulfil the same requirements: either graduation from an accredited medical school or the completion of AMC exams to demonstrate an equal level of competence to those who have successfully graduated from an accredited medical school. Thus, for instance, if a person of Indian national origin studied overseas, he/she would have to sit the AMC exams. If he/she studied in Australia, he/she would be entitled to proceed straight to an internship. Similarly, whether a person is of English national origin, Australian national origin, Indian national origin or any other national origin, the requirements remain constant.

7.5 Furthermore, despite the author's implication that the AMC has deliberately chosen not to accredit overseas medical schools for reasons associated with racial discrimination, there is no evidence to suggest that the system was intended to, or in fact works to, the detriment of persons of a particular race or national origin. Contrary to the author's complaint, the system of AMC examinations does not carry any imputation regarding the attributes of individuals of particular national origins. In particular, the need to sit for such examinations does not imply that doctors trained overseas, whether or not they have been practising in Australia, are inferior because of their race, national or ethnic origin. Instead, it simply sends the message that all graduates of medical schools will be subject to the same standard of examination before being permitted to work unconditionally in Australia.

7.6 The HREOC was satisfied that the accreditation system was not based on race. The AMC's evidence, which the HREOC accepted, was that accreditation was undertaken on the basis of efficient use of

resources. The AMC has considered it impractical to investigate for the accreditation process every university attended by applicants for registration. Given the wide range of countries from which immigrants to Australia come, there is concomitantly an extremely large number of universities all around the world from which OTDs have graduated. The AMC does not have the resources to undertake such an extensive accreditation, nor should it be expected to. The Australian Government supports the reasonableness of the allocation of the AMC's resources to accredit schools with which it has most familiarity and contact. It thus considers an examination to be an equitable system of adjudging standards of competence by persons, regardless of race or national origin. The accreditation of New Zealand medical schools, in particular, is explainable in terms of the mutual accreditation programme carried out by the Australian Medical Council and the Medical Council of New Zealand.

7.7 The State party does not accept the author's allegation that the system privileges Australian and New Zealand doctors and disadvantages doctors trained outside Australia and New Zealand. Even if (for the purposes of argument) such a benefit or disadvantage could be established, such an effect would not constitute discrimination on the basis of "national origin" or any other prescribed ground under the Convention. The group who are privileged under this scenario are those trained in Australian and New Zealand medical schools, rather than persons of particular national origin. Medical students in Australia do not share a single national origin. Similarly, those who are OTDs are not of a single national origin. Whilst the latter group are likely "not to be of Australian national origin", the Australian Government does not accept that such a broad category of persons represents a "national origin" or racial classification for the purposes of article 5 (e)(i). For the purposes of article 5 (e) (i), it would be necessary to demonstrate discrimination on the basis of a person's particular national origin—in this case, the author's Indian national origin.

7.8 The current system of examinations is clearly based on objective and reasonable criteria. It is a legitimate policy objective for the Australian Government to seek to maintain high standards of medical care for its residents and to seek to assure itself of the standards of medical competence of those seeking to work in Australia on an unsupervised basis. Thus, it is reasonable for legislatures to institute a means of supplementary exams for those trained in universities with which it is not familiar to ensure that their competence is at a comparable level to those trained within Australia and New Zealand. That the author would prefer an alternative method of evaluating competence does not detract from the reasonableness of the current system. It is within a State's discretion to take the view which has been adopted—that an examination is the best method to test for overall knowledge. The reasonableness of such a system is also demonstrated by the extent to which similar practices are adopted by other States parties to the Convention, such as the United Kingdom, Canada, the United States and New Zealand.

7.9   The need for doctors to demonstrate their competence could also be regarded as outside the realm of "discrimination" by reason of it being an inherent occupational requirement. Although the Convention does not explicitly mention such an exception, it would seem in keeping with the spirit of the Convention for the Committee to recognize that measures based on the inherent requirements of jobs do not represent discrimination, in a similar way to the recognition of the principle in article 1 (2) of the ILO Convention (No. 111) concerning Discrimination in respect of Employment and Occupation.

7.10 The State party submits that there has been no relevant impairment of the right to work or free choice of employment through the current scheme. The institution of regulatory schemes governing the prerequisites for admission to practise in a particular profession and applying equally to all does not infringe or impair an individual's right to work. Implicit in the author's complaint is that he should have the right to work as a doctor and the right to have his qualifications recognized by the health authorities in Australia without undergoing any form of external examination. In the Australian Government's view, such an argument misunderstands the nature of the internationally recognized right to work.

7.11 Under international law, the right to work does not confer a right to work in the position of one's choice. Instead, by recognizing the right to work, States parties undertake not to inhibit employment opportunities and to work towards the implementation of policies and measures aimed at ensuring there is work for those seeking it. In the current context the

Australian Government is not impairing anyone's right to work. In fact, the relevant legislative schemes merely regulate the means of practising a particular profession.

7.12 The system of admission to unrestricted practice does not impair the right of anyone to free choice of employment, let alone persons of a particular national origin. Recognition of a right to free choice of employment is designed to prevent forced labour, not to guarantee an individual the right to the particular job he/she desires. In the present context, there is no servitude or forced labour regime which impairs the choice of employment of doctors of a particular national origin. Instead, there is a system of examinations which permits entry into unrestricted practice.

7.13 Similarly, whilst counsel has attempted to argue that the author is equally placed to Australian doctors in terms of competence and that his experience should be a sufficient demonstration of competence, the State party submits that there is no evidence that doctors of Indian national origin should be treated differently to overseas-trained doctors of other national origins. Nor is there compelling evidence to suggest that the subjection of the author to the AMC examinations is unreasonable and evidence of racial discrimination. Despite counsel's reliance on the author's practice in public hospitals, the State party notes that at all relevant times, the author's practice has been circumscribed by strict supervision and limited practice requirements commensurate with his status as a conditional registrant. The State party would thus reject any implication that his work in Australia demonstrates sufficient competence to warrant automatic general registration.

7.14 The State party denies that the standard of the AMC examinations is higher than that expected of students at Australian and New Zealand medical schools. Steps have been taken to ensure the comparability of the examination system, including: (a) the appointment of a Board of Examiners with broad experience in teaching and examining undergraduates, and therefore familiar with the curricula of Australian university medical schools; (b) the use of a bank of approximately 3,000 MCQ questions mostly drawn from MCQ examination papers of the medical schools of Australian universities and questions specifically commissioned by the AMC from Australian medical schools; (c) the MCQ examination papers are marked by Educational Testing Centre at the University of

New South Wales, a major national testing authority which also provides information in relation to the statistical reliability and validity of the questions. If data indicate that a particular question fails as a discriminator of performance, or if there is evidence to suggest that a question could be misleading, the Board of Examiners is able to delete that question from the examination; (d) instructing both the MCQ and clinical examiners to the effect that the examinations should be directed to establishing whether AMC candidates have the same level of medical knowledge and medical skills as new graduates.

7.15 The past practice of adjustment of raw scores in the MCQ examination does not reflect any racial discrimination, or a racially discriminatory quota. Such adjustment was designed as a method of standardization to prevent unrepresentative results based on the particular examination.

7.16 Other than his particular complaints about his failure to pass the examinations, the author has not advanced any objective evidence to support the non-comparability of the examination standards. The only study produced by the author's counsel merely comments on perceptions of deficiencies in the standard of first year interns, rather than the comparability of the forms of examination to which OTDs and AMC-accredited medical students are subject.

7.17 Quite apart from the nature of the examinations in themselves, the author has failed to make a case that any disparity in standards of the MCQ examinations and standards at AMC-accredited universities has the purpose or effect of discriminating against persons of a particular national origin. When the figures of national origin and success rates in the MCQ are compared, there is no evidence of discrimination against persons of a particular national origin. In particular, there is no evidence that persons of Indian national origin are less likely than persons of other national origin to pass the examination. The State party provides a table of results in the 1994 exams (the last year in which the quota applied), showing that Indian students' success rates in the AMC exams are proportionate to their entry levels in the examinations. Whilst Indian doctors comprised 16.48 per cent of doctors attempting the MCQ examination in 1994, they represented 16.83 per cent of those successfully passing the MCQ examination.

7.18 The author alleges that during the period of the operation of the quota system between July 1992 and October 1995, the exclusion of OTDs such as himself from the AMC clinical examination on the basis of his quota ranking constituted racial discrimination and was a denial of his right to equal enjoyment of the right to work and free choice of employment under article 5 (e) (i).

7.19 When the Australian Health Ministers' Conference (AHMC) resolved to introduce the quota on OTDs in early 1992, the OTDs in the process of undergoing the AMC examinations numbered approximately 4,500, almost four times the number of doctors expected to graduate from Australian medical schools. In the face of such a large number of OTDs seeking to practise in Australia and mindful of the national workforce supply target (set at one doctor per 500 persons), the AHMC adopted a National Medical Workforce Strategy comprising a number of initiatives. One of them was the introduction of a quota on the numbers of OTDs who would be allowed to sit the clinical examination, having passed the MCQ examination. Thus, the AHMC requested the AMC to set a cap of 200 on the number of candidates proceeding annually to the clinical examinations. The request was made on the basis of: (a) the number of doctors needed to service the Australian community to requisite standards; (b) the cost of the provision of medical services under an open-ended funding commitment and the impact on that cost of a more than optimum number of doctors; (c) the geographic distribution of doctors; and (d) the degree to which the supply of doctors is sufficient to meet the needs of particular community groups and particular specialities.

7.20 The quota was not racially discriminatory in any form. Firstly, it applied to all OTDs regardless of national origin, with persons of a variety of national origins, including Australians, being subject to the requirement. Nor is there any evidence that the quota disproportionately affected persons of Indian national origin. In evidence before the Federal Court, for example, the proportion of doctors of Indian birth gaining entry to the quota was in fact marginally higher than the percentage of doctors of Indian birth attempting the MCQ examination. Furthermore, the quota on doctors trained overseas was complemented by the pre-existing de facto quota on students seeking entry to Australian medical schools.

7.21 Secondly, even if the quota could be considered to have benefited those who have attended Australian and New Zealand medical schools, such persons are not characterized by a national origin. Instead, they would be likely to share citizenship, a factor outside the realm of the Convention.

7.22 Thirdly, even if (for the purposes of argument) the Committee was of the view that the quota represented a distinction on the basis of national origin, the State party would submit that the quota was a reasonable measure, proportionate to meeting the State's legitimate interest in controlling the number of health-care providers and hence was not an arbitrary distinction. Such a purpose is not inconsistent with the Convention and would only infringe the Convention if such policies, designed to deal with the supply of medical professionals, disguised racial discrimination. Whilst the details of the quota were subject to some criticism by the HREOC (in that it did not provide for a waiting list, but required OTDs not initially successful in coming within the annual quota to undergo the examination again), such a factor does not make the quota unreasonable or discriminatory.

7.23 As the State party has previously noted, the quota is no longer in existence and the author has been permitted to sit for the clinical examination on several occasions. He has thus been afforded a remedy, if any was required. The State party's view remains that the subject matter is moot.

7.24 The State party further considers that the author's complaint concerning the application of the quota to all OTDs regardless of citizenship status does not fall within the terms of the Convention. Under article 1 (2) of the Convention States parties are not prohibited from discriminating on the basis of citizenship. Conversely, the imposition of a system which does not take account of citizenship cannot be the basis of complaint under the Convention.

7.25 Furthermore, the State party denies that the judgement of the Federal Court has the effect of reducing the protection accorded to Australians under the Racial Discrimination Act 1975. The issues raised by the author under this allegation relate primarily to the interpretation of domestic legislation which should not be the subject of separate investigation by the Committee. The Racial Discrimination Act 1975 remains an appropriate and effective means of eradicating racial discrimination.

7.26 Finally, the State party notes the author's allegations that Australia continues to act in violation of article 5 (e) (i) on the grounds that the AMC has raised the pass criteria for the clinical examination to compensate for the discontinuation of the quota system. The author alleges that his failure to pass the clinical examination is evidence of this practice and of the fact that he is being victimized for lodging his original complaint with the HREOC in 1995. The State party contends that this complaint continues to be subject to the investigation of the HREOC and thus remains an inappropriate subject for the Committee's examination.

*Counsel's comments*

8.1 In his response to the State party's observations counsel indicates that unlike other countries where both local graduates and overseas-trained doctors are assessed by sitting exactly the same national licensing examination, in Australia there is a differential system with one regime for overseas-trained doctors and another for Australian graduates. The Australian graduate is assessed by his/her university on the basis of what he/she has been taught. It is primarily an exercise in curriculum recall rather that an assessment of essential medical knowledge and clinical competence. The Australian Medical Council's own witnesses in the author's case before the HREOC have conceded that in undergraduate assessment the aim is to try and pass the student. Indeed, pass rates for final-year medical students in Australian universities are close to 100 per cent. On the contrary, the AMC MCQ examination purports to assess whether a doctor possesses sufficient knowledge for safe practice. In 1995 the Australian Medical Council conducted a trial in which its 1994 MCQ paper was submitted to final-year medical students at Monash University and Sydney University. The results of the trial clearly reveal that a higher assessment standard is applied to OTDs than to Australian graduates and that the quota served to disadvantage overseas doctors when compared to local graduates.

8.2 As regards the AMC clinical examination, the differential nature of the system is even more manifest. The author has attempted the AMC clinical examination on four occasions. On each occasion he has been failed. He lodged a further complaint with the HREOC, which has not issued a decision yet. In the course of the hearing, the true nature of the AMC clinical examination system has been revealed. It has been exposed as a chaotic, unstructured and unreliable assessment tool which, in form and content, departs markedly from the system used to assess students in Australian universities. Moreover, the AMC's own internal working parties have emphasized the inadequacies of its examination system and the need to improve its reliability and validity.

8.3 Counsel provides a table showing pass rates in the AMC clinical examination by country of birth during the period 1995 to 1997. The pass rate for persons born in India is 45.9 per cent, for those born in the Middle East 43.6 per cent and for those born in Asia 43.5 per cent. For those born in the United States or Canada the pass rate is 55.6 per cent, for Western Europe 62.5 per cent, for the United Kingdom and Ireland 77.1 per cent and for South Africa 81.1 per cent. Counsel wonders whether these differential pass rates are merely a reflection of the quality of medical education in the countries in question or whether conscious or unconscious perceptions of racial "compatibility" play a part. It is well established that many people make conscious or unconscious judgements about a person's competence on the basis of race and colour and if an examination system has a format that gives free rein to any prejudices that may exist, then it is not competence alone which determines the result. Counsel also quotes a number of reports and statements by Australian institutions indicating that the country needs more trained doctors and that the system of accreditation of overseas-trained doctors is unfair and discriminatory.

8.4 With respect to the quota system, counsel argues that the quota was a quantitative control designed to shut out a number of overseas-trained doctors not because they were trained overseas but because they were from overseas. There is a close correlation between place of birth and place of training in that most people are educated in their country of birth. Accordingly, a restriction purportedly based on place of training is effectively a restriction based on national origin, particularly if that restriction is in no way connected to the issue of training. He also states that in the author's 1995 case before the HREOC there was no clear evidence of an oversupply of doctors in the country. Rather, it was the increase in the number of Australian medical graduates coupled with the automatic registration of doctors from the United Kingdom (which existed until recently) which

had been the major reasons for the increase in doctors' numbers. It was also emphasized that the principal supply problem was one of geographical distribution of doctors, that the imposition of the quota was motivated by a desire to restrict the number of doctors to control the health expenditures of Commonwealth countries (and protect doctors' incomes) and that the Health Ministers' advisers were advocating immigration quotas, not examination quotas. The only reasonable conclusion to be drawn from the evidence of the Government's own witnesses and reports was that the decision to impose the quota was based not on fact and analysis but on feelings and perceptions.

8.5 The State party asserts that the author has been practising medicine in Australia under temporary registration and that he is subject to strict supervision and practice requirements while working as a practitioner in the public hospital system. This statement is totally untrue. The author has now worked as a doctor for 14 years, 10 of which have been in Australian public hospitals. He is classified as a Senior Hospital Medical Officer Year 5 and in his last position at Maroondah Hospital (a large hospital in Melbourne) he was the Night Senior, i.e., he was in charge of the whole hospital at night. Unfortunately, he is now unable to practise even under temporary registration. The Medical Board of Victoria, following advice from the Australian Medical Council regarding his examination results, has placed such tight restrictions on this registration that it has made him unemployable.

8.6 The State party asserts that the United States, Canada, the United Kingdom and New Zealand have similar examination systems to Australia. It does not say, however, that while the United States and Canada have an initial evaluating examination for overseas-trained doctors, the licensing examination is the same for both overseas-trained and locally trained doctors. Thus, there is not a differential system allowing differential standards and open to abuse, as is the case in Australia.

8.7 Counsel further states that the right to work must embrace the right to be fairly assessed to work in the occupation for which a person is qualified and not to be denied that right by reasons of a capricious assessment system or quota.

9.1 In accordance with rule 94, paragraph 6, of its rules of procedure, the Committee reconsidered the question of admissibility in the light of the observations made by the State party with respect to the Committee's decision of 19 August 1997 that declared the communication admissible. The Committee, however, did not find reasons to revoke its previous decision, since the State party's observations as well as the author's comments thereon referred mainly to the substance of the matter. In the circumstances, the Committee proceeded with the examination of the merits.

9.2 The main issue before the Committee is whether the examination and the quota system for overseas-trained doctors respect the author's right, under article 5 (e) (i) of the Convention, to work and to free choice of employment. The Committee notes in this respect that all overseas-trained doctors are subjected to the same quota system and are required to sit the same written and clinical examinations, irrespective of their race or national origin. Furthermore, on the basis of the information provided by the author it is not possible to reach the conclusion that the system works to the detriment of persons of a particular race or national origin. Even if the system favours doctors trained in Australian and New Zealand medical schools such an effect would not necessarily constitute discrimination on the basis of race or national origin since, according to the information provided, medical students in Australia do not share a single national origin.

9.3 In the Committee's view, there is no evidence to support the author's argument that he has been penalized in the clinical examination for having complained to the HREOC, in view of the fact that an independent observer, appointed by him, was present during two of his attempts.

10. The Committee on the Elimination of Racial Discrimination, acting under article 14, paragraph 7 (a), of the International Convention on the Elimination of All Forms of Racial Discrimination, is of the opinion that the facts as submitted do not disclose a violation of article 5 (e) (i) or any other provision of the Convention.

11.1 Pursuant to article 14, paragraph 7 (b), of the Convention, the Committee recommends that the State party take all necessary measures and give transparency to the procedure and curriculum established and conducted by the Australian Medical Council, so that the system is in no way discriminatory towards foreign candidates irrespective of their race or national or ethnic origin.

11.2 After considering several complaints concerning Australia under article 14 of the Convention, the Committee also recommends to the State party that every effort be made to avoid any delay in the consideration of all complaints by the Human Rights and Equal Opportunity Commission.

# Communication No. 10/1997

*Submitted by*: Ziad Ben Ahmed Habassi (represented by counsel).
*Alleged victim*: The petitioner.
*State party*: Denmark.
*Date of adoption of Opinion:* 17 March 1999.
*Subject matter:* Refusal of bank loan to non-citizens; access to effective mechanisms of protection; effective investigation.
*Procedural issues:* Exhaustion of domestic remedies.
*Substantive issues:* Right to an effective remedy against acts of racial discrimination; right to an effective investigation; discrimination based on national origin.
*Articles of the Convention:* 2 (1) (a) and (d), and 6.
*Finding*: Violation (arts. 6 and 2 (1) (d) in combination).

*Opinion*

1.   The author of the communication is Ziad Ben Ahmed Habassi, a Tunisian citizen born in 1972 currently residing in Århus, Denmark. He claims to be a victim of violation by Denmark of article 2, paragraph 1 (d), and article 6 of

the International Convention on the Elimination of All Forms of Racial Discrimination. He is represented by counsel.

## The facts as presented by the author

2.1 On 17 May 1996 the author visited the shop "Scandinavian Car Styling" to purchase an alarm set for his car. When he inquired about procedures for obtaining a loan he was informed that "Scandinavian Car Styling" cooperated with Sparbank Vest, a local bank, and was given a loan application form which he completed and returned immediately to the shop. The application form included, inter alia, a standard provision according to which the person applying for the loan declared himself or herself to be a Danish citizen. The author, who had a permanent residence permit in Denmark and was married to a Danish citizen, signed the form in spite of this provision.

2.2 Subsequently, Sparbank Vest informed the author that it would approve the loan only if he could produce a Danish passport or if his wife was indicated as applicant. The author was also informed that it was the general policy of the bank not to approve loans to non-Danish citizens.

2.3 The author contacted the Documentary and Advisory Center for Racial Discrimination (DRC) in Copenhagen, an independent institution which had been in contact with Sparbank Vest on previous occasions about the bank's loan policy vis-à-vis foreigners. In a letter dated 10 January 1996 the DRC had requested Sparbank Vest to indicate the reasons for a loan policy requiring applicants to declare that they were Danish citizens. Sparbank Vest had informed the DRC, by letter of 3 March 1996, that the requirement of citizenship mentioned in the application form was to be understood merely as a requirement of permanent residence in Denmark. Later, the DRC requested information from the bank about the number of foreigners who had actually obtained loans. On 9 April 1996 Sparbank Vest informed the DRC that the bank did not register whether a customer was a Danish citizen or not and therefore it was not in a position to provide the information requested. It also said that in cases of foreign applicants the bank made an evaluation taking into account whether the connection to Denmark had a temporary character. In the bank's experience, only by a permanent and stable connection to the country was it possible to provide the necessary service and ensure stable communication with the customer.

2.4 On 23 May 1996 the DRC reported the incident concerning the author to the police department in Skive on behalf of the author, alleging that the bank had violated the Danish Act on the prohibition of differential treatment on the basis of race. The DRC enclosed copies of its previous correspondence with Sparbank Vest. By letter dated 12 August 1996 the police informed the DRC that the investigation had been discontinued given the lack of evidence that an unlawful act had been committed. The letter indicated that the requirement of Danish citizenship had to be considered in connection with the possibility of enforcement and that the bank had given assurances that the provision would be deleted when printing new application forms.

2.5 On 21 August 1996 the DRC lodged a complaint with the State Prosecutor in Viborg, challenging the decision of the police department to consider the citizenship criterion legitimate. The author had a clear permanent connection to Denmark in view of the fact that he was married to a Danish citizen and had a regular job. The fact that the bank still insisted on documentation with regard to Danish citizenship constituted a discriminatory act which could not be justified by the bank's interest in enforcing its claim. The DRC also emphasized the fact that Sparbank Vest had not provided any information regarding foreign customers, despite the fact that such information was relevant to determine whether or not the loan policy was discriminatory. By letter dated 6 November 1996 the State Prosecutor informed the DRC that he did not see any reason to overrule the police decision.

2.6 The author indicates that the decision of the State Prosecutor is final, in accordance with section 101 of the Danish Administration of Justice Act. He also states that questions relating to bringing charges against individuals are entirely at the discretion of the police and, therefore, the author has no possibility of bringing the case before a court.

## The complaint

3.1 Counsel claims that the facts stated above amount to violations of article 2, paragraph 1 (d), and article 6 of the Convention, according to which alleged cases of discrimination have to be investigated thoroughly by the national authorities. In the present case neither the police department of Skive nor the State Prosecutor examined whether the bank's loan policy constituted indirect discrimination on the basis of national origin and race. In particular, they should have examined the following issues: first, to what extent persons applying for loans were requested to show their passports; second, to what extent Sparbank Vest granted loans to non-Danish citizens; third, to what extent Sparbank Vest granted loans to Danish citizens living abroad.

3.2 Counsel further claims that in cases such as the one under consideration there might be a reasonable justification for permanent residence. However, if loans were actually granted to Danish citizens who did not have their permanent residence in Denmark, the criterion of citizenship would in fact constitute racial discrimination, in accordance with article 1, subparagraph 1, of the Convention. It would be especially relevant for the police to investigate whether an intentional or an unintentional act of discrimination in violation of the Convention had taken place.

*State party's submission on admissibility and counsel's comments*

4.1 In a submission dated 28 April 1998 the State party notes that according to section 1 (1) of Act No. 626 (Act against Discrimination) any person who, while performing occupational or non-profit activities, refuses to serve a person on the same conditions as others due to that person's race, colour, national or ethnic origin, religion or sexual orientation is liable to a fine or imprisonment. Violation of the Act is subject to public prosecution, i.e., private individuals cannot bring a case before the courts.

4.2 If the prosecutor considers that no offence has been committed, or that it will not be possible to bring evidence sufficient for conviction and, therefore, discontinues the investigation, the injured party still has the possibility of bringing a civil action claiming compensation for pecuniary or non-pecuniary damage. An action claiming compensation for pecuniary damage is not relevant in the present case, since the loan was actually granted with the applicant's wife listed as borrower and the applicant as spouse. It would, however, have been relevant to bring a civil declaratory action against the bank claiming that it acted against the law when it refused the loan application. Such action is

recognized in domestic case-law. Accordingly, the State party considers that a civil action is a possible remedy which the applicant should have made use of and that the non-use of this remedy renders the case inadmissible.

4.3 The State party also argues that the author had the possibility of complaining to the Ombudsman of the Danish Parliament about the decision of the prosecutor. The fact that the prosecutors are part of the public administration means that their activities are subject to the Ombudsman's power to investigate whether they pursue unlawful aims, whether they make arbitrary or unreasonable decisions or whether they commit errors or omissions in other ways in the performance of their duties. The result of a complaint to the Ombudsman may be that the police and the prosecutor reopen the investigation.

4.4 The State party also argues that the communication is manifestly ill-founded. Its objections, however, are explained in its assessment of the merits of the case.

5.1 Counsel contends that the State party fails to indicate on which provision of the Danish Act on Tort it bases its claim that civil action can be taken against Sparbank Vest. He assumes that the State party refers to section 26 of the Act. However, to his knowledge, no cases relating to racial discrimination have ever been decided by Danish courts on the basis of that section. Accordingly, there is no evidence in Danish case-law to support the interpretation given by the State party.

5.2 Counsel also contends that a private party may only be liable under section 26 if there is an act which infringes national law. In the present case, however, the relevant bodies within the prosecution system did not find any reason to investigate; it would, therefore, have been very difficult to convince a court that there was any basis for liability on the part of Sparbank Vest. In those circumstances a theoretical remedy based on section 26 of the Danish Act on Tort does not seem to be an effective remedy within the meaning of the Convention.

5.3 With respect to the possibility of filing a complaint with the Ombudsman, counsel argues that such remedy is irrelevant, since the Ombudsman's decisions are not legally binding.

*The Committee's admissibility decision*

6.1 During its fifty-third session in August 1998 the Committee examined the admissibility of the communication. It duly considered the State party's contention that the author had failed to exhaust domestic remedies but concluded that the civil remedies proposed by the State party could not be considered an adequate avenue of redress. The complaint which was filed first with the police department and subsequently with the State Prosecutor alleged the commission of a criminal offence and sought a conviction under the Danish Act against Discrimination. The same objective could not be achieved by instituting a civil action, which would lead only to compensation for damages.

6.2 At the same time the Committee was not convinced that a civil action would have any prospect of success, given that the State Prosecutor had not considered it pertinent to initiate criminal proceedings regarding the applicant's claim. Nor was there much evidence in the information brought to the attention of the Committee that a complaint before the Ombudsman would result in the case being reopened. Any decision to institute criminal proceedings would still be subject to the discretion of the State Prosecutor. No possibilities would then be left for the complainant to file a case before a court.

6.3 Accordingly, on 17 August 1998, the Committee declared the communication admissible.

*The State party's observations on the merits*

7.1 The State party submits that Mr. Habassi complained to the police on 28 May 1996. On 12 August 1996 the police interviewed the credit manager of Sparbank Vest in Skive, who was notified of Mr. Habassi's complaint. According to the police report the manager stated that all loan applicants signed the same type of application form and that the Danish Bankers Association had decided that the phrase "that I am a Danish national" would be deleted when the application forms were reprinted. No further investigative steps were taken. By letter dated 12 August 1996 the Chief Constable in Skive informed the DRC that it had decided to discontinue the investigation, since it could not reasonably be assumed that a criminal offence subject to public prosecution had been committed. The letter also provided details on the possibility of filing an action for damages and enclosed guidelines on how to file a complaint. By letter of the same date the Chief Constable also informed Sparbank Vest that the investigation had been discontinued.

7.2 The State party recalls that on 21 August 1996 the DRC complained about the Chief Constable's decision to the District Public Prosecutor in Viborg. DRC stated in its complaint that it found it worrying that the Chief Constable apparently considered the requirement of nationality motivated by the need to ensure enforcement to be a lawful criterion. Mr. Habassi had a Danish civil registration number and a national register address in Denmark. That in itself ought to have been sufficient to prove his ties with Denmark. In addition, he stated on the loan application that he received a salary and had a Danish spouse. The bank's practice of demanding documentation about nationality was a discriminatory act which could not be justified by considerations of enforcement.

7.3 DRC also stated that for Mr. Habassi it was immaterial whether the refusal of the bank was based on negative attitudes towards ethnic minorities (for instance that they are poor debtors) or on genuine concern on the part of the bank about enforcement. The salient fact was that despite having satisfied all the conditions for being granted a loan, he was required (probably because of his foreign-sounding name) to provide further documentation. It was therefore Mr. Habassi's Middle East background that was the cause of the refusal and not the more formal criterion of nationality. The bank's statement that the requirement of Danish nationality would be removed from the application forms did not alter the fact that Mr. Habassi had been exposed to unlawful differential treatment against which the Danish authorities had a duty to offer protection pursuant to the Convention.

7.4 The State party also recalls that the District Public Prosecutor found no basis for reversing the Chief Constable's decision and argued, in particular, that neither the Act against Discrimination nor the Convention include nationality as an independent ground of discrimination. Against this background it must be assumed that discrimination against foreign nationals only violates the Act to the extent that it could be assimilated to discrimination on the basis of national origin or one of the other grounds listed in section 1 (1). According to the legislative history of the Act, it had to be presumed that certain forms of differential treatment could be considered lawful if they pursued a legitimate aim seen in the light of the purpose of the Act. In the processing of loan applications the applicant's ties with Denmark may be of importance, among other things, for assessing the possibility of enforcement of the creditor's claim. In consideration of this the data concerning the applicant's nationality were objectively justified.

7.5 The State party argues that the police investigation in the present case satisfies the requirement that can be inferred from the Convention and the Committee's practice. According to the Administration of Justice Act the police initiates an investigation when it can be reasonably assumed that a criminal offence subject to public prosecution has been committed. The purpose of the investigation is to clarify whether the conditions for imposing criminal liability or other criminal sanctions have been fulfilled. The police will reject an information laid if no basis is found for initiating an investigation. If there is no basis for continuing an investigation already initiated, the decision to discontinue it can also be made by the police, provided no provisional charge has been made.

7.6 In the State party's opinion, there is no basis for criticizing the Chief Constable's and the District Public Prosecutor's decisions, which were taken after an investigation had actually been carried out. The police took the information seriously and its decision was not unsubstantiated. The decision was not only based on the information forwarded by the author, including the written correspondence with the bank about its credit policy, but also on interviews with the author and a credit manager of the bank.

7.7 The State party refers to the Committee's opinion regarding communication 4/1991 in which the Committee stated that "when threats of racial violence are made and especially when they are made in public and by a group, it is incumbent upon the State to investigate with due diligence and expedition".[1] It argues, however, that the present case is of a different nature and therefore the Committee cannot reasonably set out the same requirements to investigate as in the said opinion. Even if the requirement that it is incumbent on the police to "investigate with due diligence and expedition" were to apply in the present case,

---

[1] *L.K.* v. *Netherlands*, para. 6.6.

where the loan application was actually granted, the State party considers that the requirement was met. Although the information laid did not lead to prosecution, the handling of it by the police did afford the applicant effective protection and remedies within the meaning of article 2, paragraph 1 (d), and article 6 of the Convention.

7.8 The State party further contends that there is no basis either for criticizing the legal assessment made by the prosecutor. It is noted in this connection that not every differentiation of treatment is unlawful discrimination within the meaning of the Convention. In general recommendation XIV on article 1, paragraph 1, of the Convention the Committee stated that "a differentiation of treatment will not constitute discrimination if the criteria for such differentiation, judged against the objectives and purposes of the Convention, are legitimate (...). In considering the criteria that may have been employed, the Committee will acknowledge that particular actions may have varied purposes. In seeking to determine whether an action has an effect contrary to the Convention it will look to see whether that action has an unjustifiable disparate impact upon a group distinguished by race, colour, descent or national or ethnic origin." The decisions of both the Chief Constable and the District Public Prosecutor show that the decisions were based on the fact that differentiation of treatment that pursues a legitimate aim and respects the requirement of proportionality is not prohibited discrimination.

7.9 Finally, the State party dismisses the author's claims that questions relating to the pursuance by the police of charges against individuals are entirely up to the discretion of the police and that there is no possibility of bringing the case before the Danish courts. Firstly, it is possible to complain to the relevant District Public Prosecutor; secondly, the applicant had the possibility of filing a civil action against the bank; and thirdly, the applicant had the possibility of complaining to the Ombudsman. The effect of such complaint to the Ombudsman may be that the police and the prosecutor reopen the investigation.

*Counsel's comments*

8.1 Counsel contends that the police interviewed the author but had only a brief telephone conversation with the bank. No detailed investigation, for example about the requirements concerning Danish citizens living abroad, was carried out. The police did not at all examine whether the case amounted to indirect discrimination within the meaning of the Convention. The Committee, however, stressed the duty of States parties to duly investigate reported incidents of racial discrimination in its concluding observations regarding communication 4/1991.

8.2 The State party states that the requirement of Danish citizenship was only to be seen in connection with the assessment of the ties with Denmark of the person applying for a loan in correlation, therefore, with the possibilities of subsequent judicial recovery of the amount of the loan in case of default. Counsel underlines that such reason was not mentioned by the credit manager of Sparbank Vest, as reflected in the police report. The report says that the police assistant E.P. had contacted the credit director of Sparbank Vest who was of the opinion that the bank had not done anything illegal in connection with the loan application in question, since all applicants signed the same type of application form with the formulation "that I am a Danish citizen". The bank did not mention any particular reason for its practice. It did not, in particular, declare that there was a requirement of residence due to the possibility of enforcing claims against debtors. It appears, therefore, that the reason in question had been made up by the police in Skive on their own initiative. Even if the reason came from the bank itself it appears to be highly irrelevant for an evaluation of whether the requirements of the Convention have been met.

8.3 It is clear that Danish citizenship is not a guarantee for subsequent judicial recovery of the defaulted amount if the Danish citizen lives, for example, in Tunisia. The application of a criterion of citizenship for the reason given by the police would indeed be a serious indication that indirect discrimination on grounds prohibited by the Convention had taken place. The possibilities of subsequent judicial recovery would rather justify a criterion of residence. However, with respect to such criterion counsel draws the attention of the Committee to a letter of 6 April 1995 addressed to the DRC in which the Minister of Business Affairs (Erhvervsministeren) expresses the view that a credit policy according to which no credit is granted to persons unless they have lived in Denmark for at least five years would be contrary to the discrimination rules. It is the author's conclusion that the police did not at all attempt

to clarify with the bank the real reason behind the requirement of citizenship.

8.4 Counsel states that, according to the State party, the decisions of the Chief Constable and the State Prosecutor were based on the fact that differentiation of treatment that pursues a legitimate aim and respects the requirements of proportionality is not prohibited discrimination. He argues, however, that the authorities did not in fact examine whether a legitimate aim was pursued by the bank and that in cases of alleged discrimination the decision whether or not to initiate proceedings must be taken after a thorough investigation of the alleged cases of discrimination.

*Examination of the merits*

9.1 The Committee has considered the author's case in the light of all the submissions and documentary evidence produced by the parties, as required under article 14, paragraph 7 (a), of the Convention and rule 95 of its rules of procedure. It bases its findings on the following considerations.

9.2 Financial means are often needed to facilitate integration in society. To have access to the credit market and be allowed to apply for a financial loan on the same conditions as those which are valid for the majority in the society is, therefore, an important issue.

9.3 In the present case the author was refused a loan by a Danish bank on the sole ground of his non-Danish nationality and was told that the nationality requirement was motivated by the need to ensure that the loan was repaid. In the opinion of the Committee, however, nationality is not the most appropriate requisite when investigating a person's will or capacity to reimburse a loan. The applicant's permanent residence or the place where his employment, property or family ties are to be found may be more relevant in this context. A citizen may move abroad or have all his property in another country and thus evade all attempts to enforce a claim of repayment. Accordingly, the Committee finds that, on the basis of article 2, paragraph (d), of the Convention, it is appropriate to initiate a proper investigation into the real reasons behind the bank's loan policy vis-à-vis foreign residents, in order to ascertain whether or not criteria involving racial discrimination, within the meaning of article 1 of the Convention, are being applied.

9.4 The Committee notes that the author, considering the incident an offence under the Danish Act against Discrimination, reported it to the police. First the police and subsequently the State Prosecutor in Viborg accepted the explanations provided by a representative of the bank and decided not to investigate the case further. In the Committee's opinion, however, the steps taken by the police and the State Prosecutor were insufficient to determine whether or not an act of racial discrimination had taken place.

10. In the circumstances, the Committee is of the view that the author was denied effective remedy within the meaning of article 6 of the Convention in connection with article 2 (d).

11.1 The Committee recommends that the State party take measures to counteract racial discrimination in the loan market.

11.2 The Committee further recommends that the State party provide the applicant with reparation or satisfaction commensurate with any damage he has suffered.

12. Pursuant to rule 95, paragraph 5, of its rules of procedure, the Committee would wish to receive information, as appropriate and in due course, on any relevant measures taken by the State party with respect to the recommendations set out in paragraphs 11.1 and 11.2.

# Communication No. 11/1998

*Submitted by*: Miroslav Lacko (represented by counsel, the European Roma Rights Center).
*Alleged victim*: The petitioner.
*State party*: Slovakia.
*Date of adoption of Opinion:* 9 August 2001.
*Subject matter:* Discrimination in access to a restaurant based on Roma origin; access to effective mechanisms of protection.
*Procedural issues:* Exhaustion of domestic remedies.
*Substantive issues:* Right to an effective remedy against acts of racial discrimination; discrimination based on ethnic and national origin; right of access to any place or service intended for use by the general public; State parties undertake to prevent, prohibit and eradicate all practices of racial segregation and apartheid in territories under their jurisdiction.
*Articles of the Convention:* 2, 3, 4, 5, 6 and 14 (7) (a).
*Finding*: No violation

*Opinion*

1. The petitioner is Miroslav Lacko, a Slovak citizen of Romany ethnicity. He claims to be a victim of violations by the Slovak Republic of articles 2, 3, 4, 5 and 6 of the International Convention on the Elimination of All Forms of Racial Discrimination. He is represented by the European Roma Rights Center, a non-governmental organization based in Budapest, acting as legal counsel.

*The facts as submitted by the petitioner*

2.1 On 24 April 1997 the petitioner, accompanied by other persons of Romany ethnicity, went to the Railway Station Restaurant located in the main railway station in Kosice, Slovakia, to have a drink. Shortly after entering the restaurant the applicant and his company were told by a waitress to leave the restaurant. The waitress explained that she was acting in accordance with an order given by the owner of the restaurant not to serve Roma. After requesting to speak with her supervisor, the petitioner was directed to a man who explained that the restaurant was not serving Roma, because several Roma had previously destroyed equipment in the restaurant. When the petitioner related that neither he nor his company had damaged any equipment, the person in charge repeated that only polite Roma would be served.

2.2 On 7 May 1997, the petitioner filed a complaint with the General Prosecutor's Office in Bratislava, requesting an investigation to determine whether an offence had been committed. The case was assigned to the County Prosecutor's Office in Kosice who referred the matter to the Railway Police. In the meantime the applicant also sought remedy from the Slovak Inspectorate of Commerce, responsible for overseeing the lawful operation of commercial enterprises. In a letter to the petitioner, dated 12 September 1997, the Inspectorate reported that it had conducted an investigation into the complaint during the course of which it had been observed that Roma women had been served at the restaurant and that the owner had arranged that there would be no other discrimination of any polite customers, Roma included.

2.3 By resolution dated 8 April 1998, the Railway Police Department in Kosice reported that it had conducted an investigation into the case and found no evidence that an offence had been committed. The petitioner appealed to the County Prosecutor who, in a resolution dated 24 April 1998, ruled that the decision of the Railway Police Department was valid and indicated that there was no further legal remedy available.

*The complaint*

3.1 Counsel states that the failure to remedy the discrimination in the instant case reflects the absence of any Slovak legislation, which expressly and effectively outlaws racial discrimination in access to public accommodations. Mr. Lacko has been forced to live with continuing uncertainty—dependent on the restaurant owner's racially motivated whim—as to whether he will be admitted to the restaurant on any given day. If the owner determines that on one day "polite" Roma will be served, then the applicant may be served if he is deemed sufficiently polite. If, however, the owner decides that no Roma will be served that day or that the applicant is not sufficiently polite, he will be denied service.

3.2 Counsel claims that a number of rights secured to the petitioner under the Convention have been violated, including article 2, paragraph 1 (d) taken together with article 5 (f); and articles 2, paragraph 2; 3; 4 (c); and article 6 of the Convention.

3.3 Counsel claims that Slovak criminal law has no provision applicable to the violation at issue in the instant case as required by article 2, paragraph 1 taken together with article 5 (f) of the Convention. The petitioner was denied equality before the law in that he and his Romany company suffered discrimination in access to service in the restaurant on grounds of race and/or ethnicity.

3.4 Counsel claims that by being refused service in the restaurant and told to leave solely for racial reasons, and then being told that only polite Roma would be admitted, the petitioner was subjected to policies of racial segregation. The State party's failure to provide any remedies and the absence of any legal norm expressly prohibiting non-discrimination in access to public accommodations constitute failure to comply with its obligation under article 3 of the Convention.

3.5 The State party's failure to sanction or remedy the restaurant's racially motivated discrimination against the petitioner and his Romany colleagues, in fact, promoted racial discrimination in violation of article 4 (c) of the Convention. In addition, the continued leasing of space to the restaurant by the main railway station, a public institution, further constitutes promotion by public institutions of racial discrimination.

3.6 Counsel further states that the objective of the communication is a recommendation by the Committee that: (1) the State party provide compensation for the humiliation and degradation the applicant has suffered in being subjected to racial discrimination in his access to the restaurant; (2) the State party take effective measures to ensure that racial discrimination is no longer practised at the restaurant; and (3) the State party adopt legislation expressly prohibiting, and providing effective remedies for, racial discrimination in places or services intended for use by the general public.

*Observations by the State party on admissibility*

4.1 By submission of 23 June 1999 the State party challenges the admissibility of the communication on grounds of non-exhaustion of domestic remedies. In accordance with section 30, paragraph 2, of Act No. 314/1996 on the Prosecution Authority the applicant had the possibility to file an application for review of the lawfulness of the Resolution with the Regional Prosecution Office in Kosice. A decision by the Regional Prosecution Office could have a substantial impact and result in new proceedings by the District Prosecution Office and the Railway Police.

4.2 Furthermore, the petitioner had the possibility of initiating a civil action under section 11 of the Civil Code, which states that natural persons shall have the right to the protection of their honour, human dignity, privacy, name and manifestations of personal nature. Belonging to a particular national minority or ethnic group is also one of the attributes of personality, therefore, the injured person may claim the protection of his/her personality in civil proceedings and ask the competent court to be given adequate satisfaction or granted compensation of immaterial injury. The resolution of the District Prosecution Office indicated in this respect that it was without prejudice on the entitlement of the injured party to damages that might be claimed in civil proceedings before a competent court.

4.3 Furthermore, the petitioner could have filed a complaint against the procedure and the result of the investigation carried out by the Inspectorate of Commerce, with the Central Inspectorate of the Slovak Inspectorate of Commerce or with the Ministry of Economy, to which the Slovak Inspectorate of Commerce reports. He could also have filed a complaint with the Office of the Government of the Slovak Republic, which, under section 2 of Act No. 10/1996 Coll. on the inspection in state administration, reviews the processing of petitions, complaints, communications and applications. He also failed to file a petition with the competent Trade Licence Office, in accordance with section 1 of Act No. 71/1967 Coll. on administrative procedure (the Rules of Administrative Procedure). Indeed, the District Prosecutor informed him on 3 July 1997 that he could file petitions with the above professional bodies.

4.4 The State party further submits that the communication does not make it clear which rights of the petitioner guaranteed under national law were violated, which domestic remedies were claimed and when the alleged violations took place. In his complaint with the General Prosecutor the petitioner alleged a crime of support and promotion of movements aiming at suppressing the rights and freedoms of citizens under section 260 of the Criminal Code. The Railway police suspended the examination of the case in view of the fact that it did not find grounds for such a crime and that the petitioner and his colleagues were served in the bar. In his appeal against the decision of the Railway police the petitioner did not object to the police conclusion regarding the alleged crime, but rather he claimed a violation of Act No. 634/1992 Coll. on consumer protection. Moreover, in his complaint to the Inspectorate of Commerce the petitioner sought investigation into the violation of a non-existent law on the protection of integrity. None of the complaints made it clear which violation of Act No. 634/1992 Coll. on consumer protection the petitioner claimed and what kind of remedy he sought.

4.5 According to the State party, staff from the Inspectorate of Commerce, as communicated to the petitioner by letter dated 12 September 1997, visited the restaurant accompanied by several Roma women who were duly served and in no way discriminated against. The Inspectorate carried out other subsequent visits to the restaurant but did not find any irregularity of the kind pointed out by the petitioner in his communication, nor did it receive complaints similar to Mr. Lacko's.

*Counsel's comments*

5.1 In a submission dated 2 August 1999 counsel objects to the State party's argument regarding the exhaustion of domestic remedies. He states that, according to international human rights jurisprudence, the local remedies rule requires the exhaustion of remedies that are available, effective and sufficient.

5.2 Counsel argues that a petition with the Regional Prosecution Office cannot be considered an effective remedy. Having filed a criminal complaint and waited for almost a year for the completion of the criminal investigation, having then timely appealed the conclusion of the police and having finally had his appeal rejected, the petitioner was under no obligation to pursue any further criminal remedy, especially insofar as he was expressly told that no further complaint was admissible.

5.3 Counsel states that the State party has pointed to no law or facts to suggest that a second petition would have met with any more favourable response than the criminal complaint initially filed; repeated petitions are not "effective remedies" for the purpose of admissibility requirements. Since the Resolution of the District Prosecution Office was issued on 24 April 1998, no new facts, which might have justified a renewed petition have arisen.

5.4 Counsel indicates that the petitioner was not required to seek any criminal remedy for the racial discrimination to which he was subjected, because, as a matter of law, there are no effective criminal remedies for racial discrimination in the State party. The State party has not pointed to a single criminal code provision, which expressly punishes discrimination on the grounds of race or ethnicity in access to public accommodations. The only articles of the criminal code, which address racism relate to racist speech and racially motivated violence.

5.5 Counsel objects to the State party's argument regarding the petitioner's failure to initiate civil action. It is stated that there are no effective civil or administrative remedies for racial discrimination available under Slovak law. Article 11 of the Civil Code is directed against acts of defamation or breach of privacy and makes no mention of discrimination on the grounds of race or ethnicity. Nor do any consumer protection laws contain a specific anti-discrimination provision with respect to race, which would make it possible to consider the instant case under the terms of the Convention.

5.6 The only remedies the Trade Licensing Board and the Slovak Inspectorate of Commerce could have afforded to the applicant, had they found his rights violated, would be to impose a fine on the restaurant and/or revoke its licence. These remedies are not effective or sufficient and are no substitute for the promulgation of legal norms capable of ensuring that individuals are not subjected to acts of racial discrimination.

5.7 Counsel contends that even when a given legal framework provides for a number of remedies capable of redressing the violation alleged, an individual is not required to pursue more than one. Where there is a choice of effective and sufficient remedies, it is up to the applicant to select one.

5.8 Counsel points out that the European Court has made clear that Government actions to terminate a violation of the European Convention, once one has occurred, do not in themselves erase the initial fact of the violation or render an application to the Strasbourg organs inadmissible. On the basis of that jurisprudence counsel contends that any subsequent termination of the refusal to serve the petitioner on the grounds of race in no way redresses the initial violation to which he was subjected or deprives him of victim status for the purpose of the present communication.

5.9 Finally, with respect to the State party's assertion that other Roma have been served at the Restaurant, counsel argues that such facts would in no way remedy the discrimination to which the petitioner was subjected. The fact that such rights may be arbitrarily afforded to others does not mitigate their arbitrary and discriminatory denial to the petitioner.

*The Committee's decision on admissibility*

6.1 At its 55th session in August 1999, the Committee considered the admissibility of the communication.

6.2 The Committee noted the State party's claims that the petitioner had failed to exhaust domestic remedies available to him. The Committee recalled that article 14, paragraph 7 (a), of the Convention provides that the Committee shall not consider any communication unless it has ascertained that all available domestic remedies have been exhausted. The Committee has held in its previous jurisprudence that a petitioner is only required to exhaust remedies that are effective in the circumstances of the particular case.[6]

6.3 The Committee has noted that the decision of the District Prosecutor was a final decision as far as the criminal procedure was concerned. The State party failed to demonstrate that a petition for review, which would be a remedy against the legality of the decision, could in the present case lead to a new examination of the complaint. Furthermore, the Committee finds that the facts of the claim were of such a nature that only criminal remedies could constitute an adequate avenue of redress. The objectives

---

[6] See *Anna Koptova* v. *Slovakia*, communication No. 13/1998, Opinion of 8 August 2000, para. 6.4.

pursued through a criminal investigation could not be achieved by means of civil or administrative remedies of the kind proposed by the State party. Therefore, the Committee found that no other effective remedies were available to the petitioner.

6.4 The Committee found that it lacked sufficient information to assess whether, as the petitioner stated, there was legislation in the State party guaranteeing for everyone the right of access to any place or service intended for use by the general public without distinction as to race, colour, or national or ethnic origin.

6.5 The Committee observed that the requirements for admissibility established under rule 91 of its rules of procedure had been met and decided that the communication was admissible. It requested the State party and the petitioner to provide information about domestic legislation and remedies intended to protect one's right of access to any place or service intended for use by the general public without distinction as to race, colour or national or ethnic origin, as contemplated in article 5 (f) of the Convention.

*State party's observations on the merits*

7.1 In submissions dated 25 November 1999 and 8 January 2001, the State party provides information on domestic legislation and remedies for the protection of individuals against racial discrimination in the criminal, civil and administrative fields.

7.2 The State party submits that fundamental rights are guaranteed to every person without discrimination in article 12, paragraph 2, of the Constitution. Protection of those rights can be enforced through administrative, civil and criminal procedures. Anyone is entitled to compensation of damage caused by an unlawful decision of a court, another state body or a public administration body on the basis of Act No.58/1969 Coll.

7.3 The State party further submits that administrative proceedings against the decision of a state organ commence with a complaint in which an individual or a legal entity claim to have their rights breached and request the court to review the lawfulness of the decision. The decision of the court is binding. The court can also rule on decisions of administrative bodies, which are not yet final. The State party admits that the Inspectorate of Commerce did not comply with the administrative procedure under which it is obliged to deal with the merits of the case. However, the petitioner could have filed a complaint with the Ministry of Economy, which is the central body of state administration in the field of consumer protection. He could also have filed a complaint under Act No. 58/1968 Coll. on State's liability for the unlawful decision of a state body. If the petitioner had used all the possibilities contemplated in the Slovak legal order, the restaurant owner could have been sanctioned.

7.4 Sections 11 to 17 of the Civil Code regulate the protection of personal integrity. Under section 13, a natural person has the right to have arbitrary or unlawful interference with his/her integrity stopped, the consequences of such interference removed and to be given appropriate satisfaction. If the moral satisfaction would seem insufficient because the dignity or respect enjoyed in society by the natural person was significantly harmed, this natural person is also entitled to compensation for non-pecuniary damage. The amount of compensation shall be determined by the court taking into account the magnitude of the damage and the circumstances under which the violation occurred. Part III, chapter V of the Code of Civil Procedure regulates the proceedings in matters concerning the protection of personal integrity. The system of civil remedies also distinguishes between regular remedies (appeal) and extraordinary remedies (renewal of proceedings and recourse).

7.5 The petitioner also had the option to seek the protection of his rights pursuant to sections 74, 75 and 102 of the Code of Civil Procedure, according to which a court may order preliminary measures in case it is necessary to have the situation of the parties regulated temporarily or if there is concern that the enforcement of the court decision might be endangered. Furthermore, on the basis of articles 1, 2, 12, 13, 17, 19 and 20 of the Constitution, sections 11 and 13 of the Civil Code should be interpreted as guaranteeing the protection of personal integrity against acts of racial discrimination.

7.6 The legal order of the Slovak Republic also contains legal provisions on consumer protection, in particular Act No. 634/1992 Coll.

Section 6 of this law prohibits discrimination explicitly. According to it, the seller may in no way discriminate against consumers, except when the consumer does not satisfy conditions set up under special rules, such as Act No. 219/1996 Coll. on the protection against abuse of alcoholic drinks. Public administration bodies can impose a sanction of up to 500,000 crowns for breaching these provisions. Repeated violation of the prohibition on consumer discrimination may be sanctioned with a fine up to 1 million crowns.

7.7 The Penal Code regulates protection against racial discrimination. In his criminal complaint the petitioner claimed that the acts alleged fell under section 260 of the Penal Code (support and promotion of movements aiming at suppressing the rights and freedoms of citizens). He did not invoke section 121 of the Penal Code (causing harm to a consumer) or misdemeanour under section 24 of Act No. 372/1990. Section 196, paragraph 2, stipulates that everyone who uses violence against a group of citizens or individuals or threatens them with death, damage to their health and causing a serious damage because of their political conviction, nationality, race, confession or for having no confession shall be punished.

7.8 The State party submitted that the General Prosecution Authority of the Slovak Republic asked the Regional Prosecution Office of Kosice to examine the present communication. The latter reviewed the lawfulness of the procedure applied and the decision reached by the Railway Police and the District Prosecution Office in order to determine whether the head of the restaurant had committed a crime of supporting and propagating movements leading to the suppression of civil rights and freedoms under section 260 of the Criminal Code or any other crime. After reviewing the relevant files the Regional Prosecution Office concluded that the ban issued by the head of the restaurant to serve people of Romany ethnicity justified suspicion of the crime of inciting to national or racial hatred under section 198a, paragraph 1, of the Penal Code. However, in its opinion the acts in question did not entail a degree of dangerousness for the society to be considered a crime. They nevertheless satisfied the criteria to be considered a misdemeanour under section 49, paragraph 1, letter a) of Act No. 372/1990 Coll. on

misdemeanours. It also considered that a criminal sanction against the head of the restaurant was foreclosed by the amnesty of 3 March 1998. This opinion was communicated by the Regional Prosecution Office to the petitioner in a letter dated 15 June 1999.

7.9 After reviewing the files concerned, the Prosecutor General disagreed with the legal opinion of the Regional Prosecution Office concerning the degree of dangerousness of the act. It considered that the Regional Prosecution Office had manifestly overestimated the immediate rectification by the head of the restaurant after a discussion with the petitioner. In a written instruction to the Regional Prosecution Office the Prosecutor General stated that the results of the review sufficiently justified the suspicion that the head of the restaurant had committed a crime of instigation to national and racial hatred under section 198a, paragraph 1, of the Penal Code and instructed the subordinate prosecution office accordingly.

7.10 On 19 April 2000, the Kosice District Prosecutor indicted Mr. J.T. On 28 April 2000, the court declared Mr. J.T. guilty of the crime described in article 198a, section 1, of the Penal Code and sentenced him to pay a fine of Sk 5000 or, alternatively, to serve a term of three months' imprisonment. The sentence became effective on 25 July 2000.

*Counsel's comments*

8.1 In a submission dated 17 February 2000, counsel addresses the issues raised by the State party repeating the arguments of previous submissions, including the exhaustion of civil and administrative remedies, the existing criminal remedies against discrimination in access to public accommodations, the date on which the racial discrimination at issue took place, and the petitioner's failure to invoke relevant domestic law provisions before the domestic authorities.

8.2 Counsel submits that the European Commission Against Racism and Intolerance (ECRI) has repeatedly stated that in Slovakia there are no criminal remedies for acts of discrimination as opposed to those for racist speech, thereby implicitly holding that the crime of incitement to ethnic or racial hatred itself cannot be considered as an applicable remedy for the violations at issue in the instant case. ECRI has also been unable to find any relevant case law that would suggest that any of the provisions of the Slovak Criminal Code would apply to cases of discrimination in access to public accommodations.

8.3 Counsel argues that a remedy delayed too long cannot be considered to be an effective remedy. It took almost three and a half years since the incident at issue and a communication filed with the Committee for the Slovak authorities only to indict the person responsible. This in itself, and regardless of the outcome of the proceedings at issue, amounts to a violation of article 6 of the Convention.

*Considerations of the merits by the Committee*

9. Acting under article 14, paragraph 7 (a), of the International Convention on the Elimination of All Forms of Racial Discrimination, the Committee has considered all the information submitted by the petitioner and the State party.

10. In the view of the Committee, the condemnation of Mr. J.T. and the penalty imposed, even though after a long period of time following the events, constitutes sanctions compatible with the obligations of the State party. Taking due account of this condemnation, even if delayed, the Committee makes no finding of a violation of the Convention by the State party.

11. Acting under article 14, paragraph 7 (b), of the Convention, the Committee recommends to the State party that it complete its legislation in order to guarantee the right of access to public places in conformity with article 5 (f) of the Convention and to sanction the refusal of access to such places for reason of racial discrimination. The Committee also recommends to the State party to take the necessary measures to ensure that the procedure for the investigation of violations is not unduly prolonged.

# Communication No. 13/1998

*Submitted by*: Anna Koptova (represented by counsel, the European Roma Rights Center).
*Alleged victim*: The petitioner.
*State party*: Slovakia.
*Date of adoption of Opinion*: 8 August 2000.
*Subject matter*: Expulsion from place of residence based on racial grounds; family dwellings were set on fire after their departure; access to effective mechanisms of protection; effective investigation.
*Procedural issues*: Exhaustion of domestic remedies; status of "victim".
*Substantive issues*: Right to an effective remedy against acts of racial discrimination; right to an effective investigation; discrimination based on ethnic and national origin; State parties must not engage in act or practice of racial discrimination against persons, group of persons or institutions; State parties shall take effective measures to review governmental, national and local policies, and to amend, rescind or nullify any laws and regulations which have the effect of creating or perpetuating racial discrimination; State parties undertake to prevent, prohibit and eradicate all practices of racial segregation and apartheid in territories under their jurisdiction; prohibition of public authorities or public institutions, national or local, to promote or incite racial discrimination; right to freedom of movement and residence within the border of the State.
*Articles of the Convention*: 2, 3, 4, 5, 6 and 14 (7) (a).
*Finding*: Violation (art. 5 (d) (i)).

*Opinion*

1. The author of the communication is Anna Koptova, a Slovak citizen of Romany ethnicity.

She is the director of the Legal Defence Bureau for Ethnic Minorities of the Good Romany Fairy Kesaj Foundation in Kosice and claims to be a victim of violations by the Slovak Republic of articles 2, 3, 4, 5 and 6 of the Convention. She is represented by the European Roma Rights Center, a non-governmental organization based in Budapest.

1.2 In conformity with article 14, paragraph 6 (a) of the Convention, the Committee transmitted the communication to the State party on 25 March 1999.

*The facts as submitted by the author*

2.1 The author reports that in 1981 seven Romany families from the villages of Rovne and Zbudske Dlhe, Slovak Republic, came to work in an agricultural cooperative located in the municipality of Krasny Brod. Shortly after their arrival each of the families sought and received permanent residence under Slovak Law (135/1982 Act) in what are today the municipalities of Nagov and Rokytovce (at the time part of Krasny Brod). When, at the end of 1989, the agricultural cooperative ceased operations the Romany families lost their jobs. Insofar as their living quarters at the cooperative were linked to their employment, they were compelled to leave the cooperative. Upon their departure, the authorities demolished the stables which they had occupied.

2.2 In May 1991 the Romany families returned to the municipalities where they were legally registered, i.e., Rokytovce and Nagov. For various periods over the following six years, they lived in temporary housing provided reluctantly by local authorities in the county of Medzilaborce. On more than one occasion during that period, however, anti-Roma hostility on the part of local officials and/or non-Romany residents forced the Romany families to flee. Thus, between May and December 1991 the Medzilaborce County Department of Social Affairs reserved a trailer for the families to rent. Although the families raised the money no village (Krasny Brod, Cabiny, Sukov, Rokytovce, Nagov or Cabalovce) allowed them to place the trailer on its territory. In 1993, after they had built temporary dwellings in the village of Cabiny, the dwellings were torn down by non-Romany residents. Throughout this period the Romany families were moving frequently from one town to another, in search of a permanent and secure home.

2.3 In spring 1997 the families again established temporary dwellings on agricultural land located in Cabiny. Local authorities from neighbouring villages met to discuss the situation. The mayor of Cabiny characterized as illegal the movement of Roma to Cabiny and warned of a possible negative reaction from the rest of the population. The mayors of Cabalovce and Nagov agreed to accommodate the homeless Roma. On 8 June 1997 the Municipal Council of Rokytovce, whose mayor had not been present at the above-mentioned meeting, enacted a resolution which expressly forbade the Romany families from settling in the village and threatened them with expulsion should they try to settle there. The resolution also declared that they were not native inhabitants of Rokytovce, since after the separation of Rokytovce and Krasny Brod in 1990 they had neither resided in the village nor claimed their permanent residence there. On 16 July 1997 the Municipality of Nagov adopted resolution No. 22 which also forbade Roma citizens to enter the village or to settle in shelters in the village district. The resolution explicitly provided that its effect was of permanent duration.

2.4 On 21 July 1997 the dwellings built and occupied by the Romany families in the municipality of Cabiny were set on fire. To date no perpetrator has been identified and there is no record of what, if any, steps the prosecution authorities have taken to investigate the facts.

2.5 The Kosice Legal Defence Foundation sent a letter to the General Prosecutor's Office in Bratislava requesting an investigation into the legality of Resolution No. 21 of the Municipal Council of Rokytovce and resolution No. 22 of the Municipal Council of Nagov. The letter asserted that the resolutions were acts of "public discrimination" against Roma which infringed their rights to freedom of movement and residence and to protection against discrimination. On 19 September 1997 the General Prosecutor's Office informed the Foundation that the investigation had been assigned to the County Prosecutor in Humenné.

2.6 On 24 November 1997 the Kosice Legal Defence Foundation submitted an application to the Constitutional Court of the Slovak Republic requesting annulment of both resolutions. The submission stated that these resolutions violated the human rights and fundamental freedoms not only of Romany citizens with permanent residence in the respective towns but of all Romany citizens, as well as of the Foundation itself, which could not carry out its work on behalf of Roma in the affected towns. It also stated that nine Romany families with permanent residence in the two villages in question had been forced to leave and that the resolutions constituted a general ban against Romany citizens, pursuant to which no citizen of Romany origin was allowed to enter these villages. It requested the annulment of both resolutions on the grounds that they violated the rights of non-discrimination and freedom of movement and residence, as well as the particular rights of ethnic minorities protected by the Slovak Constitution.

2.7 In its decision of 18 December 1997 the Constitutional Court dismissed the submission on the ground that, as a legal person, the Kosice Legal Defence Foundation could not suffer an infringement of the constitutional rights set forth in its application, since those rights were designed to protect only natural persons. On 29 December 1997 the District Prosecutor's Office in Humenné notified the Foundation that, in view of the Constitutional Court's ruling, it had suspended its investigation concerning the challenged resolutions.

2.8 On 5 May 1998 Ms. Koptova, together with Miroslav Lacko (another employee of the Kosice Legal Defence Foundation) and Jan Lacko, one of the Romany citizens whose dwellings were destroyed on 21 July 1997, filed another submission before the Constitutional Court. This submission challenged the Nagov resolution on the grounds that it unlawfully restricted the freedom of movement and residence of a group of people solely because they were Roma. The submission argued that not only Jan Lacko, a permanent resident of Nagov, but all Roma in Slovakia, including Ms. Koptova, suffered infringements of their rights under the Slovak Constitution to freedom of movement and residence, freedom from racial and ethnic discrimination and freedom in the choice of nationality. On the same date Julia Demeterova, a permanent resident of Rokytovce and another of the Romany citizens whose dwellings had been destroyed, filed a submission with the Constitutional Court challenging the Rokytovce resolution on the same grounds.

2.9 On 16 June 1998 the Constitutional Court issued two written opinions dismissing both petitions on similar grounds. In response to Jan Lacko's submission the Court reasoned that, as a permanent resident of Nagov, he had not provided any evidence to show that the Nagov resolution had in fact been applied in a manner which would infringe his rights. As to Miroslav Lacko and Ms. Koptova, both of whom had permanent residence outside Nagov, the Court found no evidence that either had tried to enter or move into the community of Nagov, or that the community had tried to stop them. Accordingly, the Court found, their rights had not been violated. With respect to Demeterova's submission the Court found that, as a permanent resident of Rokytovce, she had provided no evidence that the resolution had in fact been applied in a manner which infringed her rights.

2.10 Since the adoption of both resolutions at issue Anna Koptova has not gone to Rokytovce or Nagov. She fears that, as a Slovak citizen of Romany ethnicity, she would be subjected to violence if she were to enter either municipality.

*The complaint*

3.1 The author asserts that a number of rights to which she is entitled under the Convention have been violated, including the following:

Article 2 (1) (a). The institutions which have adopted the resolutions in question are local public authorities and public institutions. By maintaining the resolutions in force the Slovak Republic has engaged in acts of racial discrimination against the author and other Roma and has failed to ensure that all public authorities and public institutions, national and local, refrain from acts or practices of racial discrimination.

Article 2 1 (c). By maintaining in force the resolutions at issue the Slovak Republic has failed to take any measures to review governmental, national and local policies and to amend, rescind or nullify any laws and regulations which have the effect of creating or perpetuating racial discrimination.

Article 3. The resolutions publicly and formally refer to the author and other persons by their assumed racial/ethnic identity and single them out for special treatment. As such, the Resolutions expressly endorse policies of racial segregation and apartheid. By refusing to withdraw them the Slovak Republic has contravened its obligation to prevent, prohibit and eradicate all practices of segregation and apartheid within its jurisdiction.

Article 4 (c). By maintaining in force the resolutions at issue the Slovak Republic has failed to comply with its obligation not to permit public authorities or public institutions, national or local, to promote or incite racial discrimination against the author and other Roma.

Article 5 (d) (i). The resolutions at issue expressly forbid the author and other Roma from entering the two municipalities solely because of their status as Roma. By adopting and maintaining in force these resolutions the Slovak Republic has infringed the author's right to freedom of movement and residence.

Article 6. The author complained to local law enforcement authorities and filed formal complaints with the Constitutional Court. However, each request for a remedy was rebuffed. The ruling of 16 June 1998 by the Constitutional Court represents the final domestic decision, from which no appeal is permitted. Accordingly, all domestic remedies have been exhausted.

3.2 The author states that she is a victim of the above violations for the purposes of article 14, paragraph 1, of the Convention. Both resolutions may be reasonably understood by the author, (as, indeed, by all Roma in Slovakia) to apply to her. The author would like to be free to visit Nagov and Rokytovce, for instance in order to further the work of her organization. However, she has not entered either municipality since the resolutions were adopted, in part because she fears that they could be enforced against her. The author believes that, by publicly and formally using the term "Roma" to refer to certain unspecified persons and by singling out such persons for special and invidious treatment, the resolutions subject her, as a person of Romany ethnicity, to degrading treatment.[1]

3.3 The author further argues that, in assessing her "victim" status, the Committee should also take into consideration jurisprudence of the European Court of Human

Rights which entitles individuals to contend that a law violates their rights by itself, in the absence of an individual measure of implementation, if they run the risk of being directly affected by it.

3.4 Even though the author does not now and did not previously reside in the affected municipalities, she is among the class of persons defined by the challenged resolutions who are adversely affected by them. Both the text of the resolutions and the background of anti-Roma hostility which underlies their adoption make it reasonable to believe that the risk of additional adverse effect—i.e., that, if violated, the Resolutions might be enforced through, inter alia, physical force—is high.

3.5 Finally, the author asserts that the matter is not being examined under any other procedure of international investigation or settlement, although she notes that a separate case concerning the events giving rise to the present communication had been filed on behalf of other persons with the European Court of Human Rights.

*State party's observations on admissibility*

4.1 By submission of 23 June 1999 the State party challenges the admissibility of the communication. It informs the Committee that on 8 April 1999 the Municipal Council of Nagov and the Municipal Council of Rokytovce held extraordinary meetings, also attended by the District Prosecutor of Humenné, and decided to revoke resolution No. 22 of 16 June 1997 and resolution No. 21 of 8 June 1997 respectively. The State party therefore concludes that the communication has lost its relevance.

4.2 The State party further argues that a case concerning alleged racial discrimination against Roma caused by the adoption of the above-mentioned resolutions has been filed with the European Court of Human Rights. Although the applicants are not identical in the two cases, the subject matter is exactly the same.

4.3 According to the State party, the Roma inhabitants of Rokytovce were summoned by the District Prosecutor of Humenné by registered letters dated 20 November 1997. However, they failed to appear in the Prosecutor's Office, which means that they did not cooperate in establishing the facts of the case.

4.4 The State party also submits that the author has failed to exhaust domestic

---

[1] In so doing the author relies upon jurisprudence of the European Commission of Human Rights, in particular its decision in *East African Asians* v. *United Kingdom*, in which the Commission found that challenged immigration legislation had publicly subjected the applicants to racial discrimination and constituted an interference with their human dignity, amounting to "degrading treatment" in the sense of article 3 of the European Convention on Human Rights.

remedies. First of all, the Constitutional Court rejected the petition filed by the Legal Defence Bureau for Ethnic Minorities on the grounds that, as a legal entity, the Bureau could not challenge a violation of fundamental rights belonging to natural persons. The court, however, also noted that its decision was without prejudice to the right of natural persons to claim the violation of their fundamental rights as a result of decisions made by State or local administrative organs. On the basis of the court's decision the District Prosecutor of Humenné informed the author that her case would be discontinued. The author did not appeal the decision of the District Prosecutor, although it was possible to appeal in accordance with Act 314/1996 on the Prosecution Authority.

4.5  As for the decision of the Constitutional Court dated 16 June 1998 to reject the author's petition of 5 May 1998, the State party submits that nothing prevented the author from filing a new petition with the Constitutional Court submitting evidence of violation of her constitutional rights or a causal link between the violation of her rights and the decision of the municipal council.

4.6  Secondly, the State party submits that the author could have availed herself of the remedy provided for under section 13 of the Civil Code, according to which everyone is entitled to seek the protection of the State against violations of his/her integrity and to be given appropriate satisfaction; in the case of insufficient satisfaction, mainly because the dignity or respect that the person enjoyed in society was significantly harmed, the victim is entitled to compensation, to be determined by a court as appropriate.

4.7  The State party further submits that the resolutions of the Nagov and Rokytovce municipal councils were never implemented. During the time they remained in force no act of violence against persons belonging to the Roma minority took place and the Roma moved within the boundaries of the two municipalities without restrictions. The Roma registered as permanent residents in those municipalities when the resolutions were adopted continue to enjoy that status.

4.8  As for the author's claim that several provisions of the Convention, including article 2, paragraph 1 (a), have been violated, the State party indicates that, according to section 1, paragraphs 1 and 2, of the Act of the Slovak National Council No. 369/1990 Coll. on the Municipal System, a municipality is an independent self-governing territorial unit of the Slovak Republic and any interventions as to its powers and/or impositions of responsibilities are possible only by law. The two resolutions adopted by the municipal councils of Nagov and Rokytovce did not concern the performance of State administrative tasks transferred to the municipal level in the field of general public administration, neither did they concern security and public order affairs transferred to municipalities, in which case the control and supervision of a municipality could be applied pursuant to article 71, paragraph 2, of the Constitution.

4.9  The author never tried to move into either municipality, to acquire or rent a house or to work there. She showed no interest in visiting the municipalities in order to know the reasons for the issuing of the resolutions. She provided no evidence, to the Committee or the authorities involved in the case at the national level, that she had tried to enter the municipalities or that she had been prevented from doing so.

*Counsel's comments*

5.1  In a submission dated 2 August 1999 counsel contends that even if the challenged resolutions were withdrawn the communication is still admissible.

5.2  First of all, the author remains a "victim" within the meaning of article 14 of the Convention. The Committee could follow in this respect jurisprudence from the European Court of Human Rights according to which an applicant remains a "victim" unless the following conditions obtain: (i) there has been an acknowledgment by the domestic courts of a violation of the substance of the European Convention rights at issue; (ii) the applicant has received satisfaction with regard to the past damage suffered by reason of the violating provisions; and (iii) the applicant has received satisfaction with regard to a complaint that the violating provisions should not have been promulgated in the first place.

5.3  In the instant case none of those conditions has been satisfied: (i) at no time has the author received an acknowledgment by the domestic courts that the existence of the resolutions amounted to a violation of domestic law, of the Slovak Constitution, of the Convention or of any other treaty or international legal instrument protecting human rights; (ii) at no time has the author received satisfaction with regard to the past damage suffered by her by reason of the authorities' initial promulgation and subsequent maintenance in force of the resolutions for almost two years; (iii) at no time has the applicant received satisfaction with regard to her complaint that the resolutions should not have been issued in the first place. Accordingly, counsel concludes that the author is a "victim" within the meaning of article 14 and that the matter of the abolition of the resolutions is relevant only for the purpose of any suggestions and recommendations that the Committee might address to the State party at the conclusion of the case.

5.4 Further or alternative to the arguments made above, counsel submits that the Committee should in any event consider the author's claim for reasons of "general interest". The Committee ought to have jurisdiction to consider claims relevant to the general or public interest, even in exceptional cases where the victim requirement has not been satisfied. A case involving the promulgation and maintenance in force of resolutions banning an entire ethnic minority from residing or entering an entire municipality is precisely the kind of case that should satisfy a "general interest" rule.

5.5 Regarding the State party's argument that an application on the same matter has also been submitted to the European Court of Human Rights, counsel contends that the author had already informed the Committee about that. However, the application filed with the European Court by three other persons and alleging violations of the European Convention should in no way preclude the author from filing a separate communication before the Committee complaining that the resolutions violate the Convention. Counsel cites jurisprudence of the Human Rights Committee adopting that approach.

5.6 Furthermore, even if the author had filed a separate application with the European Court of Human Rights concerning the same matter, there is no provision in the Convention expressly barring the Committee from examining a case that is already being examined by another international body.

5.7 The substantive features and intent behind this Convention and the European Convention are totally different. The application before the European Court alleges breaches of European Convention provisions, including the prohibition of inhuman and degrading treatment and the right to freedom of movement and choice of residence. It seeks, inter alia, a declaration that certain provisions of the European Convention have been violated and an award of just compensation. By contrast, the present communication alleges separate and different violations of the Convention on the Elimination of All Forms of Racial Discrimination (which is more concerned than the European Convention with the positive duties and obligations of States parties not to discriminate on the basis of race, colour or national origin) and seeks suggestions and recommendations concerning the Government's obligation to remedy the alleged violations. The simultaneous filings of claims involving similar matters with the Committee and the European Court are founded on different legal bases and seek different legal remedies. They are not, therefore, duplicitous claims.

5.8 Counsel further objects to the State party's argument that the author did not exhaust domestic remedies. He states that, according to international human rights jurisprudence, the local remedies rule requires the exhaustion of remedies that are available, effective and sufficient. A remedy is considered available if it can be pursued by the petitioner without impediment, it is deemed effective if it offers some prospect of success and it is found sufficient if it is capable of redressing the complaint. If a remedy is not available, effective or sufficient the individual is not required to pursue it.

5.9 First of all, there is no effective remedy available in the State party for any cases of racial discrimination. In its concluding observations on the Slovak Republic, dated 4 August 1997, the Human Rights Committee noted that independent complaint mechanisms for victims of all forms of discrimination did not exist. The European Commission against Racism and Intolerance (ECRI) has also noted the absence of effective legal remedies for racial discrimination in the State party.

5.10 Secondly, the author did exhaust all remedies available. As explained in the initial submission, the Kosice Legal Defence Foundation reported the matter to the Office of the General Prosecutor, requesting an investigation into the legality of the resolutions. Upon request, the Foundation provided the County Prosecutor in Humenné with the names of five persons from Nagov and four persons from Rokytovce who felt they had been discriminated against by the two resolutions. Soon afterwards the Foundation submitted an application to the Constitutional Court requesting annulment of both the resolutions at issue. The Court dismissed the submission on the ground that, as a legal person, the Foundation could not suffer an infringement of constitutional rights designed to protect only natural persons. As a result of that ruling the District Prosecutor's Office decided to suspend its investigation, as it was not competent to examine decisions of the Constitutional Court. Subsequent to that, the present communication was filed with the Committee.

5.11 On 30 March 1999 the Departmental Secretary General of the Office of the Government of the Slovak Republic informed counsel that the Office of the General Prosecutor was reviewing the resolutions and that, if they were found illegal, a suggestion for withdrawal would be filed at the Constitutional Court, as the only organ with legal authority to withdraw resolutions of local government councils in order to guarantee their compliance with domestic and international law. On 31 May 1999 counsel was informed by the Chairman of the Committee on Human Rights and National Minorities of the Slovak Republic that the resolutions had been cancelled.

5.12 As for the State party's contention that the applicant did not cooperate with the investigation, counsel contends that whether or not the applicant failed to attend an interview at the Office of the General Prosecutor, which is not admitted, the Prosecutor was still under a domestic and international legal duty to investigate the complaint. The only circumstance in which the Prosecutor is not under such a duty is where the applicant's failure to attend the appointment would hinder the investigation. In other words, the applicant must be someone whose evidence is necessary in order to investigate the case. This exception clearly does not apply in the instant case, because the applicant's alleged failure to attend for an interview is not a hindrance to continuing investigation by the Prosecutor as to the compliance of the resolutions with domestic or international human rights norms. Indeed, despite the alleged failure of the applicant to appear for an interview, the authorities proceeded with their investigation until the decision of the Constitutional Court was promulgated.

5.13 The State party has failed to identify any basis for believing that the Office of the Prosecutor, having once rejected the complaint, would reach a different result if faced with a second, identical complaint, given the absence of new facts or law. Furthermore, on the basis of jurisprudence of the Constitutional Court, it is questionable whether the prosecutor possesses the legal power to remedy the violations of the Convention alleged in the instant case. In fact, in the letter sent to counsel on 30 March 1999, referred to above, the Government itself states that the only effective and available remedy in this case is an application to the Constitutional Court. Thus the Government has conceded that a complaint to the General Prosecutor is not an effective and available remedy because the Prosecutor's Office is not a judicial body.

5.14 Counsel also argues against the State party's contention that a civil action pursuant to article 11 of the Civil Code would be an effective remedy. The applicable provisions of the Civil Code regulate private relations, whereas the resolutions at issue are not matters of private individual rights. The municipalities that issued the resolutions are not private entities, therefore the Civil Code is inapplicable.

5.15 A civil remedy, even if available and effective, would be insufficient, insofar as a civil court in the Slovak Republic would not have legal authority to grant sufficient redress for the violations of the Convention that the applicant has suffered. Thus the civil court lacks the power to: (i) prosecute, sanction or otherwise punish the responsible municipal officials for racial discrimination; (ii) declare that the existence of the resolutions amounted to a practice of racial discrimination and that such a practice is unacceptable and illegal; (iii) declare that the existence of the resolutions amounted to a violation of human rights laid down in international human rights instruments by which the Republic of Slovakia is bound; (iv) award satisfaction with regard to a complaint that the violating provisions should not have been made in the first place; (v) order cancellation of the resolutions. Furthermore, the author should only exhaust those remedies which are reasonably likely to prove effective.

5.16 Regarding the second constitutional action, filed by the author in her personal capacity, the State party contends that the author failed to present evidence of an actual attempt to enter the territories and that the author should have filed a new petition.

According to counsel, these contentions lack merit. Insofar as the Constitutional Court had already dismissed several separate applications concerning the same resolutions, the suggestion that the author should be required to submit yet another petition, to the very same forum which had squarely rejected her claim, lacks logical or legal foundation.

5.17 As for the failure to present evidence, counsel reiterates its arguments concerning the "victim status" of the author and suggests that in assessing such status the Committee should be guided by the jurisprudence of the European Court, which entitles individuals to contend that a law violates their rights by itself, in the absence of an individual measure of implementation, if they run the risk of being directly affected by it. It is not necessary for the author to demonstrate that she was actually placed in an unfavourable position. The author has been personally affected by the resolutions in the following ways:

Inhuman and degrading treatment. The author has personally suffered degrading treatment, direct emotional harm, loss of human dignity and humiliation owing to the existence of the two resolutions, a fact not altered by their subsequent cancellation. It is therefore not unreasonable that the applicant, as any other Romany person in Slovakia, feels that she has been personally offended and publicly shamed in a way different from the moral outrage which may be felt by even the most sympathetic of non-Roma.

Subjection to undue restrictions on her personal freedoms. The author was affected by the threat of a potential use of violence; prevented from entering or settling in the vicinity of Nagov and Rokytovce, thereby violating her rights to freedom of movement and freedom to choose a residence; and prevented from having personal contact with persons in the vicinity of Nagov and Rokytovce, thereby violating her right to private life.

The author has also been directly affected by the existence of the resolutions because she is affected by the atmosphere of racial discrimination around her.

5.18 The State party asserts that the municipalities that issued the resolutions are not "public authorities" or "public institutions" and that a municipality is "an independent self-governing territorial unit of the Slovak Republic". Counsel disagrees with that view, at least with respect to governmental responsibility for ensuring compliance with the Convention. Several provisions of the Constitution and the Municipality System Act No. 369/1990 suggest that there is a direct relationship between the State and the municipality, a relationship which makes it clear that the municipalities are "public authorities" or "public institutions". The Committee itself has stated, in its general recommendation XV on article 4 of the Convention, that the obligations of a "public authority" under the Convention include the obligations of a municipality. Although municipalities may be "independent self-governing territorial units", they are still State organs and part of the State administration and, therefore, public institutions within the meaning of article 2 (1) (a) of the Convention.

5.19 As for the fact that the resolutions were cancelled, the Government measures of cancellation were not "effective measures" in the sense of article 2 (1) (c), because the cancellations were unreasonably delayed. Prior to cancellation the resolutions did violate the above-mentioned provision.

5.20 That the resolutions may not have been implemented through the particular means of criminal prosecution and conviction does not mean they did not breach the Convention. Part of the point and clearly the effect of the resolutions was to deter any Roma who might otherwise consider coming to the affected municipalities. The fact that no Roma dared to defy the resolutions would indicate that the mere passage and maintenance in force of the resolutions for almost two years succeeded in intimidating Roma and thus interfering with their rights under the Convention.

5.21 Finally, counsel provides observations by monitoring organizations documenting official and racially motivated violence and discrimination against Roma in the State party.

*Admissibility considerations*

6.1 At its fifty-fifth session the Committee examined the admissibility of the communication. It duly considered the State party's claims that the communication should be considered inadmissible on several grounds.

6.2 First of all, the State party argued that the resolutions of the municipal councils in question were revoked and, therefore, the communication had lost its relevance. The Committee noted, however, that notwithstanding their abrogation the resolutions had remained in force from July 1997 to April 1999. Accordingly, the Committee had to examine whether during that time violations of the Convention had taken place as a result of their enactment.

6.3 Secondly, the State party contended that a similar case had been filed with the European Court of Human Rights. The Committee noted in that respect that the author of the present communication was not the petitioner before the European Court and that, even if she was, neither the Convention nor the rules of procedure prevented the Committee from examining a case that was also being considered by another international body.

6.4 Thirdly, the Committee did not share the State party's view that domestic remedies had not been exhausted and considered that neither a new petition to the Constitutional Court nor a civil action would be effective remedies in the circumstances of the case.

6.5 Fourthly, the Committee was of the view, contrary to the State party, that the author could be considered a "victim" within the meaning of article 14, paragraph 1, of the Convention, since she belonged to a group of the population directly targeted by the resolutions in question.

6.6 Finally, the Committee considered that the municipal councils which had adopted the resolutions were public authorities for the purposes of the implementation of the Convention.

6.7 The Committee found that all other conditions for admissibility established under rule 91 of its rules of procedure had been met. Accordingly, it decided, on 26 August 1999, that the communication was admissible. It also decided that, in order to enable the Committee to examine the case in all its aspects, the State party and the author should provide information about domestic legislation and remedies intended to protect the right of everyone, without distinction as to race, colour, or national or ethnic origin, to freedom of movement and residence within the border of the State, in accordance with article 5 (d) (i) of the Convention.

*Further observations by the State party*

7.1 The State party admits that the investigation of the complaint carried out by the District Prosecutor's Office of Humenné was incomplete, since it did not address the substantive aspects. However, the Legal Defence Bureau for Ethnic Minorities did not make use of their legal possibility to have the lawfulness of the resolutions in question reviewed. A complaint pursuant to section 11, paragraph 1, of Act No. 314/1996 Coll.[2] to the prosecution authority or a motion by the Prosecutor-General with the Constitutional Court for incompatibility of the resolutions in question with the Constitution could have been filed. As the Legal Defence Bureau failed to utilize these possibilities, neither the regional nor the general prosecution authorities knew about the way in which the District Prosecutor's Office of Humenné had handled the complaint. The State party emphasizes that the Slovak legal order has effective, applicable, generally available and sufficient means of legal protection against discrimination.

7.2 The State party acknowledges that the adoption of the resolutions in question in 1997 created an unlawful situation which lasted until their abrogation in 1999. However, during the time they remained in force no violation of human rights took place since they were not applied against anybody. The Constitutional Court found in that respect that the applicants had provided no evidence of the violation of their rights and freedoms.[3]

7.3 The State party further submits that no direct violation of the right to freedom of movement and choice of residence, as

---

[2] Pursuant to section 30, paragraph 1.2, of this Act, the prosecutor shall, upon his own initiative or upon a petition, review the procedure or decisions by public administrative bodies, decisions of a court, prosecutor, investigator or police body for compliance with the law. The person who filed the petition may request a review as to the lawfulness of its processing with a repeated petition which shall be processed by the superior body.
Pursuant to section 11 of the same Act, prosecutors shall file protests against generally binding pieces of legislation, municipal binding regulations, guidelines, amendments, resolutions, other legal acts and decisions by public administrative bodies issued in individual cases which violate the law. If the protest was filed with the body which issued the decision, this body can either repeal the decision being challenged or replace it with a decision complying with the law. If this body does not fully accept the protest, it has the duty to submit it to a superior or monitoring body. The prosecutor may file a new protest against the decision rejecting the protest.
[3] See para. 2.9 above.

guaranteed by article 5 (d) (i) of the Convention, took place in the present case. The legal order of the Slovak Republic guarantees the equality of citizens before the law.[4] Freedom of movement and residence is also guaranteed to all persons staying in the territory of the State party regardless of their citizenship.[5] The freedom of residence is understood as the right of citizens to choose without any restrictions their place of residence. This right may only be limited as a result of a penal sanction. A ban on residence can be imposed as a sanction only for intentional crimes, can never be imposed on juveniles and cannot apply to the place where the offender has permanent residence. Restrictions to the freedom of movement and residence can only be based on a parliamentary act and never on decisions of the Government or other bodies of State administration.

### Counsel's comments

8.1 Counsel notes the State party's acknowledgement that the resolutions in question were unlawful. As a result, the only relevant issues left for the Committee to decide are, firstly, whether the applicant is a victim for the purposes of a complaint under the Convention and, secondly, whether the subsequent abolition of the resolutions affects the validity of the complaint to the Committee.

8.2 In its admissibility decision the Committee already addressed the first issue when it stated that the author could be considered a "victim" within the meaning of article 14, paragraph 1, of the Convention, since she belonged to a group of the population directly targeted by the resolutions in question.[6] The Committee also addressed the second issue when it noted that, notwithstanding their abrogation, the resolutions had remained in force from July 1997 to April 1999 and that it had to examine whether during that time violations of the Convention had taken place as a result of their enactment.[7]

8.3 Finally, counsel states that the points raised by the State party in its observations on the merits have already been addressed in his submission of 2 August 1999.

### Additional information submitted by the State party

9.1 Upon the Committee's request the State party provided copy of records of the municipal councils of Rokytovce and Nagov containing the texts of resolutions Nos. 21 and 22 respectively.

9.2 The English version of the record referring to resolution No. 21 reads as follows:

"The extraordinary meeting was convoked based on the minutes [of the meeting] of mayors of settlements of Cabina, Nagov, Cabalovce, Krasny Brod and Rokytovce in connection with Roma citizens that are homeless in the District of Medzilaborce.

"Deputies of the Municipal Council after reading and studying the Minutes have adopted the following standpoint on the matter in question:

The deputies have univocally stated and they declare herewith that those Roma are not native citizens of Rokytovce, but they are immigrants from settlements of Rovné and Zbudské. In 1981 one family moved there as employees of the JRD (Unified Agricultural Co-operative) Krásny Brod...

In 1981 they received permanent residence status from ... the former Secretary of the Municipal National Committee in Krásny Brod, as the settlement of Rokytovce did not exist as an independent settlement and it was then only a part of the settlement of Krásny Brod. The family was officially registered/ reported at a house as tenants...

In 1989 the Roma moved from the settlement to the settlement of Sukov as there was work for them there.

---

[4] Article 12, paragraph 2, of the Constitution stipulates that fundamental rights and freedoms are guaranteed to all regardless of their gender, race, colour, language, faith and religion, political or other views, national or social origin, belonging to a national minority or ethnic group, etc. Article 33 stipulates that membership in any national minority or ethnic group may not be used to the detriment of any individual. Article 34 states that citizens belonging to national minorities or ethnic groups shall be guaranteed their full development, particularly the rights to promote their cultural heritage with other citizens of the same national minority or ethnic group, receive and disseminate information in their mother tongues, form associations and create and maintain educational and cultural institutions.
[5] Art. 23 of the Constitution.

[6] See para. 6.5 above.
[7] See para. 6.2 above.

After the settlement of Rokytovce became independent in 1990, the Roma citizens did not live there; neither did they report there for permanent residence. As a result we do not count them among our citizens.

Based on findings from the registered entries in the House Book it was ascertained that of five proposed Roma that should return back to the settlement of Rokytovce, only two of them have permanent residence in Rokytovce, those being Júlia Demetrová and Valéria Demetrová.

The Municipal Council declared in conclusion that in case the Roma would forcefully move into the settlement, they would be, with the help of all citizens, evicted from the settlement."

9.3 Resolution No. 22 of 16 July 1997, as amended by resolution No. 27/98, indicates the following: "The Municipal Council cannot agree with accommodation of the Roma citizens in the cadastral territory of Nagov, as they do not have any ownership rights, nor origin, nor accommodation, nor jobs (employment) in the settlement of Nagov."

*Examination of the merits*

10.1 Having received the full texts of resolutions 21 and 22 the Committee finds that, although their wording refers explicitly to Roma previously domiciled in the concerned municipalities, the context in which they were adopted clearly indicates that other Roma would have been equally prohibited from settling, which represented a violation of article 5 (d) (i) of the Convention.

10.2 The Committee notes, however, that the resolutions in question were rescinded in April 1999. It also notes that freedom of movement and residence is guaranteed under article 23 of the Constitution of the Slovak Republic.

10.3 The Committee recommends that the State party take the necessary measures to ensure that practices restricting the freedom of movement and residence of Roma under its jurisdiction are fully and promptly eliminated.

# Communication No. 16/1999

*Submitted by*: Kashif Ahmad (represented by legal counsel).
*Alleged victim*: The petitioner.
*State party*: Denmark.
*Date of adoption of Opinion:* 13 March 2000.
*Subject matter:* Insults at school on racial grounds; access to effective mechanisms of protection; effective investigation.
*Procedural issues:* Substantiation for purposes of admissibility.
*Substantive issues:* Right to an effective remedy against acts of racial discrimination; right to an effective investigation.
*Articles of the Convention:* 2 (1) (d) and 6.
*Finding*: Violation (art. 6).

*Opinion*

1.1 The author of the communication is Kashif Ahmad, a Danish citizen of Pakistani origin born in 1980 who claims to be a victim of violations by Denmark of article 2, subparagraph 1 (d), and article 6 of the Convention. He is represented by counsel.

1.2 In conformity with article 14, paragraph 6 (a), of the Convention, the Committee transmitted the communication to the State party on 27 August 1999.

*The facts as submitted by the author*

2.1 On 16 June 1998 family members and friends had come to meet pupils after the exams at the Avedore Gymnasium, Hvidovre, as is the usual practice in Danish high schools. The author and his brother were waiting with a video camera outside an examination room, where a friend of theirs was taking an exam. While they were waiting, a teacher, Mr. K.P., asked them to leave. Since they refused the teacher informed the headmaster, Mr. O.T., who immediately called the police. Mr. O.T. publicly referred to the author and his brother as "a bunch of monkeys". When the author told Mr. O.T. that he was going to complain about the manner in which he had been treated, Mr. K.P. expressed doubts about the effectiveness of such a complaint and said that the author and his brother were a "bunch of monkeys" who could not express themselves correctly. When the police arrived the author and his friends discussed the matter with them. The police promised to have a discussion with Mr. O.T.

2.2 The same day the author received a letter in which Mr. O.T. informed him that he did not want him to be present at the official celebration to be held at the school on 19 June 1998 in the course of which he was going to receive his diploma. On 17 June 1998 the author's father went to Avedore Gymnasium in order to discuss the matter with Mr. O.T. Mr. O.T. first refused to receive him and when he finally accepted, told him that the matter had been settled and asked him to leave. Subsequently, the author learned from one of the employees at the school that Mr. O.T. had given instructions to the door guards not to let him in.

2.3 By letter dated 25 June 1998, counsel informed Mr. O.T. that the matter was a serious one and that the expressions he had used against the author amounted to a violation of section 266 (b) of the Danish Penal Code. Counsel also requested an explanation and an apology for his client. Mr. O.T. replied that the author and his brother had been noisy outside the examination rooms but he did not deny having used the racist expressions referred to above.

2.4 Counsel filed a complaint with the police of Hvidovre on 7 July 1998. By letter dated 23 September 1998 the police informed him that they had interviewed Mr. O.T. and Mr. K.P. and concluded that the expressions used were outside the scope of section 266 (b) of the Penal Code and that the case would be discontinued in accordance with section 749, subparagraph 2, of the Danish Administration of Justice Act. The letter also said that the expressions used had to be seen in connection with a tense incident. In the opinion of the police, they should not be understood as insulting or degrading in terms of race, colour, national or ethnic origin, since they could also be used towards persons of Danish origin who behaved as the author had.

2.5 By letter dated 1 October 1998 counsel requested the police to have the case brought before the State Attorney. On 30 November 1998 the State Attorney upheld the decision of the police.

2.6 Counsel claims that, in accordance with section 101 of the Administration of Justice Act, a decision by the State Attorney relating to an investigation by the police departments cannot be appealed to other authorities. As questions relating to the pursuance by the police of charges against individuals are entirely up to the discretion of the police, there is no possibility of bringing the case before a court. Furthermore, legal action by the author against Mr. O.T. and Mr. K.P. would not be effective, taking into account that the police of Hvidovre and the State Attorney had rejected the author's complaints.

2.7 Counsel further contends that the High Court of the Eastern Circuit, in a decision of 5 February 1999, held the view that an incident of racial discrimination did not in itself imply a violation of the honour and reputation of a person under section 26 of the Danish Act on Tort. According to counsel the position of the High Court, as a result of that decision, is that racial discrimination carried out politely would not in itself constitute a basis for a claim for compensation.

*The complaint*

3.1 It is submitted that the case was not examined properly by the national authorities and that the author never obtained an apology or sufficient satisfaction or reparation. As a result the State party has violated its obligations under article 2, subparagraph 1 (d), and article 6 of the Convention.

3.2 Counsel claims that neither the police department of Hvidovre nor the State Attorney examined, in particular, the following issues: (a) had Mr. O.T. and Mr. K.P. said that the author and his brother were "a bunch of monkeys" and that they could not express themselves correctly; (b) had that been used with reference to the Pakistani origin of the author and his brother; (c) had that expression amounted to a discriminatory opinion about the author and his brother. According to counsel, the police limited themselves to interviewing Mr. O.T. and Mr. K.P.; they did not even consider interviewing the author and his brother, or the six witnesses whose names and addresses were known to them.

4.1  In a submission dated 29 November 1999 the State party contends that the author has failed to establish a prima facie case for the purpose of admissibility and, accordingly, the communication should be declared inadmissible. The State party does not dispute that the other conditions for admissibility set out in article 14 of the Convention and rule 91 of the Committee's rules of procedure are satisfied. Should the Committee not declare the communication inadmissible on the above ground, the State party submits that there has been no violation of the Convention and that the communication is manifestly ill-founded.

4.2  The State party quotes excerpts from the complaint lodged by counsel with the Chief Constable of Hvidovre on 7 July 1998, the letter addressed by counsel to Avedore High School on 22 June 1998 requesting an explanation of the incident and an apology, and the response from the headmaster. It states that as a result of counsel's complaint the police interviewed Mr. K.P. on 9 September 1998.

4.3  Mr. K.P. explained to the police that the author had previously been a student of his and that there had been disagreements between them, including about the author's grades. On the examination day in question he had been corridor attendant responsible, inter alia, for peace and order. At one point he noticed two individuals in the basement at the door to the sports field and that a cup was jammed into the door to keep it open. He asked the two persons, one of whom was the author's brother, what they were doing there. They answered that they were waiting for the author, who was returning books. Mr. K.P. said that it was a strange place to be standing and that there had previously been three cases of theft at the school where that particular door had been used. The two young people started getting excited and shouted at Mr. K.P. The author, who was standing at the book return desk, turned round and insulted Mr. K.P.

4.4  Later, Mr. K.P. noticed four to six persons of foreign origin, including the author and his brother, waiting outside an examination room. There was much noise in the corridor and several times the teachers had come out of the examination rooms and requested quiet. Mr. K.P. then decided to empty the corridors. Everybody left except the group containing the author and his brother. The brother shouted

that they were not going to leave. Mr. K.P. asked them four times, quietly and peacefully, to leave the corridor but they still refused to do so. Both the author and his brother had threatening, piercing eyes, pointed with their fingers at Mr. K.P. and shouted and screamed. Mr. K.P. pressed the intercommunication system on the wall and shortly afterwards the headmaster arrived. The headmaster tried for about five minutes to talk to the group but they still refused to leave. The group, mainly led by the brother and, to some extent, the author, hurled insults and became more and more threatening, even in the presence of other teachers. As a result, the police was summoned. Mr. K.P. could not remember whether the group left by themselves after realizing that the police had been called or whether the police removed them. In any case, he noted subsequently that police were standing outside the school talking with the group. Mr. K.P. was asked whether the headmaster had said anything about "monkeys" to the group. He replied that he had heard nothing of the sort. He was asked whether he had said anything similar. He answered that he did not think so but was not able to reply definitively. If he had said something about "monkeys", it had nothing to do with race, religion, ethnic origin, etc. of the group, but had merely been used as an ordinary slang word for a "bunch" that behaved abnormally. He and Mr. O.T. had not wanted to lodge a complaint with the police about the threats received, as they were used to cultural differences and different conduct.

4.5  On 18 September 1998 the police interviewed Mr. O.T., the headmaster. He explained, inter alia, that Mr. K.P. had come to him and said that he was unable to control events on the second floor as a group of foreigners would not comply with his instructions. Upon arriving on the scene he noticed that a group of foreigners consisting of 8 to 10 persons, including the author and some of his classmates, were making a lot of noise. When he asked them to leave the author's brother started to shout, insulted him and made threatening gestures. While all this was happening the author was standing with a video camera. Mr. O.T. believes that he was recording. A group of parents who had been sitting at the end of the corridor had been very shocked. During the entire episode several adults had come to the corridor and watched the whole scene with astonishment. When asked why he did not file a complaint, Mr. O.T. explained that they were used to many different nationalities at the school and consequently they probably had a higher tolerance threshold. As for the use of the expression "bunch of monkeys", he said that he could not deny having said something like that. If so, the word "monkey" was merely used in the light of the conduct of the group and had no relation to the religious affiliation, colour, ethnic origin, etc. of the group. He could equally have used the word about a group of ethnic Danes behaving similarly. He could not remember Mr. K.P. referring to the group as "a bunch of monkeys who could not express themselves grammatically correctly".

4.6 By letter dated 23 September 1998 the Chief Constable of Hvidovre informed counsel, inter alia, of the following:

"Pursuant to section 742 (2) of the Administration of Justice Act (*retsplejeloven*), the police initiates an investigation on the basis of an information when it can reasonably be assumed that a criminal offence subject to public prosecution has been committed.

"I have had some investigation made in the case, inter alia by interviewing Mr. O.T. and Mr. K.P.

"Subsequently, I am of the opinion that the statements and the circumstances under which they may have been made fall outside the provisions of section 266 (b) of the Criminal Code.

"I have therefore decided, pursuant to section 749 (2) of the Administration of Justice Act, to discontinue the investigation and shelve the case.

"In my assessment I have attached importance to the following:

"Mr. O.T. does not entirely deny that he may have said something like the quoted statement.

"However, the statements must be seen in connection with a tense episode in the corridors of the High School, during which both Mr. K.P., the teacher, and especially Mr. O.T., the headmaster, have borne various expressions of disapproval and even had to summon the police to get peace at the examinations rooms.

"Anyway, in my opinion, the alleged statements cannot especially be perceived as insulting or degrading in relation to race, colour, national extraction or ethnic origin, as such statements could be made with the same meaning about others—also of Danish ethnic origin, that exhibit a similar conduct. The statements refer to the nature of the conduct and not to the person.

"Any claim for damages is referred to a civil action."

4.7 By letter of 1 October 1998 counsel appealed the decision to the District Public Prosecutor for Zealand through the Chief Constable of Hvidovre. He stressed, inter alia, that neither the author nor his classmates had been interviewed by the police and that a video recording existed that showed the situation about 30 minutes before the episode occurred, when a very large number of classmates and relatives of a student being examined were in the corridor. The video also showed the situation shortly before the statements in question were made, when only a quite small number of persons were present in the corridor together with Mr. K.P.

4.8 On 6 October 1998 the Chief Constable forwarded the case to the District Public Prosecutor and explained that in view of the context in which the statements in question had been made he had not found it necessary to interview the author. Although he had not seen the video he did not consider it relevant, as it did not concern the episode itself. On 30 November 1998 the District Public Prosecutor informed counsel that he concurred entirely in the assessment made by the Chief Constable and found no basis for reversing his decision.

4.9 The State party submits that the central point in the present communication is the statements allegedly made by Mr. K.P. and Mr. O.T. Those statements, if made, are not an expression of a difference of treatment that constitutes discrimination in violation of article 2 (1) and article 5 (e) (v) of the Convention. It is more relevant to assess the statements in question in relation to article 4 (a) of the Convention, which requires States parties to penalize certain categories of misconduct. To enable Denmark to ratify the Convention, section 266 (b) and other sections of the Danish Criminal Code were amended. Pursuant to section 266 (b), any person who, publicly or with the intent of dissemination to a wider circle, makes statements or any other communication by which a group of persons is threatened, insulted or exposed to indignities on the grounds of race, colour, national extraction or ethnic origin, shall be liable to punishment.

4.10 It is a condition that the statements in question be directed at a group on the basis of its race, etc. Statements aimed at a single person must, if they cannot be seen as an expression of insult or persecution of the group to which the person belongs, be assessed pursuant to the general rules of the Criminal Code on invasion of privacy and defamation of character. When assessing whether some statements must be deemed to be in violation of section 266 (b) it is necessary to make a concrete assessment of the substance of the statements, including the context in which they were made. This was done by the Chief Constable and the District Public Prosecutors in deciding to discontinue the investigation. The Government concurs entirely in those assessments and considers that the author has not substantiated or rendered probable that he was the victim of racist statements in violation of the Convention, as they were not aimed at a group because of its race or ethnic origin. Thus, the author has failed to establish a prima facie case for the purpose of admissibility of his communication.

4.11 The State party is aware that the Convention makes certain requirements of the treatment accorded by the authorities to information from private individuals concerning alleged racial discrimination contrary to the Convention.[1] However, the investigation performed by the police fully satisfied the requirements that can be inferred from the Convention as interpreted in the Committee's practice. The police had details on the substance of the alleged statements both from the author and his counsel and from the teacher and the headmaster. The author has specifically pointed out that the police should have assessed whether the statements that gave rise to the complaint had in fact been made. The State party argues that both the police and the Public Prosecutor assessed that it was not necessary to decide definitively whether the statements were in fact made as, even if they had been made, they were not criminal pursuant to section 266 (b).

4.12 The task of the police in its treatment of a complaint differs from the way a criminal case is treated by the courts. The task of the police is not to establish in a binding manner what actually happened, but to assess "whether the conditions of imposing criminal liability ... are

satisfied..." (sect. 743 of the Administration of Justice Act). The police have determined that, to be able to make this assessment, it was not necessary to decide whether the alleged statements had in fact been made, as whether they had been made or not, they were not criminal.

4.13 Moreover, the author has pointed out that the police should have determined whether the expressions used were intended to disparage the national origin of the author and whether they were racially discriminatory. According to the State party, such a determination was indeed made, as reflected in the decisions of the Chief Constable and the District Public Prosecutor.

4.14 The author has further pointed out that he, his brother and six named witnesses were not interviewed by the police. The State party argues that the statements, if they had been made, could not be considered as falling within section 266 (b) of the Criminal Code. This made it unnecessary to interview the applicant, who had given an account of his understanding of the incident in his written information. Against this background, the State party considers that it was equally unnecessary to interview the applicant's brother and the six witnesses.

4.15 The State party finds that the police did initiate a proper investigation. Thus, article 2 (1) (d), article 5 (e) (v) and article 6 of the Convention have not been violated, nor has article 4 (a).

*Counsel's comments*

5.    In a submission dated 10 January 2000 counsel argues that the State party recognizes in its response some of the essential elements which gave rise to the report by the author to the police. In previous cases the Committee has stressed the need for a thorough investigation of reported cases of racial discrimination. As explained in the initial submission, the police declined to examine the case after having interviewed only the two representatives of the high school. In order to fulfil the requirements of a thorough investigation, and in order to verify whether the questions relating to the expressions used and their status under Danish law, the police should at least have interviewed the author and/or the witnesses.

---

[1] See Opinions adopted by the Committee in *L.K.* v. *Netherlands*, *Yilmaz-Dogan* v. *Netherlands* and *Habassi* v. *Denmark*.

6.1 The State party submits that Mr. K. P. did not deny having called the author and his group "monkeys". It also submits that Mr. O.T. did not deny having said something similar. It is also established that these utterances were made in the course of a tense episode in a school corridor and in the presence of several witnesses. Thus, the Committee is of the opinion that the author was insulted in public, at least by Mr. O.T.

6.2 The District Public Prosecutor did not establish whether the author had been insulted on the grounds of his national or ethnic origin, in violation of the provision of article 2, paragraph 1 (d), of the Convention. It is the opinion of the Committee that if the police involved in the case had not discontinued their investigations, it might have been established whether the author had indeed been insulted on racial grounds.

6.3 From information submitted by the State party in its fourteenth periodic report (CERD/C/362/Add.1), the Committee gathers that on several occasions persons have been convicted by Danish courts for breaches of section 266 (b) of the Criminal Code for insulting or degrading statements similar to the ones uttered in the present case. Therefore, the Committee does not share the opinion of the State party that the statements in question do not fall within section 266 (b) of the Criminal Code.

6.4 Owing to the failure of the police to continue their investigations, and the final decision of the Public Prosecutor against which there was no right of appeal, the author was denied any opportunity to establish whether his rights under the Convention had been violated. From this it follows that the author has been denied effective protection against racial discrimination and remedies attendant thereupon by the State party.

7. The Committee considers that the author has established a prima facie case for the purpose of admissibility. It also considers that the conditions for admissibility have been satisfied. It therefore decides, under rule 91 of its rules of procedure, that the communication is admissible.

8. As for the merits, the Committee considers that, in the light of the above findings, the facts as presented constitute a violation of article 6 of the Convention.

9. The Committee recommends that the State party ensure that the police and the public prosecutors properly investigate accusations and complaints related to acts of racial discrimination which should be punishable by law according to article 4 of the Convention.

# Communication No. 17/1999

*Submitted by*: B.J. (represented by legal counsel).
*Alleged victim*: The petitioner.
*State party*: Denmark.
*Date of adoption of Opinion*: 7 March 2000.
*Subject matter*: Denial of entry into a discotheque based on nationality; access to effective mechanisms of protection; effective investigation; effective compensation.
*Procedural issues*: None.
*Substantive issues*: Right to an effective remedy against acts of racial discrimination; right to an effective investigation; right of access to any place or service intended for use by the general public; discrimination based on ethnic and national origin.
*Articles of the Convention*: 2 (1) (a), (b) and (d), 5 (f), and 6.
*Finding*: No violation.

*Opinion*

1.1 The author of the communication is Mr. B.J., a Danish engineer of Iranian origin born in 1965 who claims to be a victim of violations by Denmark of article 2, subparagraph 1 (a), (b) and (d), article 5 (f) and article 6 of the Convention. He is represented by counsel.

1.2 In conformity with article 14, paragraph 6 (a), of the Convention, the Committee transmitted the communication to the State party on 27 August 1999.

*The facts as submitted by the author*

2.1 The author has lived in Denmark since 1984 and has Danish nationality. On 1 February 1997 he went to a discotheque in Odense with his brother and a group of friends. Two of them were of Danish origin and four were not. The doorman of the discotheque, Mr. M.R.S., refused to let them in. When the author asked the reason Mr. M.R.S. replied that it was because they were "foreigners".

2.2 On 2 February 1997 the author reported the matter to the police, complaining of racial discrimination. The police assistant on duty was unwilling to accept the complaint and informed the author that the admissions policy was entirely up to the owners of the discotheque.

2.3 On 3 February 1997 the author filed a written complaint that was rejected by the police. He then appealed to the State Attorney who decided to initiate an investigation. Subsequently, the Public Prosecutor brought the case before the District Court of Odense. By decision of 20 March 1998 the Court ruled that Mr. M.R.S. was to be fined DKr 1,000 for violation of section 1, subparagraph 2, of Consolidated Act No. 626 of 29 September 1987 on racial discrimination.

2.4 The author had also requested the Public Prosecutor to file a claim for compensation in accordance with section 26 of the Act on Civil Liability. In that respect the court decided that the violation to which the author had been subjected was not of such a grave or humiliating character as to justify the granting of pecuniary compensation. Accordingly, the claim was rejected.

2.5 The author did not receive a copy of the court's judgement until the time-limit for filing an appeal to the High Court had expired. With the assistance of the Documentary and Advisory Centre on Racial Discrimination (DRC) he obtained a special permit from the High Court of the Eastern Circuit to bring the case before it. However, the High Court did not find any basis for a claim of compensation. According to its judgement, the doorman had informed the author and his friends that they could not enter the discotheque because, in accordance with the discotheque's rules, there were already more than ten foreigners inside. That information was first given to the author's brother and then to the author himself in a polite manner. In the circumstances the High Court concluded that the violation of the

author's honour committed by the doorman was not of such severity and did not involve such humiliation as to justify the granting of compensation under section 26 of the Act on Civil Liability. The Court made reference to the fact that the doorman had been fined for rejecting the author and that, accordingly, the necessary verification and condemnation of the act had taken place and the author had had sufficient satisfaction.

2.6 Judgements of the High Court in appeal cases may normally not be appealed to the Supreme Court. However, the *Proces-bevillingsnaevn* may grant a special permit if the case involves issues of principle. On 4 March 1999 the author's counsel applied to the *Procesbevillingsnaevn* for such a permit, arguing that Danish courts had never before had the possibility to interpret section 26 of the Act on Civil Liability in the light of article 6 of the Convention. The application, however, was rejected by letter of 11 May 1999 and was not brought before the Supreme Court. No further remedies are available under Danish law.

*The complaint*

3.1 According to counsel, it is undisputed that the author's exclusion from the discotheque was an act of racial discrimination. Article 6 of the Convention stipulates that effective satisfaction and reparation must be granted for any damage suffered as a result of discrimination. However, the purely symbolic fine imposed by the Odense court does not provide effective satisfaction or reparation in accordance with that provision. Furthermore, under section 26 of the Danish Act on Civil Liability it is possible to grant compensation for insult. By refusing such compensation the Danish courts have failed to apply Danish law.

3.2 Counsel further claims that by refusing the author's right to compensation the Danish courts have not fulfilled their obligations under article 2, subparagraph 1 (a), (b) and (d), of the Convention. He finally claims that by allowing the discotheque to refuse the author access on racial grounds the State party has not fulfilled its obligations under article 5 (f) of the Convention.

*State party's observations*

4.1 In a submission dated 29 November 1999 the State party recognizes that the conditions for admissibility of the communication are satisfied. However, it claims that no violation of the Convention has occurred and that the communication is manifestly ill-founded.

4.2 The State party recalls that by indictment of 3 June 1997, the Chief Constable of Odense charged the doorman in question with violation of section 1 (2), of the Act Prohibiting Discrimination on the basis of Race (Consolidated Act No. 626 of 29 September 1987), because on 2 February 1997 he refused the author admittance on the basis of the latter's colour and ethnic origin. On 20 March 1998 the District Court of Odense found the doorman guilty of the charge. Upon counsel's request, the prosecutor claimed that the doorman should pay compensation for non-pecuniary damage to the author, in accordance with section 26 of the Act on Liability in Damages *(erstatningsansvarsloven)* and article 6 of the Convention. However, the claim for compensation was dismissed by the District Court. The author filed an appeal with the Eastern High Court claiming that the offender should be ordered to pay compensation for non-pecuniary damage of DKr 10,000 with the addition of pre-judgement interest. However, the Eastern High Court upheld the judgement of the District Court.

4.3 In connection with the alleged violation of article 2 (1) (a), (b) and (d) of the Convention, the State party argues that article 2 (1) (d) is the most relevant provision, as article 2 (1) (a) and (b) do not make any independent contribution in relation to the author's complaint, which concerns discrimination committed by a private individual. The adoption of Consolidated Act No. 626 of 29 June 1987 prohibiting discrimination on the basis of race is to be seen, inter alia, as fulfilment of the obligations following from article[s] 2 (1) (d), 5 (f) and 6 of the Convention. Not only has the State party adopted law that criminalizes acts of racial discrimination such as that of which the applicant was a victim on 2 February 1997, but Danish authorities have enforced these criminal provisions in the specific case by prosecuting and penalizing the doorman.

4.4 Concerning the author's claim that the purely symbolic nature of the fine does not provide effective satisfaction or reparation, the State party claims that the Convention cannot be interpreted to mean that it requires a specific form of penalty (such as imprisonment or a fine) or a specific severity or length (such as a non-suspended custodial penalty, a suspended custodial penalty, a fine of a specific amount or the like) as the sanction for

specific types of acts of racial discrimination. In the State party's view, it is not possible to infer a requirement of a penalty of a specific type or severity from the wording of the Convention, the practice of the Committee in its consideration of communications under article 14, or from the general recommendations adopted by the Committee.

4.5 Violations of section 1 of the Act prohibiting discrimination on the basis of race are punished with "a fine, lenient imprisonment or imprisonment for a term not exceeding six months". In determining the penalty within the maximum penalty provided for by the provision, the court in question must take into account a multiplicity of elements. It thus follows from section 80 (1) of the Danish Criminal Code that, in determining the penalty, account shall be taken of the gravity of the offence and information concerning the offender's character, including his general personal and social circumstances, his conduct before and after the offence and his motives in committing it.

4.6 Determination of suitable sanctions in specific cases falls within the margin of appreciation of the State party. The national authorities have the benefit of direct contact with all the persons concerned and are better able to assess what is a suitable sanction in the specific case. Moreover, it must be up to the State party to decide what sanction must be deemed sufficiently deterrent and punitive. It is recognized, however, that the margin of appreciation should not be exercised in a manner which would impair the very essence of article 6 of the Convention.

4.7 The penalty imposed on the doorman in the present case accords with domestic case law in similar cases and can be compared with the sanctions in criminal cases concerning racist statements falling within section 266 (b) of the Criminal Code.[1] It can therefore not be considered a fine of a "purely symbolic nature".

4.8 In view of the foregoing, the State party is of the opinion that there is no basis for alleging that article 2 (1) (d), article 5 (f) or article 6 of the Convention has been violated by the conduct of the criminal proceedings against the doorman, as the judgement established

---

[1] The State party refers to several cases which are also mentioned in its fourteenth periodic report to the Committee on the Elimination of Racial Discrimination.

that the author had been the victim of a prohibited act of racial discrimination.

4.9 An individual who believes that he or she has been the subject of discrimination in violation of the Act prohibiting discrimination on the basis of race, interpreted in the light of the Convention, can, if relevant, claim compensation for pecuniary or non-pecuniary damage from the offender. However, the State party finds that it must be left to the individual State party to determine the detailed procedural rules and rules of substance for awarding compensation for non-pecuniary damage.

4.10 The right to "adequate reparation or satisfaction" is not an absolute right, but may be subject to limitations. These limitations are permitted by implication since such a right, by its very nature, calls for regulation by the State. In this respect, the States parties enjoy a margin of appreciation and can lay down limitations provided that those limitations do not restrict or reduce the right in such a way or to such extent that its very essence is impaired. In this respect guidance may be found in the jurisprudence of the European Court of Human Rights.

4.11 The State party finds that the last part of article 6 of the Convention is to be interpreted in the same way as article 5 (5) of the European Convention for the Protection of Human Rights and Fundamental Freedoms. It appears from the latter that everyone who has been the victim of arrest or detention in contravention of its provisions "shall have an enforceable right to compensation". In the interpretation of this provision the European Court has established that the provision does not involve an unconditional right to compensation, as the Contracting States have a right to demand that certain conditions be satisfied. Thus, the Court has stated that the said provision "does not prohibit the Contracting States from making the award of compensation dependent upon the ability of the person concerned to show damage resulting from the breach. In the context of article 5 (5) ... there can be no question of 'compensation' where there is no pecuniary or non-pecuniary damage to compensate".[2]

4.12 It is thus the opinion of the State party that the Convention cannot be interpreted to mean that a person who has been the subject

of an act of discrimination committed by another individual, including an act of discrimination in violation of article 5 (f) of the Convention, always has a claim for compensation for non-pecuniary damage. The fact that a person who has committed such an act is actually prosecuted and convicted can in certain cases constitute in itself "adequate reparation or satisfaction". This view is supported, inter alia, by the interpretative statement concerning article 6 of the Convention deposited by the United Kingdom when signing the Convention. The statement in question says: "The United Kingdom interprets the requirement in article 6 concerning 'reparation or satisfaction' as being fulfilled if one or other of these forms of redress is made available and interprets 'satisfaction' as including any form of redress effective to bring the discriminatory conduct to an end".

4.13 According to Danish law, it is possible both in law and in fact to be awarded compensation for pecuniary and non-pecuniary damage in case of acts of racial discrimination committed by individuals in violation of the Convention, but this presupposes that the conditions therefor are otherwise satisfied.

4.14 Pursuant to section 26 (1) of the Act on Liability in Damages, a person who is responsible for unlawful interference with another person's liberty, invasion of his privacy, damage to his self-esteem or character or injury to his person shall pay compensation for the damage to the injured person. The provision is mandatory but the condition is that the unlawful act has inflicted "damage" (in Danish *tort*) the injured party. *Tort* in the Danish sense is damage to another person's self-esteem and character, that is, the injured person's perception of his own worth and reputation. The humiliation is what motivates the claim for compensation for non-pecuniary damage. It is inherent in the requirement of "unlawful" damage that it must be culpable and that it must be of some gravity. When determining the compensation, if any, account must be taken of the gravity of the damage, the nature of the act and the circumstances in general.

4.15 The decision of the Eastern High Court refusing compensation to the author for non-pecuniary damage was based on a specific assessment of the circumstances concerning the criminal act. Thus, the Court found that the damage to the author's self-esteem had not

---

[2] *Wassink* v. *Netherlands*, application No. 12535/86, Judgement of 27 September 1990.

been sufficiently grave or humiliating to determine any compensation for non-pecuniary damage.

4.16 The fact that a person who has committed an act of racial discrimination against another individual is actually prosecuted and convicted can in certain cases constitute in itself "adequate reparation or satisfaction". The judgement of the Eastern High Court accords with this view when it states the following: "The Court further refers to the facts that the doorman has been sentenced to a fine in respect of the refusal of admittance, that the requisite determination and condemnation of the act has thus been effected and that this has afforded the applicant sufficient satisfaction".

4.17 It is thus the opinion of the State party in the specific case that the fact that the doorman was sentenced to a fine for his refusal to admit the author to the discotheque in question constitutes "adequate reparation or satisfaction".

*Counsel's comments*

5.1 In a submission dated 14 January 2000 counsel maintains that no effective remedy has been granted to the author in order to comply with the relevant provisions of the Convention, including article 6. In order to implement the Convention conscientiously the States parties must be under an obligation to ensure its effective observance. Sanctions for breaches of national provisions implementing the Convention must be effective and not only symbolic.

5.2 The State party argues that under Danish law it is possible to be awarded compensation for pecuniary and non-pecuniary damage in case of acts of racial discrimination in violation of the Convention committed by individuals, but this predisposes that the conditions therefor are otherwise satisfied. To counsel's knowledge no such court decisions exist. The present case was the first in which a claim for compensation was examined by a Danish court.

5.3 Furthermore, according to section 26 of the Danish Act on Liability compensation is granted in accordance with other statutory provisions. As no other statutory provisions exist in this field there would be no point in awaiting coming court decisions.

5.4 The decision to refuse compensation implies, as a matter of fact, that no compensation for non-pecuniary damages is granted in cases of racial discrimination if the racial discrimination has taken place "politely". Such a position is not in conformity with the Convention.

*Issues and proceedings before the Committee*

6.1 As readily recognized by the State party the Committee considers that the conditions for admissibility are satisfied. It therefore decides, under rule 91 of its rules of procedure, that the communication is admissible.

6.2 The Committee considers that the conviction and punishment of the perpetrator of a criminal act and the order to pay economic compensation to the victim are legal sanctions with different functions and purposes. The victim is not necessarily entitled to compensation in addition to the criminal sanction of the perpetrator under all circumstances. However, in accordance with article 6 of the Convention, the victim's claim for compensation has to be considered in every case, including those cases where no bodily harm has been inflicted but where the victim has suffered humiliation, defamation or other attack against his/her reputation and self-esteem.

6.3 Being refused access to a place of service intended for the use of the general public solely on the ground of a person's national or ethnic background is a humiliating experience which, in the opinion of the Committee, may merit economic compensation and cannot always be adequately repaired or satisfied by merely imposing a criminal sanction on the perpetrator.

7. While the Committee considers that the facts described in the present communication disclose no violation of article 6 of the Convention by the State party, the Committee recommends that the State party take the measures necessary to ensure that the victims of racial discrimination seeking just and adequate reparation or satisfaction in accordance with article 6 of the Convention, including economic compensation, will have their claims considered with due respect for situations where the discrimination has not resulted in any physical damage but humiliation or similar suffering.

# Communication No. 26/2002

*Submitted by*: Stephen Hagan (represented by counsel).
*Alleged victim*: The petitioner.
*State party*: Australia.
*Date of adoption of Opinion:* 20 March 2003.
*Subject matter:* Use of offensive terms in public; racial discrimination; access to effective mechanisms of protection; effective investigation.
*Procedural issues:* Inadmissibility *ratione materiae*; substantiation for purposes of admissibility; State's reservation to article 4.
*Substantive issues:* Racial discrimination; right to an effective remedy against acts of racial discrimination; right to an effective investigation; State parties shall take effective measures to review governmental, national and local policies, and to amend, rescind or nullify any laws and regulations which have the effect of creating or perpetuating racial discrimination; State parties undertake to adopt immediate and effective measures, particularly in the fields of teaching, education, culture and information, with a view to combat prejudices which lead to racial discrimination; prohibition of propaganda based on ideas or theories of superiority of one race or group of persons of one colour or ethnic origin, or which attempt to justify or promote racial hatred and discrimination in any form.
*Articles of the Convention:* 2 (1) (c), 4, 5 (d) (i) and (ix), (e) (vi) and (f), 6, and 7.
*Finding:* State party is recommended to remove a public sign that is considered racially offensive.

## Opinion

1. The petitioner, Stephen Hagan, is an Australian national, born in 1960, with origins in the Kooma and Kullilli Tribes of South Western Queensland. He alleges to be a victim of a violation by Australia of articles 2, in particular, paragraph 1 (c); 4; 5, paragraphs (d) (i) and (ix), (e) (vi) and (f); 6 and 7 of the International Convention on the Elimination of All Forms of Racial Discrimination. He is represented by counsel.

## The facts as presented

2.1 In 1960, the grandstand of an important sporting ground in Toowoomba, Queensland, where the author lives, was named the "E.S. 'Nigger' Brown Stand", in honour of a well-known sporting and civic personality, Mr. E.S. Brown. The word "nigger" ("the offending term") appears on a large sign on the stand. Mr. Brown, who was also a member of the body overseeing the sports ground and who died in 1972, was of white Anglo-Saxon extraction who acquired the offending term as his nickname, either "because of his fair skin and blond hair or because he had a penchant for using 'Nigger Brown' shoe polish". The offending term is also repeated orally in public announcements relating to facilities at the ground and in match commentaries.

2.2 On 23 June 1999, the petitioner requested the trustees of the sports ground to remove the offending term, which he found objectionable and offensive. After considering the views of numerous members of the community who had no objection to the use of the offending term on the stand, the trustees advised the petitioner by letter of 10 July 1999 that no further action would be taken. On 29 July 1999, a public meeting chaired by a prominent member of the local indigenous community, and attended by a cross-section of the local Aboriginal community, the mayor and the chair of the sports ground trust, passed a resolution "That the name 'E.S. Nigger Brown' remain on the stand in honour of a great sportsman and that in the interest of the spirit of reconciliation, racially derogative or offensive terms will not be used or displayed in future".[1]

2.3 On 11 May 2000, the petitioner brought a federal court action, on the basis that the trustees' failure to remove the offending term

---

[1] It is not clear whether the petitioner attended this meeting.

violated sections 9 (1)[2] and 18 C (1)[3] of the federal Racial Discrimination Act 1975 ("the Act"). He sought removal of the offending term from the grandstand and an apology from the trustees. On 10 November 2000, the Federal Court dismissed the petitioner's application. The Court considered that the petitioner had not demonstrated that the decision was an act "reasonably likely in all the circumstances to offend, insult, humiliate or intimidate an indigenous Australian or indigenous Australians generally". Nor was the decision an act, in the words of the statutory language, "done because of the race ... of the people of the group". Finally, the Court considered that the Act did not protect the "personal sensitivities of individuals", as it considered to be the case here, but rather "render[ed] acts against individuals unlawful only where those acts involve treating the individual differently and less advantageously than other persons who do not share the membership of the complainant's racial, national or ethnic group". On 23 February 2002, the Full Court of the Federal Court rejected the petitioner's appeal. On 19 March 2002, the High Court of Australia refused the petitioner's application for special leave to appeal.

2.4 The petitioner also pursued a complaint to the Human Rights and Equal Opportunities Commission (HREOC), which could not be pursued further because of a subsequent restriction by law of the Commission's jurisdiction to investigate certain individual complaints.

*The complaint*

3.1 The petitioner contends that the use of the offending term on the grandstand and orally in connection therewith violates articles 2, in particular, paragraph 1 (c); 4; 5, paragraphs (d) (i) and (ix), (e) (vi) and (f); 6 and 7 of the Convention. He contends that the term is "the most racially offensive, or one of the most racially offensive, words in the English language". Accordingly, he and his family are offended by its use at the ground and are unable to attend functions at what is the area's most important football venue. He argues that whatever may have been the position in 1960, contemporary display and use of the offending term is "extremely offensive, especially to the Aboriginal people, and falls within the definition of racial discrimination in article 1" of the Convention.

3.2 He clarifies that he has no objection to honouring Mr. Brown or naming a football stand in his honour, but that at the time the nickname "Nigger" was applied to Mr. Brown, non-Aboriginal Australians "either were not aware of or were insensitive to the hurt and offence that term caused to Aboriginal people". He argues further that it is not necessary to repeat Mr. Brown's nickname in order to honour him, for other stadia named after well-known athletes utilize their ordinary names, rather than their nicknames.

3.3 He argues that under article 2, paragraph 1 (c), in particular, any State party to the Convention has an obligation to amend laws having the effect of perpetuating racial discrimination. He contends that use of words such as the offending term in a very public way provides the term with formal sanction or approval. Words convey ideas and power, and influence thoughts and beliefs. They may perpetuate racism and reinforce prejudices leading to racial discrimination. The lawfulness (in terms of domestic law) of the use of this term also runs counter to the objectives of article 7, which indicates that States parties undertake to combat prejudices leading to racial discrimination.

3.4 The petitioner further argues that section 18 (1) (b) of the Act, requiring the offensive conduct to be "because of" a racial attribute is narrower than the associative terms "based on" found in the definition of racial discrimination in article 1 of the Convention.

---

[2] Section 9 of the Racial Discrimination Act 1975 (Commonwealth) provides:
**Racial discrimination to be unlawful**
(1) "It is unlawful for a person to do any act involving a distinction, exclusion, restriction or preference based on race, colour, descent or national or ethnic origin which has the purpose or effect of nullifying or impairing the recognition, enjoyment or exercise, on an equal footing, of any human right or fundamental freedom in the political, economic, social, cultural or any other field of public life."
[3] Section 18 C of the Racial Discrimination Act provides:
**Offensive behaviour because of race, colour, or national or ethnic origin**
(1) It is unlawful for a person to do an act, otherwise than in private, if:
    (a) The act is reasonably likely, in all the circumstances, to offend, insult, humiliate or intimidate another person or a group of people; and
    (b) The act is done because of the race, colour or national or ethnic origin of the other person or of some or all of the people in the group.

He characterizes that the dismissal of his complaint, inter alia on the grounds that the offensive term was not "because of" a racial attribute, was "technical".

3.5 By way of remedy, the petitioner seeks the removal of the offending term from the sign and an apology, as well as changes to Australian law to provide an effective remedy against racially offensive signs, such as the one in question.

*The State party's submissions on admissibility and merits*

4.1 By submission of 26 November 2002, the State party disputed both the admissibility and merits of the petition.

4.2 As to admissibility, the State party, while conceding that domestic remedies have been exhausted, considers the petition incompatible with the provisions of the Convention and/or insufficiently substantiated. Concerning incompatibility, the State party refers to jurisprudence of the Human Rights Committee that it will not review the interpretation of domestic law, absent bad faith or abuse of power,[4] and invites the Committee on the Elimination of Racial Discrimination to take the same approach. The State party notes that its courts and authorities considered the petitioner's complaints expeditiously and according to laws enacted in order to give effect to its obligations under the Convention. The courts, at first instance and appeal, held that the petitioner's complaints had not been made out. Accordingly, the State party submits it would be inappropriate for the Committee to review the judgements of the Federal Court and to substitute its own views. As to the specific claim under paragraph 1 (c) that the State party should amend the Racial Discrimination Act (being a law having the effect of perpetuating racial discrimination), the State party argues that this claim is incompatible with the Convention, as the Committee has no jurisdiction to review the laws of Australia in the abstract. It invites the Committee to follow the jurisprudence of the Human Rights Committee to this effect.[5]

4.3 In view of the thorough consideration and rejection of the complaint before domestic instances, the State party also argues that the petition is insufficiently substantiated, for purposes of admissibility.

4.4 On the merits, the State party disputes that the facts disclose a violation of any articles of the Convention invoked. As to the claim under article 2, the State party submits that these obligations are of general principle and programmatic in character, and therefore accessory to other articles of the Convention. Accordingly, in the same way that the Human Rights Committee only finds a violation of article 2 of the International Covenant on Civil and Political Rights[6] after finding a separate substantive violation of the Covenant, a violation of article 2 of the Convention could only arise after a violation of the other substantive articles (which is denied in its submissions under arts. 4 to 7 below).[7] Even if the Committee considers that article 2 can be directly breached, the State party submits that it has satisfied its obligations: it condemns racial discrimination, has enacted legislation and policy to make its practice by any person or body unlawful as well as to eliminate all forms of racial discrimination and actively promote racial equality, and has provided effective mechanisms of redress.

4.5 In terms of the specific paragraphs of article 2, as to paragraph 1 (a), the State party cites academic commentary to the effect that this provision does not deal with private acts of discrimination (which are referred to in subparas. (b) and (d)).[8] As the Toowomba Sports Ground Trust is a private body rather than a public authority or government agent, its acts fall outside the scope of paragraph 1 (a). As to paragraph 1 (b), the State party relies on commentary that this provision is intended to prevent any actor engaged in racial discrimination from receiving State support.[9] The State party submits that neither the establishment of the Sports Ground Trust, its continued existence, nor its response to the communication can be taken as any

[4] *Maroufidou* v. *Sweden*, communication No. 58/1979, Views adopted on 9 April 1981.
[5] *MacIsaac* v. *Canada*, communication No. 55/1979, Views adopted on 25 July 1980: "[The Committee's] task is not to decide in the abstract whether or not a provision of national law is compatible with the Covenant, but only to consider whether there is or

has been a violation of the Covenant in the particular case submitted to it."
[6] Article 2 of the Covenant sets out the right to an effective remedy for violations of the Covenant.
[7] Paras. 4.7 to 4.9 below.
[8] N. Lerner, *The UN Convention on the Elimination of All Forms of Racial Discrimination* (Alphen aan den Rijn, Netherlands, Sijthoff Noordhoff, 1980), p. 37.
[9] Ibid.

State sponsorship, defence or support of any racial discrimination committed by the Trust (which is denied).

4.6 As to paragraph 1 (c), the State party refers to its submissions below that no racial discrimination has been suffered.[10] That the petitioner's complaint under the Racial Discrimination Act was unsuccessful does not detract from the effectiveness of that legislation, nor does it suggest that the Act creates or perpetuates racial discrimination. As to paragraph 1 (d), the State party again refers to its submissions that no racial discrimination has occurred, and to its general remarks above on article 2.[11] As to paragraph 1 (e), the State party refers to commentary that this provision is "broadly and vaguely worded", leaving undefined "[w]hat 'integrationist' movements are, and what 'strengthens' racial division".[12] The State party recalls that Australia is a multicultural society, and that its laws and policies are designed to eliminate direct and indirect racial discrimination and actively to promote racial equality. It refers to its periodic reports to the Committee for in-depth description of these laws and policies. As to paragraph 2, the State party submits that the petitioner has failed to indicate how the circumstances of his case warrant the implementation of "special measures". Alternatively, it refers to its submissions that no discrimination has taken place for the conclusion that no need for "special measures" arises.

4.7 As to the petitioner's claim under article 4, the State party invokes its reservation to this article.[13] The State party recalls that pursuant to its obligations under this article, it enacted Part II A of the Racial Discrimination Act, including section 18 C, under which the petitioner filed his claim. It further argues, based on the jurisprudence of the Human Rights Committee,[14] that States parties must be accorded a certain "margin of appreciation" in implementing their Convention obligations.

4.8 The State party argues that the use of the term "because of" in section 18 of the Act, requiring a causal relationship between offensive conduct and the race, colour or national or ethnic origin of the "targeted group", is an appropriate manner to implement the obligation to prohibit the intentionally racist acts described in article 4. This is consistent with the Convention and avoids uncertainty. Accordingly, the State party argues that to use "based on" in section 18 of the Act would not give appropriate effect to article 4 of the Convention as implemented in Australian law.

4.9 The State party contends that the petitioner's complaint was not dismissed on technical grounds, but for lack of substance. The Federal Court, rejecting the contention that any use of the offending term must necessarily be racially offensive, concluded that in the context in which the offending term was used and the community perceptions of the sign on the stand, the decision of the Trust to leave the sign intact did not breach section 18 C of the Act. The State party invites the Committee to adopt the approach of the Federal Court and take into consideration the context in which the word is used in determining issues under article 4.

4.10 The State party refers to the following contextual elements: (i) the fact that the offending term is displayed as "an integral part of the name of a person who is clearly being honoured by having his name publicly attached to the stand", (ii) the Federal Court's finding that "[e]ven if the nickname 'Nigger' was originally bestowed long ago on Mr. Brown in circumstances in which it then had a racial or even a racist connotation, the evidence indicates that for many decades before the author's complaint, its use as part of the customary identifier of Mr. Brown had ceased to have any such connotation", (iii) the consultations with local indigenous persons, (iv) the evidence of a former Aboriginal rugby league personality in the area for whom the name was unproblematic and "simply part of history", and (v) the absence of any complaint (until the petitioner's) over 40 years of display at a ground often frequented by many indigenous persons despite increased

---

[10] Paras. 4.15 to 4.19 below.

[11] Para. 4.4 above.

[12] Lerner, *The UN Convention*, p. 38.

[13] The reservation provides: "The Government of Australia ... declares that Australia is not at present in a position specifically to treat as offences all the matters covered by article 4 (a) of the Convention. Acts of the kind there mentioned are punishable only to the extent provided by the existing criminal law dealing with such matters as the maintenance of public order, public mischief, assault, riot, criminal libel, conspiracy and attempts. It is the intention of the Australian Government, at the first suitable moment, to seek from Parliament legislation specifically implementing the terms of article 4 (a)."

[14] *Hertzberg et al.* v. *Finland*, communication No. 61/1979, Views adopted on 2 April 1982.

sensitivities and willingness to speak out in recent years.

4.11 In the light of the above, the State party contends that the Federal Court's conclusion (upheld on appeal) that the trustees' refusal, conveyed only after "in good faith [having] taken care to avoid offending the members of a racial group" and which "is not, on an objective view, likely to offend members of that group", was not an "act done because of the race of" any person. While accepting that the petitioner subjectively felt offended, the Committee should apply an objective test similar to that of the Federal Court in finding that there was no suggestion that the trustees were attempting to justify, promote or incite racial discrimination, contrary to article 4 of the Convention.

4.12 In terms of the specific paragraphs (a) to (c) of article 4, the State party argues that the petitioner has supplied no evidence as to how it may have violated any of these obligations, including that it may be abetting racist activities. It points to Part II A of the Act, which makes unlawful offensive behaviour based on racial hatred, and to further legislation at both State and Territory level that proscribes racial hatred and vilification, as implementing its obligations under these paragraphs. As to paragraph (a) it recalls its reservation, and, as to paragraph (c), that the Trust is not a public authority or institution.

4.13 As to the petitioner's claim, under article 5, that he is unable to enjoy functions at the sports ground, the State party refers to the jurisprudence of the European Court of Human Rights in assessing discrimination. Under that approach, there must be a clear inequality of treatment in enjoyment of the relevant right, as compared to others in an analogous position. If there is such inequality between similarly situated persons, there must be reasonable and objective justification as well as proportionality of the means applied to achieve a particular aim.[15] The State party observes that sections 9 (making racial discrimination

unlawful)[16] and 10 (ensuring equality before the law) of the Act were enacted to implement articles 2 and 5 of the Convention, and section 9 closely follows the definition of racial discrimination in article 1 of the Convention.

4.14 The State party notes that the Federal Court (upheld on appeal) interpreted the phrase "based on" section 9 (1), upon which the author relied, as not "requiring a causal relationship between the act complained of and race etc., but [that it] should rather be read as meaning 'by reference to', i.e., as capable of being satisfied by a less direct relationship than that of cause and effect". Turning to the petitioner's case in terms of section 9 (1), the Court did not consider that the trustees' decision to retain the sign was an act "based on" race. This was so for the decision was not "an act that involved treating members of the Aboriginal race differently, let alone less favourably, from other members of the community", as the offending term was simply part of the customary identifier of a well-known person which had long ceased to have any inappropriate connotation.

4.15 The Court considered that, even if the decision was based or motivated on race, these racial considerations "were taken into account to satisfy the trustees that maintenance of the sign would *not* give offence to Aboriginal persons generally, as distinct from offence to [the petitioner] personally". Thus, the Court concluded, in finding that there was no racial discrimination, that: "[I]t cannot be said that the act, even if based on race, involved any distinction etc. having either the purpose or effect of nullifying or impairing the recognition, enjoyment or exercise, on an equal footing, of any human right or fundamental freedom of the kind referred to in section". The State party therefore submits that, as found by the Federal Court, the petitioner has failed to establish that he was treated by the trustees any differently from, or less favourably than, any other person in a similar position, and therefore no racial discrimination has been established.

4.16 In terms of the specific paragraphs of article 5 invoked by the petitioner (paras. (d) (i), (d) (ix), (e) (vi) and (f)), the State party submits that as he failed to establish a racially based distinction in the circumstances of his case, no question of discrimination arises in respect of his freedom of movement,

---

[15] *Airey* v. *Ireland*, application No. 6289/73, Judgement of 9 October 1979, para. 30; *Dudgeon* v. *United Kingdom*, application No. 7525/76, Judgement of 22 October 1981, para. 67; *Van der Mussele* v. *Belgium*, application No. 8919/80, Judgement of 23 October 1983, para. 46; *The Belgian Linguistic* Case (Merits), applications Nos. 1474/62, 1677/62, 1691/62, 1769/63, 1994/63 and 2126/64, Judgement of 23 July 1968, para. 6.

[16] For full text of the provision, see footnote 2 above.

freedom of assembly or association, right to equal participation in cultural activities, or right of access to any public place or service, respectively. As to paragraph (e) (vi), the State party refers to the Committee's jurisprudence that it is beyond its mandate to ensure that this right is established, but rather to monitor its implementation once the right is granted on equal terms.[17]

4.17 On article 6, the State party notes that States possess a wide margin of discretion in fulfilling their obligation under article 6.[18] It submits that its domestic law, which provides for the filing and determination of complaints of racial discrimination and the award of remedies, including monetary compensation for successful complaints, appropriately implements the obligation under article 6. The State party emphasizes that the dismissal of the petitioner's complaint by the Federal Court is no reflection on the effectiveness of the Act's remedies against racial discrimination, or of the remedies available when complaints are successful.

4.18 In any event, the State party submits that article 6, providing for remedies, is accessory in nature and can only be found to have been violated once a separate violation of the specific rights in the Convention has been established.[19] As no other violation of the Convention has been established (under arts. 2, 4, 5 or 7), nor can there be a consequent violation of article 6.

4.19 As to the claim under article 7, the State party notes that the Act came into effect the day after the Convention entered into force for the State party. Moreover, federal, State and Territory Governments have, over the years, adopted a wide array of measures to combat effectively racial prejudice and promote racial harmony, which are detailed in the State party's periodic reports. That the petitioner was unsuccessful before the domestic courts does not detract from the immediacy or effectiveness of measures taken by the State party's Governments to combat racial prejudice and to promote racial harmony.

---

[17] *D.T. Diop* v. *France*.
[18] L. Valencia Rodríguez, "The International Convention on the Elimination of All Forms of Racial Discrimination" in *Manual on Human Rights Reporting Under Six Major International Instruments* (United Nations publication, Sales No. GV.E.97.0.16), p. 289.
[19] See para. 4.4 and footnote 4 above.

*The petitioner's comments*

5.1 By submission of 20 December 2002, the petitioner responded to the State party's observations. He confirms that he is not asking the Committee to review decisions of the domestic courts, but rather to assess compliance with the Convention of the public display and repeated use in announcements of the offending term. It is apparent from the outcome of the domestic proceedings that the State party's domestic law is cast in overly restrictive terms and does not give full effect to Convention obligations. Nor does the petitioner ask the Committee to review the State party's law *in abstracto*; rather, he complains of a specific breach of the Convention and the State party's failure to provide a corresponding remedy.

5.2 The petitioner considers that subjective views of individuals referred to by the State party who were not offended by the term in question is of no relevance, as the question is whether the offence was felt by the petitioner and his family. In any event, a considerable number of other persons shared the petitioner's views on the stand, namely the Toowoomba Day Committee, the Toowoomba Multicultural Association, over 80 people participating in a "practical reconciliation" walk and 300 persons who signed a petition. Affidavits to this effect were submitted to the Federal Court, but were not admitted as evidence on technical grounds.[20] The petitioner invites the Committee to take notice of these views. In any event, the petitioner requests the Committee to conclude that the offending term is objectively offensive, whatever the subjective views of various individuals.

5.3 As to the inferences to be drawn from the failure of his domestic proceedings, the petitioner argues that this failure derived from the State party's legislation being so narrowly drawn that it is exceedingly difficult to prove discrimination, and thus it did not give full effect to the Convention. This failure shows that the State party's law does not provide effective protection against racial discrimination. He emphasizes that he does not approach the Committee arguing a violation of domestic legislation, but rather of the Convention itself.

5.4 As to the State party's specific arguments under article 2, the petitioner observes that the

---

[20] This evidence is supplied to the Committee.

State party has taken no steps to have the offending sign removed, despite the controversy surrounding it for years. This is said to be in violation of the duty, under article 2, to eliminate and bring to an end all forms of racial discrimination. The petitioner rejects the characterization of the Sports Ground Trust as a "private body". He points out that trustees are appointed and can be removed by the Minister, and that their function is to manage land for public (community) purposes. Indeed, the State party's legislation provides that any liability of the trustees attaches to the State.[21] It is therefore a public authority or institution for Convention purposes.

5.5  As to the State party's specific arguments under article 4, the petitioner objects to the reference to its reservation. He contends that the reservation is "probably invalid" as incompatible with the object and purpose of the Convention. Even if valid, he points out that the reservation is temporally limited as it refers to the State party's intention "at the first possible moment, to seek from Parliament legislation implementing the terms of article 4 (a)". Given that the State party contends that the Part II A of the Act implements its obligations under the article, the reservation must now have lapsed.

5.6  The petitioner points out that he is not objecting to use of the offending term in the distant past, but rather its contemporary use and display. He points out that it is not necessary to repeat the offensive nickname in order to honour Mr. Brown, and it is not common in the State party for stands to feature the nicknames of famous sportspeople in addition to their proper names.

5.7  As to the State party's specific arguments under article 5, the petitioner contends that he *has* established a racially based distinction on the basis that the offending term is racially offensive and derogatory, and that white Australians are not affected as the petitioner and his family have been. The inability as a consequence of the petitioner and his family to attend the ground impaired their rights under article 5, including their right to equal participation in cultural activities. As to the State party's specific arguments under article 5, the author observes that the State party failed to identify any measure of "teaching, education, culture and information" directed at combating the trustees' discriminatory conduct, or at promoting

---

[21] Section 92 Lands Act 1994 (Queensland).

reconciliation amongst the many persons offended by the sign.

*Issues and proceedings before the Committee*

*Consideration of admissibility*

6.1  Before considering any claims contained in a petition, the Committee on the Elimination of Racial Discrimination must, in accordance with rule 91 of its rules of procedure, decide whether or not it is admissible under the Convention.

6.2  The Committee notes that the State party concedes that domestic remedies have been exhausted. As to the State party's arguments that the petition falls outside the scope of the Convention and/or is insufficiently substantiated, the Committee considers that the petitioner has sufficiently substantiated, for purposes of admissibility, that his individual claim may fall within the scope of application of the provisions of the Convention. Given the complexity of the arguments of both fact and law, the Committee deems it more appropriate to determine the precise scope of the relevant provisions of the Convention at the merits stage of the petition.

6.3  In the absence of any further objections to the admissibility of the communication, the Committee declares the petition admissible and proceeds to its examination of the merits.

*Consideration of the merits*

7.1  Acting under article 14, paragraph 7 (a), of the International Convention on the Elimination of All Forms of Racial Discrimination, the Committee has considered the information submitted by the petitioner and the State party.

7.2  The Committee has taken due account of the context within which the sign bearing the offending term was originally erected in 1960, in particular the fact that the offending term, as a nickname probably with reference to a shoeshine brand, was not designed to demean or diminish its bearer, Mr. Brown, who was neither black nor of aboriginal descent. Furthermore, for significant periods neither Mr. Brown (for 12 years until his death) nor the wider public (for 39 years until the petitioner's complaint) objected to the presence of the sign.

7.3  Nevertheless, the Committee considers that that use and maintenance of the offending term can at the present time be considered offensive and insulting, even if for an extended period it may not have necessarily been so regarded. The Committee considers, in fact, that the Convention, as a living instrument, must be interpreted and applied taking into the circumstances of contemporary society. In this context, the Committee considers it to be its duty to recall the increased sensitivities in respect of words such as the offending term appertaining today.

8. The Committee therefore notes with satisfaction the resolution adopted at the Toowoomba public meeting of 29 July 1999 to the effect that, in the interest of reconciliation, racially derogatory or offensive terms will not be used or displayed in the future. At the same time, the Committee considers that the memory of a distinguished sportsperson may be honoured in ways other than by maintaining and displaying a public sign considered to be racially offensive. The Committee recommends that the State party take the necessary measures to secure the removal of the offending term from the sign in question, and to inform the Committee of such action it takes in this respect.

# Communication No. 27/2002

*Submitted by*: Mr. Kamal Quereshi (represented by counsel, Eddie Khawaja, of the Documentation and Advisory Centre on Racial Discrimination).
*Alleged victim*: The petitioner.
*State party*: Denmark.
*Date of adoption of Opinion:* 19 August 2003.
*Subject matter:* Discriminatory statements made public by members of a political party; effective investigation; access to effective mechanisms of protection.
*Procedural issues:* Undue delay in submission of communication.
*Substantive issues:* State parties have a positive obligation to take effective action against reported incidents of racial discrimination; right to an effective remedy against acts of racial discrimination; right to an effective investigation; racial discrimination.
*Articles of the Convention:* 2 (1) (d), 4 and 6.
*Finding:* No violation.

*Opinion*

1. The petitioner is Kamal Quereshi, a Danish national born 29 July 1970 and a member of the Danish Parliament for the Socialist People's Party. He claims to be a victim of a violation by Denmark of articles 2, subparagraph 1 (d), 4 and 6 of the Convention. He is represented by counsel.

*The facts as presented*

2.1 On 26 April 2001, Pia Andersen, a member of the Executive Board of the Progressive Party, faxed a party press release to media, with the headline "No to more Mohammedan rapes!". It included the following statements:

"Cultural enrichments taking place in the shape of negative expressions and rapes against us Danish women, to which we are exposed every day ... Now it's too much, we will not accept more violations from our foreign citizens, can the Mohammedans not show some respect for us Danish women, and behave like the guests they are in our country, then the politicians in the parliament have to change course and expel all of them."

2.2 On 15 May 2001, Ms. Andersen faxed another press release, in relation to neighbourhood disturbances in Odense, which included the following:

"Engage the military against the Mohammedan terror! ... Dear fellow citizen, it is that war-like culture these foreigners enrich our country with ... Disrespect for this country's laws, mass rapes, violence, abuse of Danish women by shouting things like 'horse', 'Danish pigs' etc.. And now this civil war-like situation."

2.3 For these two actions, the Odense police charged Ms. Andersen with a violation of section 266 (b) of the Danish Criminal Code ("sect. 266 (b)").[1] She was later convicted (see para. 2.8). On 5 September 2001, the Progressive Party placed a newspaper invitation to a lecture by the former party leader, Mogens Glistrup, which read that: "The Bible of the Muhamedans requires: The infidel shall be killed and slaughtered, until all infidelity has been removed."

2.4 From 20 to 22 October 2001, the Progressive Party held its annual meeting. This meeting, of a party running for Parliament, was required by law to be broadcast on public television. A number of speakers presented the following views:

> Margit Guul (member of the party): "I'm glad to be a racist. We shall free Denmark of Mohammedans", "the black breed like rats", "they shall have a hand cut off if they steal"

> Bo Warming (member of the party): "The only difference between Mohammedans and rats is that the rats do not receive social benefits"

> Mogens Glistrup (former party leader): "Mohammedans are going to exterminate the populations in those countries they have forced themselves into"

> Peter Rindal (member of the party): "Regarding Muslim graveyards, that is a brilliant idea, and preferably of such size that they all fit in them, and preferably at once"

> Erik Hammer Sørensen (member of the party): "5th columnists are walking around among us. The ones we have received commit violence, murder and rape"

> Vagn Andersen (member of the party): "The State has given these foreigners/ strangers jobs. They work in our slaughterhouses, where they without problems can poison our food, and endanger our agricultural export. Another form of terrorism is to break into our water supply facilities and poison the water"

2.5 After witnessing this meeting, the petitioner requested the Documentation and Advisory Centre on Racial Discrimination ("DRC") to file a criminal complaint against the Progressive Party for a violation of section 266 (b). The DRC filed a complaint with the Chief Constable of the Thisted police, the city of residence of the Progressive Party leader. On 31 October 2001, the complaint was rejected on the basis that section 266 (b) did not apply to legal persons such as a political party. On 3 December 2001, the Aalborg Regional Public Prosecutor upheld this decision.

2.6 Thereupon, the petitioner requested the DRC to file a criminal complaint against each member of the executive board of the Progressive Party, for violation of sections 23 and 266 (b) of the Criminal Code. On 11 December 2001, the DRC complained that Ms. Andersen, as a member of the party's executive board, had participated in a violation of section 266 (b), as a result of the press releases, newspaper invitation and comments of the annual meeting all described above. The DRC considered it relevant that the Progressive Party had allegedly set up courses allegedly teaching members how to avoid violations of section 266 (b), by avoiding the use of certain phrases.

2.7 On 7 January 2002, the Chief Constable of the Odense police rejected the petitioner's complaint, considering that there was no reasonable evidence to support the allegation that an unlawful act had been committed.[2] The

---

[1] Section 266 (b) of the Criminal Code provides as follows:
> "(1) Any person who, publicly or with the intention of wider dissemination, makes a statement or imparts other information by which a group of people are threatened, insulted or degraded on account of their race, colour, national or ethnic origin, religion, or sexual inclination shall be liable to a fine or to imprisonment for any term not exceeding two years.
> (2) When the sentence is meted out, the fact that the offence is in the nature of propaganda activities shall be considered an aggravating circumstance."

[2] The relevant sections of the Administration of Justice Act regulating the investigation of criminal complaints provide as follows:
> 742 (2): "The police shall institute investigations upon a [criminal] report lodged or on its own initiative, when it may reasonably be presumed that a criminal offence subject to prosecution has been committed."
> 743: "The purpose of the investigation is to clarify whether the conditions for imposing criminal liability or other legal consequences under criminal law are fulfilled, and to provide information for use in the determination of the case and prepare the conduct of the case before the court."

Chief Constable considered that membership of a political party's executive does not of itself create a basis for criminal participation in relation to possible criminal statements made during the party's annual meeting by other persons.

2.8 On 22 January 2002, the DRC referred the decision to the Funen Regional Public Prosecutor, challenging the Chief Constable's rejection of the complaint on the basis stated. It contended that Ms. Andersen herself was directly involved in the dispatch of the press releases, in respect of which the Odense police had charged her with violations of section 266 (b), and that it would therefore be difficult to argue that she had not directly or indirectly called upon other party members to say similar things. Therefore, according to the DRC, the police should at a minimum have conducted an investigation to clarify these matters. On 25 January 2002, the Odense District Court convicted Ms. Andersen of offences against section 266 (b) of the Criminal Code for the publication of the press releases.

2.9 On 11 March 2002, the Funen Regional Public Prosecutor rejected the complaint, finding that neither the petitioner nor the DRC had the required essential, direct, individual or legal interest to become parties in the case. While the police had taken the view that the petitioner, on account of the nature of the complaint, his ethnic background and membership of Parliament, had standing to pursue a complaint, the State Attorney considered that these elements did not support such a conclusion.

*The complaint*

3.1 The petitioner argues that the decision of the Odense Chief Constable not to initiate an investigation constituted a violation of articles 2, subparagraph 1 (d), 4 and 6 of the Convention. Referring to the Committee's jurisprudence, he argues that States parties have a positive obligation to take serious, thorough and effective action against alleged cases of racial discrimination. The police decision that there was no information to suggest Ms. Andersen incited other speakers at the annual meeting fell short of that standard, as the police did not question

---

749 (1): "The police shall dismiss a report lodged if it deems that there is no basis for initiating investigation."

Ms. Andersen or any other speaker. Thus, the police could not examine issues such as whether the speeches could be seen as part of an organized attempt systematically to spread racist views, whether Ms. Andersen participated in the selection of the speakers, whether she had seen a transcript or knew of the content of the speeches, and whether she, as a member of the Executive Board, tried to prevent expressions of racist views.

3.2 The petitioner alleges that the decision of the Funen Regional Public Prosecutor that he had no standing violates article 6 of the Convention. He thus considers himself deprived of action in response to an act of racial discrimination to which he feels he was exposed. Even if the speeches were not directed against him, they subjected a group to which he feels connected to racial discrimination. Further, as section 266 (b) is the only criminal provision concerning racial discrimination, it is essential to hold not only individuals but also political parties, as identified by members of their Executive Board, responsible for expression of racist views.

3.3 As to the exhaustion of domestic remedies, the petitioner contends that under the State party's law, the Regional Public Prosecutor's decision cannot be appealed, and thus there is no possibility that the police will initiate criminal proceedings. He argues that private legal action brought by him directly against Ms. Andersen would not be effective, given that the police and Regional Public Prosecutor had rejected this complaint. In addition, the Eastern High Court, in a decision of 5 February 1999, has decided that racial discrimination does not, in itself, infringe a person's honour and reputation in terms of section 26 of the Act on Civil Liability.

3.4 The petitioner observes that the same matter has not been submitted to another international procedure of investigation or settlement.

*The State party's submissions on the admissibility and merits of the petition*

4.1 By submissions of 29 January 2003, the State party disputed both the admissibility, in part, and the merits of the petition.

4.2 The State party understands the petitioner's observation on the impossibility of applying section 266 (b) to legal persons as raising a separate claim, which should be declared inadmissible for failure to present the petition to the Committee within the required six months' time limit. The Aalborg Regional Public Prosecutor's decision finally to reject the complaint against the Progressive Party was taken on 3 December 2001, over six months prior to the submission of the petition, and this claim should therefore be declared inadmissible. The State party notes however that due to an amendment to the criminal code, legal persons may be held liable for offences against section 266 (b) since 8 June 2002.

4.3 On the merits of the claims concerning the handling of the complaint against Ms. Andersen by the Odense Chief Constable and in turn the Funen Regional Public Prosecutor, the State party argues that these processes fully satisfy the requirements that can be inferred from the Convention, and as interpreted in the Committee's practice. This is so even though the petitioner did not achieve the result he wanted, that is the initiation of criminal proceedings, for the Convention does not guarantee a specific outcome, but rather sets down certain requirements for the handling of such complaints, which were met in this case.

4.4 As to the decision of the Odense Chief Constable police rejecting the complaint against Ms. Andersen, the State party noted that, on the basis of the DRC's detailed report to him, he had a broad basis for deciding whether there was reason for initiating a full investigation. The State party emphasises that the Chief Constable's task was *not* to assess whether the statements made at the annual meeting involved a violation of section 266 (b), but whether it could reasonably be presumed that Ms. Andersen, as a member of the party's executive board, could be punished for participation in a violation of section 266 (b) on the grounds, inter alia, of statements made by third parties.

4.5 While at the time a criminal report had been lodged against the speakers at the conference and criminal proceedings had been separately initiated by the petitioner against Ms. Andersen concerning the two press releases, the petitioner's complaint contained no information that Ms. Andersen had encouraged others to make criminal statements or had otherwise participated in them; rather, it simply made a general allegation that as a member of the executive board, she was criminally liable for *participation*, and it was in respect of this

charge that the decision was made. It would have been open to the author to bring charges against the individuals who had personally engaged in the conduct in question. Accordingly, the State party finds no basis for criticizing the Chief Constable's decision concerning Ms. Andersen, and the dismissal of a report found to be without basis is consistent with the Convention.

4.6 Concerning the specific issues that the petitioner contends the Chief Constable should have investigated, the State party points out, on the argument that the police should have investigated whether the rostrum statements amounted to propaganda activities, that propaganda activity is considered an aggravating circumstance at the sentencing stage (see sect. 266 (b) (2)). It is not a constitutive element of the offence charged, and as it had been determined that there were not reasonable grounds to suspect Ms. Andersen had committed an offence against section 266 (b), there was no need to further investigate this aspect.

4.7 As to the further issues that the petitioner claims should have been investigated, the State party recalls that the Chief Constable dismissed the case on the ground that membership of a party's executive committee does not per se involve criminal participation in statements made by others at a party conference. As the information given to the police supplied no basis for initiating an investigation, there was no concrete reason for presuming Ms. Andersen was liable for criminal participation in, or encouragement of, statements made by third parties. There was no reason to investigate the further matters raised.

4.8 As to the argument of a violation of the right to an effective remedy protected by article 6, because of the refusal of the Funen Regional Public Prosecutor to consider the petitioner's case, the State party observes that the Regional Public Prosecutor found that the DRC had no material legal interest that would entitle it to appeal, and that it could not be assumed that the author had such interest. She further stated that a review of the case did not otherwise give rise to any comments, and, thus, she also considered the case on the merits. As the authority superior to the Chief Constable, the Regional Public Prosecutor may *proprio motu* assess the correctness of a decision on the merits even when formal entitlements to appeal are not satisfied. Indeed, on the basis of the special nature of the violation, and given that section 266 (b) of the Criminal Code relates to public statements, there may well be special reason to consider the merits of a case involving a violation of section 266 (b) despite the fact that an applicant cannot be considered party to the particular proceedings. This is what transpired in the present case. As the Regional Public Prosecutor assessed the merits of the case, the State party argues it has ensured effective protection and remedies to the petitioner, consistent with article 6 of the Convention.

4.9 The State party points out that it satisfied its obligations under article 6, in addition, by the Chief Constable's determination on whether or not an investigation should be initiated, and by providing for recourse to the independent Parliamentary Ombudsman if it was thought that the decisions of the Chief Constable or the Regional Public Prosecutor were invalid, insufficiently reasoned or contrary to the law. In addition, under section 63 of the Constitution, decisions of administrative authorities, including the Chief Constable and the Regional Public Prosecutor, may be challenged judicially before the courts on the same grounds. While this possibility exists, the State party cannot refer to an instance where this has been resorted to.

4.10 In conclusion, the State party considers that it is not possible to infer an obligation under the Convention to carry out an investigation in situations that provide no basis for it. The Administration of Justice Act provides for the appropriate remedies in accordance with the Convention, and the competent authorities fully discharged their obligations in the specific case.

*The petitioner's comments*

5.1 By letter of 10 March 2003, the petitioner responded to the State party's comments, clarifying that he did *not* contend the State party was in breach of article 6 by not providing for corporate liability under section 266 (b). Given this situation, however, it was of great importance that there be an effective investigation as to whether members of the executive board of a legal entity could be held responsible for the conduct in question.

5.2 On the merits, the petitioner contends that there is a breach of article 6 due to an inability to appeal decisions of the Regional Public Prosecutor. He refers to a previous decision of the Committee to the effect that the possibility to appeal to the Parliamentary Ombudsman did not amount to an effective remedy, for purposes of article 6.[3] The Ombudsman has full discretion as to whether to pursue a case, and the State party does not refer to a single occasion where the Ombudsman has investigated a Regional Public Prosecutor's refusal to initiate an investigation. In addition, the State party's own inability to invoke a case where judicial review under the Constitution was invoked in such a case suggests this recourse is ineffective.

5.3 As to the Regional Public Prosecutor's review of the Chief Constable's decision, the petitioner argues that both the conduct and outcome of the appeal violated article 6. Firstly, non-mandatory review of the merits of the decision is said itself to breach article 6 of the Convention, as it does not involve a *mandatory* examination of the case. Even if there was a merits review by the Regional Public Prosecutor, the petitioner considers it unclear why the case did not give rise to any comments, and the actual ground for dismissal of the appeal was the lack of standing. Thus, the rejection of the appeal also breached article 6.

5.4 The petitioner agrees that article 6 does not guarantee a specific outcome of a given case. However, his case relates not to the outcome of the investigation, but to the investigation itself. He disagrees that the Chief Constable's decision not to initiate an investigation was "acceptable", as it was based on the DRC's detailed report. In his view, the Chief Constable did not ascertain important issues; in particular, the fact that Ms. Andersen had already been indicted for disseminating racist views made an investigation into possibly organized and systematic conduct on the part of the executive board members important.

5.5 The petitioner rejects that the DRC's report contained only a "general allegation" against Ms. Andersen, as it specifically detailed an alleged criminal offence. An effective investigation would have required at least questioning the alleged perpetrator before deciding whether or not to prosecute. In addition, if membership of the executive board did not itself imply complicity in criminal conduct of the party or its members, and no complaint could be directed against the party itself, there was all the more reason

---

[3] *Habassi* v. *Denmark*, communication No. 10/1997, Opinion of 17 March 1999.

individually to assess the extent, if any, of Ms. Andersen's role in the alleged acts of racial discrimination.

5.6 The petitioner observes that criminal complaints were indeed brought against the individuals personally responsible for the conduct in question, as suggested by the State party, but contends that this does not affect the issue of Ms. Andersen's alleged participation therein, or the effectiveness of the investigation in respect of the charges against her. He thus considers that the State party has failed to show that the decision not to conduct an investigation, the Regional Public Prosecutor's rejection on formal grounds of the appeal against the Chief Constable's decision, and the inability to appeal the Regional Public Prosecutor's decision, were consistent with articles 4 and 6 of the Convention.

*Issues and proceedings before the Committee*

*Consideration of admissibility*

6.1 Before considering any claims contained in a petition, the Committee on the Elimination of Racial Discrimination must, in accordance with rule 91 of its rules of procedure, decide whether or not it is admissible under the Convention.

6.2 The Committee notes that the petitioner disclaims any contention that the inability, at the material time, to file a criminal complaint of racial discrimination was in violation of the Convention. Thus, the Committee need not decide whether such a claim would be inadmissible with reference to the six months rule applicable to the timeframe within which a petition may be brought. In the absence of any further objections to the admissibility of the petition, the Committee declares it admissible and proceeds to its examination of the merits.

*Consideration of the merits*

7.1 Acting under article 14, paragraph 7 (a), of the International Convention on the Elimination of All Forms of Racial Discrimination, the Committee has considered the information submitted by the petitioner and the State party.

7.2 The Committee notes that the present case involves two different sets of acts by different actors: on the one hand, Ms. Andersen herself transmitted press releases by facsimile, in respect of which she was subsequently convicted. On the other

hand, speakers at the party conference (of which Ms. Andersen was not one) made the series of racist statements, contrary to article 4, paragraph b, of the Convention, described in paragraph 2.4, concerning which criminal complaints were lodged (see para. 5.6).

7.3 Against this background, the Committee considers that given the complaint against Ms. Andersen in connection with the party conference was not accompanied by any evidence suggesting that she was an accomplice soliciting, directing or otherwise procuring the speakers at the party meeting to engage in the impugned conduct, it is reasonable to conclude, as did the State party's authorities, that the complaint did not make out a case that Ms. Andersen, as opposed to the speakers themselves, had engaged in any act of racial discrimination; indeed, as a matter of criminal law, liability of a member of a party's executive board could not attach, without additional evidence, in respect of statements made by third parties.

7.4 In the Committee's view, this case may accordingly be distinguished from previous cases where, on the facts, the Committee has on occasion considered that an investigation into the alleged acts of racial discrimination that had taken place was insufficient for the purposes of article 6.[4] In each of those cases, in fact, the investigation was in respect of the individual(s) directly committing the alleged act of racial discrimination, rather than a third party, with the result that *no* person was held criminally responsible for the acts in question; in the present case, on the other hand, criminal complaints *were* lodged against those directly responsible. It cannot therefore be considered that there was no effective action taken in response to the acts in question.

7.5 As to the review of the decisions not to prosecute in the present case, the Committee refers to its jurisprudence that "the terms of article 6 do not impose upon States parties the duty to institute a mechanism of sequential remedies" in cases of alleged racial discrimination.[5] Accordingly, even if article 6 might be interpreted to require the possibility of judicial review of a decision not to bring a criminal prosecution in a particular case

---

[4] See, for example, *Ahmad* v. *Denmark*, communication No. 16/1999, Opinion of 13 March 2000, and *Habassi* v. *Denmark*.

[5] *Yilmaz-Dogan* v. *Netherlands*, para. 9.4 (finding no violation of art. 6).

alleging racial discrimination, the Committee refers to the State party's statement that it is open, under national law, judicially to challenge a prosecutor's decision.

8. The Committee on the Elimination of Racial Discrimination, acting under article 14, paragraph 7, of the Convention, is of the opinion that the facts before it do not disclose a violation of the Convention inasmuch as the State party's action with respect to Ms. Anderson is concerned.

9. In the light of the State party's obligation under article 4, paragraph (b), of the Convention, however, the Committee would wish to remain apprised as to the results of the criminal complaints lodged against the speakers at the party political conference in view of the racist nature of their remarks, contrary to article 4, paragraph b, of the Convention. The Committee draws the attention of the State party to the need to balance freedom of expression with the requirements of the Convention to prevent and eliminate all acts of racial discrimination, particularly in the context of statements made by members of political parties.

# Communication No. 29/2003

*Submitted by*: Mr. Dragan Durmic (represented by the European Roma Rights Center and the Humanitarian Law Center).
*Alleged victim*: The petitioner.
*State party*: Serbia and Montenegro.
*Date of adoption of Opinion:* 6 March 2006.
*Subject matter:* Denial of entry to a club based on Roma origin; access to effective mechanisms of protection; effective investigation.
*Procedural issues:* Inadmissibility *ratione temporis*; exhaustion of domestic remedies; undue delay in submission of communication.
*Substantive issues:* Right to an effective remedy against acts of racial discrimination; right to an effective investigation; obligation to refrain from publishing information on individual petitions, prior to examination by the Committee; ongoing violations; right of access to any place or service intended for use by the general public; discrimination based on ethnic and national origin.
*Articles of the Convention:* 2 (1) (d) and 5 (f) in combination, 3, 4 (c), 6 and 14 (7) (a).
*Finding:* Violation (arts. 5 (f) and 6).

*Opinion*

1. The petitioner is Dragan Durmic, a national of Serbia and Montenegro and of Romani origin. He claims to be a victim of violations of Serbia and Montenegro of article 2, paragraph 1 (d), read together with article 5 (f), as well as articles 3, 4 (c) and 6 of the International Convention on the Elimination of Racial Discrimination. The petitioner is legally represented by the Humanitarian Law Center and the European Roma Rights Center. Serbia and Montenegro made the declaration under article 14 of the Convention on 27 June 2001.

*The facts as presented by the petitioners*

2.1 In 2000, the Humanitarian Law Center (HLC) carried out a series of "tests" across Serbia, to establish whether members of the Roma minority were being discriminated against while attempting to access public places. It was prompted to such action by numerous complaints alleging that the Roma are denied access to clubs, discotheques, restaurants, cafes and/or swimming pools, on the basis of their ethnic origin.

2.2 On 18 February 2000, two Roma individuals, one of whom the petitioner, and three non-Roma individuals, attempted to gain access to a discotheque in Belgrade. All were neatly dressed, well-behaved and were not under the influence of alcohol. Thus, the only apparent difference between them was the colour of their skin. There was no notice displayed to the effect that a private party was being held and that they could not enter without showing an invitation. The two individuals of Roma origin were denied entry to the club on the basis that it was a private party and they did not have invitations. When the petitioner asked the security guard how he may obtain an invitation there and then, he was told that it was not possible and that the invitations were not for sale. He was unwilling to inform the petitioner how he might obtain an invitation for future events. The three non-Roma individuals were all allowed to enter, despite having no invitations for the so called private party and making this clear to the security personnel at the time.

2.3 On 21 July 2000, on behalf of the petitioner, the HLC filed a criminal complaint with the Public Prosecutor's Office in Belgrade. It was directed against unidentified individuals employed by the discotheque in question on suspicion of having committed a crime under article 60 of the Serbian Criminal Code.[1] The petitioner claimed a violation of his rights as well as the rights of the other Roma individual to equality, human dignity and equal access to places intended for the use of the general public. Among the international provisions invoked, the HLC put special emphasis on article 5 (f) of the [International Convention on the Elimination of Racial Discrimination]. It requested the Public Prosecutor's Office to identify the perpetrators and initiate a formal judicial investigation against them, or file an indictment directly in the competent court.

2.4 After seven months, in the absence of any response, the HLC sent another letter to the Public Prosecutor stressing that, should the latter dismiss the criminal complaint, and if the perpetrators had been identified by that time, the petitioner and the other alleged victim wished to exercise their legal prerogative to take over the prosecution of the case in the capacity of private/subsidiary prosecutors.[2] The Public Prosecutor responded that he had

requested the police on two separate occasions in August 2000 to investigate this incident but that they had failed to do so.

2.5 On 22 October 2001, the Public Prosecutor informed the HLC that it had confirmed, through police inquiries, that there had been a private party at the disco on the date in question, allegedly organized by the owner of the establishment. He also stated that the police had ignored the order to identify and question the security personnel on the evening of the incident. No further information was received from the Public Prosecutor. According to the petitioner, under articles 153 and 60 of the Criminal Procedure Code, in circumstances where the Public Prosecutor simply ignores a criminal complaint filed by a complainant regarding a crime, the complainant can only wait for the Prosecutor's decision or, alternatively, informally urge him to take action as provided for by law.

2.6 On 30 January 2002, the petitioner filed a petition in the Federal Constitutional Court stating that, by failing to identify the perpetrators and dismissing the criminal complaint, the Public Prosecutor prevented the petitioner and alleged victim from taking over the prosecution of the case on their own behalf. More than 15 months after submitting the petition to the Federal Constitutional Court, the petitioner has not received any response and thus has obtained no redress for the violations suffered.

*The complaint*

3.1 On the issue of *ratione temporis*, the petitioner acknowledges that the incident in question predates the State party's declaration under article 14 of the Convention. However, he argues that the Socialist Federal Republic of Yugoslavia (SFRY) ratified the Convention in 1967 and following its dissolution the Convention retained its binding effect with respect to all successor states, including the State party. On 4 February 2003, the Former Republic of Yugoslavia (FRY) renamed itself the State Union of Serbia and Montenegro but remained the same subject under international law. In his view, article 14 is a simple jurisdictional clause and therefore a declaration made in accordance with this article results merely in the recognition by the State concerned of another means by which the Committee can monitor implementation of the Convention. He notes that article 14 contains no express temporal limitation which

---

[1] Article 60 provides "Whoever denies or restricts on the grounds of distinctions in nationality, race, religion, political or other affiliation, ethnicity, sex, language, education or social status the rights of citizens embodied in the Constitution, law, or other regulations or ordinances, or a ratified international treaty, or whoever grants citizens benefits or privileges on these grounds, shall be punished with a term of imprisonment of three months to five years."
[2] According to the petitioner, under domestic law, if the Public Prosecutor finds that there is reasonable suspicion that a certain person has committed a criminal offence, he will request the investigating judge to institute a formal judicial investigation. But if not, he must inform the complainant of this decision, who can in turn exercise his prerogative to take over the prosecution of the case on his own behalf.

would prevent the Committee from examining petitions on the basis of facts that had taken place prior to the date of deposit of the declaration. In any event, he argues, it is now more than 21 months following the declaration and the State party has yet to provide the petitioner with any redress. The petitioner refers to the jurisprudence of the European Court of Human Rights and of the Human Rights Committee.

3.2 As to "testing" as a technique used for the collection of evidence on allegations of discrimination, the petitioner submits that since the 1950s United States courts have recognized testing as an effective means of proving discrimination. He also refers to the jurisprudence of the [Committee] which he purports demonstrates that the Committee itself has confirmed the admissibility of such cases.[3] The petitioner also requests the opportunity to provide further clarification on this issue if the Committee considers it necessary.

3.3 The petitioner alleges that he has exhausted all effective domestic remedies available. As to constitutional remedies, he denies that there is or ever was a constitutional remedy available to individual victims of discrimination. He acknowledges that, on 27 June 2001, the FRY made a declaration under article 14, paragraph 2, of the Convention, designating the country's Federal Constitutional Court as the final domestic judicial instance entrusted with receiving and considering all complaints alleging discrimination—"*providing all other domestic remedies have already been exhausted*". However, according to the Constitution of the FRY, adopted on 27 April 1992, no such competence was ever granted. In fact, article 128 of the Constitution expressly stated that "the Federal Constitutional Court shall decide on a complaint [alleging various individual human right violations, including discrimination] only when other legal remedies are not available"—i.e., "*when the law provides no other legal remedy for a given kind of violation*".

3.4 The Federal Constitutional Court explained its competence as follows: "If dissatisfied with the final decision of the

---

[3] *Lacko* v. *Slovakia*, communication No. 11/1998, Opinion of 9 August 2001, *B.J.* v. *Denmark*, communication No. 17/1999, Opinion of 17 March 2000 and *M.B.* v. *Denmark*, communication No. 20/2000, Opinion of 13 March 2002.

Republican Labour Office, the party is entitled to institute administrative litigation before the Serbian Supreme Court ... The Court has established that the person who filed [this] constitutional complaint had recourse to other means of legal protection, of which he availed himself... For this reason ... the Court has decided to dismiss the constitutional complaint." The petitioner alleges that such legal reasoning led lawyers to conclude that constitutional complaints were indeed "a purely theoretical remedy since the Yugoslav legal system nominally provides protection in almost all cases of human rights violations." The authorities did not amend the Constitution of the FRY, nor the Federal Constitutional Court Act, which would have been necessary to formally provide for an expansion of the Federal Constitutional Court's competence to examine cases of discrimination as the final judicial instance—once an alleged victim has been unsuccessful in obtaining redress from all other/regular remedies.

3.5 On 4 February 2003, the FRY adopted a new constitution and renamed itself the State Union of Serbia and Montenegro. The former Federal Constitutional Court was to be replaced by the Court of Serbia and Montenegro. Pursuant to article 46 of the Charter, this court will also be competent to consider individual complaints alleging human rights violations, including discrimination, but, like the old Court, only "if no other recourse has been provided for". Finally, article 62 (1) of the new Court of Serbia and Montenegro Act, adopted on 19 June 2003, confirmed this understanding of the competence of the Court by providing that an individual complaint can be filed only if "no other avenue of legal redress exists" within either Serbia or Montenegro. Prior to the adoption of the new Constitutional Charter as well as subsequently, domestic legislation contained provisions affording other non-constitutional, means of redress to victims of racial discrimination—including civil and/or criminal remedies. Therefore, the petitioner argues, notwithstanding the article 14 declaration, there is no (and has never been) a constitutional remedy available to victims of discrimination. The petitioner adds that the article 14 declaration itself refers to a currently non-existent court i.e., the Federal Constitutional Court, and not to the Court of Serbia and Montenegro.

3.6 Regardless of the petitioner's view in this regard and to oppose any possible objections from the State party on exhaustion of domestic remedies, the petitioner filed a submission in the Federal Constitutional Court and, in so doing, invoked the article 14 declaration. On exhaustion of domestic remedies, he concludes that the wrong suffered by him is of such a serious nature that only a criminal remedy would provide adequate redress and that he exhausted all domestic criminal remedies, as well as the merely "hypothetically available" constitutional remedy, and still obtained no redress. For the preposition that domestic remedies have been exhausted to the extent that criminal remedies are the only effective remedies to address the kind of violations at issue, the petitioner refers to the cases of *Lacko* v. *Slovakia* and *M.B.* v. *Denmark*,[4] both found to be admissible by [the Committee], as well as jurisprudence of the European Court of Human Rights.[5]

3.7   As to the six-months rule, the petitioner submits that although he filed a complaint in the Federal Constitutional Court, this Court never considered the matter. Moreover, as a result of the adoption of the new Constitutional Charter, this Court has since ceased to exist and is yet to be replaced by the new Court of Serbia and Montenegro which, according to the petitioner, will have no competence to consider individual discrimination cases. For the petitioner, the six-month time limit has not even started running, and his communication is therefore both timely and admissible. He invokes the jurisprudence of the European Court of Human Rights, which has accepted cases when there is a continuing situation, act or omission that can be imputed to the authorities.

3.8   The petitioner submits that the allegations of violations ought to be interpreted against a backdrop of systematic discrimination of Roma in the State party, as well as the practical absence of any adequate form of redress. He claims a violation of article 2, paragraph 1 (d), read together with article 5 (f) of the Convention as the discotheque the petitioner was prevented from accessing a "place or service intended for use by the general public," on the basis of his race. The failure of the State party to prosecute the owners of the discotheque for its discriminatory practice, and

to ensure that such discrimination does not recur, is said to amount to a violation of article 5 (f), read in conjunction with article 2, paragraph 1 (d).

3.9   The petitioner refers to the Committee's general recommendation on article 5,[6] in which the Committee noted that, although article 5 "does not of itself create civil, political, economic, social or cultural rights, [it] assumes the existence and recognition of these rights. The Convention obliges States to prohibit and eliminate racial discrimination in the enjoyment of such human rights." Thus, the Committee looks to the extent to which States have ensured "the non-discriminatory implementation of each of the rights and freedoms referred to in article 5 of the Convention." Moreover, the Committee indicated that States' responsibility to ensure protection of the "rights and freedoms referred to in article 5 of the Convention" is not dependent on the good will of each Government; it is mandatory. The scope of this binding obligation is to ensure the "effective implementation" of the rights contained in article 5. Indeed, [the Committee] has held that the Convention prohibits discrimination by both private parties and public authorities. The petitioner also refers to the Human Rights Committee's interpretation of article 26, the general non-discrimination provision of the International Covenant on Civil and Political Rights on the obligation of States parties to protect against discrimination.

3.10   The petitioner claims a violation of article 3 of the Convention, as he was subjected to a form of racial segregation by being refused entry to the discotheque solely on grounds of race. The State party's failure to provide any remedies in this case constitutes a failure to comply with its obligation under article 3 to "prevent, prohibit and eradicate all practices of this nature....". He claims a violation of article 4 (c) as by failing to prosecute the owners of the discotheque or in any way remedy the alleged discrimination against the petitioner and the other alleged victim, the prosecuting authorities—the police and the Public Prosecutor's Office—have promoted racial discrimination. In its general recommendation on article 4 of the Convention, the [Committee] recalled "that the provisions of article 4 are of a mandatory character. To satisfy these obligations, States parties have not only to enact appropriate

---

[4] See footnote 3 above.

[5] *A.* v. *France*, application No. 14838/89, Judgement of 23 November 1993. See also *Yagiz* v. *Turkey*, application No. 19092/91, Judgement of 25 June 1996 75 D&R 207 as well as *Sargin and Yagci* v. *Turkey*, application No. 14116-7/88, 61 D&R 250.

---

[6] General recommendation XX (1996), para. 1.

legislation but also to ensure that it is effectively enforced."

3.11 The petitioner invokes article 6 of the Convention, as the State party has not provided him with a remedy for the discrimination he suffered, nor has it taken measures to punish the perpetrators or ensure that such discrimination does not recur. For the same reasons, the petitioner has to date been denied his right to civil compensation, which he may only claim in criminal proceedings. Due to the State party's failure to provide any remedies in the instant case, and notwithstanding the existing domestic criminal provisions prohibiting discrimination in access to public places, the petitioner has been forced to live with continuing uncertainty as to whether he will be admitted to the discotheque on any given date in the future.

*The State party's admissibility submission*

4.1 By submission of 12 August 2003, the State party submitted its response on admissibility. As to the facts, it stated that, on 20 August 2000 the Ministry of Internal Affairs was requested to collect the necessary information and to identify the persons working for the discotheque in question. Subsequent requests were made to the Ministry on 3 July and, 22 October 2001, 5 February, 2 October, and 23 December 2002, 25 February 2003 and 14 May 2003. On 4 April 2001, the Ministry submitted a report from which it transpires, based on an interview with the manager of the club, that a private party for specially invited guests was being held on the night in question. The manager could not identify the security personnel on duty that night, given the club's frequent personnel turnover. Consequently, as a result of the problems in establishing their identity the Public Prosecutor had difficulty in building up a case.

4.2 According to the State party, articles 124 and 128 of the Constitution of the Federal Republic of Yugoslavia, in force at the time of the alleged incident, laid down the competence of the Federal Constitutional Court to consider claims of violations of the rights and freedoms enshrined therein and to consider complaints "when other legal remedies are not available". It is submitted that these provisions are referred to in the article 14 declaration made by the FRY on 27 June 2001, in recognition of the competence of the Committee to receive and consider communications. The State party

acknowledges that on 30 January 2002, the petitioner submitted a complaint to the Federal Constitutional Court, as the last instance in the matter, the consideration of which was postponed by the Court on 2 December 2002. The Court has not examined this matter yet for the following reasons: following the adoption of the Constitutional Charter of the State Union of Serbia and Montenegro on 4 February 2003, the FRY ceased to exist. Under article 12 of the Law on the Implementation of the Constitutional Charter, the Federal Constitutional Court transmitted all undecided cases to the Court of Serbia and Montenegro, the competence of which in this matter is defined in article 46 of the Constitutional Charter. Considering that the judges of the Court have not been elected and that, accordingly, the Court itself has not yet been constituted, the Federal Constitutional Court continues to work, considering matters of vital importance for the functioning of the State only and leaving all other cases for consideration by the Court of Serbia and Montenegro once it is constituted and operational. In view of the fundamental changes that took place in the judicial system of the country, the prolongation of the case, the State party submits, is justifiable.

4.3 The State party contends that in April 2003, the petitioner publicly disclosed the present communication, allegedly in contravention of article 14, paragraph 4, of the Convention.

*Petitioner's comments on State party submission*

5.1 On 2 October 2003, the petitioner commented on the State party's submission. As to the conduct of the investigation, he notes that the prosecuting authorities have not even identified the security personnel more than three years after the submission of the criminal complaint and that the procedure has been prolonged. The excuse offered by the State party seems to imply that the police are dependent on the good will of the club manager in order to proceed. In addition, there is no information on the thoroughness of the investigation undertaken by the police: whether they looked into the club's internal records to establish the identity of the individuals employed at the time or whether, in the absence of such records, they informed other competent authorities in order to hold the club manager legally accountable for failing to register his employees as required by domestic labour and tax law. The police and Public Prosecutor have failed to date to contact the petitioner and/or other witnesses for the purpose of obtaining a detailed description of the security personnel in question. The petitioner invokes the jurisprudence of the United Nations Committee against Torture in support of his claim that the State party has failed to conduct a comprehensive, prompt, and ultimately effective official investigation into the incident.

5.2 The petitioner reiterates his initial arguments on the issue of exhaustion of domestic remedies. Neither he nor his legal representatives were ever informed about the alleged decision of the former Federal Constitutional Court of 2 December 2002 to postpone consideration of the case. To his knowledge, the Court simply did not respond for more than 12 months—or rather, up to the very moment when it actually ceased to exist. Indeed, he argues, the State party has not provided a copy of the Court's decision referred to and even if it did this would not address in substance any of the above issues. The petitioner submits that a long-term backlog of cases, and a change in a State's legal framework, coupled with its failure to take remedial measures, cannot be invoked as an excuse for continuing to deny redress to an individual. On the contrary, States are obliged to organize their legal systems so that they comply with the requirements of legal certainty and provide effective remedies to all victims of human rights abuse. However, in the petitioner's view, his argument is purely academic, as the only decision the Federal Constitutional Court could have adopted in this instance, would have been to reject the petitioner's communication on the grounds that there are other, non-constitutional, remedies available.

5.3 As to the claim that he violated article 14 of the Convention, the petitioner submits that the State party misinterpreted the non-disclosure guarantee contained therein. This provision imposes a burden on the State party itself to keep the names and other personal details of all petitioners confidential and relates to "the proceedings before the designated domestic anti-discrimination body only". In a situation where the petitioner himself wishes to publicize his petition submitted to the Committee, this cannot be deemed in violation of article 14, paragraph 4, of the Convention.

*Decision on admissibility*

6.1 At its sixty-fifth session the Committee examined the admissibility of the communication. As to whether the petitioner had submitted the petition within the time limit set out in rule 91 (f) of the Committee's rules of procedure, the Committee recalled that, communications must be submitted to it, except in the case of duly verified exceptional circumstances, within six months after all available domestic remedies have been exhausted. It observed that the Court of Serbia and Montenegro had not yet considered the matter and therefore the six-month rule had not yet begun to run.

6.2 As to the State party's claim that the petitioner violated article 14, paragraph 4, of the Convention, by publicly disseminating the contents of his petition, the Committee recalled that paragraph 4 provides that, "A register of petitions shall be kept by the body established or indicated in accordance with paragraph 2 of this article, and certified copies of the register shall be filed annually through appropriate channels with the Secretary General on the understanding that the contents shall not be publicly disclosed."

6.3 The Committee was of the view that the obligation to refrain from publishing information on individual petitions, prior to examination by the Committee, applies only to the Secretary General of the United Nations, specifically, acting through the Secretariat, and not to the parties to the petition who remain at liberty to publish any information at their disposal relating to a petition.

6.4 As to the question of admissibility *ratione temporis,* the Committee noted that although the incident in front of the discotheque (18/2/2000) took place before the declaration was made under article 14 (27/6/01), what had to be considered from the point of view of the State party's obligations, is not the incident itself, which took place between individuals, but the shortcomings of the competent authorities in conducting the investigation and the absence of efforts made by the State party to guarantee an effective remedy to the petitioner, in accordance with article 6 of the Convention. As the State party had so far failed to complete its investigations, to refer this case to the new Court of Serbia and Montenegro and to offer other remedies to the petitioner, the alleged violations were ongoing and had continued since the date of the incident itself and after the State party's declaration under article 14. Consequently, the Committee found that this claim was admissible *ratione temporis* under article 14.

6.5 On the question of exhaustion of domestic remedies, the Committee observed that a complaint was made to the Federal Constitutional Court on 30 January 2002 and, at least up to the date of consideration by the Committee, had not been considered either by that Court or by its successor, the new Court of Serbia and Montenegro. While noting the State party's arguments on the ongoing changes within its judicial system, the Committee observed that the petitioner had sought to have his claims of violations of the Convention by the State party adjudicated for over four and a half years, since the incident in February 2000. In this regard, the Committee noted that the State party itself had conceded that the prospect of an early review was unlikely, given that the new Court of Serbia and Montenegro had not even been constituted. The Committee recalled that in article 14, paragraph 7, of the Convention, the requirement to exhaust domestic remedies does not apply if the application of the remedies is unreasonably prolonged. It considered that the application of remedies in this case had been unduly prolonged, and thus found that the requirements of article 14, paragraph 7 (a), had been met. On 5 August 2004, therefore, the Committee declared the case admissible.

*The State party's submission on the merits and petitioner's comments thereon*

7.1 On 10 June 2005, the State party informed the Committee that officers from Vracar Police Station had again interviewed the witnesses involved in this case but could take no further action, as it was not possible to identify the person/s alleged to have committed the offence. Meanwhile, due to the application of the Statute of Limitations, the lapse of time has barred any further investigation of the case.

7.2 For the State party, even if criminal proceedings had been instituted, the petitioner would have been instructed by the Court to pursue a civil claim, due to the fact that the necessity to call expert evidence to assess the petitioners request for damages would delay the criminal proceedings and increase the costs. In cases in which claims are made for non-material damages in criminal proceedings, the claimant is instructed to pursue his/her

claim through civil proceedings. If the petitioner's complaint had reached the criminal court, it would have been dismissed because of the high standard of proof required in criminal proceedings.

7.3 According to the State party, the petitioner could have pursued civil claims for compensation. The Law on Contracts and Torts and the Law on Litigation allows a victim to institute civil proceedings independently from criminal ones. A victim may institute civil proceedings for damages in a situation where the defendant in criminal proceedings has been acquitted. The same law would also have permitted the petitioner to institute civil proceedings against the club itself for which he would not have had to identify the individual allegedly responsible for the damage. It would suffice to establish that the individuals responsible were employees of the club and that the petitioner had been prevented from gaining access to it because he is a Roma. Provided that the petitioner is successful and is awarded compensation, the Law also provides publication of the decision. The State party argues that, as the petitioner did not file such a civil claim, he has failed to exhaust domestic remedies, the case is thus inadmissible.

7.4 The State party contests the petitioner's position that the Court of Serbia and Montenegro would have taken a decision in accordance with the practice of the former Federal Constitutional Court, as the new court is not bound by the decision of another court, radical changes have taken place in the judicial system since the Constitutional Court took that position and the laws and the practice of the courts are increasingly influenced by international conventions. In any event, the Court of Serbia and Montenegro has not yet considered this matter.

8.1 On 12 October 2005, the petitioner commented on the State party's submission, arguing that the State appears to rely on the inefficiency of the administrative bodes (Vracar Police Station) entrusted with conducting criminal investigations as an excuse for the Public Prosecutor's inability to provide redress to the petitioner. The police limited themselves to recording the statements of the manager of the disco without corroborating them with any other sources. They failed to take basic investigative steps to elucidate the circumstances of the incident, such as looking into the club's internal records to establish the identity of the individuals employed at the time or, informing other competent authorities to hold the club legally accountable for failing to register its employees, as required by law.

8.2 The petitioner submits that the statute of limitations has been invoked as an excuse for the failure to enforce the law when it is the State itself which is responsible for the excessive length of the investigation. The Public Prosecutor has still not issued a decision on the complaint. Under international law, States are obliged to provide effective remedies to all victims of human rights violations and excuses such as a large backlog of cases, a change in the State's legal structure, coupled with its failure to take remedial measures, or other administrative difficulties of the State's own making, are no justification for the continued absence of redress.[7]

8.3 As to the State party's argument that if the petitioner's complaint had reached the criminal court, it would have been thrown out because of the high standard of proof required in criminal proceedings, the State are relying on the inefficiency of its investigative bodies to gather sufficient evidence. In the present case, it has not even passed the investigative stage.

8.4 As to the arguments that the State party's criminal courts are ill-equipped to determine damage for non-pecuniary harm, and that conducting forensic expertise to determine the size of non-pecuniary damage is time-consuming, the petitioner submits that the State party's courts appear to be guided by considerations of expediency rather than the desire for justice for victims of crime.

8.5 It remains unclear for the author why the State party argues that criminal remedies are inadequate remedies when a crime that caused non-pecuniary harm has been committed. A criminal court must be able to provide non-pecuniary damage to the aggrieved party, in addition to the identification and the punishment of those responsible.

8.6 As to the alternative remedies proposed by the State party, the petitioner submits that the wrong he suffered is so serious and so clearly in violation of the Convention that only a criminal remedy could have provided redress. Consequently, civil and administrative remedies alone are not sufficiently effective. He invokes the Committee's decision in *Lacko* v. *Slovakia*.[8]

8.7 On the possibility of introducing an alternative civil action for damages under articles 154 and 200 of the Law of Obligations, the petitioner argues that even if he had chosen to seek redress in a civil court, he would have been barred from doing so, as it is the practice to suspend civil proceedings for damages arising from criminal offences, until the relevant criminal proceedings have been completed. In any event, he would have been obliged to identify the respondent. As to taking a civil action against the club itself, he submits that this would not have been a substitute for a criminal action and that the individuals responsible would escape responsibility. In addition, any such legal action would be destined to fail, given the potential evidentiary difficulties that the petitioner would face.

*Consideration of the merits*

9.1 Acting under article 14, paragraph 7 (a), of the International Convention on the Elimination of All Forms of Racial Discrimination, the Committee has considered the information submitted by the petitioner and the State party.

9.2 In relation to the State party's request that the Committee should reconsider its decision on admissibility on the grounds that the petitioner has not exhausted domestic remedies by failing to institute civil proceedings against the discotheque in question, the Committee recalls its jurisprudence established in the case of *Lacko* v. *Slovakia*,[9] that objectives pursued through a criminal investigation could not be achieved by means of civil or administrative remedies of the kind proposed by the State party. Therefore, the Committee sees no reason to review its decision on admissibility of 5 August 2004.

9.3 As to the merits, the Committee considers it unreasonable that the State party, including the Public Prosecutor, appear to have accepted the claim that it was impossible to identify the personnel involved in the incident in question by reason of a high turnover of

---

[7] The petitioner refers to the judgements of the European Court of Human Rights: *Pelissier and Sassi* v. *France*, application No. 25444/94, 25 March 1999; *Zimmerman and Steiner* v. *Switzerland*, application No. 8737/79, 13 July 1983; and *Guincho* v. *Portugal*, application No. 8990/80, 10 July 1984.

[8] See footnote 3 above.
[9] See footnote 3 above.

staff without further investigation or enquiry on why such information would not be readily available.

9.4 The Committee does not share the State party's opinion that due to the Statute of Limitations it is now too late to initiate proceedings against those considered responsible, as the delays in the investigation appear to have been wholly attributable to the State party itself. This point supports the petitioner's argument that the investigation was neither conducted promptly nor effectively, as nearly six years after the incident (and apparently *after* the expiry of the time limit under the Statute of Limitations) no investigation, let alone a thorough one has been carried out. In this regard, the Committee notes that the Court of Serbia and Montenegro has still not considered the case and it is noteworthy that the State party has provided no likely date for its consideration.

9.5 The State party has equally failed to establish whether the petitioner had been refused access to a public place, on grounds of his national or ethnic origin, in violation of article 5 (f), of the Convention. Owing to the police's failure to carry out any thorough investigation into the matter, the failure of the public prosecutor to reach any conclusion, and the failure of the Court of Serbia and Montenegro even to set a date for the consideration of the case, some six years after the incident, the petitioner has been denied any opportunity to establish whether his rights under the Convention had been violated.

9.6 The Committee notes that in previous jurisprudence it has found violations of article 6 of the Convention without finding violations of any of the substantive articles.[10] The State party's response to the claims of racial discrimination was so ineffective that it had failed to ensure appropriate protection and remedies pursuant to this provision. According to article 6, "States parties shall assure to everyone within their jurisdiction effective protection and remedies, through the competent national tribunals and other State institutions, against any acts of racial discrimination which violate his human rights and fundamental freedoms contrary to this Convention." Although on a literal reading of the provision it would appear that an act of racial discrimination would have to be established before a petitioner would be entitled to protection and a remedy, the Committee notes that the State party must provide for the determination of this right through the national tribunals and other institutions, a guarantee which would be void were it unavailable in circumstances where a violation had not yet been established. While a State party cannot be reasonably required to provide for the determination of rights under the Convention no matter how unmeritorious such claims may be, article 6, provides protection to alleged victims if their claims are arguable under the Convention. In the current case, the petitioner presented such an arguable case but the State party's failure to investigate and adjudicate the case effectively prevented the determination of whether a substantive violation had occurred.

10. The Committee concludes that the State party failed to examine the petitioner's arguable claim of a violation of article 5 (f). In particular, it failed to investigate his claim promptly, thoroughly and effectively. Consequently, article 6 of the Convention has been violated.

11. The Committee recommends that the State party provide the petitioner with just and adequate compensation commensurate with the moral damage he has suffered. It also recommends that the State party take measures to ensure that the police, public prosecutors and the Court of Serbia and Montenegro properly investigate accusations and complaints related to acts of racial discrimination, which should be punishable by law according to article 4 of the Convention.

12. The Committee wishes to receive, within six months, information from the State party about the measures taken in light of the Committee's Opinion. The State party is requested to give wide publicity to the Committee's Opinion.

---

[10] *Habassi* v. *Denmark* and *Ahmad* v. *Denmark*.

# Communication No. 30/2003

*Submitted by*: The Jewish community of Oslo; the Jewish community of Trondheim; Rolf Kirchner; Julius Paltiel; the Norwegian Antiracist Centre; and Nadeem Butt (represented by counsel, Mr. Frode Elgesem).
*Alleged victim*: The petitioners.
*State party*: Norway.
*Date of adoption of Opinion:* 15 August 2005.
*Subject matter:* Nazi march and incidents of violence directed against blacks and political opponents; "hate speech"; access to effective mechanisms of protection; freedom of speech.
*Procedural issues:* Status of "victim" and "potential victim"; exhaustion of domestic remedies.
*Substantive issues:* Right to an effective remedy against acts of racial discrimination; prohibition of disseminating ideas based on racial superiority or hatred, incitement to racial discrimination, as well as all acts of violence or incitement to such acts against any race or group of persons; right to freedom of speech; "due regard" clause of article 4 of the Convention.
*Articles of the Convention:* 4, 6 and 14 (7) (a).
*Finding:* Violation (arts. 4 and 6).

*Opinion*

1.    The authors of the communication, dated 17 June 2003, are Mr. Rolf Kirchner, born on 12 July 1946, leader of the Jewish community in Oslo, Mr. Julius Paltiel, born on 4 July 1924, leader of the Jewish community in Trondheim, and Nadeem Butt, born on 16 June 1969, leader of the Norwegian Antiracist Centre (NAC). They claim to be victims of violations by Norway[1] of articles 4 and 6 of the Convention. They are represented by counsel.

*The facts as presented*

2.1  On 19 August 2000, a group known as the "Bootboys" organized and participated in a march in commemoration of the Nazi leader Rudolf Hess in Askim, near Oslo. Some 38 people took place in the march, which was routed over 500 metres through the centre of Askim, and lasted 5 minutes. The participants wore "semi-military" uniforms, and a significant number allegedly had criminal convictions. Many of the participants had their faces covered. The march was headed by Mr. Terje Sjolie. Upon reaching the town square, Mr. Sjolie made a speech, in which he stated:

*"We are gathered here to honour our great hero, Rudolf Hess, for his brave attempt to save Germany and Europe from Bolshevism and Jewry during the Second World War. While we stand here, over 15,000 Communists and Jew-lovers are gathered at Youngsroget in a demonstration against freedom of speech and the white race. Every day immigrants rob, rape and kill Norwegians, every day our people and country are being plundered and destroyed by the Jews, who suck our country empty of wealth and replace it with immoral and un-Norwegian thoughts. We were prohibited from marching in Oslo three times, whilst the Communists did not even need to ask. Is this freedom of speech? Is this democracy? ...*

*Our dear Führer Adolf Hitler and Rudolf Hess sat in prison for what they believed in, we shall not depart from their principles and heroic efforts, on the contrary we shall follow in their footsteps and fight for what we believe in, namely a Norway built on National Socialism ..."[2]*

2.2  After the speech, Mr. Sjolie asked for a minute's silence in honour of Rudolf Hess. The crowd, led by Mr. Sjolie, then repeatedly made

---

[1] Norway recognized the competence of the Committee to receive and consider communications under article 14 by declaration of 23 March 1976.

[2] The speech was recorded on video by the magazine "Monitor". It was later used in the criminal proceedings against Mr. Sjolie.

the Nazi salute and shouted "Sieg Heil". They then left the scene.

2.3 The authors claim that the immediate effect of the march appeared to be the founding of a Bootboys branch in nearby Kristiansand, and that for the next 12 months the city was "plagued" by what the authors describe as incidents of violence directed against blacks and political opponents. They further state that, in the Oslo area, the march appears to have given the Bootboys confidence, and that there was an increase in "Nazi" activity. Several violent incidents took place, including the murder by stabbing on 26 January 2001 of a 15 year old boy, Benjamin Hermansen, who was the son of a Ghanaian man and a Norwegian woman. Three members of the Bootboys were later charged and convicted in connection with his death; one was convicted of murder with aggravating circumstances, because of the racist motive of the attack. The authors state that he and one of the other persons convicted in this case had participated in the march on 19 August 2000.

2.4 The authors state that the Bootboys have a reputation in Norway for their propensity to use violence, and cite 21 particular instances of both threats and the use of violence by the Bootboys between February 1998 and February 2002. Mr. Sjolie himself is currently serving a term of imprisonment for attempted murder in relation to an incident in which he shot another gang member.

2.5 Some of those who witnessed the commemoration march filed a complaint with the police. On 23 February 2001, the District Attorney of Oslo charged Mr. Sjolie with a violation of section 135 a of the Norwegian Penal Code; this prohibits a person from threatening, insulting, or subjecting to hatred, persecution or contempt, any person or group of persons because of their creed, race, colour or national or ethnic origin. The offence carries a penalty of fines or a term of imprisonment of up to two years.

2.6 On 16 March 2001, Mr. Sjolie was acquitted by the Halden City Court. The prosecutor appealed to the Borgarting Court of Appeal, where Mr. Sjolie was convicted of a violation of section 135 a, because of the references in his speech to Jews. The Court of Appeal found that, at the least, the speech had to be understood as accepting the mass extermination of the Jews, and that this constituted a violation of section 135 a.

2.7 Mr. Sjolie appealed to the Supreme Court. On 17 December 2002, the Supreme Court, by a majority of 11 to 6, overturned the conviction. It found that penalizing approval of Nazism would involve prohibiting Nazi organizations, which it considered would go too far and be incompatible with the right to freedom of speech.[3] The majority also considered that the statements in the speech were simply Nazi rhetoric, and did nothing more than express support for National Socialist ideology. It did not amount to approval of the persecution and mass extermination of the Jews during the Second World War. It held that there was nothing that particularly linked Rudolph Hess to the extermination of the Jews; noted that many Nazis denied that the holocaust had happened; and that it was not known what Mr. Sjolie's views on this particular subject were. The majority held that the speech contained derogatory and offensive remarks, but that no actual threats were made, nor any instructions to carry out any particular actions. The authors note that the majority of the Court considered article 4 of the Convention not to entail an obligation to prohibit the dissemination of ideas of racial superiority, contrary to the Committee's position as set out in general recommendation XV.

2.8 The authors claim that the decision will serve as a precedent in cases involving s135a of the Penal Code, and that it will henceforth not be possible to prosecute Nazi propaganda and behaviour such as that which occurred during the march of 19 August 2000. Following the Supreme Court decision, the Director of Public Prosecution expressed the view that, in light of the Supreme Court's decision, Norway would be a safe haven for Nazi marches, due to the prohibition on such marches in neighbouring countries.

*The complaint*

3.1 The author's contend that they are victims of violations by the State party of articles 4 and 6 of the Convention. They allege that, as a result of the Supreme Court's judgement of 17 December 2002, they were not afforded protection against the dissemination of ideas of racial discrimination and hatred, as well as incitement to such acts, during the march of 19 August 2000; and that they were not afforded

---

[3] Section 100 of the Norwegian Constitution guarantees the right to freedom of speech.

a remedy against this conduct, as required by the Convention.

*Status as victims*

3.2   The authors argue that they are victims of the above violations because of the general inability of Norwegian law to protect them adequately against the dissemination of anti-Semitic and racist propaganda, and incitement to racial discrimination, hatred and violence. They concede that the Committee has not previously had the opportunity to consider the concept of "victim" in this context, but submit that the Committee should adopt the approach of both the United Nations Human Rights Committee and the European Court of Human Rights. They state that the "victim" requirement in the three Conventions is framed in equivalent terms, and submit that the Human Rights Committee and the European Court have recognized that, by the mere existence of particular domestic laws, a person's rights may be directly affected in a way which results in them being a victim of violations. Reference is made to the decisions of the Human Rights Committee in *Toonen* v. *Australia*[4] and *Ballantyne et al.* v. *Canada*,[5] and the decision of the European Court of Human Rights in *Dudgeon* v. *United Kingdom*.[6] In the *Toonen* case, the Human Rights Committee held that the author could claim to be a victim of a violation of his right to privacy because of the existence of a provincial law which criminalized sexual relations between consenting male adults, even though the author had not been prosecuted. An analogous result was reached by the European Court in the *Dudgeon* case. Similarly, in *Ballantyne*, a case involving the prohibition in Quebec of the use of the English language in public outdoor advertising, the Human Rights Committee found that the author could claim to be a victim, although he had not been prosecuted under the relevant legislation. The authors claim that these cases demonstrate that the "victim" requirement may be satisfied by all members of a particular group, as the mere existence of a particular legal regime may directly affect the rights of the individual victims within the group. In this instance, the authors contend that they,

together with any other Jew, immigrant or others facing an imminent risk of suffering racial discrimination, hatred or violence, can claim to be victims of violations of articles 4 and 6 of the Convention.

3.3   The authors submit that they are victims notwithstanding the absence of any direct confrontation with the participants in the march. In this regard, it must be recalled that the Convention is concerned not only with the dissemination of racist ideas as such, but also the effects of this (art. 1, para. 1). Further, it will rarely be the case that racist views are imparted directly to persons of the race concerned—it will usually be the case that the views are disseminated to likeminded people. If article 4 were not to be read in this context, it would be rendered ineffective.

3.4   The authors also refer to decisions of the European Court of Human Rights, which recognize the right of a potential victim to bring a claim against alleged human rights violation. In *Campbell and Cosans* v. *United Kingdom*,[7] the Court held that a schoolboy could claim to be a victim of a violation of article 3 of the Convention due to the existence of corporal punishment as a disciplinary measure at the school he attended, even though he himself had never been subjected to it. The general threat of being subjected to such treatment was sufficient to substantiate his claim of being a "victim". The authors contend that the existence of violent Nazi groups in Norway, together with the state of Norwegian law after the Supreme Court judgement in the *Sjolie* case, entail a real and imminent risk of being exposed to the effects of dissemination of ideas of racial superiority and incitement to racial hatred and violence, without them being protected, or provided with a remedy, as required by articles 4 and 6 of the Convention.

3.5   The authors further state that, in any event, they have already been personally affected by the alleged violations. The march and speech referred to had a serious adverse effect on Mr. Paltiel, who survived a concentration camp during the war, and who has previously had threats made on his life because of his educational work. The same considerations apply to Mr. Kirchner, whose family was also deeply affected by the persecution of Jews during the war. In addition, the petitioners which are organizations are directly affected, as it is said

---

[4] Communication No. 488/1992, Views adopted on 31 March 1994.
[5] Communications Nos. 359 and 385/1989, Views adopted on 31 March 1993.
[6] Judgement of 22 October 1981.

---

[7] Applications Nos. 7511/76 and 7743/76, Judgement of 25 February 1982.

they will no longer be able to rely on the protection of the law in conducting their work. They argue that the Supreme Court's decision hands over the task of protecting against the effects of racist advocacy to private organizations, and creates new responsibilities for those who are the targets of the racial discrimination.

*Exhaustion of domestic remedies*

3.6 The authors submit that there are no available domestic remedies to be exhausted. The decision of the Supreme Court is final and there is no possibility of appeal.

*On the merits*

3.7 In relation to the merits of the claim, the authors refer to the Committee's general recommendation XV, paragraph 3, which requires States parties to penalize four categories of misconduct: dissemination of ideas based on racial superiority or hatred; incitement to racial hatred; acts of violence against any race, and incitement to such acts. They consider that the decision of the Supreme Court is incompatible with the Committee's general recommendation in relation to article 4 in this regard.

3.8 The authors note that, in the Committee's recent concluding observations on Norway's 15th periodic report, it noted that the prohibition on dissemination of racial hatred is compatible with the right to freedom of speech; article 20 of the International Covenant on Civil and Political Rights stipulates the same. The authors invoke paragraph 6 of general recommendation XV, which states that organizations which promote and incite racial discrimination shall be prohibited, and submit that the State party's alleged failure to meet these requirements has been noted with concern by the Committee on previous occasions.[8] The authors submit that it is fully acceptable for a State party to protect democratic society against anti-democratic propaganda. In particular, they state that there is no basis for the Supreme Court's conclusion that article 4 of the Convention does not require States parties to penalize the dissemination of ideas of racial superiority, given the Committee's clear position on this issue.

3.9 The authors contend that the Supreme Court underestimated the danger of what it termed "Nazi rhetoric", and that the object of article 4 is to combat racism at its roots. As the Supreme Court minority pointed out, Mr. Sjolie's speech accepted and encouraged violent attacks on Jews, and paid homage to their mass extermination during World War II. In particular, the declaration that the group would follow in the Nazi's footsteps and fight for what they believed in had to be understood as an acceptance of and incitement to violent acts against Jews. The use of the Nazi salute made clear that the gathering was not peaceful, and, given the Bootboys' record of violence, the commemoration march was frightening and the incitement to violence evident.

3.10 The authors state that, in light of the Supreme Court's decision, section 135 a of the Penal Code is unacceptable as a standard for protection against racism. They therefore argue that the State party violated article 4 of the Convention, and consequently violated article 6, as the legal regime laid down by the Supreme Court necessarily implies that no remedies, such as compensation, can be sought.

*Observations by the State party*

4.1 By note dated 3 October 2003, the State party challenges the admissibility of the communication, and requests that the Committee address the question of admissibility separately from the merits.

4.2 It submits that the authors' communication amounts to an *actio popularis*, the aim of which is to have the Committee assess and evaluate the relationship between section 135 a of the Penal Code, as applied by the Supreme Court, and article 4 of the Convention. The State party considers that issues of such a general nature are best dealt with by the Committee under the reporting procedure. It notes that the Committee recently addressed this very issue when considering the 16th report of the State party; the Committee had noted with concern that the strict interpretation of section 135 a may not cover all aspects of article 4 (a) of the Convention and invited the State party to review this provision and provide information to the Committee in its next periodic report.[9] The State party submits that it is currently

---

[8] CERD/C/304/Add.40, para. 13, and CERD/C/304/Add.88, para. 14.

[9] CERD/C/63/CO/8, para. 12.

preparing a white paper on proposed amendments to section 100 of the Constitution, which guarantees freedom of speech, and the scope of s135 a of the Penal Code. The State party assures the Committee that its Concluding Observations will be a weighty consideration in considering relevant amendments to these provisions.

4.3 The State party submits that neither the Jewish communities of Oslo and Trondheim, nor the Antiracist Centre, can be considered "groups of individuals" for the purposes of article 14, paragraph 1. The Jewish communities are religious congregations comprising numerous members. The Antiracist Centre is a non-governmental organization which seeks to promote human rights and equal opportunity, and conducts research on racism and racial discrimination. The State party submits that, whilst the jurisprudence of the Committee is silent on this issue, a "group of individuals" should be understood as meaning a group of which every individual member could claim to be a victim of the alleged violation. What is significant is not the group per se, but those individuals who comprise it. It is the individuals, rather than the groups, which have standing.

4.4 In relation to the individual authors, Mr. Kirchner, Mr. Paltiel and Mr. Butt, the State party contends that they have not exhausted domestic remedies. It refers to the decision of the Committee in the case of *POEM and FASM* v. *Denmark*, where it noted that the petitioners had not been plaintiffs in any domestic proceedings, and considered that it was a "basic requirement" of admissibility that domestic remedies be exhausted "by the petitioners themselves".[10] The State party notes that none of the individual petitioners in the present case was a party to the domestic proceedings leading to the Supreme Court's judgement, and that the only complaint about the incident to the police was made by a local politician in the town of Askim. It states that the petitioners have not filed any complaints with the domestic authorities or made any requests for protection.

4.5 The State party contends that the authors are not "victims" for the purpose of article 14, paragraph 1. There have only been two instances in which the Committee has appeared to find that article 4 gives rise to an individual right, capable of being invoked in the context of a communication under article 14 of the Convention. In both of those cases, the racist expressions had been directed specifically at the petitioners in question, and had involved adverse effects on their substantive rights under article 5. By contrast, none of the petitioners in this case was present when the remarks were made during the commemoration march. They were not personally targeted by the remarks, nor have they specified how, if at all, their substantive rights under article 5 were affected by the comments of Mr. Sjolie. Accordingly, the State party contends that the authors are not victims for the purpose of article 14, paragraph 1.

*Comments by the petitioners*

5.1 In comments on the State party's submissions of 2 December 2003, the authors contend that the communication is truly individual in nature. They state that, in any event, the issue of inadequate protection against racist speech under article 4 had been an issue in the Committee's dialogue with the State party for some time, and that the concerns expressed by the Committee in its Concluding Observations have had little impact on the State party.

5.2 The authors reiterate that the Jewish communities and the Antiracist Centre should be considered "groups of individuals" for the purpose of article 14 of the Convention, and that they have standing to submit communications to the Committee. They note that there is nothing in the wording of article 14 which supports the interpretation that all members of the group must be able to claim victim status on their own. If such a strict reading were applied, the words "groups of individuals" would be deprived of any independent meaning. They contrast the wording of article 14, paragraph 1, with the corresponding provision in the Optional Protocol to the International Covenant on Civil and Political Rights,[11] which provides that only individuals may submit complaints for consideration by the Human Rights Committee. They contend that the expression "groups of individuals", whatever its outer limits may be, clearly covers entities that organize individuals for a specific, common purpose, such as congregations and membership organizations.

5.3 As to the requirement of exhaustion of domestic remedies, the authors claim that, in

---

[10] Communication No. 22/2002, decision of 19 March 2003, para. 6.3.

[11] Art. 1.

light of the judgement of the Supreme Court, any legal proceedings taken by them in Norway would have no prospect of success. They invoke a decision of the European Court of Human Rights to the effect that the obligation to exhaust domestic remedies did not apply in circumstances where, due to an authoritative interpretation of the law by domestic judicial authorities, any legal action by the petitioners would be pointless.[12] They argue that the same approach should be adopted by the Committee in relation to article 14 of the Convention. Thus, even if the authors had not exhausted domestic remedies, the Supreme Court dispensed with this requirement by handing down a final and authoritative interpretation of the relevant law.

5.4 On the State party's submission that they are not "victims" for the purpose of article 14, the petitioners reiterate that article 4 guarantees to individuals and groups of individuals a *right* to be protected against hate speech. Failure to afford adequate protection against hate speech is of itself a violation of the individual rights of those who are directly affected by the State's failure to fulfil its obligations. They reiterate that, just as a person's status as a potential victim may arise when people are formally required to breach the law in order to enjoy their rights, so too may it arise where the domestic law or a Court's decision impedes the individual's future enjoyment of Convention rights. They further state that, in the present case, the individual authors are public figures and leaders of their respective Jewish communities, and therefore potential victims of violations of the Convention. Mr. Paltiel has received death threats by neo-Nazi groups in the past. However, the intent of article 4 is to fight racism at its roots; there is a causal link between hate speech of the type made by Mr. Sjolie, and serious violent racist acts. Persons like Mr. Paltiel are seriously affected by the lack of protection against hate speech. It is submitted that all the authors belong to groups of obvious potential victims of hate speech, against which Norwegian law affords no protection. They claim that there is a high degree of possibility that they will be adversely affected by the violation of article 4 of the Convention.

5.5 In a further submission dated 20 February 2004, the petitioners draw the Committee's attention to the Third Report of the European Commission against Racism and Intolerance (ECRI) on Norway, dated 27 June 2003. In this report, the ECRI stated that Norwegian legislation did not provide individuals with adequate protection against racist expression, particularly in light of the Supreme Court's judgement in the *Sjolie* case. The ECRI recommended that Norway strengthen protection against racist expression through relevant amendments to its Constitution and criminal law.

*Committee's request for clarification from the State Party*

6.1 At its 64th session, the Committee instructed the Secretariat to seek clarification from the State party as to whether, under Norwegian law, any of the petitioners could have requested to become a party to the criminal proceedings instituted after the remarks made by Mr. Sjolie on the occasion of the march of the "Bootboys"; and, in the affirmative, to clarify whether intervention by the petitioners as third parties would have had any prospect of success. The request for clarification was sent to the State party on 3 March 2004; it was also transmitted for information to the petitioners.

6.2 By letter of 19 June 2004, the petitioners submitted that they had no possibility of participating in the criminal proceedings that had been instigated in relation to the "Bootboys" march; they also added that they had not suffered any pecuniary loss which could form the basis of a civil claim.

6.3 In its submission dated 19 August 2004, the State party advised that the petitioners were not at liberty to institute private criminal proceedings or to join the public prosecution against Mr. Sjolie for alleged breaches of s135a. However, it submits that the lack of such a possibility has no bearing on the question of whether the petitioners had exhausted domestic remedies, and states that the present case is indistinguishable from the Committee's decision in *POEM and FASM* v. *Denmark*, referred to in paragraph 4.3 above, where the Committee had found the communication in question to be inadmissible, as none of the petitioners had been plaintiffs in the domestic proceedings. The State party submits that there is no significant difference between Norwegian and Danish criminal procedure law as regards the possibility of

---

[12] Case of *Open Door and Dublin Well Women* v. *Ireland*, applications Nos. 14234/88 and 14235/88, Judgement of 29 October 1992.

instituting private criminal proceedings or joining a public prosecution of racist expression. In the Danish case, as in the instant case, the communication was admissible because the petitioners did not take any procedural steps to secure the conviction of the alleged perpetrator. In the Danish case, as in the present case, the petitioners had not filed complaints with the police. None of the petitioners took any steps to address the statements of Mr. Sjolie before presenting their communication to the Committee, some three years after the comments were made. The State party submits that there is no basis to distinguish the present case from the Committee's earlier decision in the Danish case.

6.4 The State party further submits that the individual petitioners, and most likely the Jewish communities, could have filed proceedings against Mr. Sjolie for criminal defamation, which is open to persons who feel targeted by denigrating or defamatory speech under articles 246 and 247 of the Criminal Code. Had they done this, the petitioners could have joined their action for criminal defamation to the criminal proceedings already underway against Mr. Sjolie. The petitioners could thereby have had an impact on the proceedings. While sections 246 and 247 are not directed specifically against discrimination, they are applicable also to racist statements. In its decision in *Sadic* v. *Denmark*,[13] the Committee noted that the notion of an "effective remedy'" for the purposes of article 6 of the Convention is "*not limited to criminal prosecutions based on provisions which specifically, expressly and exclusively penalize acts of racial discrimination.*" It extends to "*general provisions criminalizing defamatory statements, which is applicable to racist statements*". The Committee stated in the same decision that "*mere doubts about the effectiveness of available civil remedies do not absolve a petitioner from pursuing.*"

6.5 Finally, the State party submits that, should the Committee declare the communication admissible and consider it on the merits, it should bear in mind that the Government is proposing significant enhancements of the protection offered by s135a, and that a White Paper has been presented to Parliament on possible amendments to s100 of the Norwegian

---

[13] Communication No. 25/2002, Opinion of 21 March 2002, para. 6.3.

Constitution. It is too early to inform about the outcome of the legislative process, and the State party will elaborate further upon this in the course of its next periodic report to the Committee.

6.6 In their reply dated 22 August 2004, the petitioners state that the Danish case referred to by the State party is distinguishable from their own case, as the criminal proceedings in that case had been discontinued by the police, without any action being taken by the authors to press civil or criminal proceedings against the alleged perpetrator. In the present case, Mr. Sjolie's comments were held by the Supreme Court to be protected by the constitutional right to freedom of speech, and consequently any action by the authors would be futile. They further submit that the applicability of defamation law to racist speech is an unresolved issue in Norwegian law, and for this reason defamation laws are not invoked in cases dealing with racist speech. They state that it would have been untenable for the authors to seek to consolidate defamation proceedings to the criminal proceedings instituted by the authorities; they are not aware of this ever having happened before.

*Decision on admissibility*

7.1 At its 65th and 66th sessions, the Committee considered the admissibility of the communication.

7.2 The Committee noted the State party's submission that the authors had not exhausted domestic remedies because none of them complained to the authorities about Mr. Sjolie's conduct; reference was made to the Committee's decision in the *POEM and FASM* case. However, as the authors pointed out, the *POEM and FASM* case involved criminal proceedings which were discontinued by the police, without any action being taken on the part of the authors to have the proceedings re-instigated. The present case involved an authoritative decision by the highest Norwegian Court to acquit a person accused of racist statements. In the former case, the authors could have taken the initiative to protest the decision by the police to discontinue the criminal proceedings, but did not. In the present case, the authors had no possibility of altering the course of the criminal proceedings. Further, Mr. Sjolie had now been acquitted and cannot be retried. The Committee further noted that, in answer to the question asked of it by the Committee during its 64th session, the State party confirmed that the authors could not have requested to become a party to the criminal proceedings against Mr. Sjolie. The State party submitted that the authors could have taken defamation action against Mr. Sjolie. However, the authors contended that the application of defamation laws to racist speech was an unresolved issue in Norwegian law, and the Committee was not in a position to conclude that such proceedings constituted a useful and effective domestic remedy. In the circumstances, the Committee considered that there were no effective domestic remedies to be exhausted, and that according no barrier to admissibility arose in this regard.

7.3 The authors claimed that they were "victims" of alleged violations of articles 4 and 6 of the Convention because of the general inability of Norwegian law to protect them against the dissemination of anti-Semitic and racist propaganda. They also claimed that they were "victims" because of their membership of a particular group of potential victims; the authors, together with any other Jews or immigrants, faced an imminent risk of suffering racial discrimination, hatred or violence. They referred in particular to the jurisprudence of other international human rights bodies to support their argument. They invoked the decision of the Human Rights Committee in the case of *Toonen* v. *Australia*, where the very existence of a particular legal regime was considered to have directly affected the author's rights in such a way as to give rise to a violation of the International Covenant on Civil and Political Rights. They also referred to the decision of the European Court of Human Rights in *Open Door and Dublin Well Women* v. *Ireland*, in which the Court found certain authors to be "victims" because they belonged to a class of persons which might in the future be adversely affected by the acts complained of.[14] Similarly, in the present case the authors stated that, following the decision of the Supreme Court, they are at risk of being exposed to the effects of the dissemination of ideas of racial superiority and incitement to racial hatred, without being afforded adequate protection. They also submitted that the decision contributed to an atmosphere in which acts of racism, including acts of violence, are more likely to occur, and in this regard they referred to specific incidents of violence and other "Nazi" activities. The

Committee agreed with the authors' submissions; it saw no reason why it should not adopt a similar approach to the concept of "victim" status as was adopted in the decisions referred to above. It considered that, in the circumstances, the authors had established that they belong to a category of potential victims.

7.4 The Committee did not consider the fact that three of the authors are organizations posed any problem to admissibility. As has been noted, article 14 of the Convention refers specifically to the Committee's competence to receive complaints from "groups of individuals". The Committee considered that to interpret this provision in the way suggested by the State party, namely to require that each individual within the group be an individual victim of an alleged violation, would be to render meaningless the reference to "groups of individuals". The Committee had not hitherto adopted such a strict approach to these words. The Committee considered that, bearing in mind the nature of the organizations' activities and the classes of person they represent, they too satisfied the "victim" requirement in article 14.

7.5 On 9 March 2005, the Committee therefore declared the communication admissible.

*State party's submissions on the merits*

8.1 By note of 9 June 2005, the State party submits that there has been no violation of articles 4 or 6 of the Convention. It states that, consistent with the provisions of the Convention, article 135a of the Norwegian Penal Code must be interpreted with due regard to the right to freedom of expression. The State party's obligation to criminalize certain expressions and statements must be balanced against the right to freedom of expression, as protected by other international human rights instruments.[15] In the present case, the Norwegian Supreme Court carefully assessed the case following a full hearing, including arguments on the requirements of the relevant international instruments. It concluded that the proper balance of these rights resulted in there being no violation of article 135a in the present case, a conclusion which the Court considered to be consistent

---

[14] See footnote 17 below, para. 44.

[15] Reference is made to article 10 of the European Convention on Human Rights and article 19 of the International Covenant on Civil and Political Rights.

with the State party's obligations under the convention, taking account of the "due regard" clause in article 4 of the Convention.

8.2  For the State party, States must enjoy a margin of appreciation in balancing rights at the national level, and that this margin has not been overstepped in the present case. The majority of the Supreme Court found that s135a applied to remarks of a distinctly offensive character, including remarks that incite or support violations of integrity and those which entail a gross disparagement of a group's human dignity. The majority considered that the remarks had to be interpreted in the light of the context in which they were made and the likely perception of the remarks by an ordinary member of the audience.[16] The State party submits that the Committee should give due respect to the Supreme Court's interpretation of these remarks, since it had thoroughly examined the entire case.

8.3  The State party submits that the Committee's general recommendation XV should be interpreted as recognizing that the application of article 4 requires a balancing of the right to freedom of expression against the right to protection from racial discrimination.

8.4  The State party notes the Committee's decision that the authors belong to a "category of potential victims"; to the extent that the authors are "potential victims", the State party draws attention to recent changes in Norwegian law which strengthen legal protection against the dissemination of racist ideas. It argues that, following the adoption of recent changes to s100 of the Constitution and s135a of the Penal Code, the authors can no longer be considered "potential victims" of racial discrimination contrary to the

Convention; any possible violation could only relate to the period preceding the adoption of these amendments.

8.5  A completely revised version of section 100 of the Constitution entered into force on 30 September 2004, affording the Parliament greater scope to pass laws against racist speech, in conformity with its obligations under international conventions. Parliament has since used this new power to amend s135a of the Penal Code, to provide that racist remarks may be subject to prosecution even if they are not disseminated among the public. Racist statements made negligently are now also proscribed—intent need not be proved. The maximum punishment has been raised from two to three years' imprisonment. The balance between s135a and freedom of speech, however, must be weighed by the courts in each case. According to the State party, these recent amendments contradict the authors' assertion that the verdict in the *Sjolie* case would serve as a precedent, and that it will be more difficult to prosecute dissemination of ideas of racist discrimination and hatred. The State party further refers to the adoption of a new Discrimination Act, which incorporates the Convention, and provides criminal sanctions for serious cases of incitement to or participation in discrimination, thus supplementing the new provisions of s135a. The Government is also developing a new Anti-Discrimination Ombudsman with a mandate to monitor and enforce these new provisions.

8.6  The State party submits that, in light of the above changes in the State party's laws, and their effect on the authors as "potential victims", the Committee should reconsider its decision on admissibility, pursuant to rule 94, paragraph 6, of its rules of procedure, at least as far as the communication raises questions regarding the general legal effects of the Supreme Court's judgement.[17]

8.7  Finally, the State party notes that the authors have not identified how the remarks of Mr. Sjolie have had adverse effects on their enjoyment of any substantive rights protected by article 5 of the Convention.

---

[16] The State party draws the Committee's attention to the reasoning of the majority set out on pages 11 and 12 of the English version of the judgement, however the Court's conclusions in this regard are not summarized in the submission. In the judgement, the majority concludes that various remarks in question are "absurd" "defy rational interpretation", and "cliché", that they expressed no more than general support for Nazi ideology, which according to the majority did not imply support for the extermination, or other systematic and serious acts of violence against Jews. Hess, in whose memory the march was held, was not particularly associated with the Holocaust. The majority also notes that the group of Sjolie's supporters was small, and those opposing the speech were in the majority and able to voice their disapproval.

[17] The submission then reads: "The Government however trusts the Committee to undertake any required assessments at this point".

9.1 In their comments on the State party's submissions dated 4 July 2005, the authors invoke their earlier submissions, in which issues relating to the merits were addressed. They emphasize that it remains undisputed that, under Norwegian law as it presently stands, only three of the four relevant categories of racial discrimination referred to in article 4 of the Convention are penalized; contrary to article 4 and recommendation 15, dissemination of ideas based on racial superiority or hatred may go unpunished.

9.2 In relation to the State party's request for the Committee to reopen the question of admissibility of the complaint, the authors state that the Committee must review and assess the communication on the basis of the facts at the material time, and not on the basis of legislation adopted subsequently. In any event, the new legislation has not addressed the authors' main concern, namely the failure of the law to proscribe all relevant categories of misconduct under the Convention; thus the authors remain potential victims.

9.3 In respect of the "due regard" clause in article 4, the authors maintain that penalizing all four categories of misconduct is clearly compatible with any international principle of freedom of speech. For them, the Committee must undertake its own interpretation of the impugned statements, rather than defer to the interpretation adopted by the Norwegian Supreme Court.[18] In characterizing the speech, the authors note that Hess was well known as Hitler's Deputy and confidant, instrumental in the development of the Nuremberg laws. They maintain that, as the minority of the Supreme Court found, anyone with a basic knowledge of Hitler and National Socialism would have understood Mr. Sjolie's speech as an acceptance and approval of mass violence against Jews in the Nazi era.

9.4 The authors refer to jurisprudence of the [European Court of Human Rights] and the Human Rights Committee, both of which have accorded racist and hate speech little protection under the freedom of speech

provisions of their respective conventions.[19] According to the authors, the role of the due regard clause is to protect the role of the media in imparting information about issues of public importance, provided the objective is not advocacy of racial hatred. It is submitted that the State party offers a much broader level of protection to hate speech than standards established in international case law. The authors further state that the Supreme Court decision in the *Sjolie* case is already having a significant effect as a precedent, despite the entry into force of the new legislation. They provide a decision by the Oslo police dated 31 May 2005 not to prosecute the leader of a neo-Nazi organization, in relation to statements made to the effect that Jews had killed millions of "his people", that Jews should be "cleansed", and were "not human beings" but "parasites". The police dropped the case with explicit reference to the *Sjolie* case.

9.5 The authors further submit that invoking freedom of speech for racist and discriminating purposes amounts to an abuse of the right of submission. They reiterate that the balance between freedom of speech and protection from hate speech following the Sjolie decision is such that persons are afforded protection only against the most distinctive and offensive remarks, entailing severe violations of a group's dignity.

9.6 Finally, the authors note that Norway does not prohibit racist organizations and that the Supreme Court in the *Sjolie* case built on the view that such a ban would be unacceptable, contrary to the Committee's general recommendation XV, paragraph 6.

*Consideration of the merits*

10.1 Acting under article 14, paragraph 7 (a), of the International Convention on the Elimination of All Forms of Racial Discrimination, the Committee has considered the information submitted by the petitioners and the State party.

10.2 In relation to the State party's request that the Committee should reconsider its decision on admissibility pursuant to rule 94, paragraph 6, of its rules of procedure in the light of recent legislative changes, the Committee

---

[18] References are made to decisions of the [European Court of Human Rights]: *Lehideux and Isorni* v. *France*, application No. 24662/94, Judgement of 23 September 1998, paras. 50-53; and *Jersild* v. *Denmark*, application No. 15890/89, Judgement of 23 September 1994, para. 35.

[19] Particular mention is made of *Jersild* v. *Denmark*, concerning racist comments by the "Greenjackets" against Africans and foreigners, held not to be protected by freedom of speech; and *J.R.T and W.G.* v. *Canada*, communication No. 104/1981, Views adopted on 6 April 1983.

considers that it must review and assess the communication on the basis of the facts as they transpired at the material time, irrespective of subsequent changes in the law. Further, the authors have referred to at least one incident following the recent amendments to the relevant legislation where the judgement in the *Sjolie* case was apparently interpreted as a bar to the prosecution of hate speech.

10.3 The Committee has noted the State party's submission that it should give due respect to the consideration of the *Sjolie* case by the Supreme Court, which conducted a thorough and exhaustive analysis; and that States should be afforded a margin of appreciation in balancing their obligations under the Convention with the duty to protect the right to freedom of speech. The Committee notes that it has indeed fully taken account of the Supreme Court's decision and is mindful of the analysis contained therein. However, the Committee considers that it has the responsibility to ensure the coherence of the interpretation of the provisions of article 4 of the Convention as reflected in its general recommendation XV.

10.4 At issue in the present case is whether the statements made by Mr. Sjolie, properly characterized, fall within any of the categories of impugned speech set out in article 4, and if so, whether those statements are protected by the "due regard" provision as it relates to freedom of speech. In relation to the characterization of the speech, the Committee does not share the analysis of the majority of the members of the Supreme Court. Whilst the contents of the speech are objectively absurd, the lack of logic of particular remarks is not relevant to the assessment of whether or not they violate article 4. In the course of the speech, Mr. Sjolie stated that his "people and country are being plundered and destroyed by Jews, who suck our country empty of wealth and replace it with immoral and un-Norwegian thoughts". He then refers not only to Rudolf Hess, in whose commemoration the speech was made, but also to Adolf Hitler and *their* principles; he states that his group will "follow in their footsteps and fight for what (we) believe in". The Committee considers these statements to contain ideas based on racial superiority or hatred; the deference to Hitler and his principles and "footsteps" must in the Committee's view be taken as incitement at least to racial discrimination, if not to violence.

10.5 As to whether these statements are protected by the "due regard" clause contained in article 4, the Committee notes that the principle of freedom of speech has been afforded a lower level of protection in cases of racist and hate speech dealt with by other international bodies, and that the Committee's own general recommendation XV clearly states that the prohibition of all ideas based upon racial superiority or hatred is compatible with the right to freedom of opinion and expression.[20] The Committee notes that the "due regard" clause relates generally to all principles embodied in the Universal Declaration of Human Rights, not only freedom of speech. Thus, to give the right to freedom of speech a more limited role in the context of article 4 does not deprive the due regard clause of significant meaning, all the more so since all international instruments that guarantee freedom of expression provide for the possibility, under certain circumstances, of limiting the exercise of this right. The Committee concludes that the statements of Mr. Sjolie, given that they were of exceptionally/manifestly offensive character, are not protected by the due regard clause, and that accordingly his acquittal by the Supreme Court of Norway gave rise to a violation of article 4, and consequently article 6, of the Convention.

10.6 Finally, in relation to the State party's submission that the authors have failed to establish how the remarks of Mr. Sjolie adversely affected their enjoyment of any substantive rights protected under article 5 of the Convention, the Committee considers that its competence to receive and consider communications under article 14 is not limited to complaints alleging a violation of one or more of the rights contained in article 5. Rather, article 14 states that the Committee may receive complaints relating to "any of the rights set forth in this Convention". The broad wording suggests that the relevant rights are to be found in more than just one provision of the Convention. Further, the fact that article 4 is couched in terms of States parties' obligations, rather than inherent rights of individuals, does not imply that they are matters to be left to the internal jurisdiction of States parties, and as such immune from review under article 14. If such were the case, the protection regime established by the Convention would be weakened significantly. The Committee's conclusion is reinforced by the wording of article 6 of the Convention, by which States

---

[20] See para. 4.

parties pledge to assure to all individuals within their jurisdiction effective protection and a right of recourse against any acts of racial discrimination which violate their "human rights" under the Convention. In the Committee's opinion, this wording confirms that the Convention's "rights" are not confined to article 5. Finally, the Committee recalls that it has previously examined communications under article 14 in which no violation of article 5 has been alleged.

11. The Committee on the Elimination of Racial Discrimination, acting under article 14, paragraph 7, of the Convention on the Elimination of All Forms of Racial Discrimination, is of the view that the facts before it disclose violations of articles 4 and 6 of the Convention.

12. The Committee recommends that the State party take measures to ensure that statements such as those made by Mr. Sjolie in the course of his speech are not protected by the right to freedom of speech under Norwegian law.

13. The Committee wishes to receive, within six months, information from the State party about the measures taken in the light of the Committee's Opinion. The State party is requested also to give wide publicity to the Committee's Opinion.

# Communication No. 31/2003

*Submitted by*: Ms. L.R. et al. (represented by the European Roma Rights Center and the League of Human Rights Advocates).
*Alleged victim*: The petitioners.
*State party*: Slovakia.
*Date of adoption of Opinion:* 7 March 2005.
*Subject matter:* Discriminatory Council's act directed to Roma; effective investigation; access to effective mechanisms of protection; the right to housing; indirect discrimination.
*Procedural issues:* Exhaustion of domestic remedies; substantiation for purposes of admissibility.
*Substantive issues:* Right to an effective remedy against acts of racial discrimination; right to an effective investigation; right to housing; indirect discrimination; State parties must not engage in act or practice of racial discrimination against persons, group of persons or institutions; State parties shall take effective measures to review governmental, national and local policies, and to amend, rescind or nullify any laws and regulations which have the effect of creating or perpetuating racial discrimination; State parties are required to prohibit and bring to an end, by all appropriate means, racial discrimination.
*Articles of the Convention:* 2 (1) (a), (c) and (d), 4 (a), 5 (e) (iii), 6, and 14 (7) (a).
*Finding:* Violation (arts. 2 (1) (a), 5 (e) (iii) and 6).

## Opinion

1. The petitioners are Ms. L.R. and 26 other Slovak citizens of Roma ethnicity residing in Dobsiná, Slovak Republic. They claim to be victims of a violation by the Slovak Republic of article 2, paragraph 1, subparagraphs (a), (c) and (d); article 4, paragraph (a); article 5, paragraph (e), subparagraph (iii); and article 6 of the International Convention on the Elimination of All Forms of Racial Discrimination. They are represented by

counsel of the European Roma Rights Centre, Budapest, Hungary, and the League of Human Rights Advocates, Bratislava, Slovak Republic.

## The facts as presented

2.1 On 20 March 2002, the councillors of the Dobsiná municipality adopted Resolution No. 251-20/III-2002-MsZ, whereby they approved what the petitioners describe as a plan to construct low-cost housing for the Roma inhabitants of the town.[1] About 1,800 Roma live in the town in what are described as "appalling" conditions, with most dwellings comprising thatched huts or houses made of cardboard and without drinking water, toilets or drainage or sewage systems. The councillors instructed the local mayor to prepare a project aimed at securing finance from a Government fund set up expressly to alleviate Roma housing problems in the State party.

2.2 Thereupon, certain inhabitants of Dobsiná and surrounding villages established a five-member "petition committee", led by the Dobsiná chairman of the Real Slovak National Party. The committee elaborated a petition bearing the following text:

"I do not agree with the building of low-cost houses for people of Gypsy origin on the territory of Dobsiná, as it will lead to an influx of inadaptable citizens of Gypsy origin from the surrounding villages, even from other districts and regions."[2]

The petition was signed by some 2,700 inhabitants of Dobsiná and deposited with the municipal council on 30 July 2002. On 5 August 2002, the council considered the petition and unanimously voted, "having considered the factual circumstances", to cancel the earlier resolution by means of a

second resolution which included an explicit reference to the petition.[3]

2.3 On 16 September 2002, in the light of the relevant law,[4] the petitioners' counsel requested the Rožňava District Prosecutor to investigate and prosecute the authors of the

---

[3] The State party provides, with its submissions on the merits of the petition, the following full text of the resolution:
"RESOLUTION 288/5/VIII-2002-MsZ
I. After discussing the petition of 30 July 2002 and after determining the facts, the Town Council of Dobsiná, through the Resolution of the Town Council is in compliance with the law, on the basis of the citizens' petition Cancels Resolution 251-20/III-2002-MsZ approving the low-cost housing - family houses or apartment houses - development policy.
II. Tasks the Town Council commissions with elaborating a proposal for solving the existence of inadaptable citizens in the town of Dobsiná and then to discuss it in the bodies of the town and at a public meeting of the citizens.
Deadline: November 2002
Responsible: Chairpersons of commissions".
[4] The petitioners refer to
(i) article 1 of the Act on the Right of Petition, which provides:
"A petition cannot call for a violation of the Constitution of the Slovak Republic and its laws, nor deny or restrict individual rights";
(ii) article 12 of the Constitution, which provides:
(1) All human beings are free and equal in dignity and in rights. Their fundamental rights and freedoms are sanctioned; inalienable, imprescriptible and irreversible.
(2) Fundamental rights shall be guaranteed in the Slovak Republic to everyone regardless of sex, race, colour, language, belief and religion, political affiliation or other conviction, national or social origin, nationality or ethnic origin, property, descent or any other status. No one shall be aggrieved, discriminated against or favoured on any of these grounds.
(3) Everyone has the right to decide freely which national group he or she is a member of. Any influence and all manners of pressure that may affect or lead to a denial of a person's original nationality shall be prohibited.
(4) No injury may be inflicted on anyone, because of exercising his or her fundamental rights and freedoms.;
(iii) article 33 of the Constitution, which provides:
"Membership in any national minority or ethnic group may not be used to the detriment of any individual"; and
(iv) the Act on the Public Prosecution Office, which provides that the Prosecutor has a duty to oversee compliance by public administration bodies with laws and regulations, and to review the legality of binding regulations issued by public administration bodies.

---

[1] The State party provides, with its submissions on the merits of the petition, the following full text of the resolution: "On its 25th extraordinary session held on 20 March 2002 the Town Council of the town of Dobsiná adopted the following resolution from discussed reports and points:
RESOLUTION 251-20/III-2002-MsZ
After discussing the proposal by Lord Mayor Ing. Ján Vozár concerning the building of low cost housing the Town Council of Dobsiná Approves the low cost housing - family houses or apartment houses - development policy and Recommends the Lord Mayor to deal with the preparation of project documentation and acquisition of funds for this development from state subsidies."
[2] Petitioners' translation, which reflects exactly the text of the petition set out in the translated judgement of the Constitutional Court provided by the State party in annexure to its submissions on the merits. The State party suggests in its submissions on the merits that a more appropriate translation would be: "I do not agree with the construction of flats for the citizens of Gypsy nationality (ethnicity) within the territory of the town of Dobsiná, as there is a danger of influx of citizens of Gypsy nationality from surrounding area [sic] and even from other districts and regions."

109

discriminatory petition, and to reverse the council's second resolution as it was based on a discriminatory petition. On 7 November 2002, the District Prosecutor rejected the request on the basis of purported absence of jurisdiction over the matter. The Prosecutor found that "...the resolution in question was passed by the Dobsiná Town Council exercising its self-governing powers; it does not constitute an administrative act performed by public administration and, as a result, the prosecution office does not have the competence to review the legality of this act take prosecutorial supervision measures in non-penal area."

2.4 On 18 September 2002, the petitioners' counsel applied to the Constitutional Court for an order determining that articles 12 and 33 of the Constitution, the Act on the Right of Petition and the Framework Convention for the Protection of National Minorities (Council of Europe) had been violated, cancelling the second resolution of the council and examining the legality of the petition. Further information was provided on two occasions at the request of the Court. On 5 February 2003, the Court, in closed session, held that the petitioners' had provided no evidence that any fundamental rights had been violated by the petition or by the council's second decision. It stated that as neither the petition nor the second resolution constituted legal acts, they were permissible under domestic law. It further stated that citizens have a right to petition regardless of its content.

*The complaint*

3.1 The petitioners argues that the State party has violated article 2, paragraph 1, subparagraph (a), by failing to "ensure that all public authorities and public institutions, national and local, shall act in conformity with this obligation" [to engage in no act or practice of racial discrimination]. They argue, with reference to the Committee's jurisprudence that a municipal council is a local public authority,[5] and that the council engaged in an act of racial discrimination by unanimously endorsing the petition and cancelling its resolution to build low-cost but adequate housing for local Roma.

3.2 The petitioners argue that there has been a violation of article 2, paragraph 1, subparagraph (c), on the basis that the State party failed to "nullify any laws or regulations which have the effect of creating or perpetuating racial discrimination". Neither the District Prosecutor nor the Constitutional Court took measures to cancel the council's second resolution, which was itself based on a discriminatory petition. They also argue that there has been a violation of subparagraph (d) of the paragraph 1, as well as article 4, paragraph (a), on the basis that the State party failed "to prohibit and bring to an end ... racial discrimination by any persons, group or organization" by not effectively investigating and prosecuting the petition's authors. They argue that the petition's wording can be regarded as "incitement to racial discrimination", and refer to the Committee's decision in *L.K.* v. *Netherlands*,[6] where the State party was found to have insufficiently investigated a petition and verbal threats designed to stop an immigrant from moving into a subsidized home.

3.3 The petitioners contend that article 5, paragraph (e), subparagraph (iii), was violated as the State party failed to safeguard the petitioners' right to adequate housing. The local conditions, described above, are, in the petitioners' view, well below an adequate level for housing and living conditions in the State party, and would have been resolved by the original council decision proceeding rather than being cancelled, without remedy, on the basis of a discriminatory petition.

3.4 Finally, the petitioners argue a violation of article 6 in that the State party failed to provide them with an effective remedy against acts of racial discrimination inflicted both by the authors of the petition and the council's second resolution, which was motivated by and based on such discrimination. They contend that no measures have been taken (i) to cancel the second resolution, (ii) to punish the petitions' authors or (iii) to ensure that such discrimination does not recur.

3.5 As to the admissibility of the complaint, the petitioners state that no further appeal lies against the Constitutional Court's judgement and that no other international procedure of investigation or settlement has been invoked.

*The State party's submissions on the admissibility of the petition*

4.1 By submission of 26 November 2003, the State party disputed the admissibility of the

---

[5] *Koptova* v. *Slovakia*.

[6] Communication No. 4/1991.

petition on the basis of the petitioners' failure to exhaust domestic remedies. Firstly, it argues that the petitioners did not avail themselves of the possibility of challenging the District Prosecutor's decision, as provided for in section 34 of the Act on Prosecution.[7]

4.2 Secondly, with respect to the constitutional application, the State party argues that despite being urged to do so by the Constitutional Court, the petitioners did not "specify [with respect to the council's second decision] any fundamental right or freedom that was allegedly violated in conflict with the Constitution, other laws or other international instruments which are binding on the Slovak Republic". As a result, the Court held:

"The provisions of article 12, paragraphs 1 and 4, article 13, paragraphs 1 and 4, and article 35 of the Constitution exclude, in general terms, the discrimination against natural or legal persons; however, they cannot be invoked without explicitly specifying the impact of a discriminatory procedure applied by a state authority or a state administration body on a fundamental right or freedom of a natural or legal person. Analogical approach may be applied to article 33 of the Constitution which has the aim of preventing any harm (discrimination or persecution) as a direct consequence of belonging to a national minority or ethnic group ... None of the rights of the citizens, who belong to a minority and enjoy constitutional protection, entails a corresponding obligation on the part of the municipality to adopt certain decisions, i.e., the decisions on specific matters, such as construction of low-cost housing."

4.3 In the State party's view, the Court, in dismissing the complaint "as manifestly unsubstantiated on procedural grounds", did not decide on the merits, as a result of the petitioners' procedural mistake. It is thus open for the petitioners to pursue a new "substantive" complaint with the Constitutional Court. Finally, the State party argues that the petitioners did not argue a breach of the Convention before the Court, although international instruments are directly applicable and the Court can grant a remedy for breach thereof.

_The petitioners' comments_

5.1 By submission of 12 January 2004, the petitioners responded to the State party's observations. On the alleged failure to file a petition for review of the District Prosecutor's decision, they argue that this authority was the only one able to bring a criminal prosecution. The Prosecutor's decision contained no indication of a possibility of further appeal. Moreover, there is no indication that a higher prosecutor would have taken any different view from that of the Prosecutor, namely that a town or municipal council is not a "public administration body" whose decisions are reviewable for legality. This view was taken despite the rejection, by the Committee, of such an argument in the decision on the _Koptova_ case. In the absence of any change to the "firmly settled" domestic jurisprudence on this issue and in the absence of any new facts, the petitioners argue that the State party has not shown that a higher prosecutor would take any different view if the complaint was re-presented. The same conclusion on the issue of exhaustion of the proposed remedy was also shared by the Committee in the _Koptova_ case and _Lacko_ v. _Slovakia_.[8]

5.2 As to the argument that a new application should be lodged with the Constitutional Court, the petitioners point out that the judgement describes itself as final and that, in _Koptova_, the Committee rejected such an argument. Accordingly, as there is no prospect that repeated petitions to either body offer any chance of success, the petitioners claim to have exhausted all effective domestic remedies. They add that the State party's arguments should be viewed against the absence of a comprehensive anti-discrimination law; the only currently proscribed conduct is hate speech, racially motivated violence and discrimination in employment.

5.3 In response to arguments that municipal councils are not State organs, the petitioners invoke the Committee's general recommendation XV on article 4 for the contrary proposition. The Slovak Municipality System Act 1990 establishes a "direct relationship" between municipalities and the State, in terms of its subordinate financial, functional and organizational positions. Finally, in its Opinion on the _Koptova_ case, the Committee found the council to be a public authority for the purposes of the Convention.

---

[7] This section provides that: "The applicant may request a review of the lawfulness of dealing with his motion by filing a repeated motion; this new motion shall be dealt with by a superior prosecutor."

[8] Communication No. 11/1998.

Thus, the petitioners submit, the council's resolution should have been reviewed for lawfulness by the District Prosecutor and the State party's international responsibility is engaged.

5.4 The petitioners dispute the State party's argument that they did not specify the fundamental rights and freedoms violated in their petition to the Constitutional Court, arguing that they did so both in the original application and in subsequent pleadings. They claimed (i) violations of the right to equal treatment and dignity regardless of ethnic origin (art. 12), (ii) violations of the right, as a member of an ethnic group or national minority, not to suffer detriment (art. 33), (iii) violations, on the basis of ethnic origin, of their right to housing and (iv) discrimination against an ethnic group, the Roma. They point out that they continue to live in "appalling, substandard" conditions. They argue that articles 12 and 33 of the Constitution are not simply accessory provisions which, standing alone, have no substance; they confer substantive rights. They also point out that, while the domestic Constitution does not protect the right to housing, it does give precedence to international treaties such as, in addition to the Convention, the International Covenant on Economic, Social and Cultural Rights, which protects the right to housing and prohibits discrimination. Furthermore, the petitioners explicitly referred to the Council of Europe Framework Convention in their application. In any event, they argue they have complied with their obligation, under the relevant jurisprudence, to raise the substance of a complaint.

5.5 The petitioners further contend that the racial discrimination suffered by them amounts to degrading treatment proscribed in article 12 of the Constitution. They refer to the case law of the European Commission of Human Rights, which held, in the *East African Asians* case, that immigration admission denied on the basis of colour and race amounted to such a violation of article 3 of the European Convention, and constituted an affront to human dignity.[9] They also argue that, under well-established principles, if a State party decides to confer a particular benefit (that it may not necessarily have had an obligation to confer ab initio), that benefit cannot be conferred in a discriminatory fashion.[10] Thus, even if the petitioners had no initial right to housing (which they contest), it cannot be cancelled, on discriminatory grounds, subsequent to its provision.

5.6 Finally, the petitioners object to any inference that they are not "victims" on the basis that the Constitutional Court held that no violation of the Slovak Constitution had been made out. They argue that they were part of a specific group of people granted certain rights and then had them abolished. Thus, once they are, "directly targeted by the resolutions", to use the Committee's language in its Opinion on the *Koptova* case, they can be considered "victims". In addition, as the complaint lodged with the District Prosecutor did not lead to substantive review of the lawfulness of the council decision or to a criminal investigation of charges of incitement, they were victims of an absence of a remedy. The petitioners refer in this respect to the Committee's concluding observations on the State party's periodic report concerning discrimination in access to housing.[11]

*The Committee's decision on the admissibility of the petition*

6.1 At its sixty-fourth session, on 27 February 2004, the Committee examined the admissibility of the petition. As to the State party's contention that the petitioners did not renew their complaint before another prosecutor after it had been dismissed by the District Prosecutor, the Committee noted that the District Prosecutor had dismissed the case for lack of jurisdiction over an act of the municipal council. In the Committee's view, as far as the decision on lack of competence was concerned, the State party had not shown how re-presentation of the complaint would provide an available and effective remedy for the alleged violation of the Convention. Consequently, these avenues needed not be pursued for purposes of exhaustion of domestic remedies. In this regard, the Committee recalled its own jurisprudence and that of the Human Rights Committee.[12]

---

[9] 3 EHRR 76 (1973).

[10] The petitioners refer to the *Belgian Linguistics* case, 1 EHRR 252, 283.
[11] CERD/C/304/Add.110.
[12] See *Lacko* v. *Slovakia* and, with respect to the Human Rights Committee, *R.T.* v. *France*, communication No. 262/87, Decision adopted on 30 March 1989, and *Kaaber* v. *Iceland*, communication No. 674/95, Decision adopted on 11 May 1996.

6.2 With reference to the contention that the petitioners should renew their claim before the Constitutional Court, the Committee recalled its jurisprudence that where the Court dismissed a fully argued constitutional petition arguing alleged racial discrimination for failure to disclose the appearance of an infringement of rights, a petitioner could not be expected to re-present a petition to the Court.[13] In the present case, the Committee observed that the current petitioners also invoked several relevant constitutional rights alleged to have been violated, including rights of equality and non-discrimination. In the circumstances, the State party had not shown how renewal of their petition before the Constitutional Court, after it had been dismissed, could give rise to a different result by way of remedy. It followed that the petitioners have exhausted available and effective remedies before the Constitutional Court.

6.3 The Committee further recalled its jurisprudence that the acts of municipal councils, including the adoption of public resolutions of legal character such as in the present case, amounted to acts of public authorities within the meaning of the provisions of the Convention.[14] It followed that the petitioners, being directly and personally affected by the adoption of the resolution, as well as its subsequent cancellation after presentation of the petition, may claim to be "victims" for purposes of submitting their complaint before the Committee.[15]

6.4 The Committee also considered that the claims advanced by the petitioners were sufficiently substantiated, for purposes of admissibility. In the absence of any other obstacles to admissibility, the complaint was therefore declared admissible.

*The State party's request for reconsideration of admissibility and submissions on the merits*

7.1 By submission of 4 June 2004, the State party submitted a request for reconsideration of admissibility and its submissions on the merits of the petition. It argued that the petitioners have failed to exhaust domestic remedies, as they could have availed themselves of an effective remedy in the form of a petition pursuant to article 27 of the Constitution and the Right to Petition Act,

challenging the second municipal council resolution and/or the petition lodged against the initial resolution. Presentation of such a petition would have obliged the municipality to accept the petition for review and to examine the factual situation. This remedy is not subject to time-limits and is still available to the petitioners.

7.2 The State party argues that the failure of the petitioners to obtain the result that they sought from the prosecuting authorities and the courts cannot, of itself amount to a denial of an effective remedy. It refers to the decision of the European Court of Human Rights in *Lacko et al.* v. *Slovakia*[16] to the effect that a remedy, within the meaning of article 13 of the European Convention on Human Rights, "does not mean a remedy bound to succeed, but simply an accessible remedy before an authority competent to examine the merits of a complaint". It is the petitioners who should be held responsible for the failure of their claim before the Constitutional Court, on the basis that they failed to specify the fundamental right allegedly infringed by the council resolution in addition to simply invoking the general equality provision of article 12 of the Constitution.

7.3 The State party rejects the Committee's view that it was sufficient for the petitioners to plead certain relevant constitutional articles, without also pleading specific concrete injury, as both generally required by the Constitutional Court's jurisprudence and specifically requested of the petitioners by the Court in the instant case. The State party regards such a requirement of particularized injury, i.e., a pleading of a violation of a general equality/non-discrimination guarantee *in combination with* a concrete right, to be wholly consistent with the spirit of the Convention.

7.4 On the remedies actually instituted by the petitioners, the State party argues that their application of 16 September 2002 to the Rožňava District Prosecutor contended only that the petition to the council amounted to an abuse of the right to petition under the Right to Petition Act, under which a petition must not incite violations of the Constitution or amount to a denial or restriction of personal, political or other rights of persons on the grounds of their nationality, sex, race, origin, political or other conviction, religious faith or social status, and must not incite to hatred and intolerance on

---

[13] See *Koptova* v. *Slovakia*, paras. 2.9 and 6.4.
[14] Ibid., para. 6.6.
[15] Ibid., para. 6.5.

[16] Application No. 47237/99, decision of 2 July 2002.

the above grounds, or to violence or gross indecency. The petitioners neither argued how the factual circumstances amounted to such an abuse of the right to petition, nor mentioned the issue of racial discrimination, Roma ethnicity or other circumstances implicating the Convention.

7.5 In their application to the Constitutional Court, the petitioners requested a ruling that the council resolution infringed "the fundamental right of the petitioners to equal fundamental rights and freedoms irrespective of sex, race, colour, language, national origin, nationality or ethnic origin guaranteed under article 12 of the Constitution" and "the fundamental right of the petitioner to not suffer any detriment on account of belonging to a national minority or ethnic group guaranteed under article 33 of the Constitution." The State party observes that the Constitutional Court requested the petitioners inter alia to complete their complaint with information on "which of their fundamental rights or freedoms were infringed, which actions and/or decisions gave rise to the infringement, [and] which decisions of the Municipal Council they consider to be ethnically or racially motivated". The petitioners however completed their submission *without* specifying the rights allegedly violated, with the result that the Court dismissed the complaint as unfounded. In light of the above, the State party requests reconsideration of the admissibility of the petition.

7.6 On the merits, the State party argues that the petitioners failed to show an act of racial discrimination within the meaning of the Convention. Firstly, it argues that the petitioners mischaracterize the facts in important respects. It is not correct that the original resolution adopted by the municipal council approved a plan to construct low-cost housing; rather, the resolution "approv[ed] the concept of the construction of low-cost housing—family houses and/or apartment houses", making *no* mention of who would be the future dwellers, whether Roma or otherwise. It is also incorrect that the council instructed the local mayor to prepare a project aimed at securing finance from a Government fund set up expressly to alleviate Roma housing problems; rather, the resolution only recommended that the mayor, as the State party describes it, "consider preparing project

documentation and obtaining the funds for the construction from Government subsidies."[17]

7.7 The State party points out that such resolutions, as purely internal organizational rules, are not binding ordinances and confer no objective or subjective rights that can be invoked before the courts or other authorities. As a result, neither Roma nor other inhabitants of Dobsiná can claim a violation of their "right to adequate housing" or discrimination resulting from such resolutions. Similarly, the Constitutional Court held that "none of the rights granted to the citizens who belong to a minority and enjoy constitutional protection entails an obligation by a municipality to make a certain decision or perform a certain activity, such as the construction of low cost housing". The municipal resolutions, which are general policy documents on the issue of housing in the municipality, make no mention of Roma and the petitioners infer an incorrect causal link. The tentative nature of the resolution is also shown by the absence of any construction timetable, as any construction necessarily depended on Government funding.

7.8 The State party observes that the second resolution, after revoking the first resolution, instructed the council, in the words of the State party, "to prepare a proposal on addressing the existence of inadaptable citizens in the town of Dobsiná and to subsequently open the proposal for a discussion by municipal bodies and at a public meeting of the citizens."[18] This makes clear that the resolution is part of an ongoing effort to find a conceptual solution to the existence of "inadaptable citizens" in the town. As a result, policy measures taken by the municipal council to secure housing for low-income citizens clearly does not fall within the scope of the Convention. Rather, the council's activities can be viewed as a positive attempt to create more favourable conditions for this group of citizens, regardless of ethnicity. The State party observes that these actions of the municipality in the field of housing were against the background of the Slovak Government's Resolution No. 335/2001 approving a Programme for the Construction of Municipal Rental Flats for low income housing, and should be interpreted in that context.

---

[17] See the full text of the resolution set out in footnote 1 above.
[18] See the full text of the resolution set out in footnote 3 above.

7.9 The State party invokes the jurisprudence of the European Court of Human Rights in which the Court declined to entertain claims of discrimination advanced by travelling communities arising from the denial of residence permits on the basis of the public interest, such as environmental protection, municipal development and the like.[19] The State party argues that in this case local residents, committed to upgrading their municipality and properties, had legitimate concerns about certain risks including adverse social impacts arising from a mass influx of persons to low-income housing. It is noted that a number of Roma also signed the petition in question.

7.10 The State party argues that reference to other cases decided by the Committee such as *Lacko*[20] and *Koptova*[21] is inappropriate, as the facts and law of the present case differ. In particular, in *Koptova*, there was no context of an ongoing policy programme of housing development. The State party also observes that on 20 May 2004, Parliament passed a new anti-discrimination law laying down requirements for the implementation of the equal treatment principle and providing legal remedies for cases of infringement. The State party also rejects the reliance placed upon the European Court's judgements in the *East African Asians*[22] and *Belgian Linguistics*[23] cases. They emphasize that the second resolution did not cancel an existing project (and thus deprive existing benefits or entitlements), but rather reformulated the concept of how housing in the municipality would best be addressed.

7.11 On article 6, the State party reiterates its arguments developed in the context of the admissibility of the petition, namely that its courts and other instances provide complete and lawful consideration, in accordance with the requirements of due process, to any claim of racial discrimination. Concerning criminal prosecutions in the context of the petition on the basis of spreading racial hatred, the State party argues that the petitioners have failed to demonstrate that any actions of its public authorities were unlawful, or that the petition or

its contents were unlawful. A violation of the right to an effective remedy protected by article 6 has accordingly not been established.

*The petitioners' comments on the State party's submissions*

8.1 With respect to the State party's argument related to the remedy of a petition, the petitioners argue that the only legal obligation is for it to be received by the relevant authority. The Constitutional Court has held that there is no obligation for the petition to be treated and given effect to; in the Court's words, "[n]either the Constitution nor the Petition Act give concrete guarantees of acceptance or consequences of dismissal of petitions". As a result, such an extraordinary remedy cannot be regarded as an effective remedy that must be exhausted for the purposes of petitioning the Committee.

8.2 On the merits, the petitioners reject the State party's characterization of the council resolutions as being without legal effect, and refer to the Committee's admissibility decision where it was decided that "public resolutions of legal character such as in the present case" amounted to acts of public authorities. The petitioners also contest whether any Roma signed the petition against the first council resolution, stating that this is founded upon an assertion made in a letter dated 28 April 2004 by the mayor of Dobsiná to the Slovak Ministry of Foreign Affairs, without any further substantiation. In any event, the petitioners argue that the ethnicity of the persons signing the petition is irrelevant, as its content, purpose and effect is discriminatory. The petitioners also argue that the repeated use of the term "inadaptable citizens" by the State party reveals institutional prejudices against Roma.

8.3 The petitioners argue that, contrary to the State party's assertions, there is a compelling causal link between the council resolutions, the petition and discrimination in access to housing suffered by the petitioners. They argue that implementation of the social housing project would have resulted in their lives assuming a sense of dignity and alleviated dangers to their health. However, to date, the State party authorities have taken no steps to alleviate the inadequate housing situation of the petitioners. They argue that their situation is part of a wider context of discrimination in access to housing at issue in the State party and submit a number of reports

---

[19] *Chapman* v. *United Kingdom*, application No. 27238/95, Judgement of 18 January 2001, and *Coster* v. *United Kingdom*, application No. 24876/94, Judgement of 18 January 2001.
[20] See footnote 8 above.
[21] See footnote 5 above.
[22] See footnote 9 above.
[23] See footnote 10 above.

of international monitoring mechanisms in support.[24]

8.4 The petitioners reject the argument that the State party authorities were under no obligation in the first place to provide housing, referring to the obligations under article 11 of the International Covenant on Economic, Social and Cultural Rights (right to "an adequate standard of living ... including ... housing"). In any event, they argue that the principle developed in the *Belgian Linguistics* case stands not only for the principle that when a State party decides to confer a benefit it must do so without discrimination, but also for the principle that having decided to implement a certain measure—in this case to pursue the housing scheme—a State party cannot later decide not to implement it and base itself on discriminatory considerations.

*Issues and proceedings before the Committee*

*Review of consideration of admissibility*

9.1 The State party has requested the Committee on the Elimination of Racial Discrimination, under rule 94, paragraph 6, of the Committee's rules of procedure, to reconsider its decision on admissibility. The Committee must therefore decide whether the petition remains admissible in the light of the further submissions of the parties.

---

[24] The petitioners cite the Committee's own concluding observations, dated 1 June 2001, on the State party (CERD/C/304/Add.110) [Note of the Committee: The Committee's most recent concluding observations on the State party are dated 10 December 2004 (CERD/C/65/CO/7)]. The petitioners also cite the Third Report on the State party of the European Commission against Racial Intolerance, dated 27 June 2003, a Report on the Situation of Roma and Sinti in the OSCE Area, dated April 2000, by the Organization for Security and Co-operation in Europe, the 2004 Report on Human Rights in the OSCE Region by the International Helsinki Federation, the 2001-2 World Report of Human Rights Watch, the concluding observations, dated 22 August 2003, of the Human Rights Committee on the State party (CCPR/CO/78/SVK), the concluding observations, dated 19 December 2002, of the Committee on Economic, Social and Cultural Rights (E/C.12/1/Add.81), the Opinion on Slovakia, dated 22 September 2000, adopted by the Advisory Committee on the Framework Convention for the Protection of National Minorities and the 2003 Country Reports (Slovakia) on Human Rights Practices of the Department of State, United States of America.

9.2 The Committee notes that the State party's request for reconsideration raises the possible remedy of a petition to the municipal authority, advancing the matters currently before the Committee. The Committee observes, however, that under the State party's law, the municipal authority is solely under an obligation to receive the petition, but not to consider it or to make a determination on the outcome. In addition, the Committee observes that it is fundamental to the effectiveness of a remedy that its independence from the authority being complained against is assured. In the present case however the petition would re-present the grievance to the same body, the municipal council, that had originally decided on it. In such circumstances, the Committee cannot regard the right of petition as a domestic remedy that must be exhausted for the purposes of article 14, paragraph 7 (a), of the Convention.

9.3 As to the State party's remaining arguments, the Committee considered that these generally recast the arguments originally advanced to it in the course of the Committee's initial consideration of the admissibility of the petition. The Committee has already resolved these issues at that point of its consideration of the petition; accordingly, it would be inappropriate for the Committee to review its conclusions at the current stage of its deliberations.

9.4 In conclusion, therefore, the Committee rejects the State party's request for a reconsideration of the admissibility of the petition and proceeds to its consideration of the merits thereof.

*Consideration of the merits*

10.1 Acting under article 14, paragraph 7 (a), of the International Convention on the Elimination of All Forms of Racial Discrimination, the Committee has considered the information submitted by the petitioner and the State party.

10.2 The Committee observes, at the outset, that it must determine whether an act of racial discrimination, as defined in article 1 of the Convention, that has occurred before it can decide which, if any, substantive obligations in the Convention to prevent, protect against and remedy such acts, have been breached by the State party.

10.3 The Committee recalls that, subject to certain limitations not applicable in the present case, article 1 of the Convention defines racial discrimination as follows: "any distinction, exclusion, restriction or preference based on race, colour, descent, or national or ethnic origin, which has the purpose or effect of nullifying or impairing the recognition, enjoyment or exercise, on an equal footing, of human rights and fundamental freedoms in the political, economic, social, cultural or any other field".

10.4 The State party argues firstly that the resolutions of the municipal council challenged make no reference to Roma, and must thus be distinguished from the resolutions at issue in, for example, the *Koptova*[25] case that were racially discriminatory on their face. The Committee recalls that the definition of racial discrimination in article 1 expressly extends beyond measures which are explicitly discriminatory, to encompass measures which are not discriminatory at face value but are discriminatory in fact and effect, that is, if they amount to indirect discrimination. In assessing such indirect discrimination, the Committee must take full account of the particular context and circumstances of the petition, as by definition indirect discrimination can only be demonstrated circumstantially.

10.5 In the present case, the circumstances surrounding the adoption of the two resolutions by the municipal council of Dobsiná and the intervening petition, presented to the council following the its first resolution make abundantly clear that the petition was advanced by its proponents on the basis of ethnicity and was understood as such by the council as the primary if not exclusive basis for revoking its first resolution. As a result, the Committee considers that the petitioners have established a distinction, exclusion or restriction based on ethnicity, and dismisses this element of the State party's objection.

10.6 The State party argues, in the second instance, that the municipal council's resolution did not confer a direct and/or enforceable right to housing, but rather amounted to but one step in a complex process of policy development in the field of housing. The implication is that the second resolution of the council, even if motivated by ethnic grounds, thus did not amount to a measure "nullifying or impairing the recognition, enjoyment or exercise, on an equal footing, of human rights and fundamental freedoms in the political, economic, social, cultural or any other field",

---

[25] See footnote 5 above.

within the meaning of article 1, paragraph 1, in fine. The Committee observes that in complex contemporary societies the practical realization of, in particular, many economic, social and cultural rights, including those related to housing, will initially depend on and indeed require a series of administrative and policy-making steps by the State party's competent relevant authorities. In the present case, the council resolution clearly adopted a positive development policy for housing and tasked the mayor with pursuing subsequent measures by way of implementation.

10.7 In the Committee's view, it would be inconsistent with the purpose of the Convention and elevate formalism over substance, to consider that the final step in the actual implementation of a particular human right or fundamental freedom must occur in a non-discriminatory manner, while the necessary preliminary decision-making elements directly connected to that implementation were to be severed and be free from scrutiny. As a result, the Committee considers that the council resolutions in question, taking initially an important policy and practical step towards realization of the right to housing followed by its revocation and replacement with a weaker measure, taken together, do indeed amount to the impairment of the recognition or exercise on an equal basis of the human right to housing, protected by article 5 (c) of the Convention and further in article 11 of the International Covenant on Economic, Social and Cultural Rights. The Committee thus dismisses the State party's objection on this point.

10.8 In light of this finding that an act of racial discrimination has occurred, the Committee recalls its jurisprudence set out in paragraph 6.3, supra, of its consideration of the admissibility of the petition, to the effect that acts of municipal councils, including the adoption of public resolutions of legal character such as in the present case, amounted to acts of public authorities within the meaning of Convention provisions. It follows that the racial discrimination in question is attributable to the State party.

10.9 Accordingly, the Committee finds that the State party is in breach of its obligation under article 2, paragraph 1 (a), of the Convention to engage in no act of racial discrimination and to ensure that all public authorities act in conformity with this obligation. The Committee also finds that the State party is in breach of its obligation to guarantee the right of everyone to equality before the law in the enjoyment of the right to housing, contrary to article 5, paragraph (e) (iii), of the Convention.

10.10 With respect to the claim under article 6, the Committee observes that, at a minimum, this obligation requires the State party's legal system to afford a remedy in cases where an act of racial discrimination within the meaning of the Convention has been made out, whether before the national courts or in this case the Committee. The Committee having established the existence of an act of racial discrimination, it must follow that the failure of the State party's courts to provide an effective remedy discloses a consequential violation of article 6 of the Convention.

10.11 The Committee considers that the petitioners' remaining claims do not add substantively to the conclusions set out above and accordingly does not consider them further.

11. The Committee on the Elimination of Racial Discrimination, acting under article 14, paragraph 7, of the Convention on the Elimination of All Forms of Racial Discrimination, is of the view that the facts before it disclose violations of article 2, paragraph 1 (a), article 5, paragraph (e) (iii), and article 6 of the Convention.

12. In accordance with article 6 of the Convention, the State party is under an obligation to provide the petitioners with an effective remedy. In particular, the State party should take measures to ensure that the petitioners are placed in the same position that they were in upon adoption of the first resolution by the municipal council. The State party is also under an obligation to ensure that similar violations do not occur in the future.

13. The Committee wishes to receive, within ninety days, information from the Government of the Slovak Republic about the measures taken to give effect to the Committee's Opinion. The State party is requested also to give wide publicity to the Committee's Opinion.

# Communication No. 32/2003

*Submitted by*: Mr. Emir Sefic (represented by the Documentation and Advisory Centre on Racial Discrimination).
*Alleged victim*: The petitioner.
*State party*: Denmark.
*Date of adoption of Opinion*: 7 March 2005.
*Subject matter*: Refusal of car insurance based on language spoken; access to effective mechanisms of protection; effective investigation.
*Procedural issues*: Exhaustion of domestic remedies.
*Substantive issues*: Right to an effective remedy against acts of racial discrimination; right to an effective investigation; State parties have a positive obligation to take effective action against reported incidents of racial discrimination; discrimination based on race, ethnic and national origin.
*Articles of the Convention*: 2 (1) (d), 5, 6 and 14 (7) (a).
*Finding*: No violation.

*Opinion*

1. The petitioner is Mr. Sefic Emir, a Bosnian citizen, currently residing in Denmark, where he holds a temporary residency and work permit. He claims to be a victim of violations by Denmark of articles 2, paragraph 1 (d), 5 and 6, of the International Convention on the Elimination of All Forms of Racial Discrimination. He is represented by the Documentation and Advisory Centre on Racial Discrimination (DRC), a non-governmental organization, based in Denmark.

*The facts as presented by the petitioner:*

2.1 On 22 July 2002, the petitioner contacted Fair Insurance A/S to purchase insurance covering loss of and damage to his car, as well as third-party liability insurance. He was told that they could not offer him insurance, as he did not speak Danish. The conversation took place in English and the sales agent FULLY understood his request.

2.2 Late July 2002, the petitioner contacted the DRC, which requested confirmation of the petitioner's allegations from Fair Insurance A/S. In the meantime, the petitioner contacted the company again and was rejected on the same grounds. By letter dated 23 September 2002, Fair Insurance A/S confirmed that the language requirement was necessary to obtain any insurance offered by the company for the following reasons:

"... ensure that we cover the need of the customer to the extent that we can ensure that both the coverage of the insurance and the prices are as correct as possible ... ensure that the customer understands the conditions and rights connected to every insurance ... ensure that the customer in connection with a damage claim particularly when it is critical (accident, fire, etc.) can explain what has happened in order that he/she can be given the right treatment and compensation.

To fulfil these demands it is ... of the utmost importance that the dialogue with the customers is carried out in a language that both the customer and we are familiar with and that for the time being we can only fulfil this requirement and offer service to our customers in Danish. The reason being that we as a young (3.5 years) and relatively small company have limited resources to employ persons in our customer services department with knowledge of insurance issues in languages other than Danish or develop or maintain material on insurances in languages other than Danish."

2.3 On 8 October 2002, the DRC filed a complaint with the Danish Financial Supervisory Authority, which monitors financial companies. By letter of 25 November 2002, the Supervisory Authority replied that the complaint should be made to the Board of Appeal of Insurances ("the Board"). However, the Supervisory Authority would consider whether a general policy of rejection on the basis of language was in accordance with Danish law. It pointed out that, under section 1 (1) in the Instruction on Third-Party

Liability Insurances for Motor Vehicles (No. 585, 9 July 2002), the company was legally obliged to offer any customer public liability insurance.

2.4 On 12 December 2002, the DRC filed a complaint with the Board and specifically asked whether the language requirement was compatible with the Act against Discrimination. On 31 January 2003, the Board informed the DRC that it was highly unlikely that it would consider the legality of the requirement in regard to any other legislation other than the Act on Insurance Agreements. However, the case was being given due consideration. The letter also contained a response, of 29 January 2003, from Fair Insurance A/S to the Board, which stated as follows:

"Regarding the Act on Insurance Agreements ... we are clearly aware of the fact that anybody accepting our conditions of insurance can demand to be offered third-party liability insurance. We regret that Emir Sefic was not offered third-party liability insurance that he could have claimed. On this basis we have explained in more detail to our employees the legal rules in regard to the liability insurance."

2.5 On 10 January 2003, the Supervisory Authority informed the DRC that its assessment would be based on section 3 of the Act on Financial Business, in its determination on whether Fair Insurance A/S had complied with "upright business activity and good practice". On 11 March 2003, it informed the DRC that it was of the view that the requirement did not violate section 3. The Supervisory Authority did not consider whether the language requirement violated any other legislation, in particular the Act against Discrimination.

2.6 On 12 December 2002, the DRC filed a complaint with the Commissioner of the Police of Copenhagen ("the Commissioner"). On 24 April 2003, the Commissioner informed the DRC that "it appears from the material received that the possible discrimination only consists of a requirement that the customers can to speak Danish in order for the company to arrange the work routines in the firm. Any discrimination based on this explanation and being objectively motivated is not covered by the prohibition in section 1 (1) of the Act against Discrimination."

2.7 On 21 May 2003, the DRC filed an appeal with the Regional Public Prosecutor of

Copenhagen ("the Prosecutor"). On 13 June 2003, the Prosecutor rejected the complaint under section 749 (1) of the Administration of Justice Act. He explained that the language requirement, "was not based on the customer's race, ethnic origin or the like, but in the wish to be able to communicate with the customers in Danish, as the company has no employees who in regard to insurances in other languages than Danish have skills. Discrimination based on such a clear linguistic basis combined with the information given by the company is not in my opinion covered by the Act on the prohibition of differential treatment based on race etc. Moreover, it is my view that the Fair Insurance A/S's acknowledgement of the fact that the company was obliged to offer a third-party liability insurance to Emir Sefic, in accordance with the Act on Insurance Agreements, is of no relevance in regard to the question whether the Act on the prohibition of differential treatment based on race etc... I have based this on the information provided by Fair Insurance A/S that it was due to a mistake that no third-party liability insurance was offered to Emir Sefic."

2.8 The petitioner argues that he has exhausted domestic remedies. Any decision by the Regional Prosecutors relating to the investigation by the police departments cannot be appealed to other authorities. As questions relating to the pursuance by the police of charges against individuals are entirely up to the discretion of the police, there is no possibility of bringing the case before the Danish Courts. He submits that a civil claim under the Act on Civil Liability would not be effective, as both the Commissioner and the Prosecutor have rejected his complaint. Furthermore, the Eastern High Court, in a decision of 5 February 1999, has held that an incident of racial discrimination does not in itself imply a violation of the honour and reputation of a person under section 26 of the Act on Civil Liability. Thus, racial discrimination in itself does not amount to a claim for compensation by the person offended.

*The complaint*

3.1 As to the definition of discrimination under article 1, subparagraph 1, of the Convention, the petitioner argues that, although a language requirement is not specifically included in this definition, discrimination may conflict with the obligation laid down in the Convention, especially under circumstances where the requirement in fact constitutes discrimination based, inter alia, on national or ethnic origin,

race or colour, as the requirement has such an effect. Further, any language requirement used with the purpose of excluding, inter alia, customers of a specific national or ethnic origin would be contrary to article 1 of the Convention. Such a requirement should also have a legitimate aim and respect the requirement of proportionality in order to constitute a legal ground for discrimination.

3.2 The petitioner claims that the State party has violated article 2, subparagraph 1 (d), and 6, by not providing effective remedies against a violation of the rights relating to article 5. He refers to the Committee's decisions in *L.K.* v. *Netherlands* and *Habassi* v. *Denmark*,[1] in which it was established that States parties have a positive obligation to take effective action against reported incidents of racial discrimination. The petitioner submits that the language requirement cannot be considered as an objective requirement; and argues that the Danish authorities could not come to such a conclusion without initiating a formal investigation. They merely based their claim on the letter from Fair Insurance A/S of 23 September 2003, the DRC's complaint to the Commissioner of 12 December 2003 and the appeal to the Prosecutor of 21 May 2003. Neither the Commissioner nor the Prosecutor examined whether the language requirement constituted direct or indirect discrimination on the basis of national origin and/or race.

3.3 The petitioner highlights the following questions and issues, which in his view the Danish authorities failed to consider in examining whether the language requirement constituted racial discrimination: Firstly, to what extent the petitioner and Fair Insurance A/S were able to communicate in the present case. As the latter did understand the petitioner sufficiently to reject his claim, the authorities should have examined whether Fair Insurance A/S had understood the needs of the petitioner, to ensure that he understood the conditions and rights connected to each insurance and that he would be able to inform the company about the relevant facts in connection with a potential damage claim. Secondly, the authorities should have examined the extent to which the situation concerning language skills in regard to statutory insurance (the third-party liability insurance) differed from the situation in regard to voluntary insurance (the insurance covering

_____

[1] Communication No. 4/1991 and communication No. 10/1997, Opinion of 17 March 1999.

loss of and damage to a car.) As the third-party insurance is statutory, the company is obliged, even if the costumer only speaks English, as in the present case, to provide an offer and accept any customer who accepts its conditions. An investigation "could" have uncovered whether Fair Insurance A/S was able to "communicate on a sufficient basis" the demands, requirements and rights connected to the statutory insurance to the petitioner.

3.4 Thirdly, the authorities should have examined whether Fair Insurance A/S had any customers who were unable to speak Danish. If this were the case (especially relating to the statutory insurance), it would be of interest to reveal how the company communicated with such customers, and why the company could not communicate with other potential customers requesting other insurances. In addition, the petitioner claims that the failure by the Commissioner and the Prosecutor to interview him and Fair Insurance A/S further demonstrates that no proper investigation was carried out to try and establish whether the reasons given by Fair Insurance A/S were correct. The petitioner argues that there "may" have been other reasons for the language requirement and refers to a test case conducted by a television show, which revealed that Fair Insurance A/S offered insurance at a higher price to an individual of non-Danish national origin than a person of Danish national origin.

*State party's submission on the admissibility and merits*

4.1 On 18 December 2004, the State party provided commented on the admissibility and merits. On admissibility, it submits that, although the petitioner has exhausted available remedies under criminal law, there remain two civil actions which he has not pursued. Thus, the case is inadmissible for failure to exhaust domestic remedies. Firstly, the petitioner could bring an action against Fair Insurance A/S, claiming that it acted in contravention of the law by exposing him to racial discrimination, and thus request damages for both pecuniary and non-pecuniary loss.

4.2 The State party argues that this case differs from the *Habassi*[2] decision, in which the Committee found that the bringing of a civil action in a case of alleged discrimination contrary to the Act against Discrimination was

not an effective remedy, as unlike the petitioner in that case, the petitioner in the current case claims that he has suffered a financial loss, as he subsequently had to take out insurance with another insurance company at a higher premium. The same argument is made to distinguish the current case from the Committee's decision in the case of *B.J.* v. *Denmark*.[3]

4.3 The second civil remedy is an action against Fair Insurance A/S under the rules of the Danish Marketing Practices; under section 1 (1) thereof, a private business may not perform acts contrary to "good marketing practices". The petitioner could have submitted that Fair Insurance A/S had acted in contravention of the Act against Discrimination in its treatment of his insurance application and had thus also acted in contravention of "good marketing practices". The petitioner could have claimed damages under general rules of Danish Law, both for the financial loss allegedly suffered by him and for non-pecuniary loss. Acts contrary to this Act can be prohibited by judgement and give rise to liability in damages.

4.4 As to the merits, the State party submits that there has been no violation of the Convention. It acknowledges that States parties have a duty to initiate a proper investigation when faced with complaints about acts of racial discrimination, which should be carried out with due diligence and expeditiously and must be sufficient to determine whether or not an act of racial discrimination has occurred.[4] However, in the State party's view, it does not follow from the Convention or the Committee's case law that an investigation has to be initiated in all cases reported to the police. If no basis is found to initiate an investigation, the State party finds it to be in accordance with the Convention to dismiss the report. In the present case, the Commissioner and the Prosecutor received a detailed written report enclosing a number of annexes from the DRC illustrating the case sufficiently to conclude, without initiating any investigation, whether it could reasonably be presumed that a criminal offence subject to public prosecution had been committed.

---

[2] Communication No. 10/1997.

[3] Communication No. 17/1999.
[4] The State party refers to the Committee's jurisprudence on this issue: *Yilmaz-Dogan* v. *Netherlands*, *L.K.* v. *Netherlands*, *Habassi* v. *Denmark*, and *Ahmad* v. *Denmark*.

4.5 As to the petitioner's argument that the Commissioner should have investigated whether the language requirement constituted direct or indirect discrimination, the State party submits that the Act against Discrimination does not make this distinction, but refers to the person who "refuses to serve" another person on the same conditions as others on account of race, nationality etc. It was, therefore, not decisive in itself to clarify whether direct or indirect discrimination had occurred, but rather whether section 1 of the Act against Discrimination had been violated intentionally, whether the alleged discrimination contrary to the Act was direct or indirect. As to the petitioner's reference to the television survey, the State party finds this of no relevance to this context.

4.6 As to whether the Commissioner should have investigated the extent to which the petitioner and Fair Insurance A/S could communicate, the State party argues that it was not decisive to clarify whether the petitioner and Fair Insurance A/S had been able to communicate adequately, but rather whether section 1 of the Act against Discrimination had been violated intentionally. As the language requirement is due to the lack of resources to hire staff with insurance expertise in languages other than Danish and to the fact that it is a telephone-based company, the State party considers the requirement to be objectively justified, as the question involves the purchase of an insurance policy, which implies contractual rights and obligations, and the contents and consequences of which both the buyer and seller must be able to understand with certainty. It is therefore, considered irrelevant to initiate an investigation of the extent to which the petitioner and Fair Insurance A/S were able to communicate in a language other than Danish. In this connection, the Government notes the decision of the Financial Supervisory Authority that this language policy does not violate section 3 of the Financial Business Act No. 660 of 7 August 2002, as the measure involved is a practical measure resulting from limited resources.

4.7 As to whether the Commissioner should have investigated the extent to which the situation concerning language skills in regard to statutory insurance differed from the situation in regard to voluntary insurance, the State party submits that it follows from Fair Insurance A/S's letter of 22 January 2003 that the company acknowledges that the petitioner should have been offered third-party liability insurance when he contacted the company. The State party notes that the task of the Commissioner was not to consider whether Fair Insurance A/S had a general practice contrary to the Act against Discrimination, but rather whether it had specifically violated the Act in connection with the petitioner's application, and thus committed a criminal act of racial discrimination.

4.8 As to whether the Commissioner should have investigated the extent to which Fair Insurance A/S had customers who are unable to speak Danish, the State party submits that in its letter of 19 September 2002, Fair Insurance A/S informed the DRC that the company has many customers with an ethnic background other than Danish, but that these customers speak Danish. In this light, it was not considered necessary to investigate any further.

*Petitioner's comments on State party's submission*

5.1 On 27 February 2004, the petitioner responded to the State party's submission. On its admissibility arguments, he submits that the Habassi decision clearly indicates that "the civil remedies proposed by the State party could not be considered an adequate avenue of redress ... (because) ... The same objective could not be achieved by [instituting] a civil action, which would lead only to compensation for damages".....and thus not to a criminal conviction. Furthermore, the Committee was of the opinion that it was not "convinced that a civil action would have any prospect of success ..." He submits that he has a right to an effective remedy against racial discrimination, as defined in article 1 and 5 of the Convention.

5.2 As to the Danish Marketing Practices Act, the petitioner submits that this Act has nothing to do with racial discrimination and a decision in relation to this Act is not a "remedy" against such a violation of the petitioner's rights. In addition, the petitioner claims that if this civil legislation covered the situation in the current case there would have been no necessity for the State party to adopt a new Act on Equal Treatment, which was implemented and took effect on 1 July 2003—after the incident addressed in the present case. The petitioner maintains his arguments on the merits.

*Issues and proceedings before the Committee*

*Consideration of admissibility*

6.1 Before considering any claims contained in a petition, the Committee on the Elimination of Racial Discrimination must, in accordance with rule 91 of its rules of procedure, decide whether or not it is admissible under the Convention.

6.2 The Committee notes that the State party objects to the admissibility of the complaint on the grounds of failure to exhaust civil domestic remedies. The Committee recalls its jurisprudence[5] that the types of civil remedies proposed by the State party may not be considered as offering an adequate avenue of redress. The complaint, which was filed with the police department and subsequently with the Public Prosecutor alleged the commission of a criminal offence and sought a conviction of the company Fair Insurance A/S under the Danish Act against Discrimination. The same objective could not be achieved by instituting a civil action, which would result only in compensation for damages awarded to the petitioner. Thus, the Committee considers that the petitioner has exhausted domestic remedies.

6.3 In the absence of any further objections to the admissibility of the communication, the Committee declares the petition admissible and proceeds to its examination of the merits.

*Consideration of the merits*

7.1 The Committee has considered the petitioner's case in the light of all the submissions and documentary evidence produced by the parties, as required under article 14, paragraph 7 (a), of the Convention and rule 95 of its rules of procedure. It bases its findings on the following considerations.

7.2 The issue before the Committee is whether the State party fulfilled its positive obligation to take effective action against reported incidents of racial discrimination, with regard to the extent to which it investigated the petitioner's claim in this case.[6] The petitioner claims that the requirement to speak Danish as a prerequisite for the receipt of car insurance is not an objective requirement and that further investigation would have been necessary to find out the real reasons behind this policy. The Committee notes that it is not contested that he does not speak Danish. It observes that his claim together with all the evidence provided by him and the information about the reasons behind Fair Insurance A/S's policy were considered by both the police department and by the Public Prosecutor. The latter considered that the language requirement "was not based on the customer's race, ethnic origin or the like", but for the purposes of communicating with its customers. The Committee finds that the reasons provided by Fair Insurance A/S for the language requirement, including the ability to communicate with the customer, the lack of resources for a small company to employ persons speaking different languages, and the fact that it is a company operating primarily through telephone contact were reasonable and objective grounds for the requirement and would not have warranted further investigation.

8. In the circumstances, the Committee on the Elimination of Racial Discrimination, acting under article 14, paragraph 7 (a), of the International Convention on the Elimination of All Forms of Racial Discrimination, is of the opinion that the facts as submitted do not disclose a violation of the Convention by the State party.

---

[5] *Habassi* v. *Denmark.*

[6] *L.K.* v. *Netherlands* and *Habassi* v. *Denmark.*

# Communication No. 34/2004

*Submitted by*: Mohammed Hassan Gelle (represented by counsel, the Documentation and Advisory Centre on Racial Discrimination).
*Alleged victim*: The petitioner.
*State party*: Denmark.
*Date of adoption of Opinion:* 6 March 2006.
*Subject matter:* Racial discriminatory statements made by a Member of Parliament against individuals of Somali origin; access to effective mechanisms of protection; effective investigation; freedom of expression.
*Procedural issues:* Substantiation for purposes of admissibility; inadmissibility *ratione materiae*; exhaustion of domestic remedies.
*Substantive issues:* Right to an effective remedy against acts of racial discrimination; right to an effective investigation; discrimination based on ethnic and national origin; State parties are required to prohibit and bring to an end, by all appropriate means, racial discrimination; freedom of expression.
*Articles of the Convention:* 2 (1) (d), 4, 6 and 14 (7) (a).
*Finding:* Violation (arts. 2 (1) (d), 4 and 6).

## Opinion

1.1  The petitioner is Mr. Mohammed Hassan Gelle, a Danish citizen and resident of Somali origin, born in 1957. He claims to be a victim of violations by Denmark of articles 2, paragraph 1 (d), 4 and 6 of the Convention. He is represented by counsel, Mr. Niels-Erik Hansen of the Documentation and Advisory Centre on Racial Discrimination (DRC).

1.2  In conformity with article 14, paragraph 6 (a), of the Convention, the Committee transmitted the communication to the State party on 3 June 2004.

## Factual background

2.1  On 2 January 2003, the daily newspaper *Kristeligt Dagblad* published a letter to the editor by Ms. Pia Kjærsgaard, a member of the Danish Parliament (*Folketinget*) and leader of the Danish People's Party (*Dansk Folkeparti*). The letter was given the title "A crime against humanity" and stated:

> "How many small girls will be mutilated before Lene Espersen, Minister of Justice (Conservative People's Party), prohibits the crime? [...]
>
> But Ms. Espersen has stated that she needs further information before she can introduce the bill. Therefore, she is now circulating the bill for consultation among 39 organizations that will be able to make objections.

> Now, it is all according to the book that a Minister of Justice wants to consult various bodies about a bill of far-reaching importance. The courts, the Director of Public Prosecutions, the police etc. must be consulted.

> But I must admit that I opened my eyes wide when, on Ms. Espersen's list of 39 organizations, I saw the following: the Danish-Somali Association [...], the Council for Ethnic Minorities [...], the Danish Centre for Human Rights [...], the National Organization for Ethnic Minorities [...] and the Documentation and Advisory Centre on Racial Discrimination [...].

> I have to ask: What does a prohibition against mutilation and maltreatment have to do with racial discrimination? And why should the Danish-Somali Association have any influence on legislation concerning a crime mainly committed by Somalis? And is it the intention that the Somalis are to assess whether the prohibition against female mutilation violates their rights or infringes their culture?

> To me, this corresponds to asking the association of paedophiles whether they have any objections to a prohibition against child sex or asking rapists whether they have any objections to an increase in the sentence for rape. For every day that passes until the period of

124

consultation expires and the bill can be adopted, more and more small girls will be mutilated for the rest of their lives. In all decency, this crime should be stopped now. [...]"

2.2 The petitioner considered that this comparison equated persons of Somali origin with paedophiles and rapists, thereby directly offending him. On 28 January 2003, the DRC, on the petitioner's behalf, reported the incident to the Copenhagen police, alleging a violation of section 266 (b)[1] of the Criminal Code.

2.3 By letter of 26 September 2003, the Copenhagen police notified the DRC that, in accordance with section 749, paragraph 1,[2] of the Administration of Justice Act, it had decided not to open an investigation into the matter, since it could not reasonably be presumed that a criminal offence subject to public prosecution had been committed.[3] The letter stated:

"In my opinion, the letter to the editor *cannot* be taken to express that Somalis are lumped together with paedophiles and rapists and that the author thereby links Somalis with authors of serious crimes. Female mutilation is an old Somali tradition that many today consider a crime due to the assault [...] against the woman. I understand Ms. Kjærsgaard's statements to mean that the criticism is aimed at the fact that the Minister wants to consult a group that many people believe to be committing a crime by performing this mutilation. Although the choice of paedophiles and rapists must be considered offensive

examples, I find that there is no violation within the meaning of section 266 (b)."

2.4 On 6 October 2003, the DRC, on the petitioner's behalf, appealed the decision to the Regional Public Prosecutor who, on 18 November 2004, upheld the decision of the Copenhagen police:

"I have also based my decision on the fact that the statements do not refer to all Somalis as criminals or otherwise as equal to paedophiles or rapists, but only argue against the fact that a Somali association is to be consulted about a bill criminalizing offences committed particularly in the country of origin of Somalis, [which is] why Ms. Kjærsgaard finds that Somalis cannot be presumed to comment objectively on the bill, just as paedophiles and rapists cannot be presumed to comment objectively on the criminalization of paedophilia and rape. The statements in question can also be taken to mean that Somalis are only compared with paedophiles and rapists as concerns the reasonableness of allowing them to comment on laws that affect them directly, and not as concerns their criminal conduct.

Moreover, I have based my decision on the fact that the statements in the letter to the editor were made by a Member of Parliament in connection with a current political debate and express the general political views of a party represented in Parliament.

According to their context in the letter to the editor, the statements concern the consultation of the Danish-Somali Association among others, in connection with the bill prohibiting female mutilation.

Although the statements are general and very sharp and may offend or outrage some people, I have considered it essential [...] that the statements were made as part of a political debate, which, as a matter of principle, affords quite wide limits for the use of unilateral statements in support of a particular political view. According to the *travaux préparatoires* of section 266 (b) of the Criminal Code, it was particularly intended not to lay down narrow limits on the topics that can become the subject of political debate, or on the way the topics are dealt with in detail.

---

[1] Section 266 (b) of the Danish Criminal Code reads: (1) Any person who, publicly or with the intention of wider dissemination, makes a statement or imparts other information by which a group of people are threatened, insulted or degraded on account of their race, colour, national or ethnic origin, religion or sexual inclination shall be liable to a fine or to imprisonment for any term not exceeding two years. (2) When the sentence is meted out, the fact that the offence is in the nature of propaganda activities shall be considered an aggravating circumstance."
[2] Section 749 of the Administration of Justice Act reads, in pertinent parts: "(1) The police shall dismiss a report lodged if it deems that there is no basis for initiating an investigation. (2) [...] (3) If the report is dismissed or the investigation is discontinued, those who may be presumed to have a reasonable interest therein must be notified. The decision can be appealed to the superior public prosecutor [...]."
[3] See sect. 742, para. 2, of the Administration of Justice Act.

To give you a better understanding of section 266 (b), I can inform you that the Director of Public Prosecutions has previously refused prosecution for violation of this provision in respect of statements of a similar kind. [...]

My decision is final and cannot be appealed, cf. section 101 (2), second sentence, of the Administration of Justice Act."[4]

*The complaint*

3.1 The petitioner claims that the Regional Public Prosecutor's argument that Members of Parliament enjoy an "extended right to freedom of speech" in the political debate was not reflected in the preparatory works of section 266 (b) of the Criminal Code, which gives effect to the State party's obligations under the Convention. In 1995, a new paragraph 2 was amended to section 266 (b), providing that "the fact that the offence is in the nature of propaganda activities shall be considered an aggravating circumstance." During the reading of the bill in Parliament, it was stated that, in such aggravated circumstances, prosecutors should not exercise the same restraint in prosecuting incidents of racial discrimination as in the past.

3.2 The petitioner submits that, during the examination of the State party's thirteenth periodic report to the Committee, the Danish delegation stated that "a systematic" or "a more extensive dissemination of statements may speak in favour of applying section 266 (b) (2)."

3.3 The petitioner quotes further statements by Pia Kjærsgaard, including one published in a weekly newsletter of 25 April 2000: "Thus a fundamentalist Muslim does in fact not know how to act cultivated and in accordance with Danish democratic traditions. He simply does not have a clue about what it means. Commonly acknowledged principles such as speaking the truth and behaving with dignity and culture—also towards those whom you do not sympathize with—are unfamiliar ground to people like M.Z."

3.4 The petitioner claims a full investigation of the incident and compensation as remedies for the alleged violation of articles 2, paragraph 1 (d), 4 and 6 of the Convention.

3.5 The petitioner claims that he has exhausted all available effective remedies, given that, under section 749, paragraph 1, of the Danish Administration of Justice Act, the police has full discretion whether or not to open criminal proceedings, subject to appeal to the Regional Public Prosecutor, whose decision is final and cannot be appealed to another administrative authority (as explicitly stated in the Regional Public Prosecutor's decision of 18 November 2004) or to a court. Direct legal action against Ms. Kjærsgaard would have been futile in the light of the rejection of his criminal complaint and of a judgement dated 5 February 1999 of the Eastern High Court of Denmark, which held that an incident of racial discrimination does not in itself amount to a violation of the honour and reputation of a person under section 26[5] of the Torts Act.

*State party's observations on admissibility and merits and petitioner's comments*

4.1 On 6 September 2004, the State party made its submissions on the admissibility and, subsidiarily, on the merits of the communication.

4.2 On admissibility, the State party submits that the petitioner failed to establish a *prima facie* case for purposes of admissibility,[6] since the statements in Ms. Kjærsgaard's letter to the editor of the *Kristeligt Dagblad*, rather than comparing Somalis with paedophiles or rapists, reflected her criticism of the Minister's decision to consult an association in the legislative process which, in her opinion, could not be considered objective with regard to the proposed bill. It concludes that the statements were racially non-discriminatory, thus falling outside the scope of application of articles 2, paragraph 1 (d), 4 and 6 of the Convention.

---

[4] Section 101, paragraph 2, of the Administration of Justice Act reads, in pertinent parts: "The decisions of the Regional Public Prosecutors on appeals cannot be appealed to the Director of Public Prosecutions or to the Minister of Justice."

[5] Section 26, paragraph 1, of the Torts Act reads: "(1) A person who is liable for unlawful violation of another person's freedom, peace, character or person shall pay compensation to the injured party for non-pecuniary damage."
[6] The State party refers to *C.P.* v. *Denmark*, communication No. 5/1994, paras. 6.2 and 6.3, as an example of a case which was declared inadmissible by the Committee on that ground.

4.3 The State party further submits that the communication is inadmissible under article 14, paragraph 7 (a), of the Convention, as the petitioner has not exhausted all available domestic remedies: article 63 of the Danish Constitution provides that decisions of administrative authorities may be challenged before the courts. Therefore, the petitioner would have been required to challenge the validity of the Regional Public Prosecutor's decision not to initiate a criminal investigation at court. Given that the petitioner considers himself directly offended by Ms. Kjærsgaard's statements, he could also have initiated criminal proceedings under section 267, paragraph 1,[7] of the Criminal Code, which generally criminalizes defamatory statements. Pursuant to section 275, paragraph 1,[8] these offences are subject to private prosecution, a remedy that was considered to be effective by the Committee in *Sadic* v. *Denmark*.

4.4 Subsidiarily, on the merits, the State party disputes that there was a violation of articles 2, paragraph 1 (d), and 6 of the Convention, because the Danish authorities' evaluation of Ms. Kjærsgaard's statements fully satisfied the requirement that an investigation must be carried out with due diligence and expedition and must be sufficient to determine whether or not an act of racial discrimination has taken place.[9] It did not follow from the Convention that prosecution must be initiated in all cases reported to the police. Rather, it was fully in accordance with the Convention to dismiss a report, e.g., in the absence of a sufficient basis for assuming that prosecution would lead to conviction. In the present case, the decisive issue of whether Ms. Kjærsgaard's statements fell under section 266 (b) of the Criminal Code did not give rise to any questions of evidence. The Regional Public Prosecutor merely had to make a legal evaluation, which he did both thoroughly and adequately.

4.5 The State party reiterates that Ms. Kjærsgaard's statements were devoid of any racist content. Thus, it is immaterial whether they were made by a Member of Parliament in the context of a current political debate on female genital mutilation. Therefore, no issue of an "extended" right to freedom of speech of Members of Parliament, allegedly encompassing even racist remarks, arises under article 4 of the Convention.

4.6 The State party adds that section 266 (b) satisfies the requirement in the Convention to criminalize racial discrimination[10] and that Danish law provides sufficient remedies against acts of racial discrimination.

5.1 On 25 October 2004, the petitioner replied that the title of Ms. Kjærsgaard's letter to the editor of the *Kristeligt Dagblad* ("A crime against humanity") sweepingly and unjustly accuses persons of Somali origin living in Denmark of practising female genital mutilation. Given that the offensive character of Ms. Kjærsgaard's statements was explicitly acknowledged by the Danish authorities (see paras. 2.3 and 2.4), the State party should withdraw its argument that the communication was prima facie inadmissible.

5.2 The petitioner argues that the possibility, under article 63 of the Danish Constitution, to challenge the decision of the Regional Public Prosecutor judicially is not an effective remedy within the meaning of article 6 of the Convention, because the deadline for initiating criminal proceedings under section 266 (b) of the Criminal Code would have expired by the time the courts refer the matter back to the police. The Committee must have been unaware of this fact when deciding on the case of *Quereshi* v. *Denmark*.[11] The Danish authorities' assumption that Members of Parliament enjoy an "extended" right to freedom of speech in the context of a political debate was not confirmed by the Danish courts and therefore requires clarification by the Committee.

---

[7] Section 267, paragraph 1, of the Criminal Code reads: "Any person who violates the personal honour of another [person] by offensive words or conduct or by making or spreading allegations of an act likely to disparage him in the esteem of his fellow citizens, shall be liable to a fine or to imprisonment for any term not exceeding four months."

[8] Section 275, paragraph 1, of the Criminal Code reads: "The offences contained in this Part shall be subject to prosecution, except for the offences referred to in sections [...] 266 (b)."

[9] The State party refers, inter alia, to *Habassi* v. *Denmark* and to *Ahmad* v. *Denmark*.

[10] The State party refers to its 14th (CERD/C/362/Add.1, paras. 135-143) and 15th (CERD/C/408/Add.1, paras. 30-45) periodic reports to the Committee, describing the background and practical application of section 266 (b).

[11] Communication No. 27/2002, opinion of 19 August 2003.

*Issues and proceedings before the Committee*

*Consideration of admissibility*

6.1 Before considering any claims contained in a petition, the Committee on the Elimination of Racial Discrimination must, in accordance with rule 91 of its rules of procedure, decide whether or not it is admissible under the Convention.

6.2 With regard to the State party's objection that the petitioner failed to establish a prima facie case for purposes of admissibility, the Committee observes that Ms. Kjærsgaard's statements were not of such an inoffensive character as to ab initio fall outside the scope of articles 2, paragraph 1 (d), 4 and 6 of the Convention. It follows that the petitioner has sufficiently substantiated his claims, for purposes of admissibility.

6.3 On the issue of exhaustion of domestic remedies, the Committee recalls that the petitioner brought a complaint under section 266 (b) of the Criminal Code, which was rejected by the Copenhagen police and, on appeal, by the Regional Public Prosecutor. It notes that the Regional Public Prosecutor stated that his decision of 18 November 2004 was final and not subject to appeal, either to the Director of Public Prosecutions or to the Minister of Justice.

6.4 As to the State party's argument that the petitioner could have challenged the decision of the Regional Public Prosecutor not to initiate a criminal investigation under section 266 (b) of the Criminal Code before the courts, in accordance with article 63 of the Danish Constitution, the Committee notes the petitioner's uncontested claim that the statutory deadline for initiating criminal proceedings under section 266 (b) would have expired by the time the courts refer the matter back to the police. Against this background, the Committee considers that judicial review of the Regional Public Prosecutor's decision under article 63 of the Constitution would not have provided the petitioner with an effective remedy.

6.5 On the State party's argument that the petitioner should have initiated private prosecution under the general provision on defamatory statements (section 267 of the Criminal Code), the Committee recalls that, in its Opinion in *Sadic* v. *Denmark*,[12] it had

indeed required the petitioner in *that* case to pursue such a course. In that case, however, the facts fell outside the scope of section 266 (b) of the Criminal Code, on the basis that the disputed comments were essentially private. In that light, section 267, which could capture the conduct in question complemented the scope of protection of section 266 (b) and was a reasonable course more appropriate to the facts of that case. In the present case, however, the statements were made squarely in the public arena, which is the central focus of both the Convention and section 266 (b). It would thus be unreasonable to expect the petitioner to initiate separate proceedings under the general provisions of section 267, after having unsuccessfully invoked section 266 (b) in respect of circumstances directly implicating the language and object of that provision.[13]

6.6 As to the possibility of instituting civil proceedings under section 26 of the Torts Act, the Committee notes the petitioner's argument that the Eastern High Court of Denmark, in a previous judgement, held that an incident of racial discrimination does not in itself constitute a violation of the honour and reputation of a person. Although mere doubts about the effectiveness of available civil remedies do not absolve a petitioner from pursuing them,[14] the Committee observes that by instituting a civil action the petitioner would not have achieved the objective pursued with his complaint under section 266 (b) of the Criminal Code to the police and subsequently to the Regional Public Prosecutor, i.e., Ms. Kjærsgaard's conviction by a criminal tribunal.[15] It follows that the institution of civil proceedings under section 26 of the Torts Act cannot be considered an effective remedy that needs to be exhausted for purposes of article 14, paragraph 7 (a), of the Convention, insofar as the petitioner seeks a full criminal investigation of Ms. Kjærsgaard's statements.

6.7 In the absence of any further objections to the admissibility of the petitioner's claims, the Committee declares the petition admissible, insofar as it relates to the State

---

[12] Decision on admissibility of 19 March 2003, paras. 6.2-6.4.

[13] See *Kamal Quereshi* v. *Denmark (II)*, communication No. 33/2003, Opinion of 9 March 2005, para. 6.3.

[14] See *Sarwar Seliman Mostafa* v. *Denmark*, communication No. 19/2000, Decision on admissibility of 10 August 2001, para. 7.4.

[15] See *Emir Sefic* v. *Denmark*, communication No. 32/2003, Opinion of 7 March 2005, para. 6.2.

party's alleged failure fully to investigate the incident.

*Consideration of the merits*

7.1 Acting under article 14, paragraph 7 (a), of the International Convention on the Elimination of All Forms of Racial Discrimination, the Committee has considered the information submitted by the petitioner and the State party.

7.2 The issue before the Committee is whether the State party fulfilled its positive obligation to take effective action against reported incidents of racial discrimination, having regard to the extent to which it investigated the petitioner's complaint under section 266 (b) of the Criminal Code. This provision criminalizes public statements by which a group of people are threatened, insulted or degraded on account of their race, colour, national or ethnic origin, religion or sexual inclination.

7.3 The Committee observes that it does not suffice, for purposes of article 4 of the Convention, merely to declare acts of racial discrimination punishable on paper. Rather, criminal laws and other legal provisions prohibiting racial discrimination must also be effectively implemented by the competent national tribunals and other State institutions. This obligation is implicit in article 4 of the Convention, under which State parties "undertake to adopt immediate and positive measures" to eradicate all incitement to, or acts of, racial discrimination. It is also reflected in other provisions of the Convention, such as article 2, paragraph 1 (d), which requires States to "prohibit and bring to an end, by all appropriate means," racial discrimination, and article 6, guaranteeing to everyone "effective protection and remedies" against acts of racial discrimination.

7.4 The Committee notes that the Regional Public Prosecutor dismissed the petitioner's complaint on the ground that Ms. Kjærsgaard's letter to the editor did not refer to all Somalis as criminals or otherwise as equal to paedophiles or rapists, but only argued against the fact that a Somali association is to be consulted about a bill criminalizing offences committed particularly in the country of origin of Somalis. While this is a possible interpretation of Ms. Kjærsgaard's statements, they could however also be understood as degrading or insulting to an entire group of people, i.e., persons of Somali descent, on account of their national or ethnic origin and not because of their views, opinions or actions regarding the offending practice of female genital mutilation. While strongly condemning the practice of female genital mutilation, the Committee recalls that Ms. Kjærsgaard's choice of "paedophiles" and "rapists" as examples for her comparison were perceived as offensive not only by the petitioner, but also were acknowledged to be offensive in character in the letter of 26 September 2003 from the Copenhagen police. The Committee notes that although these offensive references to "paedophiles" and "rapists" deepen the hurt experienced by the petitioner, it remains the fact that Ms. Kjærsgaard's remarks can be understood to generalize negatively about an entire group of people based solely on their ethnic or national origin and without regard to their particular views, opinions or actions regarding the subject of female genital mutilation. It further recalls that the Regional Public Prosecutor and the police from the outset excluded the applicability of section 266 (b) to Ms. Kjærsgaard's case, without basing this assumption on any measures of investigation.

7.5 Similarly, the Committee considers that the fact that Ms. Kjærsgaard's statements were made in the context of a political debate does not absolve the State party from its obligation to investigate whether or not her statements amounted to racial discrimination. It reiterates that the exercise of the right to freedom of expression carries special duties and responsibilities, in particular the obligation not to disseminate racist ideas,[16] and recalls that general recommendation XXX recommends that States parties take "resolute action to counter any tendency to target, stigmatize, stereotype or profile, on the basis of race, colour, descent, and national or ethnic origin, members of 'non-citizen' population groups, especially by politicians [...]."[17]

7.6 In the light of the State party's failure to carry out an effective investigation to determine whether or not an act of racial discrimination had taken place, the Committee concludes that articles 2, paragraph 1 (d), and 4 of the Convention have been violated. The lack of an effective investigation into the

_____

[16] General recommendation XV (1993) on organized violence based on ethnic origin (art. 4), para. 4.
[17] General recommendation XXX (2004) on discrimination against non-citizens, para. 12.

petitioner's complaint under section 266 (b) of the Criminal Code also violated his right, under article 6 of the Convention, to effective protection and remedies against the reported act of racial discrimination.

8. The Committee on the Elimination of Racial Discrimination, acting under article 14, paragraph 7, of the Convention on the Elimination of All Forms of Racial Discrimination, is of the view that the facts before it disclose violations of article 2, paragraph 1 (d), article 4 and article 6 of the Convention.

9. The Committee on the Elimination of Racial Discrimination recommends that the State party should grant the petitioner adequate compensation for the moral injury caused by the above-mentioned violations of the Convention. Taking into account the Act of 16 March 2004, which, inter alia, introduced a new provision in section 81 of the Criminal Code whereby racial motivation constitutes an aggravating circumstance, the Committee also recommends that the State party should ensure that the existing legislation is effectively applied so that similar violations do not occur in the future. The State party is also requested to give wide publicity to the Committee's opinion, including among prosecutors and judicial bodies.

10. The Committee wishes to receive from Denmark, within six months, information about the measures taken to give effect to the Committee's opinion.

# Communication No. 38/2006

*Submitted by*: Zentralrat Deutscher Sinti und Roma et al. (represented by counsel, the Zentralrat Deutscher Sinti und Roma and Verband Deutscher Sinti und Roma—Landesverband Bayern).
*Alleged victim*: The petitioners.
*State party*: Germany.
*Date of adoption of Opinion:* 22 February 2008.
*Subject matter:* Racial discriminatory statements against Sinti and Roma published in a journal; access to effective mechanisms of protection; effective investigation.
*Procedural issues:* Status of "victim"; substantiation for purposes of admissibility; exhaustion of domestic remedies.
*Substantive issues:* Right to an effective remedy; prohibition of disseminating ideas based on racial superiority; prohibition of public authorities or public institutions, national or local, to promote or incite racial discrimination.
*Articles of the Convention:* 4 (a) and (c), 6, and 14 (7) (a).
*Finding:* No violation.

*Opinion*

1.1 The petitioners are the association *Zentralrat Deutscher Sinti und Roma*, acting on its own behalf and on behalf of G.W.; the association *Verband Deutscher Sinti und Roma—Landesverband Bayern*; R.R.; and F.R. They claim to be victims of a violation by Germany[1] of articles 4 (a) and (c); and 6 of the Convention on the Elimination of All Forms of Racial Discrimination. They are represented by counsel.

1.2 In conformity with article 14, paragraph 6 (a), of the Convention, the Committee transmitted the communication to the State party on 14 September 2006.

*Factual background*

2.1 Detective Superintendent G.W., a member of the Sinti and Roma minority, wrote an article entitled "Sinti and Roma—Since 600 years in Germany", which was published in the July/August 2005 issue of the journal of the

---

[1] The Convention was ratified by Germany on 16 May 1969 and the declaration under article 14 was made on 30 August 2001.

Association of German Detective Police Officers (BDK), "The Criminalist". In the October 2005 issue of the journal, a letter to the editor written by P.L., vice-chairman of the Bavarian section of the BDK and Detective Superintendent of the Criminal Inspection of the city of Fürth, was published as a reply to Weiss' article. The authors indicated that "The Criminalist" was a journal distributed to more than 20,000 members of one of the biggest police associations in Germany. The text of the letter by P.L. reads as follows:

*"With interest I read the article by colleague W., himself also a Sinti, but I cannot leave this non-contradicted. Even at a time where minority protection is put above everything else and the sins of the Nazi-era still affect ensuing generations, one need not accept everything that is so one-sided. As an officer handling offences against property I have dealt repeatedly with the culture, the separate and partly conspirative way of living as well as the criminality of the Sinti and Roma. We infiltrated the life of criminal gypsies through working groups and also with the help of undercover agents ("Aussteiger"). We were told by Sinti that one feels like a "maggot in bacon" ("Made im Speck") in the welfare system of the Federal Republic of Germany. One should use the rationalization for theft, fraud and social parasitism without any bad conscience because of the persecution during the Third Reich. The references to the atrocities against the Jews, homosexuals, Christians and dissidents who did not become criminal, were considered not relevant. As W. states there are no statistics about the share of criminal Sinti and Roma in Germany. If they existed, he could not have written such an article. But it is sure that this group of people, even if only about 100,000, occupies the authorities disproportionately by comparison.*

*Who for example commits nationwide thefts largely to the disadvantage of old people? Who pretends to be a police officer to steal the scarce savings of pensioners which were hidden for the funeral in the kitchen cupboard or in the laundry locker? Who shows disabled and blind persons tablecloths and opens the door to accomplices? What about the trick with the glass of water and the paper trick? Is it really a prejudice when citizens complain about the fact that Sinti drive up with a Mercedes in front of the social welfare office? Is it not true that hardly any Roma works regularly and pays social insurance? Why does this group separate itself in such a way*

*and for example intermarries without the registry office? Why are fathers of Sinti children not named to the youth welfare office? (...)*

*Whoever does not want to integrate but lives from the benefits of and outside this society cannot claim a sense of community. My lines do not only reflect my opinion as I learned by talking to many colleagues. They are not only a record of prejudices, generalizations ("Pauschalisierungen") or accusations but a daily reality of criminal activity.*

*It is totally incomprehensible for me that a police officer who knows about this situation is so partial in his argumentation. His origins excuse him partly and his career deserves praise, but he should stick to the truth."*

2.2 The authors claimed that P.L.'s letter contained numerous discriminatory statements against Sinti and Roma. They argue that P.L. used racist and degrading stereotypes, going as far as stating that criminality was a key characteristic of Sinti and Roma. In particular, they noted that the terms "maggot" and "parasitism" were used in the Nazi propaganda against Jews and Sinti and Roma. The authors claim that such a publication fuels hatred against the Sinti and Roma community, increases the danger of hostile attitude by police officers, and reinforces the minority's social exclusion.

2.3 In November 2005, after a public protest organized by the *Zentralrat Deutscher Sinti und Roma*, the Bavarian Ministry of the Interior suspended P.L. from his function in the police commissariat of Fürth, stating that generally negative statements about identifiable groups of the population, like the Sinti and Roma in the present case, were not acceptable.

2.4 On 24 November 2005, the *Zentralrat Deutscher Sinti und Roma* and R.R. lodged a complaint with the District Attorney of Heidelberg, and on 1 December 2005, the *Verband Deutscher Sinti und Roma - Landesverband Bayern* and F.R. filed a complaint before the District Attorney of Nürnberg-Fürth. Both complaints were then transferred to the competent authority: the District Attorney of Neuruppin in Brandenburg. The District Attorney of Neuruppin dismissed the first complaint on 4 January 2006 and the second one on 12 January 2006 with the same reasoning, namely that the elements constitutive of the offence under article 130 of the German Criminal Code were missing, refusing to charge P.L. with an offence under the German Criminal Code (GCC).

2.5 On 12 January 2006, the authors lodged an appeal with the General Procurator (*Generalstaatsanwaltschaft*) of the Land of Brandenburg against the two decisions of the District Attorney of Neuruppin. This was dismissed on 20 February 2006.

2.6 On 20 March 2006, the authors appealed to the Supreme Court of Brandenburg. Their appeal was rejected on 15 May 2006. As regards the individuals, the Court found the claim to be without merits. As regards the *Zentralrat Deutscher Sinti und Roma* and *Verband Deutscher Sinti und Roma— Landesverband Bayern*, the Supreme Court found the claim inadmissible on the grounds that, as associations, their rights could only have been affected indirectly.

2.7 The authors argue that, since the judicial authorities refused to initiate criminal proceedings, German Sinti and Roma were left unprotected against racial discrimination. By so doing, the State party would be tolerating a repetition of such discriminatory practices. The authors highlight a similar case involving discriminatory public statements against Jews, in which the Supreme Court of the Land of Hessen had stated that, in the past, the terms "parasite" and "social parasitism" had been used maliciously and in a defamatory way against Jews, and held that such public statements denied members of a minority the right to be considered as equals in the community.

*The complaint*

3. The authors claim that Germany violated their rights as individuals and groups of individuals under articles 4 (a) and (c); and 6 of the Convention on the Elimination of All Forms of Racial Discrimination, as the State party does not afford the protection under its Criminal Code against publications which contain insults directed against Sinti and Roma.

*State party's observations on the admissibility and merits of the communication*

4.1 On 26 January 2007, the State party commented on the admissibility and merits of the communication. On admissibility, it submits that the *Zentralrat Deutscher Sinti und Roma* and *Verband Deutscher Sinti und Roma— Landesverband Bayern* have no standing to

submit a communication under article 14 (1) of the Convention. It submits that only individuals or groups of individuals who assert that they are victims of a violation of a right set forth in the Convention can submit communications to the Committee. Neither of these two associations claims to be a victim of State action or lack thereof, and that they cannot be accorded personal dignity. In addition, the present communication distinguishes itself from a previous decision adopted by the Committee,[2] inasmuch as the complainants here do not claim impairment of their work and do not claim to be victims as organizations.

4.2 The State party submits that all complainants have failed to substantiate their claims under article 4 (a) and (c) of the Convention, and that none of them has exhausted domestic remedies as required by article 14 (2) of the Convention. It adds that the domestic remedies include an appeal to the Federal Constitutional Court and that none of the complainants made use of this option. It would not have been clear from the outset that a constitutional complaint would fail for lack of prospect of success. The State party submits that the Brandenburg Supreme Court, in its decision of 15 May 2006, only rejected the application by the two first complainants as inadmissible because of lack of victim status. It submits that, at least in respect of the complainants that are natural persons, the Federal Constitutional Court could have examined the assessment made by the Brandenburg Supreme Court with respect to the right of freedom of expression, protected by article 5 of the German Basic Law. As regards W., the State party notes that he did not file a criminal action although this option was open to him. For that reason alone, he did not exhaust domestic remedies that were both available and potentially effective.

4.3 On the merits, the State party denies that there was a violation of articles 4, paragraph (a) and (c) and 6 of the Convention. As regards article 4 (a), it maintains that all categories of misconduct under that provision are subject to criminal sanctions under German criminal law, particularly through the offence of incitement to racial or ethnic hatred ("*Volksverhetzung*") in article 130 of the GCC.[3]

---

[2] See *The Jewish community of Oslo et al.* v. *Norway*, communication No. 30/2003, Opinion of 15 August 2005.
[3] Article 130. Incitement to racial or ethnic hatred.
(1) Whoever, in a manner that is capable of disturbing the public peace: 1. incites hatred against

In addition, the GCC contains other provisions that criminalize racist and xenophobic offences, e.g., in article. 86 (dissemination of propaganda by unconstitutional organizations) and article 86 (a) (use of symbols by unconstitutional organizations). The obligations arising from article 4, paragraph (a), of the Convention have thus been completely fulfilled by article 130 of the GCC; there is no protection gap in this respect. That some discriminatory acts are not covered by the provision is not contrary to the Convention. The list in article 4, paragraph (a), of the Convention does not enumerate all conceivable discriminatory acts, but rather acts in which violence is used or where racist propaganda is the goal.

4.4 The State party adds that in accordance with general recommendation XV, paragraph 2, article 130 of the GCC is effectively enforced. Under German criminal law, the principle of mandatory prosecution applies, by which prosecutorial authorities must investigate a suspect ex officio and bring public charges when necessary. In the present case, the State party submits that prosecutorial authorities reacted immediately, and that the situation was investigated thoroughly until the proceedings were terminated by the District Attorney of Neuruppin.

4.5 Regarding the interpretation and application of article 130 of the GCC, the State party notes that the District Attorney of Neuruppin, the Brandenburg General Prosecutor and the Brandenburg Supreme Court did not find that the elements constitutive of the offences under article 130 or article 185 GCC were met. These decisions show that not every discriminatory statement fulfils the elements of the offence of incitement to racial or ethnic hatred, but that there must

---

segments of the population or calls for violent or arbitrary measures against them; or 2. assaults the human dignity of others by insulting, maliciously maligning, or defaming segments of the population, shall be punished with imprisonment from three months to five years. (2) Whoever: 1. with respect to writings (art. 11, para. 3), which incite hatred against segments of the population or a national, racial or religious group, or one characterized by its folk customs, which call for violent or arbitrary measures against them, or which assault the human dignity of others by insulting, maliciously maligning or defaming segments of the population or a previously indicated group: (a) disseminates them; (...).

be a certain targeting element for incitement of racial hatred. The State party recalls that all the above decisions referred to the wording of the letter as "inappropriate", "tasteless" and "outrageous and impudent". The State party points out that the central question is whether the courts correctly interpreted the relevant provisions of the GCC. It recalls that States parties have some discretion in the implementation of the obligations arising from the Convention and particularly as regards the interpretation of their national legal standards. With respect to the consequences suffered by P.L., it indicates that disciplinary measures were indeed taken against him.

4.6 On article 4 (c) of the Convention, the State party denies that it violated this provision. It points to the fact that "The Criminalist" is not published by a public authority or institution, but by a professional association. The author of the letter published it as a private person, and not in his official capacity. The absence of public charges and of a conviction by public prosecutorial authorities cannot be considered to be a violation of this provision, as promotion or incitement requires significantly more than merely refraining from further criminal prosecution.

4.7 Finally, with respect to article 6 of the Convention, the State party maintains that in the present case the criminal prosecution authorities acted quickly and fully discharged their obligation of effective protection through the prompt initiation of an investigation against P.L. After an in-depth examination the authorities concluded that the offence of incitement to racial or ethnic hatred could not be established and closed the proceedings.

*Petitioner's comments*

5.1 On 7 March 2007 the authors commented on the State party's submission. They note that the German authorities did not investigate the matter ex officio, but that they were prompted to act by a complaint from one of the complainants (*Zentralrat Deutscher Sinti und Roma*). They add that, to the present day, the police union has not disassociated itself in any way from the article of P.L.

5.2 The authors claim that, although the organizations which co-authored the complaint have not been attacked by name in P.L.'s article, their own rights are harmed by such a sweeping criminalization of the entire Sinti and

Roma minority. They claim that the derogation of the social reputation of the minority has consequences for the reputation and the possibility of the organizations to exert political influence, especially since they act publicly as advocates of the minority and are funded by the State party to do so.

5.3 On exhaustion of domestic remedies, the authors claim that a complaint to the Federal Constitutional Court would not only be declared inadmissible but would have no prospect of success, based on that Court's established jurisprudence. They state that they know of no case in which the Federal Constitutional Court accepted a complaint against a decision concerning a legal enforcement procedure.

5.4 As regards the provisions of the GCC, the authors doubt that articles 130 and 185, with their strict requirements, are sufficient to combat racist propaganda effectively. They doubt that the intent of the responsible party "to incite hatred against segments of the population" (as required by art. 130) is absent in the present case, given that P.L. is a police officer.

5.5 The authors reiterate that characterizations made in the article represent an attack on the human dignity of members of the Sinti and Roma communities, and that they cannot be considered to be a "permissible statement of opinion", nor the "subjective feelings and impressions of a police officer". Had those characterizations been made against Jews, massive judicial intervention would have resulted. The authors add that the State party approves of its police officers globally criminalizing an entire population group. The approval of such public statements carries the danger that other police officers adopt a similar attitude against Sinti and Roma.

*Additional comments by the parties*

6. By submissions dated 31 May 2007 and 16 November 2007, the State party generally reiterated the points made in the initial submission. In particular, it states that article 130 of the GCC has been successfully used in the past to act against instances of extreme right-wing extremist propaganda. By submission of 27 June 2007, the complainants replied to the State party's comments, restating the arguments previously offered.

*Issues and proceedings before the Committee*

7.1 Before considering any claims contained in a petition, the Committee on the Elimination of Racial Discrimination must, in accordance with rule 91 of its rules of procedure, decide whether or not it is admissible under the Convention.

7.2 The Committee notes that two legal entities are among the authors of the complaint: the *Zentralrat Deutscher Sinti und Roma* and the *Verband Deutscher Sinti und Roma—Landesverband Bayern.* The Committee takes note of the State party's objection that, a legal person as opposed to an individual or a group of individuals is not entitled to submit a communication or to claim victim status under article 14, paragraph 1. It equally notes the authors' argument that the organizations submit the complaint on behalf of their members, as "groups of individuals" of the German Sinti and Roma community, and that their own rights are harmed by the statements in the impugned article. The Committee does not consider the fact that two of the authors are organizations to be an obstacle to admissibility. Article 14 of the Convention refers specifically to the Committee's competence to receive complaints from "groups of individuals", and the Committee considers that, bearing in mind the nature of the organizations' activities and the groups of individuals they represent, they do satisfy the "victim" requirement within the meaning of article 14 (1).[4]

7.3 On the issue of exhaustion of domestic remedies, the Committee notes that the State party argues that the complainants failed to lodge an appeal with the Federal Constitutional Court. The authors in turn maintain that such an appeal would have no prospect of success and refer to the established jurisprudence of the Court. They argue, and the State party concedes, that individuals have no right under German law to face the State to initiate criminal prosecution. The Committee has previously held that a petitioner is only required to exhaust remedies that are effective in the circumstances of the particular case.[5] It follows that, with the exception of W., the petitioners have fulfilled the requirements of article 14 (7) (a).

---

[4] See *The Jewish community of Oslo et al.* v. *Norway*, para. 7.4.
[5] See *Lacko* v. *Slovakia*, para. 6.2, and *Koptova* v. *Slovakia*, para. 6.4.

7.4 As regards W., the Committee notes that he did not file criminal charges nor was a party to the proceedings before the Brandenburg Supreme Court. Thus, the complaint is inadmissible with respect to W. because of non-exhaustion of domestic remedies.[6]

7.5 As regards article 4 (c) of the Convention, the Committee accepts the State party's contention that the BDK is a professional union and not a State organ, and that P.L. wrote the impugned letter in his private capacity. The Committee thus finds this claim inadmissible.

7.6 In light of the above, the Committee declares the case admissible inasmuch as it relates to articles 4 (a) and 6 of the Convention and proceeds to examine the merits.

7.7 On the merits, the main issue before the Committee is whether the provisions in the GCC provide effective protection against acts of racial discrimination. The petitioners argue that the existing legal framework and its application leave Sinti and Roma without effective protection. The Committee had noted the State party's contention that the provisions of its Criminal Code are sufficient to provide effective legal sanctions to combat incitement to racial discrimination, in accordance with article 4 of the Convention. It considers that it is not the Committee's task to decide in abstract whether or not national legislation is compatible with the Convention but to consider whether there has been a violation in the particular case.[7] The material before the Committee does not reveal that the decisions of the District Attorney and General Prosecutor, as well as that of the Brandenburg Supreme Court, were manifestly arbitrary or amounted to denial of justice. In addition, the Committee notes that the article in "The Criminalist" has carried consequences for its author, as disciplinary measures were taken against him.[8]

8. The Committee on the Elimination of Racial Discrimination, acting under article 14, paragraph 7, of the Convention on the Elimination of All Forms of Racial Discrimination, is of the view that the facts before it do not disclose a violation of articles 4 (a) and 6 of the Convention.

9. Notwithstanding, the Committee recalls that P.L.'s article was perceived as insulting and offensive not only by the petitioners, but also by the prosecutorial and judicial authorities who dealt with the case. The Committee wishes to call the State party's attention to (i) the discriminatory, insulting and defamatory nature of the comments made by P.L. in his reply published by "The Criminalist" and of the particular weight of such comments if made by a police officer, whose duty is to serve and protect individuals; and (ii) general recommendation XXVII, adopted at its fifty-seventh session, on discrimination against Roma.

---

[6] See POEM and FASM v. Denmark, para. 6.3.
[7] See Er v. Denmark, communication No. 40/2007, Opinion of 8 August 2007, para. 7.2.

[8] See para. 2.3.

# Communication No. 39/2006*

*Submitted by*: D.F. (not represented by counsel).
*Alleged victim*: The petitioner.
*State party*: Australia.
*Date of adoption of Opinion*: 22 February 2008.
*Subject matter*: Discriminatory act directed to New Zealand citizens residing in Australia; discrimination based on national origin.
*Procedural issues*: Substantiation for purposes of admissibility, status of "victim".
*Substantive issues*: Discrimination based on national origin; right to public health, medical care, social security and social services.
*Articles of the Convention*: 2 (1) (a) and 5 (e) (iv).
*Finding*: No violation.

\* See also *D.R.* v. *Australia*, communication No. 42/2008, Opinion of 14 August 2009.

*Opinion*

The petitioner is D.F., a New Zealand citizen now residing in Australia. He claims to be a victim of violations by Australia of article 2, paragraph 1 (a), and article 5 (e) (iv), of the International Convention on the Elimination of All Forms of Racial Discrimination. He is not represented.

*The facts as presented by the petitioner*

2.1 On 30 June 1970, at the age of 6, the petitioner and his family immigrated to Australia. As a New Zealand citizen, he was automatically deemed to be a permanent resident upon arrival and exempted from any visa requirements. In 1973, his status was that of an "exempt non-citizen" under the bilateral Trans-Tasman Travel Arrangement between Australia and New Zealand, which allows citizens of both countries to live in either country indefinitely. In 1994, the petitioner was automatically granted a Special Category Visa (SCV), which allowed him to remain indefinitely in Australia, as long as he remained a New Zealand citizen. In 1998, he was temporarily seconded overseas by his employer. He had then resided in Australia for 28 continuous years and had married an Australian. He regularly returned to Australia during his temporary absence and identifies himself as an Australian. He does not specify when he returned to Australia.

2.2 On 26 February 2001, the enactment of a bilateral social security agreement between Australia and New Zealand was announced. On the same day, the State party introduced national measures regarding social security benefits, amending the Social Security Act (1991) (SSA), and restricting access to the full range of social security payments to New Zealand citizens, unless they held permanent visas. This new act, known as the Family and Community Services Legislation Amendment (New Zealand Citizens) Act 2001, entered into force on 30 March 2001. According to the petitioner, this revised act was adopted unilaterally by the State party and not for the legitimate purpose of implementing the bilateral agreement.

2.3 The main amendment to the 1991 Act related to the meaning of the term "Australian resident", which defines eligibility for most social security benefits under the SSA. Prior to the amendment, the definition of "Australian resident" included Australian citizens, New Zealand citizens (SCV holders) and permanent visa holders. The amendment introduced a new class of non-citizen under social security law: the "protected" SCV holders, who retained their rights to social security, while all other SCV holders lost certain rights in this area. Those New Zealanders who were in Australia on 26 February 2001, and those absent from Australia on that day but who had been in Australia for a period totalling 12 months in the two years prior to that date and who subsequently returned to Australia, continued to be treated as Australian residents for the purposes of the Act, as they were now considered "protected" SCV holders. Other New Zealand citizens had to meet normal migration criteria to become an "Australian resident" for the purposes of the Act. The petitioner was not in Australia on the pertinent date and did not fulfil the transitional arrangements, as he was absent from the State party for more than 12 months in the 2 years immediately prior to and including 26 February 2001. He thus lost his status as an "Australian resident" for the purposes of the revised Act. In addition, and in conjunction with the revised Act, ministerial powers afforded under Subsection 5A (2) of the Citizenship Act 1948 were used to remove citizenship eligibility from New Zealand citizens who are not "protected" SCV holders and who do not have permanent resident status. According to the petitioner, the aim was to ensure that he was unable to regain his status as an "Australian resident" for the purpose of eligibility for social security by becoming an Australian citizen under section 5A (2) of the Citizenship Act 1948,[1] which now deprives him of eligibility for Australian citizenship.

2.4 Since the petitioner lost his status as an "Australian resident" for the purposes of social security benefits and citizenship, he is now required to apply for and obtain a permanent residence visa if he wishes to regain his previous rights. He would then be required to wait two additional years (waiting period fro new arrivals regarding eligibility for social security), even though he has already resided in Australia for over 30 years. The petitioner has not yet attempted to apply for such a visa. He argues that the new legislation places him in a precarious situation, should he become sick, injured or unemployed. Although he admits that, prior to the passage of the bill, New Zealand citizens were given preferential treatment to citizens from other countries, he argues that the withdrawal of "the positive discrimination" towards New Zealand citizens for the purposes of creating equality between them and other non-citizens was never announced as an objective of the Act in question and did not in fact achieve that aim.

2.5 In May 2006, the petitioner lodged a complaint with the Human Rights and Equal Opportunities Commission (HREOC), regarding the withdrawal of benefits and rights to social security and citizenship under the revised legislation. On 21 June 2006, his complaint was rejected, on the grounds that: it could not proceed with any complaint under the [International Convention on the Elimination of Racial Discrimination];

---

[1] Australian Citizenship Permanent Resident Status (New Zealand Citizens) Declaration 2001.

discrimination on the ground of a person's citizenship or visa status was not a ground covered under the Racial Discrimination Act (1975), and the HREOC Act does not cover complaints where the events complained of are the result of the direct operation of legislation.

*The complaint*

3. The petitioner claims that he has exhausted domestic remedies by virtue of his complaint to the HREOC. He claims that the Family and Community Services Legislation Amendment (New Zealand Citizens) Act 2001, which amended the Social Security Act (1991) (SSA), discriminated against him on the basis of his New Zealand nationality, by withdrawing entitlements to social security and citizenship, in violation of article 5 (e) (iv) of the Convention. By so doing, the State party also committed an act of racial discrimination against a group of persons, of which he is a member, in violation of article 2 (1) (a), of the Convention.

*The State party's submission on admissibility and merits*

4.1 On 1 May 2007, the State party submits that the communication is inadmissible, as the petitioner is unable to demonstrate that he is a victim of a violation of either article 2, paragraph 1 (a), or article 5 (e) (iv), of the Convention. It denies that the Family and Community Services Legislation Amendment (New Zealand Citizens) Act 2001, discriminates against New Zealand citizens living in Australia on the basis of their national origin. It submits that the Act amends legislation which previously allowed New Zealand citizens living in Australia as holders of "Special Category Visas" to receive certain social security payments without having to apply for permanent residence in Australia or Australian citizenship. Subject to transitional arrangements, New Zealand citizens arriving in the State party must now meet the definition of "Australian resident" that applies to all entrants to Australia before being eligible for certain Australian Government funded social security payments. These changes do not affect the ability of New Zealand nationals residing in Australia to have automatic access to other benefits such as employment services, health care, public housing and primary and secondary education.

4.2 According to the State party, under the terms of the new legislative amendments, no distinction is applied with respect to access to social security between New Zealand citizens and people of other nationalities who live in Australia. The limitation on the petitioner's ability to access certain social security benefits is not based on his national origin but on the fact that he is neither a permanent resident nor an Australian citizen. Previously New Zealand citizens received preferential treatment; the subsequent withdrawal of such advantages does not constitute discrimination, as it merely places New Zealand citizens on an equal footing with people of other nationalities who are neither permanent residents nor Australian citizens. It is open to the petitioner, as with all migrants to Australia, to apply for a permanent residence visa. Persons who have held a permanent residence visa for two years are eligible to receive certain social security payments, such as unemployment benefits.

4.3 The State party dismisses as misleading the allegation that New Zealand citizens who had been residing in the State party but were temporarily absent at the time the amendments came into force, i.e., 26 February 2001, "lost their rights", unlike New Zealand citizens who were present in the State party at that time and could avail themselves of the transitional arrangements in the legislative amendments. It submits that extensive transitional arrangements were put in place for New Zealand citizens temporarily absent from Australia on 26 February 2001. These arrangements provided a regime for many New Zealand citizens to continue to receive the benefits available under the pre-February 2001 arrangements. In particular, the changes did not apply to New Zealand citizens who were temporarily absent from the State party if they had been in Australia for a period, or periods, of 12 months in the previous two years immediately before 26 February 2001. For those New Zealand citizens who were intending to reside in Australia at the time of the changes, a three-month period of grace applied from 26 February 2001 (i.e., three months to commence or recommence residing in Australia). A six-month period of grace applied to those New Zealand citizens temporarily absent from Australia on 26 February 2001, and who were in receipt of social security payments. A 12-month period of grace applied to those New Zealand citizens, resident in Australia but temporarily absent, who were unable to return to Australia in the three-month period and were not in receipt of a social security payment.

4.4 On the merits, the State party submits that the petitioner has failed to substantiate his claims of racial discrimination and that the communication is thus without merit. It notes that the legislative amendments do not affect the petitioner's access to employment services, health care, public housing and primary and secondary education or family tax benefits nor do they affect the petitioner's right to obtain gainful employment in Australia. New Zealand citizens are still permitted to travel, live and work indefinitely under the terms of the Trans-Tasman Travel Arrangement. In this respect, they continue to access a significant relative advantage over citizens of other countries under the Trans-Tasman Travel arrangements.

*Petitioner's comments on State party submission*

5.1 The petitioner notes that the State party does not contest the admissibility of the complaint as far as it concerns exhaustion of domestic remedies. He argues that although the State party admits that, as a New Zealand citizen he can remain "indefinitely" within the State party, he is not a "permanent resident" for the purposes of the amended legislation. In his view, any distinction based on whether a person holds a SCV (as in his case) or a permanent residence visa is a distinction based upon "legal formalism"—as it ignores the fact that both visas afford indefinite/ permanent residence. He argues that rather than comparing his situation to that of a minority group of non-citizens (those who do not have permission to indefinitely reside in Australia and thus never had the same rights to social security as the petitioner), his situation should be compared to that of the majority who are also indefinitely residing in Australia, i.e., Australian citizens.

5.2 In the petitioner's view, the argument of "equality through deprivation" is illogical, as it can be used to claim that any group is "advantaged" over a more deprived group. He notes that the State party has used this argument on several recent occasions years to justify the progressive limitation of the right to social security for non-citizens, including, the extension of a two-year waiting period to New Zealand citizens before they became eligible to receive most social security benefits, to ensure that they too are now "equal" to permanent visa holders. As to the suggestion that he may apply for a "permanent visa", he argues that the possibility of changing his immigration status to one that is less discriminatory does not address the claim that he is discriminated against because of his current status as the holder of a Special Category Visa—particularly given that his current visa pertains directly to his nationality. In addition, there is no guarantee that he will be granted one.[2]

5.3 The petitioner affirms that New Zealand citizens retain other advantages under the terms of the Trans-Tasman Travel Arrangement, but, in his view, this does not absolve the State party from discriminating against New Zealand citizens under the new amended legislation. As to the arguments on the transitional arrangements, he submits that the fact that he was potentially eligible for a limited period to apply to regain his rights does not negate the fact that he lost them in the first place. In any event, he argues that the deadline to regain his rights was inadequate, as was the method of informing those who were absent from the State party at the date of the legislative amendments. He notes that the State party failed to offer any observations pertaining to the deprivation of his eligibility for Australian citizenship based upon his nationality.

*Issues and proceedings before the Committee*

6.1 Before considering any claim contained in a communication, the Committee on the Elimination of all Forms of Racial Discrimination must decide, pursuant to article 14, paragraph 7 (a), of the Convention,

---

[2] He refers to the Committee's concluding observations on Australia (sixty-sixth session, 21 February-11 March 2005), in which it raised a concern with respect to the limited public services offered to refugees and stated that "differential treatment based on citizenship or immigration status would constitute discrimination if the criteria for such differentiation, judged in the light of the objectives and purposes of the Convention, are not applied pursuant to a legitimate aim, and are not proportional to the achievement of that aim. He also refers to general comment No. 3 on article 9 of the [International] Covenant on Economic, Social and Cultural Rights, which states that "......any deliberately retrogressive measures [...] would require the most careful consideration and would need to be fully justified by reference to the totality of the rights provided for in the Covenant and in the context of the full use of the maximum available resources."

whether or not the current communication is admissible.

6.2 The Committee notes that the State party has not disputed the petitioner's argument that he has exhausted domestic remedies and thus considers that he has done so, for purposes of admissibility.

6.3 The Committee notes the State party's argument that the petitioner has not demonstrated that he is a "victim" within the meaning of the Convention, as his lack of entitlement to social security benefits was not based on his national origin but rather on the fact that he is neither a permanent visa-holder nor an Australia citizen. The Committee notes, however, that the petitioner was affected by the amendments to the Act in question and thus could be considered a "victim" within the meaning of article 14, paragraph 1, of the Convention. The question of whether the petitioner was discriminated against on the basis of his national origin and the State party's arguments in that regard relate to the substance of the petition and, for this reason, should be considered on the merits. The Committee finds no other reason to consider the petition inadmissible and therefore moves to its consideration on the merits.

7.1 The Committee notes that the State party contests the petitioner's claim that he is discriminated against on the basis of his national origin with respect to the distribution of social security benefits. It observes that prior to the entry into force of the Family and Community Services Legislation Amendment (New Zealand Citizens) Act of 2001, New Zealand citizens residing in Australia had the same rights to social security benefits as Australian citizens. These benefits were granted to New Zealand citizens on the basis of their nationality. Pursuant to the Act of 2001, these benefits were withdrawn from the petitioner and all other New Zealand citizens who were not entitled to, or in possession of, "protected" Special Category Visas or permanent resident visas. Thus, the distinction which had been made in favour of New Zealand citizens no longer applied. The provisions of the Act of 2001 did not result in the operation of a distinction, but rather in the removal of such a distinction, which had placed the petitioner and all New Zealand citizens in a more favourable position compared to other non-citizens.

7.2 The provisions of the 2001 Act put New Zealand citizens on a more equal footing with other non-citizens, and they can apply on the same terms for a permanent resident's visa or Australian citizenship, the receipt of either of which would bring them within the definition of "Australian resident" for the purposes of receiving the benefits in question. In this context, the Committee notes that the petitioner has neither argued nor demonstrated that the implementation of the Act of 2001 itself results in distinctions based on national origin. He has failed to show that his national origin would be an impediment to receiving a permanent resident's visa or Australian citizenship, that the majority of visa holders are non-citizens of national origins different to himself, or indeed that he has been refused such a visa on the grounds of his national origin. For these reasons, the Committee concludes that the Act in question does not make any distinctions based on national origin and thus finds no violation of either article 5 (e) (iv) or 2 (1) (a) of the Convention.

8. The Committee on the Elimination of Racial Discrimination, acting under article 14, paragraph 7 (a), of the International Convention on the Elimination of All Forms of Racial Discrimination, is of the opinion that the facts as submitted do not disclose a violation of any of the provisions of the Convention.

# Communication No. 40/2007

*Submitted by*: Murat Er (represented by counsel, Ms. Line Bøgsted).
*Alleged victim*: The petitioner.
*State party*: Denmark.
*Date of adoption of Opinion:* 8 August 2007.
*Subject matter:* Ethnic discriminatory practice in school with respect to educational and training possibilities; access to effective mechanisms of protection; legal aid.
*Procedural issues:* Inadmissibility *ratione personae*; status of "victim"; substantiation for purpose of admissibility; right to education.
*Substantive issues:* Discrimination based on ethnic grounds; right to an effective remedy against acts of racial discrimination; right to an effective investigation.
*Articles of the Convention:* 2 (1) (d), 5 (e) (v) and 6.
*Finding:* Violation (arts. 2 (1) (d), 5 (e) (v) and 6).

*Opinion*

1. The communication, dated 20 December 2006, is submitted by Mr. Murat Er, a Danish citizen of Turkish origin born in 1973. He claims that Denmark has violated article 2, paragraph 1 (d); article 5, paragraph (e) (v); and article 6 of the International Convention on the Elimination of All Forms of Racial Discrimination. He is represented by counsel, Ms. Line Bøgsted.

*Factual background*

2.1 The petitioner was a carpenter student at Copenhagen Technical School at the time of the events. As part of the study programme, students were offered the possibility of doing traineeships in private companies. On 8 September 2003, the petitioner accidentally saw a note in a teacher's hands, where the words "not P" appeared next to the name of a potential employer applying for trainees to work in his company. When asked about the meaning of that note, the teacher explained to him that the P stood for "perkere" ("Pakis") and that it meant that the employer in question had instructed the school not to send Pakistani or Turkish students for training in that company. That same day, the petitioner complained orally to the school inspector, arguing that the school collaborated with employers that did not accept trainees of a certain ethnic origin. The inspector stated that is was the school's firm policy "not to accommodate wishes from employers only to accept ethnic Danes as trainees" and that he was not aware of cases where this had happened. On 10 September 2003, the petitioner filed a written complaint with the school management board. He claims that, ever since his complaint was filed, he has been treated badly by school staff and students and was assigned to projects which he would normally not be expected to carry out at the school.

2.2 From October to December 2003, the petitioner worked as a trainee in a small carpenter business. Upon his return to the school, he was informed that he had to start a new traineeship with another company four days later, although he was enrolled in a course that started two weeks later. A journeyman, with whom he worked at this new company, informed him that the School had asked the company if it would accept to send "a Black". Back at the school, he started a new course. On the second day of the course, he asked the teacher for help with some drawings, which he did not obtain. He contends that the frustration experienced as a result of the discriminatory treatment received at the school led to his dropping the course and becoming depressive. He sought medical help and was referred to Bispebjerg Hospital, where he was treated with antidepressants. He abandoned the idea of becoming a carpenter and started working as a home carer.

2.3 The petitioner contacted an independent institution, the Documentation and Advisory Centre on Racial Discrimination (DACoRD), and asked for assistance. He complained that the school had agreed to the employer's request and stated that he had experienced reprisals from the school staff since he had complained about this. DACoRD then filed a complaint on behalf of the petitioner to the Complaints Committee on Ethnic Equal Treatment (established under Act No. 374, of 28 May 2003, on Ethnic Equal Treatment), arguing that the school's practice consisting in agreeing to employers' requests to send only trainees of Danish origin constituted direct discrimination.

2.4 The Complaints Committee examined the case and exchanged correspondence with the school and with DACoRD. In the correspondence, the school admitted that unequal treatment based on ethnicity might have occurred in isolated cases, but that this was not the general practice of the school. By decision of 1 September 2004, the Complaints Committee considered that, in that particular case, a staff member of the school had followed discriminatory instructions and thus violated section 3 of the Danish Act on Ethnic Equal Treatment. It specified, however, that section 3 was not violated by the school as such. The Committee further considered that section 8 of the referred Act (prohibition of reprisals for complaints aimed at enforcing the principle of equal treatment) did not appear to have been violated, although it noted that it did not have the competence to interrogate witnesses where evidence was lacking. It concluded that this issue was for the Danish tribunals to determine and recommended that free legal aid be granted for the case to be brought before a court.

2.5 A civil claim was filed in the City Court of Copenhagen, seeking compensation of DKr 100,000 (€13,500 approximately) for moral damages incurred as a result of ethnic discrimination. On 29 November 2005, the City Court considered that the evidence produced did not prove that either the school or its staff members were willing to meet discriminatory requests from employers and that, therefore, there was no reason to set aside the inspector's statement. It further found that the petitioner was not among the students to whom a traineeship was to be allocated on 8 September 2003 as he was undergoing an aptitude test between 1 September and 1 October after having failed the first main course and could only subsequently be considered for a traineeship, which he obtained as of 6 October 2003. It concluded that the petitioner could not be considered to have been subjected to differential treatment on the basis of his race or ethnic origin, nor that he was a victim of reprisals by the defendant because of the complaint filed by him. The petitioner contends that, under Act on Ethnic Equal Treatment, the burden of proof should have been on the staff member and not on him.

2.6 The petitioner appealed the judgement of the Copenhagen City Court to the High Court of Eastern Denmark. He did not obtain legal aid to appeal the case and DACoRD subsequently assisted him to appeal the case. One of the witnesses called before the High Court was a school staff member in charge of contacts between the school and potential employers. He stated that he had chosen not to send a student of ethnic origin other than Danish to the company, because "the school had received before negative feedbacks from students of other ethnic origin who had been training with the company. They had felt maltreated because employees at the company had used abusive language." The school argued that the complainant had not experienced reprisals as a consequence of his complaint, but that he simply was not qualified enough to be sent for training. In the petitioner's view, this argumentation is irrelevant, since the school had already admitted to have refrained from sending students of an ethnic background other than Danish to certain employers. The High Court decided that it had not been proved that the complainant had been subjected to discrimination or had experienced reprisals as a consequence of his complaint and confirmed the judgement of the City Court. According to the complainant, the High Court based its decision on the statement made by the school that the complainant did not have the necessary qualifications to be sent to training. The school was acquitted and the complainant was required to pay the procedural costs amounting to DKr 25.000 (€3,300 approximately). This amount was covered by DACoRD.

2.7 Under Danish law, a case can only be tried twice before national courts. If the case is of significant importance, there is the possibility to apply for leave to appeal to the Supreme Court. After the judgement of the High Court of Eastern Denmark, the complainant indeed applied for leave to appeal. On 5 December 2006, his application was dismissed.

*The complaint*

3.1 The petitioner claims that Denmark has violated article 2, paragraph 1 (d); article 5 (e) (v); and article 6 of the Convention.

3.2 He contends that, as a consequence of the school's discriminatory practice, he was not offered the same possibilities of education and training as his fellow students and no remedies were allegedly available to address this situation effectively, in violation of article 5 (e) (v) of the Convention. Furthermore, he experienced a financial loss as a result of national procedures.

3.3 The petitioner claims that Danish national legislation does not offer effective protection to victims of discrimination based on ethnicity, as required by article 2, subparagraph 1 (d) of the Convention, and does not meet the requirements of article 6. According to the petitioner, this resulted in his claims being dismissed. He further claims that the legislation is not interpreted by Danish courts in accordance with the Convention, since the concept of shared burden of proof and the right to obtain an assessment of whether discrimination based on ethnicity has taken place are not enforced.

*State party's observations on the admissibility and merits of the communication*

4.1 On 17 April 2007, the State party submitted observations on the admissibility and merits of the case. It claims that the communication is inadmissible *ratione personae* because the petitioner is not a "victim" for the purposes of article 14 of the Convention. It refers to the Human Rights Committee's case-law on article 1 of the Optional Protocol to the International Covenant on Civil and Political Rights on "victim status".[1] Under this case-law, the victim must show that an act or an omission of a State party has already adversely affected his or her enjoyment of a right or that such an effect is imminent, for example, on the basis of existing law and/or judicial or administrative practice. The State party submits that its alleged failure to provide effective protection and effective remedies against the reported act of racial discrimination does not constitute and imminent violation of the petitioner's rights under the articles of the Convention invoked.

4.2 The State party claims that the complaint is based on the Copenhagen Technical School's alleged practice of complying with discriminatory requests from certain employers who apparently refused to accept trainees with an ethnic origin other than Danish for traineeships. However, the State party contends that the petitioner was never in a position where he was directly and individually subjected to and/or affected by this alleged discriminatory practice and therefore has no legal interest in contesting it. It notes that the reason why the applicant did not start his traineeship in September 2003 was, as established by both the Copenhagen City Court and the High Court of Eastern Denmark, solely his lack of professional qualifications. He had failed the examination after his first year of training and was thus ineligible for a traineeship in September 2003 but had to undergo a one-month aptitude test at the

---

[1] The State party invokes the Human Rights Committee's Views in *E.W. et al.* v. *Netherlands*, communication No. 429/1990, of 8 April 1993, para. 6.4; *Bordes and Temeharo* v. *France*, communication No. 645/1995, of 22 July 1996. para. 5.5; and *Aalbersberg et al.* v. *Netherlands*, communication 1440/2005, of 12 July 2006, para. 6.3.

School. It concludes that the School's treatment of the applicant with regard to the traineeship was merely based on objective criteria. In the State party's view, this statement is confirmed by the fact that the petitioner started a traineeship on 6 October 2003, after having completed the relevant aptitude test.

4.3 The State party maintains that, even if it were concluded that the School and/or certain staff members acted in a racially discriminatory manner in some cases when allocating traineeships to students, there was no discrimination in the petitioner's case and had thus no existing or imminent effects on the applicant's enjoyment of his rights under the Convention.

4.4 On the merits, the State party contends that both the protection offered to the applicant and the remedies available to address his claim of racial discrimination fully satisfy the Convention's requirements under articles 2, paragraph 1 (d); 5 (e) (v) and 6. It notes that the Convention does not guarantee a specific outcome of the complaints of alleged discrimination but rather sets out certain requirements for the national authorities' processing of such cases. The judgements of both the City Court and the High Court are based on the Danish Act on Ethnic Equal Treatment, which offers comprehensive protection against racial discrimination under Danish law. It notes that this Act entered into force on 1 July 2003 to implement EU Council Directive 2000/43/EC, yet it is not the only instrument that recognizes the principle of equal treatment. The State party adapted its legislation back in 1971 to meet its obligations pursuant to the Convention.[2]

4.5 According to the State party, the petitioner's submissions, particularly his claims under article 2, paragraph 1 (d) and article 6 of the Convention, are phrased in abstract and general terms. It recalls the Human Rights Committee's established practice that, when examining individual complaints under the Optional Protocol, it is not its task to decide in abstract whether or not the national law of a State party is compatible with the Covenant, but only to consider whether there is or has been a violation of the Covenant in the

particular case submitted to it.[3] It further recalls that the issue is to determine whether the applicant was offered effective protection and remedies against an alleged and concrete act of racial discrimination. It considers that the more general and abstract issues raised by the petitioner should more rightly be dealt with by the Committee, in connection with the examination of Denmark's periodic report under article 9 of the Convention.

4.6 The State party recalls that article 2, paragraph 1 (d), is a policy statement and that the obligation contained therein is, by its nature, a general principle. In the State party's view, this article does not impose concrete obligations on the State party and, even less, specific requirements on the wording of a possible national statute on racial discrimination. On the contrary, State parties enjoy a significant margin of appreciation in this regard. Concerning article 5 (e) (v), the State party notes that, although being more concrete in obliging States parties to guarantee equality before the law in relation to education and training, it also leaves a significant margin of appreciation to them with regard to the implementation of this obligation.

4.7 The State party notes that the Act on Ethnic Equal Treatment offers individuals a level of protection against racial discrimination which, in certain aspects, such as the rule of shared burden of proof of section 7 and the explicit protection against victimization of section 8, goes further than the protection required by the Convention. It notes that this law was effectively implemented by both national courts in examining the petitioner's case. It further notes that both the City Court and the High Court thoroughly assessed the evidence submitted and heard the petitioner and all key witnesses. Therefore, these Courts had an adequate and informed basis for assessing whether the petitioner had been a victim of racial discrimination. The State party adds that the petitioner's complaint was also examined by the Complaints Committee for Ethnic Equal Treatment and, even if this does not constitute an "effective remedy" within the meaning of article 6, by the Technical School at a Manager's meeting, which resulted in a warning to the training instructor and a written reply to the petitioner.

---

[2] The State party refers to its initial and second report to [the Committee] (CERD/C/R.50/Add.3 and CERD/C/R.77/Add.2).

[3] The State party refers to the Human Rights Committee's Views in *MacIsaac* v. *Canada*, para. 10.

4.8    According to the State party, the fact that the applicant was not granted legal aid in the High Court proceedings does not imply that these proceedings cannot be considered an effective remedy.

4.9    With regard to the petitioner's claim that the Danish courts do not interpret Danish legislation in accordance with the Convention, the State party notes that this is a general statement and does not refer to the petitioner's own case.[4] It further notes that, in any event, it is not the Committee's task to review the interpretation of Danish law made by national courts. Nevertheless, the State party contends that both national courts in the petitioner's case delivered reasoned decisions and applied the rule of shared burden of proof. It recalls that this rule, recognized in section 7 of the Danish Act on Ethnic Equal Treatment, provides for a more favourable burden of proof for alleged victims of discrimination than the Convention. It provides that if a person presents facts from which it may be presumed that there has been direct or indirect discrimination, it is incumbent on the other party to prove that there has been no breach of the principle of equal treatment. By contrast, under the Convention, it is up to the applicant to provide prima facie evidence that he or she is a victim of a violation of the Convention.[5] The State party concludes that the fact that the petitioner's complaint under the Act invoked was unsuccessful does not imply that this instrument is ineffective.

*Petitioner's comments*

On 28 May 2007, the petitioner challenged the State party's argument that because he did not prove that he was more qualified than the 14 students who obtained a traineeship in September 2003 he could not be considered as a victim. He notes that, when a traineeship was earmarked for "Danes", the number of traineeships left to students of non-Danish origin was reduced accordingly, being discriminated de facto irrespective of whether they could in the end obtain one of the remaining internships or not. He claims that this fact was not taken into consideration by the High Court, which only decided on the issue of whether the petitioner was qualified and thus eligible for the traineeship in September 2003. He contends that, by not making any assessment on whether or not race discrimination took place, the Danish Court violated his right to an effective remedy guaranteed by articles 2 and 6, in relation to article 5 (e) (v), of the Convention.

5.1    The petitioner contends that the fact that the teacher at the Copenhagen Technical School admitted before the High Court that he chose not to send a student of non-Danish origin to the company shows that the principle of equal treatment was violated.

*Issues and proceedings before the Committee*

*Decision on admissibility*

6.1    Before considering any claims contained in a petition, the Committee on the Elimination of Racial Discrimination must, in accordance with rule 91 of its rules of procedure, decide whether or not it is admissible under the Convention.

6.2    The Committee notes the State party's allegation that the communication is inadmissible *ratione personae* because the petitioner does not qualify as a victim under 14 of the Convention. It further notes the Human Rights Committee's Views invoked by the State party with regard to the "victim status" and the State party's contention that the petitioner was not individually affected by the school's alleged discriminatory practice of complying with employers' requests to exclude non-ethnic Danish students from being recruited as trainees because he did not qualify for a traineeship in September 2003 and that he therefore has no legal interest in contesting it.

6.3    The Committee does not see any reason not to adopt a similar approach to the concept of "victim status" as in the Human Rights Committee's Views referred to above, as it has done in previous occasions.[6] In the case under examination, it notes that the existence of an alleged discriminatory school practice consisting in fulfilling employers' requests to exclude non-ethnic Danish students from traineeships would be in itself sufficient to justify that all non-ethnic Danish students at the school be considered as potential victims

---

[4] The State party invokes the Committee's Views in *Michel Narrainen* v. *Norway*, communication No. 3/1991, of 15 March 1994, paras. 9.4 and 9.5.
[5] The State party invokes the Committee's Views in *C.P.* v. *Denmark*, paras. 6.2 and 6.3; and *K.R.C.* v. *Denmark*, communication No. 23/2002, of 14 August 2002, para. 6.2.

[6] In this regard, see the Committee's Opinion in *The Jewish community of Oslo and others* v. *Norway*, para. 7.3 in fine.

of this practice, irrespective of whether they qualify as trainees according to the school's rules. The mere fact that such a practice existed in the school would be, in the Committee's view, enough to consider that all non-ethnic Danish students, who are bound to be eligible for traineeships at some point during their study programme, be considered as potential victims under article 14, paragraph 1, of the Convention. Therefore, the Committee concludes that the petitioner has established that he belongs to a category of potential victims for the purposes of submitting his complaint before the Committee.

*Consideration on the merits*

7.1 The Committee has considered the petitioner's case in the light of all the submissions and documentary evidence produced by the parties, as required under article 14, paragraph 7 (a), of the Convention and rule 95 of its rules of procedure. It bases its findings on the following considerations.

7.2 The petitioner claims that Danish national legislation does not offer effective protection to victims of ethnic discrimination as required by article 2, paragraph 1 (d), of the Convention, and that Danish courts do not interpret national legislation in accordance with the Convention. The Committee notes the State party's allegation that the petitioner's claims are abstract and do not refer to his own case. It considers that it is not the Committee's task to decide in abstract whether or not national legislation is compatible with the Convention but to consider whether there has been a violation in the particular case.[7] It is also not the Committee's task to review the interpretation of national law made by national courts unless the decisions were manifestly arbitrary or otherwise amounted to a denial of justice.[8] In light of the text of the judgements of both the City Court of Copenhagen and the High Court of Eastern Denmark, the Committee notes that the petitioner's claims were examined in accordance with the law that specifically regulates and penalizes acts of racial or ethnic discrimination and that the

decisions were reasoned and based on that law. The Committee therefore considers that this claim has not been sufficiently substantiated.

7.3 In respect of the author's claim that, as a result of the school's practice, he was not offered the same possibilities of education and training as his fellow students, the Committee observes that the uncontroversial fact that one of the teachers at the school admitted having accepted an employer's application containing the note "not P" next to his name and knowing that this meant that students of non-Danish ethnic origin were not to be sent to that company for traineeship is in itself enough to ascertain the existence of a de facto discrimination towards all non-ethnic Danish students, including the petitioner. The school's allegation that the rejection of the petitioner's application for traineeship in September 2003 was based on his academic records does not exclude that he would have been denied the opportunity of training in that company in any case on the basis of his ethnic origin. Indeed, irrespective of his academic records, his chances in applying for an internship were more limited than other students because of his ethnicity. This constitutes, in the Committee's view, an act of racial discrimination and a violation of the petitioner's right to enjoyment of his right to education and training under article 5, paragraph e (v), of the Convention.

7.4 With regard to the petitioner's allegation that the State party failed to provide effective remedies within the meaning of article 6 of the Convention, the Committee notes that both national Courts based their decisions on the fact that he did not qualify for an internship for reasons other than the alleged discriminatory practice against non-ethnic Danes—namely, that he had failed a course. It considers that this does not absolve the State party from its obligation to investigate whether or not the note "not P" written on the employer's application and reported to be a sign recognized by a school teacher as implying exclusion of certain students from a traineeship on the basis of their ethnic origin, amounted to racial discrimination.[9] In the light of the State party's failure to carry out an effective investigation to determine whether or

---

[7] *Vid.* the Human Rights Committee's Views in *MacIsaac* v. *Canada*, para. 10

[8] *Vid.* the Human Rights Committee's Views in *Mulai* v. *Guyana*, communication No. 811/1998, para. 5.3; *Smartt* v. *Guyana*, communication No. 867/1999, para. 5.7; *Arutyunyan* v. *Uzbekistan*, communication No. 917/2000, para. 5.7, among others.

---

[9] In this regard, see the Committee's Opinion in *Mohammed Hassan Gelle* v. *Denmark*, communication No. 34/2004, of 6 March 2006, para. 7.5.

not an act of racial discrimination had taken place, the Committee concludes that articles 2, paragraph 1 (d), and 6 of the Convention have been violated.

8. In the circumstances, the Committee on the Elimination of Racial Discrimination, acting under article 14, paragraph 7 (a), of the International Convention on the Elimination of All Forms of Racial Discrimination, is of the opinion that the facts as submitted disclose a violation of articles 2, paragraph 1 (d); 5, paragraph (e) (v); and 6 of the Convention by the State party.

9. The Committee on the Elimination of Racial Discrimination recommends that the State party grant the petitioner adequate compensation for the moral injury caused by the above-mentioned violations of the Convention. The State party is also requested to give wide publicity to the Committee's opinion, including among prosecutors and judicial bodies.

10. The Committee wishes to receive, within 90 days, information from the Government of Denmark about the measures taken to give effect to the Committee's Opinion.

# Communication No. 41/2008*

*Submitted by*: Mr. Ahmed Farah Jama (represented by counsel, Mr. Niels Erik Hansen).
*Alleged victim*: The petitioner.
*State party*: Denmark.
*Date of adoption of Opinion*: 21 August 2009.
*Subject matter*: Racial discriminatory statements made by a victim of a crime; effective investigation; access to effective mechanisms of protection.
*Procedural issues*: Exhaustion of domestic remedies; compatibility with the provisions of the Convention; status of "victim"; inadmissibility *ratione materiae*.
*Substantive issues*: State parties have a positive obligation to take effective action against reported incidents of racial discrimination; right to an effective remedy against acts of racial discrimination; right to an effective investigation; prohibition of disseminating ideas based on racial superiority.
*Articles of the Convention*: 2 (1) (d), 4, 6 and 14 (7) (a).
*Finding:* No violation.

* See also *Saada Mohamad Adan* v. *Denmark*, communication No. 43/2008, Opinion of 13 August 2010.

*Opinion*[1]

1.1 The petitioner is Mr. Ahmed Farah Jama, a Somali citizen living in Denmark, born in 1963. He claims to be a victim of violations by Denmark of article 2, paragraph 1 (d), article 4 and article 6 of the International Convention on the Elimination of All Forms of Racial Discrimination. He is represented by counsel, Mr. Niels Erik Hansen.

1.2 In conformity with article 14, paragraph 6 (a), of the Convention, the Committee transmitted the communication to the State party on 3 March 2008.

*The facts as submitted by the petitioner*

2.1 On 18 February 2007, the Danish newspaper *Sobdagsavisen* published an interview with Ms. Pia Merete Kjærsgaard, a member of parliament and the leader of the Danish People's Party. Among other issues, she referred to an incident which had taken place in 1998, when she was attacked in an area of Copenhagen called Norrebro by a

---

[1] Pursuant to rule 90 of the Committee's rules of procedure, Committee member Mr. Peter did not participate in the adoption of the present Opinion.

group of individuals. In particular, she said: "Suddenly they came out in large numbers from the Somali clubs. There she is, they cried, and forced the door to the taxi open and then beat me ... I could have been killed; if they had entered I would have been beaten up. It was rage for blood." The petitioner claims that no Somalis were involved in the incident in question, and that this was a new false accusation by Ms. Kjærsgaard against the Somalis living in Denmark.

2.2 The petitioner filed a complaint requesting the police to investigate whether Ms. Kjærsgaard's statement constituted a crime under section 266 (b) of the Criminal Code.[2] He claims that the persons who actually attacked Ms. Kjærsgaard were never arrested by the police and their identity and nationality were never established. Furthermore, at the time Ms. Kjærsgaard had not indicated that the authors of the attack were Somalis and none of the newspaper articles published or witnesses stated that Somalis were involved. He recalls that in the past Ms. Kjærsgaard had made public statements accusing Somalis of paedophilia and gang rape of Danish women.[3]

2.3 In a decision dated 25 June 2007, the Commissioner of Police, with the consent of the Regional Public Prosecutor, rejected the complaint, as it seemed unlikely that a crime had been committed. The decision indicated that the statement was a mere description of the acts that took place and that the context in which it was made had been taken into consideration. It also indicated that, because the Regional Public Prosecutor had been involved in the proceedings, any appeal against it should be forwarded to the Prosecutor-General.

2.4 The petitioner appealed to the Director of Public Prosecutions on 10 July 2007. On

18 September 2007, the Director dismissed the case, as he considered that the petitioner had no right to appeal. He held that the petitioner had neither a personal nor a legal interest in the case and therefore could not be considered a party to it. Only the parties were entitled to appeal the decision. Those reporting the crime, those affected by the crime, witnesses and so on were considered parties only if they had a direct, personal and legal interest in the matter. Lobby organizations, companies or other entities or persons handling the interests of others or the interests of the general public on an idealistic, professional, organizational or similar basis could not normally be considered parties to a criminal case, unless they had received a power of attorney from a party. Accordingly, the Documentation and Advisory Centre on Racial Discrimination (DACoRD), which was acting on behalf of the petitioner, could not be considered entitled to appeal.

*The complaint*

3.1 The petitioner claims that the absence of a proper investigation by the police and the Regional Public Prosecutor constitutes a violation of article 2, paragraph 1 (d), and article 6 of the Convention. The argument in the decision of 25 June 2007 that Ms. Kjærsgaard's statement was a mere description of the acts that took place in 1998 implied that the police had not even consulted their own files on the case. If they had, they would have learned that the suspect in the 1998 incident was a white male.

3.2 The petitioner further claims that the State party did not fulfil its obligation, under article 4 of the Convention, to take effective action regarding an act of hate speech against Somalis living in Denmark. He considers that the act in question constitutes racist propaganda and therefore falls within the scope of section 266 (b) (2) of the Criminal Code. Furthermore, he refers to a statement made by a police officer to the media according to which it was uncontested that people had swarmed out of the Somali clubs when Ms. Kjærsgaard was attacked in 1998. By confirming the false accusation made by Ms. Kjærsgaard, this statement may also constitute a violation of article 4, as it would make the accusations more credible and stir up hatred against Somalis living in Denmark.

3.3 Finally, the petitioner claims that the denial of his right to appeal violates his right to an effective remedy. The ongoing public

---

[2] This provision reads as follows:
(1)    Any person who, publicly or with the intention of wider dissemination, makes a statement or imparts other information by which a group of people are threatened, insulted or degraded on account of their race, colour, national or ethnic origin, religion or sexual inclination shall be liable to a fine or to imprisonment for a term not exceeding two years.
(2)    When the sentence is meted out, the fact that the offence is in the nature of propaganda activities shall be considered an aggravating circumstance.
[3] See *Gelle* v. *Denmark*.

statements against Somalis have a negative effect on his daily life in Denmark. A study published by the Danish Board for Ethnic Equality in 1999 indicated that Somalis living in Denmark constituted the ethnic group most likely to suffer from racist attacks in the street (verbal abuse, violent attacks, spitting in the face, etc.). As a black person of Somali origin, he has to be on the alert when he enters into public spaces, fearing racist attacks and abuse. Thus, he considers himself a victim in the present case and has a personal interest in it.

*State party's observations on admissibility and the merits*

4.1 On 3 June 2008, the State party submitted observations on the admissibility and merits of the communication. It argues that the petitioner has failed to establish a prima facie case for the purpose of admissibility and that he did not exhaust domestic remedies.

4.2 The State party states that on 16 March 2007 the Documentation and Advisory Centre on Racial Discrimination, on behalf of the petitioner, reported Ms. Kjærsgaard to the police for violation of section 266 (b) of the Criminal Code. On 25 June 2007, the Commissioner of the West Copenhagen Police decided, pursuant to section 749 (1) of the Danish Administration of Justice Act, not to initiate an investigation. The Commissioner indicated that Ms. Kjærsgaard's statement did not "constitute an aggravated insult and degradation of a group of persons that can be considered to fall within the scope of section 266 (b) of the Criminal Code. I have emphasized in particular the nature of the statement, which is a description of a specific sequence of events, as well as the context in which it was made (…). Hence, as the statement cannot be considered to fall within the scope of section 266 (b) of the Criminal Code, there is no basis for initiating any investigation". The decision was issued after endorsement by the Regional Public Prosecutor for North Zealand and West Copenhagen.

4.3 As a result of the appeal filed by DACoRD on behalf of the petitioner, the Director of Public Prosecutions obtained an opinion from the Regional Public Prosecutor dated 20 July 2007. The Prosecutor stated, inter alia, that in his view the statements did not fall within the scope of section 266 (b) of

the Criminal Code, whether or not it could actually be proved who had assaulted Ms. Kjærsgaard in 1998. Accordingly, it would have made no difference to his decision on the matter if he had had police reports on the 1998 incident or on the questioning of Ms. Kjærsgaard at his disposal.

4.4 The communication should be declared inadmissible in its entirety because the petitioner has failed to establish a prima facie case. One of the themes of the interview with Ms. Kjærsgaard to the *Sondagsavisen* dealt with what it is like to have to live under police protection and, in that connection, the 1998 incident was mentioned. The statements are in the nature of a description of a specific sequence of events, as part of a description of how Ms. Kjærsgaard perceived the incident. She only stated in the interview that the attackers came out from "the Somali clubs", but did not express any attitude or make any degrading statement about persons of Somali origin. The statements in question therefore cannot be considered racially discriminating, and they thus fall outside the scope of article 2, paragraph 1 (d), article 4 and article 6 of the Convention.

4.5 In the communication to the Committee, the petitioner referred to a statement of Ms. Kjærsgaard ("I could have been killed; if they had got in, I would have been beaten to a pulp at least. It was a killing rage.") This statement was not included in the complaint lodged by the petitioner with the police, nor was it subsequently reported to the Danish authorities. Since the applicant has thus not exhausted domestic remedies in this respect, this part of the communication should be declared inadmissible.

4.6 It appears that the petitioner considers himself to be a victim of a racist attack and that he has an interest in the case because the ongoing statements affect his life in a negative way. According to section 267 (1) of the Criminal Code, any person who violates the personal honour of another by offensive words or conduct or by making or spreading allegations of an act likely to disparage him in the eyes of his fellow citizens, is liable to a fine or to imprisonment for a term not exceeding four months. Further, according to section 268, if an allegation has been made or disseminated in bad faith, or if the author had no reasonable ground to regard it as true, he is guilty of defamation. Pursuant to section 275 (1) of the Criminal Code, these offences are subject to private prosecution. The State party recalls the Committee's Opinion in communication No. 25/2002, *Sadic* v. *Denmark*, in which the Committee recognized that the institution of proceedings under section 267 (1) of the Criminal Code could be regarded as an effective remedy which the petitioner had failed to exhaust. It also recalls communication No. 34/2004, *Gelle* v. *Denmark*, where the Committee held that the case in question concerned statements that were made squarely in the public arena and that it would thus be unreasonable to expect the petitioner to institute separate proceedings under the general provision of section 267, after having unsuccessfully invoked section 266 (b) in respect of circumstances directly implicating the language and object of that provision. Finally, the State party recalls the decision of the Human Rights Committee declaring inadmissible communication No. 1487/2006, *Ahmad* v. *Denmark*, concerning the publication of an article called "The Face of Muhammad" in a Danish newspaper on 30 September 2005. The Director of Public Prosecutions decided against bringing criminal prosecutions in respect of the publications at issue pursuant to sections 140 and 266 (b) of the Criminal Code. Subsequently, Mr. Ahmad, on behalf of the Islamic Community of Denmark, instituted private criminal proceedings against the editors of the newspaper under sections 267 and 268 of the Code. Eventually, the editors were acquitted. The judgement was subsequently appealed to the High Court, where the case was still pending when the Human Rights Committee declared it inadmissible for failure to exhaust domestic remedies. According to the State party, this decision should be taken into account when assessing whether the present communication should be declared inadmissible. It does not follow from article 2, paragraph 1 (d), and article 6 of the Convention that the petitioner is entitled to a specific remedy. The crucial factor is that a remedy is available.

4.7 Regarding the merits, the State party finds that no violation of article 2, paragraph 1 (d), article 4 or article 6 took place. The assessment carried out by the Commissioner of the West Copenhagen Police fully satisfies the requirements that can be inferred from the Convention as interpreted in the Committee's practice. The question in the present case was solely whether Ms. Kjærsgaard's statements could be considered to fall within the scope of section 266 (b) of the Criminal Code. There were thus no problems with the evidence and the public prosecutor simply had to perform a legal assessment of the statements in question. This legal assessment was thorough and adequate, although it did not have the outcome sought by the petitioner. In his refusal to initiate an investigation, the public prosecutor placed particular emphasis on the nature of Ms. Kjærsgaard's statements as a description of a specific sequence of events and on the fact that the statements were made as part of Ms. Kjærsgaard's description of the 1998 events.

4.8 According to the guidelines on the investigation of violations of section 266 (b) of the Criminal Code, issued by the Director of Public Prosecutions, "in cases where a report of a violation of section 266 (b) of the Criminal Code is lodged with the police, the person who issued the written or oral statement should normally be interviewed, inter alia, to clarify the purpose of the statement, unless it is obvious that section 266 (b) of the Criminal Code has not been violated". The reason why the case files concerning the 1998 incident were not reviewed and that Ms. Kjærsgaard was not interviewed is that the statements did not fall within the scope of the said section, regardless of whether it could be proved who had allegedly assaulted her in 1998. Ms. Kjærsgaard simply stated that her attackers came out from "the Somali clubs", and did not make any disparaging or degrading remarks about persons of Somali origin. In that light, obtaining the police reports on the 1998 incident was irrelevant to the decision on the matter. Nothing in the present case could provide the public prosecutor with a basis for establishing that Ms. Kjærsgaard had criminal intent to make disparaging statements about a specific group of people. Consequently, the public prosecutor's handling of the case satisfies the requirements that can be inferred from article 2, paragraph 1 (d), and article 6 of the Convention, taken together with the Committee's practice.

4.9 The State party rejects the claim that by confirming the false accusation made by Ms. Kjærsgaard, the police may also be in violation of article 4. The fact that the Commissioner dismissed the report cannot be taken to mean that it was determined whether the statements about the 1998 incident were true or false. In fact, the Commissioner did not give any opinion on this matter because he considered that the statements fell outside the scope of section 266 (b).

4.10 Regarding the petitioner's claim that neither he nor DACoRD was able to appeal the Commissioner's decision, the Convention does not imply a right for citizens to appeal the decisions of national administrative authorities to a higher administrative body. Nor does the Convention address the question of when a citizen should be able to appeal a decision to a superior administrative body. Hence, the Convention cannot be considered a bar to a general rule to the effect that it is normally only the parties to a case or others with a direct, essential, individual and legal interest in the case who are entitled to appeal a decision about criminal prosecution.

4.11 The State party refers to Notice No. 9/2006 issued by the Director of Public Prosecutions, according to which police commissioners must notify him of all cases in which a report of a violation of section 266 (b) is dismissed. This reporting scheme builds on the ability of the Director of Public Prosecutions, as part of his general supervisory powers, to take a matter up for consideration to ensure proper and uniform enforcement of section 266 (b). In the present case, the Director found no basis for exceptionally disregarding the fact that neither DACoRD nor the applicant was entitled to appeal the decision. Furthermore, in its appeal, DACoRD did not give any reason, either in its own right or on behalf of the petitioner, as to why it considered itself entitled to appeal. The State party concludes that the petitioner did have access to an effective remedy.

*Petitioner's comments on the State party's submission*

5.1 On 18 August 2008, the petitioner commented on the State party's submission. He held that Ms. Kjærsgaard's description of the 1998 events was incorrect, as nobody (Somalis or non-Somalis) came out of the Somali clubs when she arrived in her taxi. No Somalis were involved, either as bystanders or aggressors, and no Somalis participated in the planning and execution of the attack. Refugees from Somalia have been one of the main targets, along with other groups, of the ongoing racist propaganda of the Danish People's Party. In spite of this, the police did not acknowledge that the statement was false.

5.2 In connection with the claims related to articles 2 and 6 of the Convention, the police should have interviewed Ms. Kjærsgaard in the course of the investigation in order to clarify why her statement was different from that made in 1998. At that time she had not indicated that her attackers came out of the Somali clubs. Furthermore, he insists that in being denied the right to appeal he was also denied the right to an effective remedy.

5.3. The petitioner disagrees with the State party's argument that no prima facie case has been established. As to the argument that domestic remedies were not exhausted in connection with Ms. Kjærsgaard's statement that "she could have been killed", the petitioner confirms that no such statement was included in his report to the police. However, the police could have included it in its investigation, as it was mentioned in the article in question. The decision by the police not to investigate further means that they did not find a violation in connection with that phrase either.

5.4 The petitioner argues that his case is not comparable to communication No. 1487/2006, *Ahmad* v. *Denmark*, submitted to the Human Rights Committee. This communication concerns religious discrimination against Islam and thus does not fall within the scope of the Convention. Furthermore, in communication No. 1487/2006, the legal standing of the authors in connection with the appeal was never questioned.

5.5 Regarding the State party's observations on the merits, the petitioner rejects the argument that Ms. Kjærsgaard's statement does not fall within the scope of section 266 (b) of the Criminal Code. False accusations against an ethnic group have always been covered by that provision, as well as by article 4 of the Convention. If the public prosecutor had consulted the 1998 file, it would not have been "obvious", as the State party suggested, that the statement did not fall within the scope of section 266 (b).

*Issues and proceedings before the Committee*

*Consideration of admissibility*

6.1 Before considering any claim contained in a communication, the Committee on the Elimination of All Forms of Racial Discrimination must decide, pursuant to article 14, paragraph 7 (a), of the Convention, whether or not the communication is admissible.

6.2 With regard to the State party's objection that the petitioner failed to establish a prima facie case for the purposes of admissibility, the

Committee observes that Ms. Kjærsgaard's statement was not of such a character as to fall ab initio outside the scope of article 2, paragraph 1 (d), article 4 and article 6 of the Convention. The Committee also notes the petitioner's claim that the ongoing public statements against Somalis have a negative effect on his daily life and considers that he satisfies the "victim" requirement within the meaning of article 14, paragraph 1, of the Convention. It thus follows that the petitioner has sufficiently substantiated his claims for the purposes of admissibility.

6.3 Regarding the petitioner's claim that he was not given the opportunity to appeal the decision of the police commissioner, the Committee does not consider it within its mandate to assess the decisions of domestic authorities regarding the appeals procedure in criminal matters. This part of the communication is therefore inadmissible *ratione materiae* under article 14, paragraph 1, of the Convention.

6.4 On the issue of exhaustion of domestic remedies, the State party claims that part of Ms. Kjærsgaard's statement was not included in the petitioner's report to the police, in particular the sentences: "I could have been killed; if they had got in, I would have been beaten to a pulp at least. It was a killing rage." The Committee considers, however, that these sentences are closely linked to those in which she referred to the authors of the attack. Even if they were not referred to specifically by the petitioner, they are part of the claim which constituted the gist of his report to the police. Accordingly the Committee does not share the State party's view that the petitioner did not exhaust domestic remedies with respect to that part of the statement.

6.5 The Committee takes note of the State party's argument that the applicant is not entitled to a specific remedy, and that private prosecution is possible under sections 267 (1) and 268 of the Criminal Code. The Committee notes, however, that the statements were made in the public arena, which is the central focus of both the Convention and section 266 (b) of the Criminal Code, and that the petitioner's choice of remedy was not a controversial issue at the national level. It would thus be unreasonable to require the petitioner to initiate also proceedings under sections 267 (1) and 268, after having unsuccessfully invoked section 266 (b) in respect of circumstances directly implicating the language and object of that provision.[4]

6.6 In the absence of any further objections to the admissibility of the communication, the Committee declares the communication admissible, insofar as it relates to the State party's alleged failure fully to investigate the incident.

*Consideration of the merits*

7.1 Acting under article 14, paragraph 7 (a), of the International Convention on the Elimination of All Forms of Racial Discrimination, the Committee has considered the information submitted by the petitioner and the State party.

7.2 The issue before the Committee is whether the State party fulfilled its positive obligation to take effective action against reported incidents of racial discrimination, having regard to the extent to which it investigated the petitioner's complaint under section 266 (b) of the Criminal Code. This provision criminalizes public statements by which a group of people are threatened, insulted or degraded on account of their race, colour, national or ethnic origin, religion or sexual inclination.

7.3 The Committee recalls its earlier jurisprudence[5] according to which, it does not suffice, for the purposes of article 4 of the Convention, merely to declare acts of racial discrimination punishable on paper. Rather, criminal laws and other legal provisions prohibiting racial discrimination must also be effectively implemented by the competent national tribunals and other State institutions. This obligation is implicit in article 4 of the Convention, under which States parties undertake to adopt immediate and positive measures to eradicate all incitement to, or acts of, racial discrimination. It is also reflected in other provisions of the Convention, such as article 2, paragraph 1 (d), which requires States to prohibit and bring to an end, by all appropriate means, racial discrimination, and article 6, which guarantees to everyone effective protection and remedies against any acts of racial discrimination.

---

[4] See *Quereshi* v. *Denmark*, communication No. 33/2003, Opinion of 9 March 2005, para. 6.3, and *Gelle* v. *Denmark*, para. 6.3.
[5] See *Gelle* v. *Denmark*, paras. 7.2 and 7.3.

7.4 The Committee notes the petitioner's claim that the reference in Ms. Kjærsgaard's statement, in the newspaper interview published on 17 February 2007, to the fact that her aggressors in the 1998 incident came out of the Somali clubs constituted an act of racial discrimination, as no Somalis were involved in the incident in question. The Committee also notes that the Commissioner of the West Copenhagen Police asserts that he examined the claim and concluded that Ms. Kjærsgaard's statement was merely a description of a specific sequence of events, in that she stated that the aggressors came out of the Somali clubs but did not make any disparaging or degrading remarks about persons of Somali origin. The Committee considers that, on the basis of the information before it, the statement concerned, despite its ambiguity, cannot necessarily be interpreted as expressly claiming that persons of Somali origin were responsible for the attack in question. Consequently, without wishing to comment on Ms. Kjærsgaard's intentions in making the statement, the Committee cannot conclude that her statement falls within the scope of article 2, paragraph 1 (d), and article 4 of the Convention, or that the investigation conducted by the national authorities into the 1998 incident did not meet the requirements of an effective remedy under the Convention.

8. In the circumstances, the Committee on the Elimination of Racial Discrimination, acting under article 14, paragraph 7 (a), of the International Convention on the Elimination of All Forms of Racial Discrimination, considers that it is not in a position to state that there has been a violation of the Convention by the State party.

9. On the basis of rule 95, paragraph 1, of its rules of procedure, the Committee would nevertheless like to draw attention to earlier recommendations formulated in the course of its consideration of individual communications, in which it called on States parties to:

- Ensure that the police and judicial authorities conduct thorough investigations into allegations of acts of racial discrimination as referred to in article 4 of the Convention[6]

- Draw attention of politicians and members of political parties to the particular duties and responsibilities incumbent upon them pursuant to article 4 of the Convention with regard to their speeches, articles or other forms of expression in the media.[7]

---

[6] *Dragan Durmic* v. *Serbia and Montenegro*, communication No. 29/2003, Opinion of 6 March 2006.
[7] *Kamal Quereshi* v. *Denmark*, communication No. 27/2002, Opinion of 19 August 2003; *P.S.N.* v. *Denmark*, communication No. 36/2006, Decision of 8 August 2007; *A.W.R.A.P.* v. *Denmark*, communication No. 37/2006, Opinion of 8 August 2007.

# II. Decisions declaring a communication inadmissible

## Communication No. 5/1994

*Submitted by*: C.P. (the petitioner is not represented by counsel).
*Alleged victim*: The petitioner and his son, M.P.
*State party*: Denmark.
*Declared inadmissible:* 15 March 1995.
*Subject matter:* Dismissal on racial grounds; discrimination based on colour and race grounds; physical violation and psychological harassment; effective investigation; access to effective mechanism of protection.
*Procedural issues:* Exhaustion of domestic remedies; substantiation for purpose of admissibility.
*Substantive issues:* Right to an effective remedy against acts of racial discrimination; right to an effective investigation; right to equal treatment before the tribunals and all other organs administering justice.
*Articles of the Convention:* The petitioner did not invoke specific provisions of the Convention.

*Decision on admissibility*

1. The author of the communication is C.P., an American citizen of African origin living in Roskilde, Denmark. He submits the communication on his behalf and on behalf of his son, and contends that they have been the victims of racial discrimination by the municipal and police authorities of Roskilde and the Danish judicial system. He does not invoke specific provisions of the International Convention on the Elimination of All Forms of Racial Discrimination.

*The facts as submitted by the author*

2.1 The author is an African American, who has been residing in Denmark since 1963; he married a Danish citizen in 1963, who later left him and from whom he is now divorced. From 1964 to 1972, he worked for a chemicals company in Roskilde; from 1972 to an unspecified date, he worked for Kodak Inc., as shop steward in a warehouse. In September 1990, he was elected shop steward at the Roskilde Technical School. He contends that starting in October 1990, students of the school began to display signs of racism towards him; the school authorities allegedly did not intervene. Mr. P. claims that a number of students, with the blessing of their teacher, carved a racially offensive inscription and cartoon into a red brick. The inscription ran approximately as follows: "A coal black man hanging from a gallows, with large red lips". Under this was inscribed the word "nigger". This brick and other, similar ones, allegedly were openly displayed in the author's working area. Again, the school authorities failed to intervene and allowed the display to continue.

2.2 On 19 November 1990, the author participated in a meeting of the School Staff Council; at the meeting, he showed two of the bricks and asked the school's support in fighting or suppressing this form of racism. To his surprise, the director of the school criticized him for raising the issue; no measures were taken to identify the students responsible for the "display". The author adds that after the meeting, the school director, head teacher and technical manager refused to talk to him.

2.3 In January 1991, the author was informed that he was to leave immediately, with 10 minutes' notice only, the area where he had been working since being hired by the school. He attributes this to the hostile and discriminatory attitude of the school superintendent and others towards him. Still in January 1991, the author was asked to carry out certain tasks in the school cafeteria, during student breaks. Here, he allegedly was again confronted with the racist remarks and slogans of the students directed towards him; when he asked the school director to be removed from the area, the latter refused. In May 1991, after what the author refers to as "months of racial harassment", the school director and technical manager dismissed him.

2.4 As to the events concerning his son, the author submits the following: on 20 July 1991, the author's son M., then 15 years old, was stopped on his bicycle at a traffic light by a group of four young men aged 17 and 18, who severely beat him, using, inter alia, beer bottles. M. sustained a number of injuries (nose, front, cheeks and jaw), which have since necessitated numerous plastic surgery interventions; the last such intervention was in 1994. According to the author, all four men had previously made racist slurs and remarks to his son and that, in 1988, they had tried to drown him in a lake in a public park. This previous incident had been reported to the police which did not, according to the author, investigate it but dismissed it as a "boyish joke".

2.5 The author immediately reported the incident of 20 July 1991 to the police. He complains that the police requested to see his residence permit and a copy of his rental agreement instead of swiftly investigating the matter; according to him, the police was reluctant to investigate the incident expeditiously and thoroughly, which allegedly had to do with his colour. Two of his son's assailants were briefly kept in police custody for interrogation; another was remanded in custody for another week.

2.6 The author claims that the court proceedings against his son's aggressors were biased, and that the defendants were allowed to "distort" the evidence in the case. Eventually, one received a suspended prison sentence of 60 days, whereas two others were sentenced to pay 10 daily fines of 50 and 100 Danish kroners (DKr), respectively. According to the author, the outcome of the case was at odds with the medical evidence presented and the doctor's testimony in court. Mr. P. complains about an alleged "judicial cover-up" of the case, noting that the mother of one of the defendants works for the Roskilde District Court. The author's attempts to have the case removed from the docket of the Roskilde District Court and moved to another venue in Copenhagen were unsuccessful. In his initial submission, the author does not state whether he appealed the sentence against his son's aggressors pronounced by the District Court.

2.7 Concerning his dismissal from the Roskilde Technical School, the author notes that he filed a complaint for "racial harassment and unlawful dismissal". This complaint was heard on 8 and 9 April 1992, 11 months after the dismissal; it appears that, initially, the case was to be heard in January 1992. The author asserts that the school director and the technical manager "conspired" to distort and blur all the evidence. The judge dismissed the author's complaint, in a reasoned judgement of 29 pages, adding that Mr. P. was not entitled to monetary compensation but to have his court and legal fees waived. According to the author, the judge refused to grant leave to a higher tribunal. On 10 June 1992, therefore, the author wrote to the Attorney-General, who advised him to submit the case to the Civil Rights Department. By letter dated 3 February 1993, the Department replied that the deadline for filing an appeal had expired. The author suspects that, since he had told his legal representative that he wanted to appeal, all the parties involved are "conspiring that he [should] not bring a racism case against ... the Danish Government".

2.8 Finally, the author refers to a malpractice suit which he filed against his lawyer. It transpires from his submissions that a panel of lawyers and judges, which included a judge of the Danish Supreme Court, has also dismissed this complaint.

*The complaint*

3.1 The author complains that he and his son have been victims of racial discrimination on the part of the Roskilde police and judicial authorities, and concludes that the judicial system and legal profession have shown much solidarity in covering up and dismissing his own and his son's case. He contends that there is no domestic law which would protect non-citizens and non-whites from racial harassment and unlawful dismissal in Denmark.

3.2 The author seeks: (a) a ruling under whose terms he is given a new hearing in his suit for unlawful dismissal against the Roskilde Technical School; (b) the Committee's recommendation that the aggressors of his son be re-indicted and prosecuted/tried once again for the offence of 20 July 1991; and (c) a condemnation of the attitude of the police and judicial authorities involved in the case.

4.1 In its submission under rule 92 of the Committee's rules of procedure, the State party divides the complaint into the suit for unlawful dismissal filed by Mr. P. and the criminal proceedings against the presumed aggressors of his son.

4.2 As to the first issue, the State party observes that, in April 1992, the Roskilde Court heard the complaint filed by the author on 19 November 1991 with a request that he be awarded DKr 100,000 for unlawful dismissal, and that it delivered its judgement on 5 May 1992. It notes that the author's claim, based on section 26 of the Liability for Damages Act, was founded partly on the argument that the Technical School had not taken any measures in connection with the appearance of the bricks with typically racist motives, partly on the claim that the school had remained passive vis-à-vis the author's request to discuss the matter in the Cooperation Committee, partly on the claim that the school had reacted to the author's grievances by transferring him to a post including work as a canteen watchman, and that the school had later dismissed him without any valid reason.

4.3 The State party notes that the Court, in its judgement, found that the author had not submitted the matter involving the display of the bricks to the school authorities until several weeks after Mr. P. had first seen the bricks. This delay, the Court held, contributed significantly to impeding the investigations into who was responsible for the display. On that ground, it concluded that the mere fact that investigations were slack was not in itself sufficient to hold the school liable for damages.

4.4 The Court, in its judgement, characterized as "very unfortunate" the failure of the school to take up Mr. P.'s complaints for detailed discussion of the incident in the Cooperation Committee when asked to do so, but found that this alone did not give rise to liability for damages. The Court further held that, at the time of Mr. P.'s transfer to another post, his dismissal would have been justified for financial reasons. The Court argued that the school could not be blamed for having tried to keep Mr. P. at work through transfer to another job which, in the judges' opinion, was not "obviously degrading", as claimed by the author.

4.5 The Court further observed that the fact that it did not become known until the examination of witnesses during the court hearing that the principal of the school had indeed had one of the bricks in his possession and had shown them to some of his assistants could not—however unfortunate this might appear—be deemed an unlawful act giving rise to the liability of the school.

4.6 With regard to the issue of exhaustion of domestic remedies by Mr. P., the State party gives the following information:

Pursuant to section 368 of the Administration of Justice Act, the author could appeal the judgement of the Roskilde Court to the Eastern Division of the Danish High Court.

Under section 372 (1), the time allowed for appeal is four weeks from the day the judgement is given. Sections 372 (2) and 399 (2) regulate some exceptions to this rule and allow for appeals even after the expiration of this period.

4.7 By letter of 25 May 1992 addressed to the Ministry of Justice, the author outlined the circumstances which led to the proceedings before the Roskilde Court and its judgement in the case. No information was given in this letter as to when judgement had been given, nor were details given about the nature of the legal action. On 9 June 1992, the Ministry of Justice informed the author that it could not intervene in, or change, decisions handed down by courts of law. In this letter, the Ministry advised the author that he could appeal the judgement to the Eastern Division of the High Court and informed him about the statutory deadlines for the filing of such an appeal.

4.8 On 10 June 1992, the author petitioned the Department of Private Law in the Ministry of Justice for permission to appeal after the expiration of the period allowed for appeal (sect. 372 (2) of the Administration of Justice Act). The Department then obtained the documents in the case as well as a statement from the author's lawyer, P.H. In a letter dated 18 September 1992, P.H. stated that he had sent a copy of the judgement of 5 May to the author on 6 May 1992, advising him that, in his opinion, there was not ground for appeal. As the lawyer did not hear from Mr. P., he wrote to him again on 19 May, requesting him to contact him telephonically. According to the lawyer, Mr. P. did not contact him until after the expiration of the appeal deadline, informing him that he indeed did want to appeal the judgement; in this connection, the author told P.H. that he had not reacted earlier because he had been in the United States. The lawyer then explained the operation of section 372 of the Administration of Justice Act to him.

4.9 After completing its review of the case, the Department of Private Law refused, by letter dated 3 February 1993, to grant permission to appeal the judgement of the Court of Roskilde to the Eastern Division of the Danish High Court. Against this background, the State party contends that the author's complaint must be declared inadmissible on the ground of non-exhaustion of domestic remedies. It is due to the author's own actions and/or negligence that the judgement of 5 May 1992 was not appealed in time.

4.10 In this context, the State party notes that Mr. P. contacted the Department of Private Law once again on the same matter on 7 January 1994. His letter was interpreted by the Department as a request for reconsideration of the issue. By letter of 16 March 1994, the Department maintained its decision of 3 February 1993. By letter of 7 June 1994 addressed to the Department of Private Law rather than to the Supreme Court of Denmark, the author applied for legal aid for the purpose of filing an application with the Supreme Court, so as to obtain permission for an extraordinary appeal under section 399 of the Administration of Justice Act. On 9 August 1994, the Department informed him that an application to this effect had to be examined at first instance by the County of Roskilde, where his application had thus been forwarded to.

4.11 With regard to the events of 20 July 1991 involving the author's son, the State party refers to the transcript of the hearing before the Court of Roskilde, which shows that the incident opposing M.P. to three young residents of Roskilde was thoroughly examined, and evidence properly evaluated, by the Court. It notes that during the proceedings, medical certificates were obtained concerning the injuries sustained by M.P. On 25 November 1991, the Chief Constable of Roskilde filed charges against the three offenders, M.M.H., A.A.O. and J.V.B. The case was heard before the Roskilde Court with the assistance of a substitute judge of the City Court of Copenhagen, as one of the accused was the son of a clerk employed by the Roskilde Court. Additionally, there were two lay judges, as the case involved an offence punishable by the loss of liberty

(sect. 686 (2) of the Administration of Justice Act).

4.12 On 27 January 1992, the Court of Roskilde handed down its judgement in the case. The Chief Constable of Roskilde found the punishment imposed on M.M.H. (60 days' suspended prison sentence) too lenient. He therefore recommended to the public prosecutor for Zealand that the sentence against Mr. H. be appealed to the Eastern Division of the High Court, with a view to having an unconditional prison term imposed on Mr. H. The public prosecutor followed the advice and appealed, and the Eastern Division of the High Court, composed of three professional and three lay judges, heard the case on 3 June 1992. The Court concluded that given the violent nature of Mr. H.'s attack on M.P., an unconditional prison sentence of 40 days should be imposed.

4.13 As regards Mr. P.'s allegations submitted to the Committee on behalf of his son, the State party argues that they are inadmissible, partly because they fall outside the scope of the Convention, partly because they are manifestly ill-founded. It notes that the communication does not give any details about the nature of the violations of the Convention in relation to the way in which the authorities and tribunals handled the criminal case against the three persons accused of violence against M.P.

4.14 The State party denies that, because of the race and colour of M.P., the courts gave the three offenders a lighter sentence than others would have received for similar use of violence. It points out that no importance whatsoever was attached, in the proceedings either before the Roskilde Court or those before the Eastern Division of the High Court, to this element. It is submitted that on the contrary, both the courts and the police of Roskilde took the case against the three individuals accused of aggressing M.P. very seriously: this appears both from the sentence imposed on Mr. H. and from the fact that he was remanded in custody after the incident, upon order of the Court of Roskilde of 21 July 1991.

4.15 The State party further recalls that the prosecution authorities felt that the sentence of the Court of Roskilde was too lenient with regard to one of the aggressors, which is why this sentence was appealed to the Eastern Division of the High Court, which increased the sentence from 60 days' imprisonment (suspended) to 40 days' unconditional imprisonment. In this connection, it is noted that an unconditional sentence is exactly what the prosecution had called for initially.

4.16 Finally, as regards the question of damages to M.P., the State party notes that in the judgement of 27 January 1992 of the Roskilde Court, he was awarded DKr 3,270, which Mr. H. was required to pay. According to the decision of the Eastern Division of the High Court, of 3 June 1992, Mr. H. had paid this amount by that time. Damages awarded by this sentence covered only pain and suffering, while M.P.'s request that the offenders' liability to pay damages to him should be included in the sentence was referred to the civil courts. Pursuant to section 993 (2) of the Administration of Justice Act, claims for damages may be brought before the (civil) courts for decision. The State party ignores whether the author's son has in fact instituted (civil) proceedings in this matter.

5.1 In his comments, dated 25 January 1995, the author takes issue with most of the State party's arguments and reiterates that he was denied his civil rights, as were his son's. He again refers to the trial against the three individuals who had aggressed his son as "a farce", and complains that the lawyer assigned to represent his son never told the latter what to expect, or how to prepare himself for the hearing. Mr. P. complains that the judge was biased in allowing the accused to present their version of the incident one after the other without interference from the Court. He dismisses several passages in the judgement as "directly misleading" and complains that a professional judge was allowed to ask his son "subjective questions" and using his answers against him. He further asserts that by concluding that, on the basis of the testimonies heard by the court, it was impossible to say who exactly started the fight, the Court "protect[ed] racist attitudes of the whites" and used a "camouflage excuse to find the accused innocent".

5.2 The author further refers to what he perceives as a miscarriage of justice: what exactly the miscarriage consists in remains difficult to establish, but it would appear that the author objects in particular to the way the judge interrogated his son and allowed the testimony of the accused to stand. The author strongly objects to the decision of the prosecution not to appeal the sentences against two of the accused. The author sums up the Court's attitude as follows: "I ask how can a judge determine a fair decision without hearing all the evidence or even worse just listening to the criminals explaining unless he wanted to pass a lenient sentence. Which he did. Very unprofessional".

5.3 As to the proceedings concerning the allegedly racist and unlawful dismissal from employment at the Roskilde Technical School, the author reiterates his version of the events and submits that he has "exhausted every possible known means to be heard and appeal [his] case". He contends that the school was not justified in dismissing him out of financial considerations, as it had recently expanded its facilities and could have used the services of a shop steward. He alleges that before the Court, the director of the Technical School committed perjury.

5.4 The author emphatically asserts that the delays in appealing the decision of the Roskilde Court should not be attributed to him. He notes that he had trusted his lawyer to handle the issue of the appeal; contrary to the assertion of the State party and his former representative, he contends that he did contact his lawyer to confirm that he wanted to appeal "at all cost", even though his lawyer had advised him that the chances of succeeding on appeal were slim. He blames his lawyer for having acted evasively at around the time—i.e., during the first days of June 1992—when the deadline for appealing the decision of the Court of Roskilde was approaching. Furthermore, the author once again, even if indirectly, accuses his representative of malpractice and suspects that the lawyer struck a deal with the judge not to have the venue of the case transferred to the Copenhagen High Court.

5.5 In conclusion, the author contends that the State party's submission is replete with "preposterous inconsistencies" and dismisses most of its observations as "misleading", "incorrect", "untrue" or "direct misleading". It is obvious that he contests the evaluation of evidence made by the Courts in both cases—his action against the Technical School and the criminal case against the aggressors of his son—and is convinced that the cases were dismissed because of racist attitudes of all concerned vis-à-vis himself and his son. He complains that there is "no affirmative action against racism in Denmark today".

## Issues and proceedings before the Committee

6.1 Before considering any claims contained in a communication, the Committee on the Elimination of Racial Discrimination must, in accordance with rule 91 of its rules of procedure, determine whether or not it is admissible under the International Convention on the Elimination of All Forms of Racial Discrimination.

6.2 The Committee has noted the arguments of the parties in respect of the issue of exhaustion of domestic remedies concerning Mr. P.'s claim of unlawful dismissal by the Technical School of Roskilde. It recalls that the Court of Roskilde heard the complaint on 19 November 1991 and delivered its reasoned judgement on 5 May 1992; said judgement was notified to the author by his lawyer on 6 May 1992. The author affirms that he did convey to his lawyer in time that he wanted to appeal this judgement, and he blames the lawyer for having acted negligently by failing to file the appeal within statutory deadlines. The Committee notes that the file before it reveals that the author's lawyer was privately retained. In the circumstances, this lawyer's inaction or negligence cannot be attributed to the State party. Although the State party's judicial authorities did provide the author with relevant information on how to file his appeal in a timely manner, it is questionable whether, given the fact that the author alleged to have been the victim of racial harassment, the authorities have really exhausted all means to ensure that the author could enjoy effectively his rights in accordance with article 6 of the Convention. However, since the author did not provide prima facie evidence that the judicial authorities were tainted by racially discriminatory considerations and since it was the author's own responsibility to pursue the domestic remedies, the Committee concludes that the requirements of article 14, paragraph 7 (a), of the International Convention on the Elimination of All Forms of Racial Discrimination, are not met.

6.3 As to the part of the author's case relating to the criminal proceedings against the aggressors of his son, the Committee notes that the police took these aggressors into custody after the author had reported the incident of 20 July 1991, and that the Chief Constable of the Roskilde police subsequently requested that they be criminally prosecuted. It also observes that the fact that one of the accused was the son of a Court clerk was duly taken into account, in that the authorities nominated a substitute judge from another venue to sit on the case. Moreover, it must be noted that the Chief Constable of Roskilde recommended, after judgement in the case had been passed, that the sentence against one of the offenders be appealed, with a view to increasing the sentence against Mr. H.; the public prosecutor for Zealand complied with this request, and the Eastern Division of the High Court imposed a term of unconditional imprisonment on Mr. H. After a careful review of available documents in the case of the author's son, the Committee finds that these documents do not substantiate the author's claim that either the police investigation or the judicial proceedings before the Court of Roskilde or the Eastern Division of the High Court were tainted by racially discriminatory considerations. The Committee concludes that no prima facie case of violation of the Convention has been established in respect of this part of the communication, and that, therefore, it is equally inadmissible.

7. The Committee on the Elimination of Racial Discrimination therefore decides:

(a) That the communication is inadmissible;

(b) That this decision shall be transmitted to the State party and to the author.

# Communication No. 7/1995

*Submitted by*: Paul Barbaro (the petitioner is not represented by counsel).
*Alleged victim*: The petitioner.
*State party*: Australia.
*Declared inadmissible:* 14 August 1997.
*Subject matter:* Dismissal on racial grounds; discrimination based on ethnic and national origin.
*Procedural issues:* Exhaustion of domestic remedies; substantiation for purposes of admissibility.
*Substantive issues:* Discrimination based on ethnic and national origin; right to equal treatment before the tribunals and all other organs administering justice; right to work, to free choice of employment, to just and favourable conditions of work, to protection against unemployment, to equal pay for equal work, to just and favourable remuneration.
*Articles of the Convention:* 1 (1), 5 (a) and (e) (i), and 14 (7) (a).

*Decision on admissibility*

1.    The author of the communication is Paul Barbaro, who is of Italian origin and currently resides in Golden Grove, South Australia. He contends that he has been a victim of racial discrimination by Australia, although he does not invoke the provisions of the International Convention on the Elimination of All Forms of Racial Discrimination. Australia made the declaration under article 14, paragraph 1, of the Convention on 28 January 1993.

*The facts as presented by the author*

2.1  On 25 June 1986, the author obtained temporary employment at the Casino of Adelaide, South Australia; he initially worked as a bar porter, and subsequently as an attendant. On 16 April 1987, the Liquor Licensing Commissioner (LLC) of the South Australian Liquor Licensing Commission, which is responsible for supervising the observance of the rules governing the management of the Adelaide Casino, and must ensure that its operations are subject to continued scrutiny, withdrew the author's temporary employment licence and refused to approve his permanent employment with the Casino. A hearing, during which the LLC questioned the author on a number of points and discussed his concerns, was held on 30 April 1987.

2.2  In September 1993, well over six years later, the author complained to the Australian Human Rights and Equal Opportunities Commission (HREOC), claiming that the Liquor Licensing Commissioner's decision had been unlawful under sections 9 and 15 of Australia's Race Discrimination Act of 1975. He argued, inter alia, that the Liquor Licensing Commissioner had decided against his obtaining a permanent contract because of his and his family's Italian (Calabrian) origin, because some of his relatives were allegedly involved in criminal activities, notably trafficking of illegal drugs, of which he did not know anything. Mr. Barbaro contends that this attitude effectively restricts the possibilities for employment for Italians who are not themselves criminals but who may have relatives that are. In support of his argument, the author refers to letters of support from Peter Duncan, M.P., who seriously questioned and denounced this perceived practice of "guilt by association".

2.3  The author refers to similar cases in which the ethnic background of applicants for employment in licensed casinos was adduced as a reason for not approving employment. In particular, he refers to the case of Carmine Alvaro, decided by the Supreme Court of South Australia in December 1986, who was refused permanent employment because of his family's involvement in the cultivation and sale of illegal drugs. In this case, the LLC had stated that he had been advised by the police that they had received information that one of the drug families of the area would attempt to place a "plant" at the Casino.

2.4 The HREOC forwarded the author's complaint to the South Australian Attorney-General's Department for comments. The latter informed the HREOC that the "sole reason for refusing [the author's] employment was to ensure the integrity of the Adelaide Casino and public confidence in that institution". Reference was made in this context to a report from the Commissioner of Police, which stated:

"Paul Barbaro has no convictions in this state. He is a member of a broad family group which, in my opinion, can only be described as a major organized crime group ... Eighteen members of this group have been convicted of major drug offences ... The offences are spread across four States of Australia. All are of Italian extraction. All are related by marriage or direct blood lines."

2.5 There were some discrepancies between the author's and the LLC's assertions in respect of the degree of some of the relationships, in particular the relationships established by the marriages of the author's siblings. The author emphasized that he had maintained a certain autonomy from his relatives and that he did not know personally many of the people listed in the Police Commissioner's report. He also insisted that he knew nothing of his relatives' previous drug-related offences.

2.6 On 30 November 1994, the Racial Discrimination Commissioner of the HREOC rejected the author's claims concerning his unlawful dismissal, having determined that it was the author's perceived or actual relationships with individuals who have criminal records, and not his Italian ethnic origin, which was the basis for the LLC's decision. The Race Discrimination Commissioner stated that "[T]he fact that [he] and [his] family members are of Italian origin or descent is not germane" to the solution of the case.

2.7 On 7 December 1994, the author appealed for review of the Racial Discrimination Commissioner's decision. By decision of 21 March 1995, the President of the HREOC confirmed the decision of the Racial Discrimination Commissioner, holding that there was no evidence that the author's ethnic background had been a factor in the LLC's decision.

*The complaint*

3.  Although the author does not invoke any provision of the Convention, it transpires from his communication that he claims a violation by the State party of articles 1, paragraph 1, and 5 (a) and (e) (i) of the Convention.

*State party's submission on the admissibility of the communication and author's comments thereon*

4.1 By submission of March 1996, the State party challenges the admissibility of the communication on several grounds. It first supplements the facts as presented by the author. Thus, the State party notes that when obtaining temporary employment in 1986, the author gave the Police Commissioner for South Australia written authorization to release to the LLC particulars of all convictions and other information that the Police Department may have had on him. On 25 June 1986, Mr. Barbaro acknowledged in writing that the granting of temporary employment was subject to all enquiries made concerning his application for approval as a Casino employee being concluded to the satisfaction of the LLC, and that temporary approval could be withdrawn at any time.

4.2 On 30 April 1987, the author, accompanied by his lawyer and two character witnesses, attended a hearing before the LLC, during which the LLC explained his concern that the author had an association with an organized crime group. The author was given an opportunity to comment on the evidence which had been provided to the LLC by the Police Commissioner.

4.3 In relation to the author's complaint before the HREOC, the State party notes that after the dismissal of Mr. Barbaro's complaint by the Race Discrimination Commissioner, the author gave notice of appeal to have the decision reviewed under section 24AA 9 (1) of the Race Discrimination Act (RDA), the President of the HREOC, Sir Ronald Wilson, a former High Court judge, confirmed the decision in accordance with section 24AA 2 (b) (i) of the RDA, holding that there was no evidence that the author's ethnic origin constituted a ground for the alleged discrimination.

4.4 The State party contends that the case is inadmissible as incompatible with the provisions of the Convention, on the basis of rule 91 (c) of the Committee's rules of procedure, as the Committee is said to lack the competence to deal with the communication. In this context, the State party affirms that Australian law and the RDA conform with the provisions of the Convention. The RDA was enacted by the Federal Government and implements articles 2 and 5 of the Convention by making racial discrimination unlawful and ensuring equality before the law (sects. 9 and 10). The wording of section 9 closely follows the wording of the definition of racial discrimination in article 1 of the Convention. Section 15 of the RDA implements the provisions of article 5 of the Convention in relation to employment. Moreover, the HREOC is a national authority established in 1986 for the purpose of receiving and investigating alleged breaches of the RDA. Members of the HREOC are statutory appointees and as such enjoy a high degree of independence. HREOC investigated the author's case thoroughly and found no evidence of racial discrimination.

4.5 In the light of the above, the State party argues that it would be inappropriate for the Committee to effectively review the decision of the HREOC. While it concedes that the issue of whether the decision of the HREOC was arbitrary, amounted to a denial of justice or violated its obligation of impartiality and independence, would fall within the Committee's jurisdiction, it contends that the author did not submit any evidence to this effect. Rather, the evidence contained in the transcript of the hearing before the LLC and the correspondence with the HREOC indicate that the author's claim was considered within the terms both of the RDA and the Convention.

4.6 The State party further submits that the complaint is inadmissible on the basis of lack of substantiation, arguing that the author did not provide any evidence that his treatment amounted to a "distinction, exclusion, restriction, or preference based on race, colour, descent, or national or ethnic origin which [had] the purpose or effect of nullifying or impairing the recognition, enjoyment, or exercise, on an equal footing, of human rights..." (art. 1, para. 1, of the Convention). There is said to be no evidence that the author's ethnic or national origin was a factor in the decision of the LLC to refuse a permanent appointment to the author; rather, he was concerned to fulfil his duty to ensure

that the operations of the casino were subject to constant scrutiny and to guarantee public confidence in the casino's lawful operation and management.

4.7 Finally, the State party claims that the author failed to exhaust available domestic remedies, as required by article 14, paragraph 7 (a), of the Convention, and that he had two available and effective remedies which he should have pursued in relation to his allegation of unfair dismissal. Firstly, it would have been open to the author to challenge the decision of the President of the HREOC in the Federal Court of Australia, pursuant to the Administrative Decisions (Judicial Review) Act of 1977 (ADJR Act). The State party emphasizes that the decision of the HREOC President *was* reviewable under the ADJR Act: grounds for review are listed in section 5 of the Act; they include grounds that there is no evidence or other material to justify the taking of the decision, and that the adoption of the decision was an improper exercise of power. The State party argues that this review mechanism is both available and effective within the meaning of the Committee's admissibility requirements: thus, pursuant to any application under the ADJR Act, the Court may set aside the impugned decision, refer it back to the first instance for further consideration subject to directions, or declare the rights of the parties.

4.8 According to the State party, the author could also have challenged the LLC's decision in the Supreme Court of South Australia, by seeking judicial review under Rule 98.01 of the South Australian Supreme Court Rules. Under Rule 98.01, the Supreme Court may grant a declaration in the nature of *certiorari* or *mandamus*. Under Rule 98.09, the Supreme Court may award damages on a summons for judicial review. It is submitted that an action for judicial review pursuant to Rule 98 was an available remedy in the instant case.

4.9 The State party concedes that the author was not obliged to exhaust local remedies which are ineffective or objectively have no prospect of success. It refers in this context to the decision of the Full Court of the Supreme Court of South Australia in the case of *R. v. Seckler ex parte Alvaro* ("*Alvaro's case*"), decided on 23 December 1986. The material facts of that case were similar to the author's: the respondent was the LLC of South Australia, the same person as in the author's case, and the matter at issue was the respondent's refusal to approve the plaintiff's employment. By majority, the Supreme Court of South Australia held that the plaintiff was not entitled to relief. In the State party's opinion, the judicial precedent provided by the decision in *Alvaro's case* did not excuse the author from exhausting the remedy available by way of judicial review; it adds that "unlike an established legal doctrine, a single majority judgement in a relatively new area of law does not meet the test of obvious futility required in order to countenance non-exhaustion of an available remedy".

4.10 Still in the same context, the State party rejects as too broad an interpretation the argument that exhaustion of domestic remedies cannot be required if the remedies available probably would not result in a favourable outcome. Therefore, judicial review under Rule 98 of the Supreme Court Rules is said to be both an available and an effective remedy, to which the author did not resort. The State party notes that the author did not file his claim within the six months of the grounds for review first arising (7 November 1987), as is required under Rule 98.06 of the Supreme Court Rules. Thus, while barred from pursuing this remedy now because of the expiration of statutory deadlines, the State party observes that failure to pursue the remedy in a timely manner must be attributed to the author. Reference to the jurisprudence of the Human Rights Committee is made.

5.1 In comments dated 28 April 1996, the author rebuts the State party's arguments and dismisses them as irrelevant to the solution of his case. He questions the credibility of the State party's arguments in the light of the letters of support he received from a Member of Parliament, Mr. Peter Duncan.

5.2 In the author's opinion, the Committee *does* have competence to deal with the merits of his claims. He contends that the HREOC did not examine his complaint with the requisite procedural fairness. In this context, he notes, without giving further explanations, that the RDA allows complainants to attend a hearing at some designated location to present arguments in support of the complaint, and that this did not occur in his case. The result, he surmises, led to an uninformed decision of the HREOC which was not compatible with the provisions of the Convention.

5.3 The author notes that the President of the HREOC, Sir Ronald Wilson, who dismissed his claim on 21 March 1995, had been a judge in the Supreme Court of South Australia when the decision in *Alvaro's case* was handed down in December 1986. He now argues that there was a conflict of interest on the part of the President of the HREOC, who had determined the merits of a factually comparable case in the Supreme Court of South Australia before dealing with the author's own case. In the circumstances, the author argues that the decision of the HREOC was tainted by bias and arbitrariness and that the Committee has competence to deal with his case.

5.4 The author reiterates that there is sufficient evidence to show that his case falls prima facie within the scope of application of article 1, paragraph 1, of the Convention. He argues that "[a]s with normal practices of institutionalized racism a clear and precise reason [for termination of employment] was not given nor required to be given". He further contends that it is difficult to see how the acts of State agents in his case did *not* amount to a "distinction" within the meaning of the Convention, given the terms of the Police Commissioner's report to the LLC from 1987, where it was explicitly stated that the author was "a member of a broad family group ... All are of Italian extraction". From this reasoning, the author asserts, it is clear that individuals with his background are precluded from enjoying or exercising their rights on an equal footing with other members of the community. He also refers to a judgement in the case of *Mandala and Anor* v. *Dowell Lee*, ((1983) All ER, 1062), where it was held that blatant and obviously discriminatory statements are generally not required when investigating instances of race distinctions, since direct evidence of racial bias is often disguised.

5.5 As to the requirement of exhaustion of domestic remedies, the author observes that the decision handed down by the President of the HREOC on 21 March 1995 and transmitted to him on 24 March 1995 failed to mention any possible further remedies. He notes that the RDA itself is silent on the possibility of judicial review of decisions adopted by the President of the HREOC by the Federal Court of Australia.

5.6 Finally, the author contends that the possibility of judicial review of the decision of the LLC to refuse him permanent employment under the rules of the Supreme Court of South Australia is not realistically open to him. He argues that the judgement of the Supreme Court of South Australia in *Alvaro's case does* constitute a relevant precedent for the determination of his own case, all the more so since the State party itself acknowledges that *Alvaro's case* presented many similarities to the author's. If adding the fact that the President of the HREOC who dismissed the author's appeal had previously been involved in the determination of *Alvaro's case*, the author adds, then the possibility of challenging his decision before the Supreme Court successfully was remote.

6.1 By further submission of 22 July 1996, the State party in turn dismisses as partial or incorrect several of the author's comments. It notes that the author was partial in choosing quotes from the Police Commissioner's report and that the complete quotes indicate that the operative factor in the LLC's decision concerning Mr. Barbaro's suitability for casino employment was his association with 18 members of his family who had been convicted of major drug-related offences. Ethnicity was only raised by the Police Commissioner as one factor, combined with others such as family association and the type of offences; the author's ethnic background was relevant only in so far as it assisted in defining this cluster of associations.

6.2 The State party concedes that in Australian employment practice, associates of applicants for employment are generally not considered a relevant factor in the determination of suitability for employment. In the instant case, it *was* relevant because the LLC was not an employer but a statutory officer. His statutory role was to ensure the constant scrutiny of casino operations, a role recognized by the Supreme Court of South Australia in *Alvaro's case*. In short, the LLC was entrusted with maintenance of the internal and external integrity of the casino. Like an employer, however, he was subject to the provisions of the RDA of 1975; in the instant case, the State party reiterates that the fact that there were drug offenders in the author's extended family was a proper justification for the LLC's decision.

6.3 The State party agrees in principle with the author's assertion that obvious and blatant expressions of racial discrimination are not required when investigating instances of race distinctions. It notes in this context that prohibition of indirectly discriminatory acts or unintentionally discriminatory acts is an established principle of Australian law. However, the State party re-emphasizes that decisions in Mr. Barbaro's case rested on grounds other than race, colour, descent or national or ethnic origin.

6.4 The State party contends that the author's comments raise new allegations about the fairness of the procedures before the HREOC, especially as regards his claim that he was denied due process since he was not afforded an opportunity to attend a hearing to present his complaint. The State party argues that the author did not exhaust domestic remedies in this respect and that he could have filed an application for judicial review of this allegation under the ADJR. In any event, the State party continues, procedural fairness did not require the personal attendance of Mr. Barbaro to present his complaint. In the case of the HREOC, the grounds for dismissing complaints prior to conciliation are set out in section 24 (2) of the RDA. They are:

(a) If the Race Discrimination Commissioner is satisfied that the discriminatory act is not unlawful by reason of a provision of the RDA;

(b) If the Commissioner is of the opinion that the aggrieved person does not desire that the inquiry be made or continued;

(c) If the complaint has been made to the Commission in relation to an act which occurred more than 12 months prior to the filing of the claim;

(d) If the Commissioner is of the opinion that the complaint under consideration is frivolous, vexatious, misconceived or lacking in substance.

In the author's case, the President of the HREOC dismissed the complaint on the basis of section 24 (2) (d) of the RDA.

6.5 The State party dismisses as totally unfounded the author's argument that the decision of the HREOC was biased because of an alleged conflict of interest on the part of the President of the HREOC. The State party points to the long-standing involvement of the President of the HREOC in the legal profession and adds that for someone with the profile and the background of the President of the HREOC, it is indeed likely that he will consider at different times issues which are related in law or in fact. The State party emphasizes that a previous encounter with a similar (factual or legal) issue does not result in a conflict of interest. Further evidence of bias is required, which the author has patently failed to provide.

6.6 As to Mr. Barbaro's contention that he was not informed of the availability of domestic remedies after the HREOC's decision of 21 March 1995, the State party notes that neither the Convention nor the Australian RDA of 1975 impose an obligation to indicate all available appellate mechanisms to a complainant.

6.7 Finally, concerning the letters of support sent to the HREOC on the author's behalf by a Member of Parliament, Mr. Peter Duncan, formerly a parliamentary secretary to the Attorney-General, the State party recalls that Federal Parliamentarians frequently write to the HREOC on behalf of their constituents, advocating the rights of their constituents in their role as democratically elected representatives. The State party contends that this role must be distinguished from both the investigative role of the independent HREOC and the executive role of the parliamentary secretary to the Attorney-General. In the instant case, it was clear that the M. P. acted on the author's behalf in his representative role. More importantly, the purpose of the letters was to urge a thorough investigation of the author's complaints by the HREOC. Once a final decision in the case had been taken, Mr. Duncan did not write again.

7. During its forty-ninth session, in August 1996, the Committee considered the communication but concluded that further information from the State party was required before an informed decision on admissibility could be adopted. Accordingly, the State party was requested to clarify:

(a) Whether the author would have had the opportunity, in the event that complaints under the Administrative Decisions (Judicial Review) Act and pursuant to Rule 98.01 of the Rules of the Supreme Court of South Australia had been dismissed, to appeal further to the Federal Court of Australia, or whether he could have complained directly to the Federal Court of Australia;

(b) Whether the State party consistently does, or does not, inform individuals in the author's situation of the availability of judicial remedies in their cases.

8.1 In reply, the State party notes that Mr. Barbaro would have had the opportunity to appeal to the Federal Court of Australia and subsequently the High Court of Australia in the event that a complaint under the ADJR Act had been dismissed. Under section 8, the Federal Court of Australia has jurisdiction to hear applications under the ADJR Act; applications may be filed in respect of decisions to which the Act applies, and decisions of the President of the HREOC fall within the definition of "decision(s) to which this Act applies" (sect. 3 (1)). The author thus had the right to seek judicial review of the President's decision before a single judge of the Federal Court of Australia on any of the grounds listed in section 5 of the ADJR Act relevant to his case, within 28 days of the decision of the HREOC President. If an application before a single Federal Court judge had been unsuccessful, the author would have had the right to seek leave to appeal to the full Federal Court.

8.2 If unsuccessful in the full Federal Court of Australia application, the author would have been further entitled to seek special leave to appeal to the High Court of Australia under Order 69A of the High Court Rules; criteria for granting special leave to appeal are listed in section 35A of the federal Judiciary Act 1903. If special leave to appeal were granted, a three-week period from the granting of special leave to appeal would apply for the filing of the notice of appeal.

8.3 The State party further notes that the author would have had an opportunity to appeal to the full court of the Supreme Court of South Australia and thereafter the High Court of Australia if a complaint under Rule 98.01 of the Rules of the Supreme Court of South Australia had been dismissed by a single judge (sect. 50 of the Supreme Court Act, 1935 (South Australia)). Mr. Barbaro would have had to lodge an appeal within 14 days of the single judge's decision. If an appeal to the full court of South Australia had been unsuccessful, Mr. Barbaro could have sought special leave from the High Court of Australia to appeal against the decision of the full court of the Supreme Court of South Australia pursuant to section 35 of the Federal Judiciary Act, 1903.

8.4 The State party reiterates that the Convention does not impose an obligation to indicate all available appeal mechanisms to a complainant. There is no statutory obligation to provide individuals with information about possible judicial remedies under federal or South Australian law; nor is it the practice of the federal Government or the Government of South Australia to advise individuals about possible appeal rights. There are, however, some obligations to inform individuals of their appeal rights: thus, under the federal Race Discrimination Act, 1975, where the Race Discrimination Commissioner decides not to enquire into an action in respect of which a complaint was filed, he or she must inform the complainant for that decision, of the *ratio decidendi* and of the complainant's rights to have this decision reviewed by the HREOC President (sect. 24 (3)). In Mr. Barbaro's case, this obligation was met. It is, moreover, the practice of the HREOC to advise verbally any complainant who has manifested a desire to challenge a decision of the Commission's president of other avenues of appeal. There is no evidence that the HREOC deviated from this practice in the author's case.

8.5 The State party notes that Mr. Barbaro does not appear to have sought legal advice on appeals and remedies available to him; it adds that it is common knowledge that a system of publicly funded legal aid exists in Australia, as well as a national network of Community Legal Centres, including in South Australia. Both Legal Aid and Community Legal Centres would have provided free legal advice about possible appeal mechanisms to individuals in the author's situation. Mr. Barbaro's failure to avail himself of such free legal advice cannot be attributed to the State party; reference is made to the Committee's jurisprudence that it is the author's own responsibility to exhaust domestic remedies.[1]

9.1 In his comments, the author concedes that the Race Discrimination Commissioner informed him of his right of review of her decision under section 24AA (1) of the Race Discrimination Act. He submits, however, that the President of the HREOC did not inform him of the possibilities of any avenues of appeal against his decision communicated to the author on 24 March 1995; he contends that the HREOC President, a former High Court judge,

---

[1] See *C.P.* v. *Denmark*, para. 6.2.

should have informed him of possible remedies. Mr. Barbaro adds that, as a layman, he could not have been aware of any other possible judicial remedies against the decision of the HREOC President.

9.2 The author reaffirms that an application to the Supreme Court of South Australia under Rule 98.01 of the Court's Rules would have been futile, given the Supreme Court's earlier judgement in *Alvaro's case*.

9.3 Finally, with regard to the State party's reference to the availability of legal advice from Community Legal Centres, Mr. Barbaro submits that "such assistance is only available in extreme situations and ... only of the matter involves an indictable offence".

*Issues and proceedings before the Committee*

10.1 Before considering any claims contained in a communication, the Committee on the Elimination of Racial Discrimination must decide, pursuant to article 14, paragraph 7 (a), of the Convention, whether or not the case is admissible.

10.2 The State party contends that the author's claims are inadmissible on the basis of failure to substantiate the racially discriminatory nature of the LLC's decision of May 1987. The Committee notes that the author has made specific allegations, notably in so far as they relate to passages in the report of the Police Commissioner of South Australia which had been made available to the LLC, to support his contention that his national and/or ethnic background influenced the decision of the LLC. In the Committee's opinion, the author has sufficiently substantiated, for purposes of admissibility, his claims under article 5 (a) and (e) (i), read together with article 1, paragraph 1, of the Convention.

10.3 The State party has also claimed that the author has failed to exhaust domestic remedies which were both available and effective, since he could have challenged the decision of the President of the HREOC under the Administrative Decisions (Judicial Review) Act, and the decision of the LLC pursuant to Rule 98.01 of the Rules of the Supreme Court of South Australia. The author has replied that (a) he was not informed of the availability of those remedies, and (b) that the precedent established by the judgement in *Alvaro's case* would have made an appeal to the Supreme Court of South Australia futile.

10.4 The Committee begins by noting that the author *was* legally represented during the hearing before the LLC on 30 April 1987. It would have been incumbent upon his legal representative to inform him of possible avenues of appeal after the LLC's decision to terminate the author's employment. That the author was not informed of potential judicial remedies by the judicial authorities of South Australia did not absolve him from seeking to pursue avenues of judicial redress; nor can the impossibility to do so now, after expiration of statutory deadlines for the filing of appeals, be attributed to the State party.

10.5 The Committee further does not consider that the judgement of the Supreme Court of South Australia in *Alvaro's case* was necessarily dispositive of the author's own case. Firstly, the judgement in *Alvaro's case* was a majority and not a unanimous judgement. Secondly, the judgement was delivered in respect of legal issues which were, as the State party points out, largely uncharted. In the circumstances, the existence of one judgement, albeit on issues similar to those in the author's case, did not absolve Mr. Barbaro from attempting to avail himself of the remedy under rule 98.01 of the Supreme Court Rules. Finally, even if that recourse had failed, it would have been open to the author to appeal to Federal court instances. In the circumstances, the Committee concludes that the author has failed to meet the requirements of article 14, paragraph 7 (a), of the Convention.

11. The Committee on the Elimination of Racial Discrimination therefore decides:

(a) That the communication is inadmissible;

(b) That this decision shall be communicated to the State party and to the author.

# Communication No. 9/1997

*Submitted by*: D.S. (the petitioner is not represented by counsel).
*Alleged victim*: The petitioner.
*State party*: Sweden.
*Declared inadmissible:* 17 August 1998.
*Subject matter:* Discrimination on job selection process; discrimination based on ethnic grounds; access to effective mechanism of protection.
*Procedural issues:* Exhaustion of domestic remedies.
*Substantive issues:* Right to work, to free choice of employment, to just and favourable conditions of work, to protection against unemployment, to equal pay for equal work, to just and favourable remuneration; right to an effective remedy against acts of racial discrimination; discrimination based on ethnic grounds.
*Articles of the Convention:* 2, 3, 5 (e) (i), 6 and 14 (7) (a).

*Decision on admissibility*

1. The author of the communication (initial submission dated 15 February 1997) is D.S., a Swedish citizen of Czechoslovak origin, born in 1947, currently residing in Solna, Sweden. She claims to be a victim of violations by Sweden of articles 2, 3, 5 (e) (i) and 6 of the International Convention on the Elimination of All Forms of Racial Discrimination.

*The facts as submitted by the author*

2.1 In April 1995, the National Board of Health and Welfare advertised a vacancy for a post of researcher/project coordinator with the National Board of Health and Welfare (*Socialstyrelsen*). In the vacancy announcement, the Board looked for applicants who would be able to collect and process material from investigative studies, and follow up, in the field of public health and medical care, the structure, content and quality of medical care in hospitals. The vacancy announcement stipulated that applicants for general research jobs should have a good knowledge of and experience in the subject area and a good knowledge of techniques and measures used to measure, describe, evaluate and judge the efficacy and results of an activity. Another requirement was that applicants should have a basic academic degree, if possible supplemented by further courses in the field of research and evaluation and with experience in the subject area. Other requirements included the ability to cooperate with others, power of initiative and ease of oral and written expression. Proficiency in another language was considered an additional asset.

2.2 One hundred and forty-seven individuals applied for the vacancy, including the author and S.L. On 10 November 1995, the National Board of Health and Welfare decided to appoint S.L. as researcher and project coordinator to the Board; she assumed her duties with effect from 1 October 1995. The author appealed to the Government against this decision, considering that her qualifications were superior to those of S.L., and that she had been refused the post because of her foreign origin.

2.3 On 14 March 1996, the Government annulled the National Board's decision to appoint S.L. to the post and referred the matter back to the Board for reconsideration. The Government's decision was based on the fact that at the time of S.L.'s appointment, the latter had not yet earned an academic degree (although she was studying for one at that time). Therefore, S.L. did not formally satisfy the requirements for the position as specified by the National Board in the vacancy announcement. The National Board's decision in the case was found to be formally incorrect.

2.4 Shortly afterwards, the National Board of Health and Welfare re-advertised the post of researcher to the Board. The vacancy announcement now stipulated that the Board was looking for a person to work on the MARS (Medical Access and Result System) project to assist in the collection and the processing of material from investigations and studies and in the evaluation of the public health and medical care structure. The work would involve contacts with medical experts to draw up catalogues and prepare material for multimedia presentations. As to the qualifications, the announcement now required "a basic academic degree *or equivalent*, as well as experience in the subject area". Other

requirements included the ability to cooperate and work in a team, the power of initiative, and ease of oral and written expression. A good knowledge of English was required.

2.5 A total of 83 individuals applied for the re-advertised post, inter alia, the author and S.L. The National Board of Health and Welfare invited four of them for an interview, including the author and S.L. Their qualifications were assessed thoroughly. On 20 May 1996, the Board decided once again to appoint S.L. as a researcher to the Board. On 6 June 1996, the author filed another appeal with the Government against this decision, claiming that she was better qualified than S.L. and referring to the fact that she had more relevant academic education and greater work experience.

2.6 The National Board of Health and Welfare prepared a detailed opinion to the Government on the issue. In its opinion, it justified the change of criteria in the re-advertisement of the vacancy and emphasized that the selection process had been careful. The Board observed that on the basis of this process, it was concluded that S.L. was deemed to have the best qualifications for the post, including personal suitability; the Board added that S.L. had by then earned an academic degree in behavioural science. The author was considered the least qualified of the four applicants who had been shortlisted.

2.7 On 12 September 1996, the Government rejected the author's appeal, without giving reasons. The author appealed against this decision as well; in January 1997, this appeal was also dismissed, on the ground that the Government had, by its decision of September 1996, finalized the examination of the matter and therefore concluded the proceedings.

*The complaint*

3.1 The author complains that she has been discriminated against in her search for employment on the basis of her national origin and her status as an immigrant. In that context she claims that:

— Major parts of vacancy announcements of the type she applied for are tailor-made for an individual who is already chosen in advance, usually a Swedish citizen born in the country;

— Qualification requirements are higher for immigrants than they are for Swedes;

Employers generally discriminate against immigrants in their employment policy, in that they will choose Swedes who in principle are overqualified for a certain job, whereas they will reject immigrants who are overqualified for the same post. During the interviews for the re-advertised post, the author claims, she was told that she was overqualified;

- During the interviews for the vacant post with the National Board of Health and Public Welfare, the interviewers allegedly displayed an openly negative attitude vis-à-vis the author. In fact, the author dismisses the entire interview as "false play".

3.2 The author claims that the only possibility of solving her situation and that of immigrants in Sweden who seek employment in general, would be to take measures of affirmative action, such as establishing quotas for immigrants for high-level posts, so that immigrants with higher education may obtain the possibility to work.

3.3 The author rejects as another sign of discrimination vis-à-vis her as an immigrant that the National Board considered her the least qualified and suitable of the four applicants shortlisted for the re-advertised post. She reiterates that her academic qualifications were far superior to those of S.L. (master's degree as compared with a bachelor's degree).

*The State party's observations*

4.1 In its submission under rule 92 of the Committee's rules of procedure, the State party challenges the admissibility of the communication.

4.2 The State party notes that the relevant sources of legal protection against ethnic discrimination in Sweden are the Instrument of Government, the Act of Public Employment and the Act against Ethnic Discrimination. The Instrument of Government lays down the basic principle that public power shall be exercised with respect for the equal worth of all (chap. one, sect. 2). Courts, public authorities and other performing functions within the public administration shall observe, in their work, the equality of all before the law and maintain objectivity and impartiality. When deciding on appointments within the State administration,

only objective factors such as experience and competence shall be taken into account.

4.3 The Act of Public Employment reiterates the principles laid down in the Instrument of Government to the extent that when making appointments to administrative positions, the guiding factors shall be experience and competence. As a general rule, competence is valued higher than experience. Authorities must also consider objective factors that correspond to objectives of the overall labour market, equal opportunities and social and employment policies. Decisions concerning the filling of vacant posts are excluded from the normal requirement that administrative authorities must provide reasons for their decisions. The rationale for this exception is concern for the unsuccessful applicant(s), sparing him/her/them the negative evaluation such reasons might imply. Under section 35 of the Government Agencies and Institutions Ordinance, appeals against the authorities' decisions may be filed with the Government. An appeal against a decision by the National Board of Health and Welfare in matters of employment can also be filed with the Government, under section 14 of the 1996 Ordinance relating to the National Board of Health and Welfare. There are no further remedies available against the Government's decision.

4.4 Labour disputes may also be tried under the Act against Ethnic Discrimination of 1994, which aims at prohibiting discrimination in working life. Under the Act, ethnic discrimination takes place when a person or group of persons is/are treated unfairly in relation to others, or are in any way subjected to unjust or insulting treatment on the grounds of race, colour, national or ethnic origin or religious belief.

4.5 Pursuant to the terms of the Act, the Government has appointed an Ombudsman against Ethnic Discrimination whose mandate is to ensure that ethnic discrimination does not occur in the labour market or other areas of society. The Ombudsman should assist anyone subjected to ethnic discrimination and help safeguard the applicant's rights. He must make special efforts to prevent job applicants from being subjected to ethnic discrimination (sect. 4). If so directed by the Ombudsman, an employer is required to attend meetings and supply information pertaining to the employer's relations with job applicants and employees. Should the employer fail to comply with the

Ombudsman's directives, the latter may levy a fine (sects. 6 and 7).

4.6 This legislation, which applies to the overall labour market, has two major thrusts. The first is the prohibition of discrimination in relation to applicants for vacancies, which is relevant to the present case. The other prohibition of discrimination covers the treatment of employees. The provision which covers the treatment of job applicants provides that any employer must treat all applicants for a post equally and that, when appointing an applicant, he may not subject other applicants to unfair treatment on account of their race, colour, national or ethnic origin or religious belief (sect. 8). This provision applies if the employer chooses someone other than the individual subjected to discrimination. Discriminatory behaviour in the recruitment process is not per se covered by the prohibition, but if, as a result, this behaviour has led to the employment of another person, the employer will be held accountable for his actions. For any treatment to constitute unlawful discrimination, it must have been motivated by differences which are not based on objective criteria. Employment considerations made by the employer must appear to be acceptable and rational to an outsider if it is to be shown that objective reasons motivated the employer's decision. Any employer who violates the prohibition of discrimination is liable to pay damages. Job applicants who are victims of discrimination may be awarded damages, to be paid by the employer.

4.7 Under section 16 of the Act against Ethnic Discrimination, cases of discrimination in employment will be examined pursuant to the Act on Litigation in Labour Disputes. Disputes shall be handled before the Labour Court, as a court of first and last instance, if they are brought by an employer's organization or an employees' organization, or by the Ombudsman. If the dispute is brought by an individual employer or a job applicant it shall be heard and adjudicated by a District Court. Appeals may be lodged with the Labour Court, which is the final instance.

4.8 The State party submits that the author has failed to exhaust available domestic remedies, as required by article 14, paragraph 7 (a), of the Convention. It contends that contrary to the views apparently held by the author, it is possible to file actions before a court in cases of ethnic discrimination and damages based on ethnic discrimination in

working life. Such an action would have been based on article 24 of the Act on Ethnic Discrimination.

4.9 The State party notes that the author does not appear to have had any contact with the office of the Ombudsman against Ethnic Discrimination, although the Ombudsman would be entitled to lodge a case about discrimination and damages on her behalf. Thus, Swedish law provides for effective judicial remedies in the author's situation. It would have been possible for the author to file an action based on non-observance of the Act on Ethnic Discrimination before the courts, and there is nothing to indicate that her complaint would not have been examined properly and thoroughly, in accordance with applicable procedures. For the Government, therefore, the case is inadmissible for failure to exhaust available domestic remedies.

4.10 Regarding the question of legal aid that might be available to persons wishing to file a case with a court, the State party indicates that under the 1972 and 1997 Legal Aid Acts it is possible to give legal aid to any natural person in a legal matter if he or she is deemed to be in need of such assistance and his or her annual income does not exceed a specific limit. In legal aid matters the claimant shall contribute to the cost in proportion to his or her ability. Legal aid may, however, not be given if it is not deemed reasonable having regard to the importance and nature of the matter and the value of the subject being disputed as well as all other circumstances in the case. Such a situation could occur if a petition does not contain reasons for the claim as prescribed by law or if the claim otherwise is deemed to be manifestly unfounded.

*Author's comments*

5.1 With respect to the requirement of exhaustion of domestic remedies, the author notes that she was not informed about any remedies other than appeals directed to the Government. Thus, the decision of 12 September 1996 informing her of the Government's dismissal of her appeal did not mention the possibility of an appeal to the Labour Court, either with the assistance of a union or that of the office of the Ombudsman. Nor did the Government inform her of this possibility after she appealed the decision of 12 September 1996. The author emphatically asserts that she considered government organs "the last authorities" in her case with respect to appellate remedies. She states that after reading an article in the newspaper on the possibility of appealing to the Labour Court she contacted her Union. The latter, however, would not take up her case.

5.2 According to the author, an appeal for assistance to the Office of the Ombudsman against Ethnic Discrimination would have been futile. She asserts that the Ombudsman himself has never filed any case on behalf of an individual with the Labour Court, and that he himself has voiced serious doubts about the applicability and effectiveness of the Act against Ethnic Discrimination of 1994. She further states that she had applied for assistance from the Ombudsman on several other occasions, without success.

5.3 As to an appeal to a District Court, the author notes that this would not have been an effective remedy either. She states that in 1993 she applied for a job she did not obtain. She brought the case before a District Court claiming discrimination and requested legal aid. The District Court decided that it had no competence to examine decisions on appointments in the labour market and dismissed the case as well as the legal aid request in December 1994. By then the Act against Ethnic Discrimination which, according to the State party, provides job applicants with the possibility of filing cases before district courts, was already in force. The court's decision also indicated that the case had no prospects of success.

5.4 Moreover, the author asserts that an appeal would have incurred financial outlays which she, as an unemployed person, could not afford. In her view, if resort to a tribunal is not free of charge, she has no judicial remedy. Even so, for her, the issue is not how many judicial instances she may appeal to, but whether the existing law against ethnic discrimination may offer her a remedy; in her opinion, it does not.

*Admissibility considerations*

6.1 Before considering any claims contained in a communication, the Committee on the Elimination of Racial Discrimination must decide, pursuant to article 14, paragraph 7 (a), of the Convention, whether or not the current communication is admissible.

6.2 The State party contends that the author's claims are inadmissible for failure to exhaust domestic remedies, since she could have (a) sought the intercession of the Ombudsman against Ethnic Discrimination in her case; and/or (b) challenged the decision not to appoint her to the vacant post in a District Court with a possibility of appeal to the Labour Court. The author has replied that she was never informed about the possibility of the latter avenue and that appeals to the Ombudsman and the courts would in any event have failed, since the applicable legislation is deficient.

6.3 The Committee notes that the author was aware of the possibility of a complaint to the Ombudsman against Ethnic Discrimination; she did not avail herself of this possibility, considering it to be futile, and because of alleged previous negative experiences with his office. She learned about the possibility of filing an action with the Labour Court and started preparations to this effect but desisted, apparently because her trade union did not support her in this endeavour as it did not find merits in her claim. She further considers that there was no real possibility of obtaining redress in a District Court because of a negative experience regarding a previous case that she had filed with a District Court.

6.4 The Committee concludes that, notwithstanding the reservations that the author might have regarding the effectiveness of the current legislation to prevent racial discrimination in the labour market, it was incumbent upon her to pursue the remedies available, including a complaint before a District Court. Mere doubts about the effectiveness of such remedies, or the belief that the resort to them may incur costs, do not absolve a complainant from pursuing them.

6.5 In the light of the above, the Committee considers that the author has failed to meet the requirements of article 14, paragraph 7 (a), of the Convention.

7. The Committee on the Elimination of Racial Discrimination therefore decides:

   (a) That the communication is inadmissible;

   (b) That this decision shall be communicated to the State party and the author of the communication.

# Communication No. 18/2000

*Submitted by*: F.A. (represented by counsel, the non-governmental organization Organisasjonen Mot Offentlig Diskriminering).
*Alleged victim*: The petitioner.
*State party*: Norway.
*Declared inadmissible:* 17 April 2001.
*Subject matter:* Discrimination based on national origin, colour and race; effective investigation.
*Procedural issues:* Undue delay in submission of communication; status of "victim"; substantiation for purposes of admissibility.
*Substantive issues:* Discrimination based on national origin, colour and race; right to an effective remedy against acts of racial discrimination.
*Article of the Convention:* 1 (1).

*Decision on admissibility*

1. The author of the communication, Mr. F.A., claims to be the victim of a violation of the Convention by Norway. He is represented by the non-governmental organization Organisasjonen Mot Offentlig Diskriminering (OMOD). OMOD brought the general situation to the attention of the Committee for the first time on 6 December 1999. In a letter dated 12 April 2000 OMOD submitted additional information and formally requested that the Committee consider the communication under article 14 of the Convention. The communication was transmitted to the State party on 13 September 2000.

*The facts as submitted by the author*

2.1 The author reported that he went to the housing agency "Eiendom Service" and paid a fee which entitled him to have access to the lists of vacant accommodation. In checking the lists he found that about half of the housing advertisements clearly indicated that persons from certain groups were not desired as tenants. Statements like "no foreigners desired", "whites only", "only Norwegians with permanent jobs" punctuated the housing lists.

2.2 On 28 June 1995 the author informed the Oslo police about this situation and requested that charges be brought against the owner of the agency on the basis of section 349a of the Norwegian Penal Code, which reads as follows:

> "Any person who in an occupational or similar activity refuses any person goods or services on the same conditions as apply to others because of his religion, race, colour of skin, or national or ethnic origin, shall be liable to fines or imprisonment for a term not exceeding six months ...
>
> The same penalty shall also apply to any person who incites or is in any other way accessory to any act mentioned in the previous paragraph."

2.3 The police took more than two years to investigate the case. During that time they never visited the housing agency in question in order to collect evidence. Finally, on 3 December 1997, the police ordered the agency's owner to pay NKr 5,000, or alternatively to serve 10 days in prison, for contravention of section 349a of the Penal Code. The decision was based on the fact that in the period between December 1995 and January 1996 the owner, through her firm, Eiendoms Service, had sold lists of accommodation to rent in which it was stated that certain accommodation was only available to Norwegians in regular employment.

2.4 The owner appealed the decision to the Oslo City Court, which, in a judgement of 15 July 1998, decided to acquit her. An appeal against this judgement was filed with the High Court, which rejected it on 18 January 1999. The High Court noted that although the situation fell under section 349a of the Penal Code, the owner had acted in involuntary ignorance of the law. The case was further appealed to the Norwegian Supreme Court, which, in a ruling of 27 August 1999, declared that the acts in question were not covered by section 349a and rejected the appeal.

*The complaint*

3.    The author claims that the facts described amount to violation by the State party of the rights to which he is entitled under article 1, paragraph 1, of the Convention.

*Observations submitted by the State party*

4.1    By submission of 13 December 2000 the State party challenges the admissibility of the communication. It claims that the author has failed to file a communication within the time limit set out in rule 91 (f) of the Committee's rules of procedure. This provision reads as follows: "With a view to reaching a decision on the admissibility of a communication, the Committee ... shall ascertain: ... (f) That the communication is, except in the case of duly verified exceptional circumstances, submitted within six months after all available domestic remedies have been exhausted". The Supreme Court's judgement was delivered on 27 August 1999. The author, who was an OMOD employee, knew about it on the same date. Therefore, the communication should have been submitted to the Committee no later than 27 February 2000.

4.2    The State party claims that the letter from OMOD of 6 December 1999 is purely of a general nature and devoid of any content that may help to qualify it as a communication from or on behalf of an alleged victim of a violation. The author's name is not even mentioned in it. The letter does draw the Committee's attention to the Supreme Court's judgement of 27 August 1999, however, this is not sufficient to turn it into an individual communication. Furthermore, the author was not a party to the criminal proceedings, which were based on charges of a general nature initiated by OMOD and not linked to alleged wrongdoings against Mr. F.A. Moreover, the issues raised in the letter were dealt with in the dialogue between the Committee and the State party under the Committee's reporting procedure. They are also being seriously addressed by the Norwegian authorities.

4.3    The State party further argues that the allegation of violation of the Convention is not satisfactorily substantiated for the purpose of admissibility. For instance, the letters of 6 December 1999 and 12 April 2000 do not indicate the provisions of the Convention allegedly violated or the precise object of the communication. In these circumstances, it is not possible for the State to provide an adequate response. Neither is it explained in the letters whether the alleged violation is related to the landlords' discrimination or to the agency's activity. In respect of the former, it would be important to know whether the accommodation in question is in the landlords' private houses or whether it was rented out as part of a larger commercial activity. In respect of the latter, the Norwegian courts considered that the firm Eiendoms Service did not discriminate against its customers.

4.4    The High Court judgement describes the modus operandi of the firm, an agency for private accommodation rentals. According to the judgement, landlords informed the agency of the accommodation available and the agency listed the offers in a card-index which provided factual information on the accommodation offered. A rubric called "Landlord's wishes" was also included in the card index. If the accommodation-hunters were interested in a particular offer in the card index they had to contact the landlord themselves for any further action. Eiendoms Service was not involved in showings, preparation of contracts, etc. The Court found that certain landlords who made use of Eiendoms Service had rejected persons of foreign origin as tenants; however, Eiendoms Service did not have any responsibility in respect of the landlord's preferences. The Court considered that section 349a of the Penal Code as supported by the *travaux préparatoires* did not apply to the services offered by a private landlord when a business person is the agent for those services. There was no evidence that the agency's owner had any objections or prejudice against, for example, people with a different skin colour. On the contrary, she had often assisted foreigners in finding accommodation. The State party claims that the author has not explained the reasons why he disagrees with the Court's conclusions.

*Counsel's comments*

5.1 Counsel refers to the objections raised by the State party on the basis of rule 91 (f) of the Committee's rules of procedure and argues that the possible shortcomings pointed out by the State party should not exceed what one can expect from a small NGO without legal expertise such as OMOD. Protection from violations by way of bodies like [the Committee] should be an option for everybody, not only for people with legal expertise.

5.2 The purpose of the letter from OMOD dated 6 December 1999 was to request the Committee to treat the Supreme Court judgement of 27 August 1999 as an individual complaint under article 14 of the Convention. In the letter, OMOD explicitly requested the Committee to carry out an individual evaluation of the Supreme Court's ruling in relation to the Convention. If the communication was only meant as a general communication from an NGO, as suggested by the State party, it would have been included in the report which OMOD prepares regularly in response to Norway's periodic reports to the Committee. It is true that the author used the opportunity to point to possible large-scale consequences which the judgement may have with regard to the protection of ethnic minorities against racial discrimination and the status of the Convention in Norway. This information, however, should be interpreted as complementary to the individual complaint put forward.

5.3 The letter from OMOD dated 12 April 2000 confirmed that the purpose of its letter of 6 December 1999 was to have the judgement treated as an individual complaint under article 14 of the Convention, and should be regarded as part of the communication submitted on 6 December 1999.

5.4 Counsel agrees that the letter of 6 December 1999 did not indicate the provisions in the Convention that had been violated. However, he considers that the allegations of violations of the Convention should be enough to declare the case admissible. In the letter of 12 April 2000 OMOD claims that the Supreme Court, in its judgement "refused to give F.A. the rights inherent in article 1.1". Among those rights are the rights referred to in article 5 (e) (iii), 5 (f) and 6, which are especially relevant to the case of Mr. F.A. Furthermore, it was Mr. F.A. who reported Eiendoms Service to the police. Subsequently,

the police brought the case to the High Court and the Supreme Court.

5.5 Counsel claims that the object of the communication is the failure of the Supreme Court to comply with its obligations under the Convention. He also claims that the alleged violation of the Convention is related to the activities of the housing agency, not the landlords.

5.6 Regarding the State party's claim that OMOD did not substantiate its claim that the conclusion of the Supreme Court was unwarranted, counsel argues that the agency's owner indeed refused a person "goods or services on the terms applicable to others". The author was not at all offered the same service as ethnic Norwegians. In fact, he was offered a smaller number of vacant flats than other customers owing to his ethnic origin, yet he had to pay exactly the same fee to have access to the index cards. Furthermore, the author was not informed beforehand that this was the case. This difference in treatment is illegal, regardless of whether it is made on behalf of somebody else, for example a landlord. The owner of the housing agency had written the discriminatory texts on the index cards and knew what that meant to persons of minority background.

5.7 Counsel further argues that the commercial activity of Eiendoms Service cannot be categorized as being within "the private sphere". The agency offered a general service to the public which fits the description of article 5 (f) of the Convention. The activity of Eiendoms Service is therefore a clear case of discrimination in the public sphere, not the private one.

*Admissibility considerations*

6.1 Before considering the substance of a communication, the Committee on the Elimination of Racial Discrimination examines whether or not the communication is admissible pursuant to article 14, paragraph 7 (a) of the Convention and rules 86 and 91 of its rules of procedure.

6.2 The State party contends that the author's claims are inadmissible because of his failure to submit a communication within the time limit set out in rule 91 (f) of the Committee's rules of procedure. The Committee recalls that, according to this provision, communications must be submitted to it, except in the case of duly verified exceptional circumstances, within six months after all available domestic remedies have been exhausted.

6.3 The Committee notes that the Norwegian Supreme Court adopted its final decision on the facts that constitute the object of the present communication on 27 August 1999. The author submitted the communication under article 14 of the Convention on 12 April 2000, i.e., more than six months after the date of exhaustion of domestic remedies. Prior to that date, on 6 December 1999, the decision of the Norwegian Supreme Court had been brought to the Committee's attention, but there was no indication that the author had intended to submit a communication under article 14 of the Convention. The general terms in which the letter of 6 December 1999 was drafted suggested that the author wished to submit the facts for the consideration of the Committee within the framework of its activities under article 9 of the Convention.

6.4 Furthermore, the Committee has found no exceptional circumstances that would justify not applying the six-month requirement stipulated in rule 91 (f) of the rules of procedure.

7. The Committee on the Elimination of Racial Discrimination therefore decides:

(a) That the communication is inadmissible;

(b) That this decision shall be communicated to the State party and the author of the communication.

8. The Committee takes this opportunity to urge the State party to take effective measures to ensure that housing agencies refrain from engaging in discriminatory practices and do not accept submissions from private landlords which would discriminate on racial grounds. The Committee recalls in this respect its concluding observations on the fifteenth periodic report of Norway, in which it expressed concern that persons seeking to rent or purchase apartments and houses were not adequately protected against racial discrimination on the part of the private sector. In this connection, the Committee recommended that Norway give full effect to its obligations under article 5 (e) (iii) of the Convention.

# Communication No. 19/2000

*Submitted by*: Sarwar Seliman Mostafa (represented by counsel).
*Alleged victim*: The petitioner.
*State party*: Denmark.
*Declared inadmissible:* 10 August 2001.
*Subject matter:* Access to effective mechanism of protection; discrimination based on racial grounds.
*Procedural issues:* Substantiation for purposes of admissibility; exhaustion of domestic remedies.
*Substantive issues:* Right to an effective remedy against acts of racial discrimination.
*Articles of the Convention:* 6 and 14 (7) (a).

*Decision on admissibility*

1. The petitioner (initial submission dated 12 April 2000) is Mr. Sarwar Seliman Mostafa, an Iraqi citizen currently residing in Denmark, together with his wife and daughter. He claims that his rights under article 6 of the Convention have been violated by Denmark. He is represented by counsel.

*The facts as submitted by the petitioner*

2.1 The petitioner was registered as an applicant for renting an apartment with the Danish housing company DAB (*Dansk Almennyttigt Boligselskab*). On 8 June 1998 the DAB informed him that an apartment was available and asked him whether he would be interested in it. The petitioner confirmed that he was interested. However, under the existing legislation the municipality of Hoje Tastrup had to approve the contract. In a letter of 16 June

1998 the municipality informed the petitioner that his application had not been approved due to social housing criteria.

2.2 In a letter of 22 June 1998, the petitioner asked the municipality to reconsider its decision. He stated that he had a good job as an engineer and also worked as an interpreter; his wife, who was also an engineer, was training as a kindergarten employee and they both spoke Danish; their daughter attended a Danish kindergarten.

2.3 In a letter dated 3 July 1998 the municipality informed the petitioner that the case would not be reopened and that his complaint had been forwarded to the Social Appeals Board (*Det Sociale Ankenaevn*).

2.4 On 8 July 1998, the petitioner contacted the non-governmental organization Documentary and Advisory Centre on Racial Discrimination (DRC). The petitioner informed the staff of the centre that when he contacted the municipality on 1 July 1998 and explained that he would submit a letter from the doctor's family supporting his application in view of the fact that his daughter suffered from asthma, the municipality officer replied that even if he sent the letter, his application would be rejected.

2.5 The petitioner reported the case to the police of Glostrup, which in a decision of 24 November 1998 refused to investigate the matter under the Danish Act on Racial Discrimination. In a decision of 29 April 1999 the State Attorney for Sealand concluded that there was no reason for changing the decision of the police. The petitioner also brought the case before the Parliamentary Ombudsman who, in a decision of 4 November 1998, indicated that the petitioner should wait for the decision of the Social Appeals Board.

2.6 In a letter dated 1 October 1998 the Social Appeals Board informed the petitioner that the Municipality of Hoje Tastrup had decided to change its previous decision rejecting the petitioner's application. Later on, on 12 October 1999, the Ministry of Housing and Urban Affairs informed the DRC that the family was invited to contact the municipality.

2.7 In a letter of 27 November 1999 the Social Appeals Board informed the DRC that the apartment to which Sarwar Seliman Mostafa was to be approved had been assigned to another person, therefore it would be impossible to give Sarwar Seliman Mostafa full satisfaction in his request as neither the Appeals Board nor the Municipality had legal authority to cancel a rental agreement made by the housing company. Furthermore, on 26 January 2000 the housing company informed the DRC that the applicable legislation did not make it possible for the company to change the decision which had been annulled by the Social Appeals Board.

2.8 The Social Appeals Board adopted its final decision on the matter on 15 March 2000. It concluded that the municipality's decision of 16 June 1998 was invalid, as Sarwar Seliman Mostafa did fulfil the conditions for approval to the housing facility.

*The complaint*

3. Counsel claims that the State party has breached its obligations under article 6 of the Convention. He states that, despite the decision of the Social Appeals Board, the petitioner has still not been provided with an appropriate apartment and that the Danish legislation does not provide for adequate satisfaction in cases like the one under consideration. Since neither the police of Glostrup nor the State Attorney were willing to interfere in the case, there is no possibility for the petitioner to make use of any further remedies at the national level.

*Observations by the State party*

4.1 By a submission of 13 December 2000, the State party challenges the admissibility of the communication. It recalls that on 1 September 1998 the municipality had decided to alter its decision of 16 June 1998 and informed the Social Appeals Board that it had decided to approve the petitioner for the dwelling applied for or a corresponding one. As a result the Board considered that the appeal had become moot and, on 1 October 1998, notified the petitioner accordingly. However, in the light of, inter alia, a request from the Parliamentary Ombudsman, the Board decided subsequently to consider the appeal concerning the decision of 16 June 1998. In its decision of 15 March 2000 the Board found that the decision of 16 June 1998 was invalid, although it had been modified by the decision of 1 September 1998.

4.2 The State party further recalls that in a letter of 12 October 1999 addressed to the DRC, the Ministry of Housing and Urban Affairs stated that Hoje-Taastrup local authority's administration of the rules on approval of tenants for non-profit housing in general was contrary to the rules in force, as the local authority used unlawful criteria such as whether the tenant was a refugee or an immigrant. She indicated that, in the future, she would be very alert to the manner in which local authorities administered the approval scheme and continue her efforts to ensure that the local authorities do not violate national or international law regarding racial discrimination.

4.3 Having acknowledged that the decision of 16 June 1998 was unlawful according to Danish law, the State party examines the consequences of such acknowledgment, in light of the petitioner's claims under article 6 of the Convention. The State party understands those claims to mean that, as a result of the wrongful act and on the basis of article 6 of the Convention, the petitioner should (a) have had the apartment which he had been wrongfully refused; or (b) have had a similar dwelling assigned to him; or (c) have received financial compensation.

4.4 Options (a) and (b) are not possible. A non-profit housing organization such as the DAB is not part of the local authority, but an independent legal entity whose activities are governed by specific rules. When a local authority refuses to approve a person as a tenant, the non-profit housing organization will offer the apartment in question to another person on the waiting list. This means that the apartment will not be vacant when it is subsequently established that the local authority's refusal to approve the applicant was wrongful. Article 6 of the Convention cannot be interpreted to mean that the Convention would require specific performance in such a situation.

4.5 The State party interprets article 6 as having two parts. The first one concerns the provision of "effective protection and remedies" and the second one the provision of "adequate reparation or satisfaction". The first part imposes on the States parties a positive obligation to introduce remedies that are available, adequate and effective and that: (i) protect the citizens against acts of racial discrimination contrary to the Convention; (ii) make it possible for the citizens to have established whether they have been subjected to racial discrimination contrary to the Convention; and (iii) make it possible for the citizens to have the acts of racial discrimination brought to an end. The State party considers that this part of article 6 is not

relevant for assessing whether the applicant is entitled to specific performance.

4.6 The second part applies to situations where a person has been subjected to racial discrimination. In such cases the States parties must ensure that the victim has access to "adequate reparation or satisfaction". That means that the act or omission constituting racial discrimination is brought to an end and that the consequences for the victim are remedied in such manner that the state of affairs prior to the violation is restored to the widest extent possible. There will always be cases in which it is not possible to restore the situation prior to a violation. This may be due to the fact, for example, that the racially discriminatory act or omission is delimited in time and place and therefore cannot be reversed (such as a racist statement), or that the interests of innocent third parties should also be protected. In such cases one has to determine whether there have been attempts to remedy the consequences for the victim of the racially discriminatory act or omission.

4.7 The present case is one of those where it is impossible to restore the situation prior to the violation. The apartment for which the petitioner was wrongfully refused approval as a tenant has been let to a third party and regard for the interests of such party is a crucial argument against subsequently calling into question the legal relationship between that party and the non-profit housing organization. To the extent that the petitioner claims that on the basis of article 6 he is entitled to specific performance, the State party finds that the communication should be declared inadmissible on the ground that no prima facie case of violation of the Convention has been established in respect of this part of the communication.

4.8 Furthermore, neither the Social Appeals Board nor any other authority [has] the possibility of assigning another dwelling to a person whom a local authority has wrongfully refused to approve as a tenant of a non-profit dwelling. Apart from cases where a local authority can assign a non-profit dwelling for the purpose of solving urgent social problems, it is the non-profit housing organization itself who allocates vacant dwellings to applicants. In practice, the person in question will remain on the waiting list and will have an apartment offered when one becomes vacant, whereupon the local authority will approve the person, unless new circumstances have arisen as a result of which the person no longer satisfies the conditions for approval. In this case, however, the petitioner had chosen to have his name removed from the waiting list of the DAB in Hoje-Taastrup.

4.9 Regardless of the wrongful conduct of the Hoje-Taastrup municipality, it was the petitioner's own choice not to remain on the list, as a result of which it became impossible for the DAB to offer him another dwelling. To the extent that the petitioner claims that as a consequence of article 6 of the Convention he should have been offered another and corresponding dwelling without otherwise satisfying the general conditions for obtaining one, including being on the waiting list, the communication should be declared inadmissible, as no prima facie case of violation of the Convention has been established in respect of this part of the communication.

4.10 As for the question of damages, the State party argues that the issue has not been brought before the Danish courts and, therefore, the petitioner has failed to exhaust domestic remedies. For this purpose it is irrelevant that the police and the public prosecutor rejected the petitioner's claims.

4.11 The local authority's refusal to approve the petitioner as a tenant raised two different issues: First, whether the refusal constituted a criminal offence and second whether the refusal was otherwise wrongful, including whether the local authority had used unlawful criteria such as the petitioner's race, colour, descent or national or ethnic origin. The police and the public prosecutor only had to assess the first issue, while the second one was assessed by other authorities, including the Social Appeals Board.

4.12 The State party claims that the decisions of the police and the public prosecutor were decisive in the context of the criminal proceedings, but did not in any way preclude the petitioner from instituting civil proceedings. In connection with such proceedings the petitioner would have been able to refer, inter alia, to the decision of the Social Appeals Board and the opinion of the Ministry of Housing and Urban Affairs. If the petitioner believes that he has suffered a pecuniary or non-pecuniary loss, the institution of civil proceedings will be an effective remedy. Damages do not depend, directly or indirectly, on the outcome of criminal proceedings.

4.13 It follows from the general rules of Danish law on damages in tort that administrative authorities may incur liability in damages for actionable acts and omissions. It is therefore possible to claim damages for losses suffered by a person because of an invalid administrative decision. Cases in dispute are dealt with by ordinary courts in connection with civil proceedings against the administrative authority in question.

*Counsel's comments*

5.1 Counsel argues that the fact that neither the Social Appeals Board nor any other authority have the possibility to assign another appropriate dwelling to a person who has wrongfully been refused approval as a tenant of a non-profit dwelling only demonstrates the failure of Danish legislation to provide effective reparation in a case like the one under consideration.

5.2 Counsel refers to the State party's statement in paragraph 4.8 above that the person in question would remain on the waiting list and have an apartment offered when one becomes vacant. He claims that the petitioner was not aware of that practice and that the letter of 1 September 1998 from the Municipality of Hoje-Taastrup to the Social Appeals Board was never sent to the petitioner or the DRC.

5.3 Counsel disagrees with the State party's statement that it was possible for the petitioner to claim damages for losses suffered or for tort and says that Danish courts have refused to apply rules on damages in tort in cases of discrimination. The fact that a person has been subjected to discrimination does not automatically entitle that person to damages in tort. In this respect he provides copy of a decision of 4 August 2000 concerning a case in which discrimination was established where the Copenhagen City Court did not find that the act of discrimination entitled the victims to damages in tort. Counsel reiterates that all domestic remedies have been exhausted.

5.4 Counsel further submits that the Convention is not incorporated into domestic law and expresses doubts as to whether the Danish courts would apply the Convention in a dispute between private parties.

6.1 In response to a request by the Committee to furnish additional information on effective remedies available to the author for the implementation of the decision of the Social Appeals Board dated 15 March 2000, or for receiving compensation, the State party, by note of 6 July 2001, affirms that the institution of a civil action against the Hoje-Taastrup local authority for compensation for pecuniary or non-pecuniary damage is an available and effective remedy. The author had the possibility of instituting an action before the ordinary courts based on the Hoje-Taastrup local authority's decision of 16 June 1998 and invoking the Convention on the Elimination of All Forms of Racial Discrimination. In this connection the State party refers to the practical effect of the Committee's recommendation in a prior case No. 17/1999 *Babak Jebelli* v. *Denmark*, which illustrates that Danish courts interpret and apply section 26 of the Act on Liability in Damages Act in the light of article 6 of the Convention. Accordingly, the State party concludes that the communication should be declared inadmissible because the author has not exhausted available and effective domestic remedies.

6.2 On 18 July 2001, counsel informed the Committee that he had no further comments to the additional information from the State party.

*Admissibility considerations*

7.1 Before considering the substance of a communication, the Committee on the Elimination of Racial Discrimination examines whether or not the communication is admissible, pursuant to article 14, paragraph 7 (a) of the Convention and rules 86 and 91 of its rules of procedure.

7.2 The Committee notes that the petitioner brought his claim before the police and the State Attorney who, in a decision of 29 April 1999, refused to investigate the matter under the Danish Act on Racial Discrimination. Parallel to that, the Social Appeals Board examined the case and concluded, on 15 March 2000, that the decision of the Municipality not to approve the author as a tenant was invalid. In the meantime, the municipality had decided to alter its previous decision and approve the petitioner for the apartment applied for or an equivalent one.

The Social Appeals Board informed the petitioner of the new municipality's decision by letter of 1 October 1998.

7.3 The Committee notes that, despite the new decision of the municipality and the one of the Social Appeals Board, the petitioner was not provided with an apartment equivalent to the one initially applied for, nor granted compensation for the damages caused to him as a result of the first decision of the municipality. The Committee notes, however, that the petitioner did not meet one of the conditions required to be assigned an equivalent apartment, namely, to remain on the waiting list. This failure cannot be attributed to the State party. In the circumstances, the petitioner could not obtain redress in the form of assignment of the original or of an equivalent dwelling. He could, however, have sought compensation.

7.4 As to the question of damages, the State party argues that the petitioner did not institute civil proceedings and, therefore, has not exhausted domestic remedies. Despite the arguments given by the petitioner and the reference to previous jurisprudence of the Danish courts, the Committee considers that doubts about the effectiveness of such proceedings cannot absolve a petitioner from pursuing them. Accordingly, the Committee considers that, by not exhausting the available domestic remedies, the petitioner has failed to meet the requirements or article 14, paragraph 7 (a) of the Convention.

8. The Committee on the Elimination of Racial Discrimination therefore decides:

(a) That the communication is inadmissible;

(b) That this decision shall be communicated to the State party and to the petitioner.

9. In accordance with rule 93, paragraph 2, of the Committee's rules of procedure, a decision taken by the Committee that a communication is inadmissible may be reviewed at a later date by the Committee upon a written request by the petitioner concerned. Such written request shall contain documentary evidence to the effect that the reasons for inadmissibility referred to in paragraph 7 (a) of article 14 are no longer applicable.

# Communication No. 21/2001

*Submitted by*: D. S. (the petitioner is not represented by counsel).
*Alleged victim*: The petitioner.
*State party*: Sweden.
*Declared inadmissible:* 10 August 2001.
*Subject matter:* Discriminatory housing advertisement; discrimination based on nationality; access to effective mechanism of protection.
*Procedural issues:* Exhaustion of domestic remedies.
*Substantive issues:* Right to an effective remedy against acts of racial discrimination; right to freedom of movement and residence within the border of the State.
*Articles of the Convention:* 2 (2), 5 (e) (i), 6 and 14 (7) (a).

## Decision on admissibility

1.   The petitioner (initial submission dated 9 July 2001) is D.S., a Swedish citizen of Czechoslovak origin, born in 1947, currently residing in Solna, Sweden. She claims to be a victim of violations by Sweden of articles 2, paragraph 2, 5 (e) (i) and 6 of the International Convention on the Elimination of All Forms of Racial Discrimination. The petitioner is not represented by counsel.

## The facts as submitted by the petitioner

2.1  On 30 November 1999, the petitioner applied for a position as "an investigator" at Ungdomstyrelsen in Stockholm. This organization carries out, among other things, investigative studies at the request of the Government or on its own initiative, on the conditions of life of young people. The vacancy announcement said that it was looking for two new staff members and that the requirements were a university degree in social science, experience of public investigative work, knowledge of the methodology of investigation, English, and experience using statistical material. Experience in research work and in development, follow-up and evaluation were also required. Good knowledge of oral and written Swedish and ability to co-operate and work independently were also prerequisites for the posts.

2.2  Ungdomstyrelsen decided to appoint A.K, I.A, and S.Z to the posts. It appears that a third post was also made available after the announcement. On 6 March 2000, the petitioner appealed the decision to the Government claiming that she had been discriminated against.

2.3  On 6 July 2000, the Government rejected the petitioner's appeal. The Government did not give reasons for the decision. The petitioner appealed against this decision as well and this appeal was similarly dismissed, on the ground that the Government's decision, of 6 July 2000, could not be appealed and that there was no other reason to re-examine the petitioner's appeal.

2.4  The petitioner also filed a complaint with the Ombudsman against Ethnic Discrimination who refused to take any action in her case, as he claimed that it had no merits. The Ombudsman stated that Ungdomstyrelsen chose individuals for the post on the basis of their education, and professional experience and saw no reason to question the employer's judgement. The petitioner states that she has not brought the case to the District Court as she claims that the new law against ethnic discrimination does not apply to individuals who allege discrimination at the recruitment stage, and even if it were applicable she could not afford to do so.

## The complaint

2.   The petitioner claims that she has been discriminated against by Sweden on the basis of her national origin and her status as an immigrant, in the refusal by Ungdomstyrelsen to offer her a job. In this context, she objects to the Ungdomstyrelsen's decision to offer the jobs in question to A.K, I.A, and S.Z, all of

Swedish origin, who she claims are less qualified than she for the post.

*Issues and proceedings before the Committee*

4.1 Before considering any claim contained in a communication, the Committee on the Elimination of all Forms of Racial Discrimination must decide, pursuant to article 14, paragraph 7 (a), of the Convention, whether or not the current communication is admissible.

4.2 The Committee notes that, although the petitioner was aware that she could have challenged the decision in the District Court not to appoint her to the vacant post, she did not do so, as she believes that the legislation is deficient and claims that she could not afford to take such an action.

4.3 The Committee concludes that, notwithstanding the reservations that the petitioner might have regarding the effectiveness of the current legislation to prevent racial discrimination in the labour market, it was incumbent upon her to pursue the remedies available, including a complaint

before the District Court. The Committee recalls that doubts about the effectiveness of such remedies, does not absolve an petitioner from pursuing them. With respect to the petitioner's claim that she could not issue proceedings in the District Court due to lack of funds, the Committee notes that the petitioner has provided no further information in this regard and therefore cannot conclude that the expenses involved would have been a grave impediment excusing her from the obligation to exhaust domestic remedies.

4.4 In light of the above, the Committee considers that the petitioner has failed to meet the requirements of article 14, paragraph 7 (a), of the Convention.

5. The Committee on the Elimination of Racial Discrimination therefore decides:

(a) That the communication is inadmissible;

(b) That this decision shall be communicated to the petitioner and, for information, to the State party.

# Communication No. 22/2002

*Submitted by*: POEM and FASM (represented by counsel).
*Alleged victim*: The petitioner.
*State party*: Denmark.
*Declared inadmissible:* 15 April 2003.
*Subject matter:* Racial discriminatory statement made by a member of parliament; access to effective mechanism of protection; effective investigation.
*Procedural issues:* Exhaustion of domestic remedies; inadmissibility *ratione personae*.
*Substantive issues:* Right to an effective remedy against acts of racial discrimination; State parties have a positive obligation to take effective action against reported incidents of racial discrimination.
*Articles of the Convention:* 2 (1) (d), 4, 6 and 14 (7) (a).

*Decision on admissibility*

1. The authors of the communication (hereafter, the petitioners), dated 8 August 2001, are POEM (Umbrella Organization for the Ethnic Minorities), and FASM (Association of Muslim Students). They claim a violation by Denmark of article 2, paragraph 1 (d), article 4 and article 6 of the Convention. They are represented by counsel.

*The facts as presented by the petitioners*

2.1 The first petitioner, the Umbrella Organization for the Ethnic Minorities (hereafter, POEM), is a Danish organization that promotes ethnic equality in all spheres of society including through full civil and political rights for ethnic minorities. The organization currently comprises 30 members representing most of ethnic and national minorities in the State party.

2.2 The second petitioner, the Association of Muslim Students (hereafter, FASM), is also a Danish organization that raises awareness on Muslim issues and deals with the negative effects caused by—so-called—Islamophobic politicians and the media on the image of Islam. The organization currently comprises more than 100 members, all students and practising Muslims students who, for the most part, were born and raised in Denmark.

2.3 POEM represents a number of Muslim organizations and other organizations which, although not Muslim, comprise members of ethnic and national groups with a Muslim background. FASM is an all-Muslim organization. Therefore, when Islamophobic and other prejudicial statements against Muslims are made public, both the petitioners and their members, including the non-Muslims, are affected.

2.4 The incident of racial discrimination raised by the petitioners relates to a statement made by the leader of the Danish People's Party (Dansk Folkeparti, hereafter DPP) and Member of Parliament, Pia Kjærsgaard, on 19 June 2000 in her weekly newsletter which was disseminated on the party's website and through a press release:

> Behind this lurks the phenomenon which becomes ever more obvious in all its horror: that the multiculturalization of Denmark brings trouble in its train like gang and group formation, mass rape and complete indifference to the principles on which the Danish legal system is built.
>
> [...]
>
> The phenomenon of mass rape is also new in a Danish context and is linked with a cultural perception of Danish girls as prostitutes who can be defiled without shame, while the same boys and guys are brought up to murder a sister if she breaches the family and cultural codes.

2.5 On 20 June 2000, the Documentation and Advisory Centre on Racial Discrimination (DRC) reported the statement to the Copenhagen Police, alleging a violation of section 266 (b) of the Criminal Code (hereafter, section 266 (b)).[1]

2.6 By letter of 21 July 2000, the Copenhagen Police informed the DRC that the case was discontinued. This decision indicated that, according to the *travaux préparatoires* of the provision, the purpose of section 266 (b) is neither to limit the topics that can make the object of a political debate nor to decide the way these topics are addressed. Political statements, although they may be perceived by some as offending, are part of dialectic where, traditionally, there are wide limits to the use of generalization and simplified allegations. The above-mentioned weekly newsletter consists in an observation on the scale of penalties for crimes of violence, which is legitimate in a political debate. Finally, although the statement could be considered as offensive, an important weight should be given in the present case to considerations related to the freedom of expression and of political debate.

2.7 By letter of 21 August 2000, the DRC requested that the case be brought before the Regional Public Prosecutor. The DRC argued that statements similar to that made by Pia Kjærsgaard had led to convictions and that neither the *travaux préparatoires* of section 266 (b) nor article 4 of the Convention provided for an extended freedom of expression for Members of Parliament or for observations made in a political debate. The petitioners are therefore of the opinion that statements forming part of a serious debate should be assessed regardless of whom has made them.

2.8 By letter of 31 August 2000, the Regional Public Prosecutor upheld the decision of the Copenhagen Police. He stressed that he had carefully considered the balance between the insulting character of the statement and the right to freedom of expression and that it must be accepted, to a certain degree, that, in order to secure a free and critical debate, statements may be offending to individuals or groups. Regardless of the degrading and insulting character of the statement for individuals of a different cultural background, the allegations

---

[1] Section 266 (b) of the Danish Criminal Code reads:
> 1. Any person who publicly or with the intention of disseminating it to a wide circle of people, makes a statement or imparts other information threatening, insulting or degrading a group of persons on account of their race, colour, national or ethnic origin, belief or sexual orientation shall be liable to a fine or imprisonment for any term not exceeding two years.
> 2. When the sentence is meted out, the fact that the offence is in the nature of propaganda activities shall be considered an aggravating circumstance.

made in the statement are not serious enough to justify a derogation from the freedom of expression.

2.9 By letter of 4 October 2000, the DRC wrote to the Director of Public Prosecutions and requested a review of the Regional Public Prosecutor's decision of 31 August 2000. The DRC also requested an opinion on the question of the existence of an extended freedom of expression for Members of Parliament and for observations being made in a political debate. The DRC further asked whether the Regional Public Prosecutor's decision was consistent with the Danish judicial practice and obligations under the Convention.

2.10 By letter of 8 February 2001, the Director of Public Prosecutions decided that there were no grounds for reviewing the decision of the Regional Public Prosecutor.

*The complaint*

*Exhaustion of domestic remedies*

3.1 The petitioners argue that, according to section 749, paragraph 1 of the State party's Administration of Justice Act, the police decides whether it will investigate the reported incidents. The decision may be referred to the Regional Public Prosecutor and his/her decision is final. Nevertheless, the State party itself stated in its fourteenth periodic report to the Committee that all cases related to section 266 (b) should be notified to the Director of Public Prosecutions. The petitioners have thus made such a notification in order to exhaust all domestic remedies.

3.2 The petitioners also contend that a direct legal action against Pia Kjærsgaard would not be effective in the absence of further investigation by the police or Regional Public Prosecutor. Moreover, the State party's Eastern High Court decided on 5 February 1999 that an incident of racial discrimination does not in itself imply a violation of the honour and reputation of a person under section 26 of the Act of Civil Liability.

*Alleged violation of article 2, paragraph 1 (d), together with article 6*

3.3 The petitioners allege that the State party has violated its obligations under article 2, paragraph 1 (d) taken together with article 6 of the Convention because, the Director of Public Prosecutions having the exclusive competence

to initiate legal action in this type of incident, the alleged victims of such an incident are not entitled to bring the case before a court, and have therefore no means of redress, if the Director of Public Prosecutions discontinues a case.

3.4 The petitioners refer to the decision in case No. 4/1991 (*L.K.* v. *Netherlands*) where the Committee emphasized that the State parties have a positive obligation to take effective action against reported incidents of racial discrimination.

3.5 Referring also to the fourteenth periodic report of the State party to the Committee, the petitioners complain that while all cases in which a provisional charge has been brought under section 266 (b) must be submitted for decision to the Director of Public Prosecutions, those that are rejected without a provisional charge are only notified to the same authority. Moreover, the petitioners contend that there is, in the State party's procedure related to acts of racial discrimination, an inequality of arms, because in cases where charges have been brought, both the Regional Public Prosecutor and the Director of Public Prosecutions have a right to review the decision, while in cases where no charge is brought, the case is only brought to the Regional Public Prosecutor.

*Alleged violation of article 2, paragraph 1 (d), together with articles 4 and 6*

3.6 The petitioners allege that the State party has violated its obligations under article 2, paragraph 1 (d) taken together with articles 4 and 6 of the Convention because, the decision of the Director of Public Prosecutions implying that the initial decision of the Copenhagen Police is in compliance with article 266 (b), the State party allows an extended right to freedom of expression for Members of Parliament and for observations being made during a political argumentation, regardless whether statements are racist or prejudicial.

3.7 In this regard, the petitioners point out to the State party's thirteenth periodic report where it was stated:

> 24. Section 266 (b) of the Penal Code, which is described in detail in Denmark's last periodic report (paras. 34-41), was amended by Act No. 309 of 17 May 1995 with the addition of a new subsection 2, according to which it must be considered an aggravating circumstance when meting out the punishment "that the count

is in the nature of propaganda". The amendment entered into force on 1 June 1995.

25. During the readings of the bill in the Danish parliament (*Folketinget*) it was declared that in these especially aggravated cases the prosecutors should not in future exhibit the same restraint with regard to prosecuting as previously.

26. Whether "propaganda" is present in a specific case will depend on an overall assessment stressing in particular whether there has been a systematic dissemination of discriminating statements, etc., including dissemination to foreign countries, with a view to influencing public opinion. It could speak in favour of referring a count to section 266 (b) (2) if the violation was committed by several persons jointly, especially if the persons in question belong to the same party, association or other organization, and manifestations of the relevant nature form part of the activities of the organization in question. Also, a more extensive dissemination of statements may speak in favour of applying section 266 (b) (2). In this respect it is relevant whether the statements were put forward in a medium involving greater dissemination, for example a printed publication, radio, television or another electronic medium.

3.8 In order to illustrate the State party's practice in this regard, the petitioners explain that the founder of the extreme right wing "Progress Party" (*Fremskridtsparteit*) Mogens Glistrup, although he made continuous allegations that could have fallen under section 266 (b), was never charged under the said provision before he left the Parliament. On 23 August 2000, no longer a Member of Parliament, Mogens Giltrup was convicted by the Supreme Court under section 266 (b) (1) to seven days conditional imprisonment for racist allegations made on television but was not convicted under section 266 (b) (2). The petitioners underline that the Court then held that the consideration of an extended right to freedom of expression for politicians concerning controversial public matters could not constitute a basis for acquitting the defendant.

3.9 With regard to Pia Kjærsgaard, the petitioners argue that, on 27 August 1998, she wrote the following statement in a weekly newspaper:

> The majority of our foreign citizens come from Africa and Asia, and this group is by and large Mohammedan. [...] and in addition to this comes a long series of expenses for aliens, such as expenses to maintain public law and order and security. [...] I maintain the point that the expenses incurred by aliens—and not the private consumption of Danish citizens—is the ultimate and decisive cause of the destruction of the Danish Welfare State. [...] Immigrants are to a large extent not capable of supporting themselves, just as aliens are far more criminal than the average population.

3.10 In another weekly newsletter of 25 April 2000, where she compared Muslim parliamentary candidates with Lenin who used the support of minor socialist parties and brutally crushed them once in power, Pia Kjærsgaard held:

> Thus a fundamentalist Muslim does in fact not know how to act [in dignity and in a cultivated way] in accordance with Danish democratic traditions. He simply does not have a clue about what it means. Commonly acknowledged principles such as speaking the truth and behaving with dignity and culture—also towards those whom you do not sympathize with—are unfamiliar ground to people like of M.Z.

3.11 By contrast, a few members of the youth branch of the DPP were charged with violation of section 266 (b) for having published the following ad: *Mass rapes—gross violence—insecurity—forced marriages—suppression of women—gang crime. That is what a multi-ethnic society has to offer us. Is that what you want?*

3.12 The work of the Progress Party and of the DPP being to promote a restrictive immigration policy—particularly concerning Muslims—mainly based on Islamophobia since three decades, the petitioners consider that it constitutes propaganda to racial hatred against Muslims in Denmark. It is thus the opinion of the petitioners that when the State party grants an extended freedom of expression to parliamentarians, who are protected from prosecutions, it allows racist propaganda and does not provide Muslims with sufficient protection.

3.13 The petitioners allege that the State party has violated its obligations under articles 4 and 6 of the Convention because, the Copenhagen Police having failed to carry out a proper investigation, the petitioners have been deprived of the opportunity to establish whether their rights under the Convention had been violated. The State party has therefore failed to provide the petitioners with effective protection against racial discrimination.

3.14 Referring to case No. 16/1999 (*Kashif Ahmad* v. *Denmark*), the petitioners stress that while the incidents have been reported on 20 June 2000, the decision of the police was transmitted a month later, on 21 July 2000. Similarly, the Attorney-General decided to uphold the police's decision 10 days after the case was brought to his attention by the DRC. The petitioners argue that it is highly unlikely that the Regional Public Prosecutor could investigate the matter and carry out investigation in 10 days, in particular, in order to assess the existence of "propaganda", to investigate all previously reported incidents concerning Pia Kjærsgaard. They further mention that they have never been questioned by the authorities in relation to their complaint.

3.15 To further support this allegation, the petitioners emphasize that the Regional Public Prosecutor has not responded properly to the different arguments developed in the complaint, the decision merely referring to the Copenhagen Police's decision and reproducing almost standard paragraphs. This demonstrates that the Regional Public Prosecutor did not investigate the matter.

*Alleged general violation of the Convention*

3.16 The petitioners argue that the State party has failed to comply with the principles of the Convention as a whole because it provides for more extensive protection for victims of defamation than for victims of racial discrimination.

3.17 While according to the Public Prosecution, political statements of a similar nature to that of the present case should be seen as legitimate contributions to the general political debate, the petitioners stress that, by contrast, a journalist, Lars Bonnevie, who wrote that Pia Kjærsgaard was promoting "apparent racist views" was convicted of defamation and sentenced to a fine and compensation.

3.18 In conclusion, the petitioners request the Committee to recommend to the State party to carry out a full investigation of this case and pay appropriate compensation to the victims.

*Observations by the State party*

4.1 By submission of 28 January 2002, the State party made its observations on the admissibility and merits of the case.

*On the admissibility*

4.2 The State party considers that the communication should be declared inadmissible *ratione personae* under article 14, paragraph 1, of the Convention because the petitioners are legal persons and not individuals or groups of individuals. It refers in this respect to the jurisprudence of the Human Rights Committee in cases Nos. 502/1992 and 737/1999. Moreover, the fact that the petitioners comprise a certain number of members and work for the interests of Muslims and other ethnic minorities does not entitle them to submit a communication under article 14 of the Convention.

4.3 Moreover, the petitioners have not submitted powers of attorney from one or more individuals claiming to be victims of a violation and authorizing them to submit such a communication.

4.4 Finally, the State party argues that the petitioners have not participated in the domestic proceedings. The report of 20 June 2000 was only made by the DRC who later on appealed to the Regional Public Prosecutor on behalf of seven named individuals.

*On the merits*

*Alleged violation of article 2, paragraph 1 (d), together with article 6*

4.5 With regard to the alleged violation of article 2, paragraph 1 (d) together with article 6, the State party is of the opinion that it cannot be inferred from the Convention that investigations should be carried out in situations which do not require it and consider that the Danish authorities have therefore fulfilled their obligations.

4.6 Furthermore, the State party considers that although proceedings in cases of alleged racial discrimination have to be carried out in compliance with the provisions of the Convention, the Convention does not specify which authority should decide to initiate prosecution or at what level of the hierarchy the decision should be taken.

4.7 For the same reasons, the State party argues that the notification of the case to the Director of Public Prosecutions cannot raise an issue under the Convention and has the only aim of ensuring a uniform prosecution practice and to collect case law in the field.

*Alleged violation of article 2, paragraph 1 (d), together with articles 4 and 6*

4.8 With regard to the alleged violation of article 2, paragraph 1 (d) together with articles 4 and 6, the State party contends that article 4 of the Convention provides that State parties undertake to declare any dissemination of ideas based on racial superiority or hatred an offence punishable by law but that State parties shall, at the same time, act according to article 19 of the Universal Declaration of Human Rights as well as article 5 (d) (viii) of the Convention.

4.9 The State party considers that the allegations made by the petitioners according to which the absence of conviction of Mogens Glistrup under section 266 (b) (2) implies that racist propaganda is accepted in Denmark was not substantiated, as the petitioners do not refer to particular incidents that have been reported to the police without any result. Moreover, in relation with the Supreme Court's judgement referred to by the petitioners, the State party indicates that since the charge under section 266 (b) (2) have been dismissed on procedural grounds, the judgement cannot be considered as reflecting an acceptance in Denmark of racist propaganda made by politicians.

4.10 The State party further explains that section 266 (b) has been amended in order to comply with its obligations under article 4 of the Convention. Concerning the relationship to the freedom of expression, it is mentioned in the *travaux préparatoires* that:

*On the other hand it is necessary to give due regard to the freedom of expression which should apply, also in comments on racial groups, etc., and which article 4 of the Convention had in view, among other things by its reference to the Universal Declaration of Human Rights. In this regard, it should first be*

*mentioned that, according to the draft, the criminal offences are limited to statements and other messages made "in public or with intent to dissemination to a wider circle". Furthermore, the statements referred to above—particularly the words "insulted or exposed to indignities"—must be interpreted to mean that offences of minor gravity are kept outside the criminal field. Outside the provision fall scientific theories put forward on differences of race, nationality or ethnicity, which presumably the Convention cannot have been intended to encompass. As mentioned above (...) there will probably also, concerning statements that were not made in a scientific context proper, but otherwise as part of an objective debate, be occasion to reckon with an area of impunity* (emphasis added by the State party).

4.11 Therefore, the State party has to apply section 266 (b) taking into account the offender's right to freedom of expression as set forth in article 19 of the International Covenant on Civil and Political Rights and article 10 of the European Convention on Human Rights.

4.12 The State party refers thereafter to a number of cases decided by the European Court of Human Rights, stating that the latter attaches an important weight to freedom of expression, especially when expressions are made as part of a political or social debate. In the case *Jersild* v. *Denmark* concerning a journalist who had been convicted under section 266 (b) for having made racist statements, the European Court of Human Rights held that the protection against racist statements had to be balanced against the freedom of expression. Concerning the relationship with the Convention, the Court stated that:

Denmark's obligation under article 10 [of the European Convention] must be interpreted, to the extent possible, so as to be reconcilable with its obligation under the United Nations Convention. In this respect it is not for the Court to interpret the "due regard" clause in article 4 of the United Nations Convention, which is open to various constructions. The Court is however of the opinion that its interpretation of article 10 of the European Convention in the present case is compatible with Denmark's obligations under the United Nations Convention.

4.13 This balance is also made in the State party's case law. In the above-mentioned Supreme Court's case concerning Mogens

Glitrup, the court found that Glistrup's statements could not objectively be justified and the extensive freedom of expression for politicians could not lead to acquittal in this case.

4.14 The State party then explains that the newsletter of 19 June 2000 was related to the level of punishment in case of rapes and gang rapes following the case of a 14-year-old girl who had been raped by several men of non-Danish ethnic background. The debate took place in the context of a proposed legislative amendment purporting to increase the punishment for rape committed by several perpetrators jointly and attracted great public interest.

4.15 The State party finds that the statement made by a Member of Parliament should be considered therefore as part of the public debate on this issue and are not of the same aggravated nature as the statements for which Mogens Glistrup was convicted by the Supreme Court.

4.16 The State party further considers that the content of the statement made in the newsletter is not disproportionate to the aim pursued, which is to take part in the debate on the issue of punishment for certain offences. The Copenhagen Police and the Regional Public Prosecutor made thus a correct balancing between article 4 of the Convention and the right to freedom of expression by deciding in advantage of the latter.

*Alleged violation of articles 4 and 6 of the Convention*

4.17 With regard to the alleged violation of articles 4 and 6 of the Convention, the State party considers that the question that had to be decided by the relevant authorities was whether Pia Kjærsgaard had violated section 266 (b) because of the statement made in the newsletter of 19 June 2000. It did not concern other statements from this person nor did it concern generally the principle of the scope of freedom of expression for Members of Parliament.

4.18 Concerning the obligation to investigate acts of racial discrimination, the State party, referring to a number of decisions taken by the Committee, considers that the investigation conducted by the police in the present case fully satisfied the obligations that can be inferred from the Convention. On the basis of the report made by the DRC, another report

was drafted and no further investigative steps were taken because the decision consisted in a legal assessment of the content of the newsletter, i.e., whether it constituted a violation of section 266 (b).

4.19 The State party also indicates that the petitioners were not questioned because they were not part of the domestic proceedings and that neither the DRC nor the seven persons named by the latter were questioned because such interviews were not relevant for the investigation, as the outcome of the case depended solely on a legal assessment.

4.20 The same argumentation is valid for the decision taken by the Regional Public Prosecutor.

4.21 Moreover, the State party considers that, since the statements were not considered to be in violation of section 266 (b) (1), neither the Copenhagen Police nor the Regional Public Prosecutor should consider whether propaganda in the sense of section 266 (b) (2) was involved, because this subsection only provides for an aggravating circumstance of acts under section 266 (b) (1).

*Alleged general violation of the Convention*

4.22 Concerning the alleged general violation of the Convention because individual victims of defamation would be better protected than groups of victims of defamation, degradation and insults, the State party contends that the object of the legal provisions on defamation is to protect the honour of specific individuals against offensive words and acts while the object of section 266 (b) is to protect groups of persons who are threatened, insulted or exposed to indignities on the grounds of race, colour, national extraction, ethnic origin, religion or sexual orientation. The two provisions are applied differently in view of their different contents and purposes.

4.23 Furthermore, both provisions complement each other as, for example, an individual can be charged for defamation even if the conditions for a charge under 266 are not met.

*Author's comments*

5.1 By submission of 14 May 2002, the petitioners made their comments on the State party's observations.

5.2 With regard to the admissibility of the communication, the petitioners are of the opinion that article 14 of the Convention does not prevent non-governmental organizations to submit communications to the Committee. Contesting that POEM and FASM are legal persons, they argue that these organizations are non-governmental organizations which represent a group of people and are thus entitled to submit a communication under article 14.

5.3 The petitioners further contend that the objective of article 14 is to exclude communications from individuals who are not subject to the jurisdiction of the State party. The petitioners consider also that article 14 of the Convention should be interpreted along the terms of article 34 of the European Convention of Human Rights,[2] which expressly provides for the right for non-governmental organizations to apply before the European Court of Human Rights.

5.4 Alternatively, the petitioners note that the powers of attorney from individual members of POEM and FASM, submitted together with their present comments, make clear that those individuals as well as the organizations that represent them appointed DRC to submit the communication to the Committee.

5.5 With regard to the alleged violation of article 2, paragraph 1 (d), together with article 6, the petitioners maintain that cases concerning section 266 (b) are treated differently whether the police intends to dismiss a report or to prosecute.

5.6 The petitioners explain that if the Regional Public Prosecutor had decided to charge Pia Kjærsgaard, she would have been entitled to receive a third opinion on the matter since the Director of Public Prosecutions takes the final decision in such cases. By contrast, the alleged victims do not have the same right if the Regional Public Prosecutor decides to dismiss the case. The Director of Public Prosecutions will only be notified of the decision to dismiss. In the opinion of the petitioners, this constitutes a differential treatment that is incompatible with the

Convention and, in particular, with article 2, paragraph 1 (d).

5.7 With regard to the alleged violation of article 2, paragraph 1 (d) together with articles 4 and 6, the petitioners agree with the State party and the European Court of Human Right's decision in *Jersild* v. *Denmark* that a fair balance has to be assessed between freedom of expression and protection against racist statements. However, in the present case, it appears that the Regional Public Prosecutor found that the statement was degrading and insulting individuals with another ethnic background but that it was not severe enough to limit the freedom of expression. The petitioners consider that the Regional Public Prosecutor should have decided that the statement fell under section 266 (b), alongside a precedent judgement of 10 April 1996 in a similar case. In the present case, freedom of expression could not constitute a justification to dismiss the case.

5.8 The petitioners therefore conclude that politicians in Denmark are entitled to make statements that fall under section 266 (b) without being charged while others, non-politicians, would be charged for similar statements. The petitioners asked the Director of Public Prosecutions to comment on this point of view which they consider as having no justification and being contrary to article 2, paragraph 1 (d), article 4 and 6 of the Convention.

5.9 The petitioners further indicate that, while they do not dispute that the European Court gives a wider margin to freedom of expression for politicians, the same holds true for journalists. In this regard, they refer again to the case of Lars Bonnevie, who was convicted of defamation on 29 April 1999 for having claimed that Pia Kjærsgaard was promoting "apparent racist views". In the same line, the petitioners refer to a decision of the Court of Aarhus which convicted a politician, Karen Sund, for having stated that "[o]ne cannot cooperate with the Danish People's Party because the leader of the party has a racial point of view".

5.10 Finally, the petitioners contend that it is for the courts to draw the line between freedom of expression and protection from racist remarks and not the police or the Regional Public Prosecutor. This is even more justified, because of the independence of the judiciary, in cases where the alleged offender is a politician.

---

[2] Article 34 of the European Convention on Human Rights reads:
The Court may receive applications from any person, non-governmental organization or group of individuals claiming to be the victim of a violation by one of the High Contracting Parties of the rights set forth in the Convention or the protocols thereto. The High Contracting Parties undertake not to hinder in any way the effective exercise of this right.

5.11 With regard to the alleged violation of articles 4 and 6, the petitioners reiterate that the case has not been investigated thoroughly and individually.

*Issues and proceedings before the Committee*

6.1 Before considering any claims contained in a communication, the Committee on the Elimination of Racial Discrimination must decide, pursuant to article 14 of the Convention and rules 86 and 91 of its rules of procedure, whether or not the communication is admissible.

6.2 The Committee notes the State party's argument that none of the petitioners were plaintiffs in the domestic proceedings and that the report to the Copenhagen Police was only submitted by the DRC.

6.3 The Committee considers that it is a basic requirement under article 14, paragraph 7 (a) that domestic remedies have to be exhausted by the petitioners themselves and not by other organizations or individuals. The Committee

finds therefore that communication is inadmissible under article 14, paragraph 7 (a), of the Convention.

7. Notwithstanding the above, the Committee calls the State party's attention to the content of paragraph 115 of the Programme of Action adopted by the World Conference against Racism, Racial Discrimination, Xenophobia and Related Intolerance in Durban (South Africa) on 8 September 2001, which "underlines the key role that politicians and political parties can play in combating racism, racial discrimination, xenophobia and related intolerance and encourages political parties to take concrete steps to promote equality, solidarity and non-discrimination in society, inter alia by developing voluntary codes of conduct which include internal disciplinary measures for violations thereof, so their members refrain from public statements and actions that encourage or incite racism, racial discrimination, xenophobia and related intolerance".

# Communication No. 25/2002

> *Submitted by*: Ahmad Najaati Sadic (represented by the Documentation and Advisory Centre on Racial Discrimination).
> *Alleged victim*: The petitioner.
> *State party*: Denmark.
> *Declared inadmissible*: 16 April 2003.
> *Subject matter:* Insults on racial grounds in public; effective investigation; access to effective mechanism of protection; discrimination based on national origin.
> *Procedural issues:* Exhaustion of domestic remedy; inadmissibility *ratione materiae.*
> *Substantive issues:* Right to an effective remedy against acts of racial discrimination; right to an effective investigation.
> *Articles of the Convention:* 2 (1) (d), 6 and 14 (7) (a).

*Decision on admissibility*

1.1 The petitioner is Mr. Ahmad Najaati Sadic, a Danish citizen of Iraqi origin, born in 1955, who claims to be a victim of violations by Denmark of article 2, paragraph 1 (d), and article 6 of the Convention. He is represented by counsel, the Documentation and Advisory Centre on Racial Discrimination (DRC).

1.2 In conformity with article 14, paragraph 6 (a), of the Convention, the Committee transmitted the communication to the State party on 16 August 2002.

*Facts of the case*

2.1 On 25 July 2000, the petitioner was working on a construction site in a public housing area in Randers, Denmark, for the company "Assentoft Painters and Decorators" owned by Jesper Christensen. When the petitioner approached Mr. Christensen to claim overdue payments, their conversation developed into an argument during which Mr. Christensen reportedly made the following comments to the petitioner: "Push off home, you Arab pig", "Immigrant pig", "Both you and all Arabs smell", "Disappear from here, God damned idiots and psychopaths." The argument between the complainant and Mr. Christensen was overheard by at least two other workers, Mr. Carsten Thomassen and Mr. Frank Lasse Hendriksen.

2.2 On 1 March 2001, the DRC, on behalf of the petitioner, informed the police in Aarhus of the incident, arguing that section 266 (b)[1] of the Danish Criminal Code had been violated by the petitioner's by then former employer.

2.3 On 9 July 2001, Frank Lasse Henriksen was interviewed by telephone by the police of Randers. The interview report states:

> "The witness stated that he was working when his boss, Mr. Christensen, came and presented a new apprentice; also present was the victim, Ahmad. A discussion/quarrel arose between Mr. Christensen and the victim, and the discussion concerned holiday pay, wages and missing wage slips [...]. [T]he witness went to Mr. Christensen, who at this point was angry about the quarrel with the victim, and felt—at least he said so—that, if the witness felt like the victim, he could consider himself sacked. The witness was so infuriated with the treatment that he took his boss at his word. Mr. Christensen now shouted that it was all just about an Arab bastard—which, in the witness's opinion, was far too rude. According to the witness, Mr. Christensen went far beyond the line. The witness was read the racist statements mentioned in the complaint and stated that they corresponded to what Mr. Christensen had called the victim. After this, the witness immediately left the workplace and has not worked for Mr. Christensen since [...]".

2.4 On 12 July 2001, Carsten Thomassen was interviewed by telephone by the police of Aarhus. The interview report states:

> "On the relevant day, at about 10.30 a.m., Mr. Sadic and his boss were standing on the external gallery on the first floor— below the witness. The witness could hear that they were quarrelling about both work and money. However, the witness had only heard fragments of the quarrel, in which both parties had obviously become 'over-excited'. At some stage, the witness heard Mr. Christensen say something like: 'You can just go home'— 'black bastard'. The witness could not hear what Mr. Sadic said as he did not speak Danish very well and was difficult to understand—particularly when he was upset, as in that moment. However, to a large extent, the witness took the quarrel to be one that may arise once in a while at the workplace [...]."

2.5 Mr. Christensen was interviewed by the police of Randers on 23 July 2001, without any charges being brought against him and without prejudice to his right to refuse testimony. The interview report states:

> "Mr. Christensen stated that, on the relevant day, he had a quarrel with the victim about payment for overtime [...]. Mr. Christensen and the victim [...] used abusive language [...]. Mr. Christensen never used [...] words like 'Arab bastard', 'Paki bastard', 'Arabs smell', etc., towards the victim. Mr. Christensen was confronted with the witness statement of Mr. Henriksen. To this, Mr. Christensen stated that he had previously sacked Mr. Henriksen due to disagreements. [...] After Mr. Henriksen had been sacked, he left the workplace and, consequently, cannot have overheard the conversation with the victim. [...] On the basis of the information presented, Mr. Christensen cannot admit [a] violation of section 266 (b) of the Criminal Code. [...]."

2.6 By letter of 24 August 2001, the Chief Constable of the Aarhus police informed the DRC that the investigation of the case had been discontinued, stating that it could not reasonably be presumed that a criminal offence subject to ex officio prosecution had been committed. The discontinuation of the investigation was mainly based on the fact that the argument between the petitioner and Mr. Christensen had taken place at work, "where only two other persons were present". Apart from the question whether or not Mr. Christensen had made the statements in question, the Chief Constable found that, in

---

[1] Section 266 (b) of the Criminal Code reads, in pertinent parts:
"(1) Any person who, publicly or with the intention of wider dissemination, makes a statement or imparts other information by which a group of people are threatened, insulted or degraded on account of their race, colour, national or ethnic origin, religion, or sexual inclination shall be liable to a fine or to imprisonment for any term not exceeding four months.
(2) [...]
(3) [...]."

any event, these statements had not been made publicly or with the intention of wider dissemination. As to a claim for damages, the petitioner was advised to pursue civil proceedings.

2.7 On 28 September 2001, the petitioner appealed the decision to discontinue investigations before the Regional Public Prosecutor in Viborg, arguing that the petitioner's former employer had made his statements on a construction site in a public housing area and, therefore, had at least accepted the possibility that other people would hear his comments. Moreover, the petitioner referred to several judgements of Danish courts which construed the requirement, in section 266 (b) of the Criminal Code, of statements being made publicly quite broadly. He challenged the Chief Constable's finding that only two other persons were present at the incident. The petitioner quoted from a written statement in which Mr. Thomassen asserted that "[o]n Tuesday, 25 July 2000, at about 10.30 a.m., I, Carsten Thomassen, was standing together with three other colleagues [...] on the external gallery for a short break, when, to our great surprise, we overheard a conversation/quarrel between the master [...] and Ahmad".

2.8 By letter of 27 November 2001, the Regional Public Prosecutor of Viborg dismissed the appeal, arguing that, although it could not be established with certainty that only two other persons were present at the incident, the statements by Mr. Christensen were made in connection with a dispute between the petitioner and his employer at a stage where both parties had become over-excited and that the witnesses were some distance away from the exact place of the quarrel and only heard fragments of the dispute. Given that "this was only a loud-voiced quarrel which others happened to overhear—at a distance [...]", the Regional Public Prosecutor concluded that the employer's statements could not be considered public. Since the argument was not likely to disturb the public peace or cause a nuisance to other people present, the police regulations had not been violated either. The petitioner was thus advised to pursue any claim for damages through civil proceedings. The decision of the Regional Public Prosecutor was final and could not be appealed.

*The complaint*

3.1 The petitioner claims that he has exhausted domestic remedies, as there is no possibility to appeal the decision of the Regional Public Prosecutor and he cannot bring the case before the Danish courts. He submits that, under section 275 of the Danish Criminal Code, violations of section 266 (b) are subject only to prosecution ex officio and that direct legal action against his former employer would have been without prospect, given that the police and the Regional Public Prosecutor had rejected his complaint. In support of the latter claim, the petitioner submits that, pursuant to a decision of the Eastern High Court dated 5 February 1999, an incident of racial discrimination does not in itself constitute a violation of the honour and reputation of a person within the meaning of section 26 of the Liability for Damages Act.

3.2 The petitioner claims that the State party has violated its obligations under articles 2, paragraph 1 (d), and 6 of the Convention by not investigating effectively to what extent the construction site was accessible to the public, how many people were present at the incident and to what extent it would have been possible for others to overhear the employer's statements. The petitioner argues that, following the decision of the Committee in *L.K. v. Netherlands* (case No. 4/1991, Opinion adopted on 16 March 1993), States parties have a positive obligation under the above provisions to take effective action against reported incidents of racial discrimination.

3.3 By reference to another case decided by the Committee *(Kashif Ahmad v. Denmark)* (case No. 16/1999, Opinion adopted on 13 March 2000) [in which racist comments were made in a hallway outside a classroom], the petitioner submits that the State party did not claim in that case that the statements had not been made publicly and that a violation was found by the Committee. He furthermore refers to two cases in which Danish courts found violations of section 266 (b) of the Criminal Code in what he considers similar circumstances.

3.4 The petitioner asks the Committee to request the State party to carry out a full investigation into the incident reported by him and to award him financial compensation, in accordance with article 6 of the Convention.

*The State party's submission on the admissibility and the merits of the communication*

4.1 By note verbale of 20 November 2002, the State party made its submissions on the admissibility and, subsidiarily, on the merits of the communication.

4.2 On admissibility, the State party submits that the petitioner failed to exhaust domestic remedies. Contrary to violations of section 266 (b), which are subject to prosecution ex officio, violations of section 267[2] of the Criminal Code—the general provision on defamatory statements which supplements section 266 (b)—are prosecuted only at the request of the individual concerned, pursuant to section 275[3] of the Criminal Code. The petitioner could have requested the institution of criminal proceedings under section 267 against his employer and, by doing so, could have obtained a decision on whether his former employer had made the reported statements and, subject to fulfilling the conditions of section 267, a conviction of Mr. Christensen.

4.3 The State party contends that the institution of criminal proceedings under section 267 of the Criminal Code is an effective remedy. Moreover, the decision of the Danish authorities to discontinue investigations under section 266 (b) was without prejudice to the effectiveness of that remedy, since neither the Chief Constable nor the Regional Public Prosecutor had taken any position on the question whether Mr. Christensen had made the statements complained of. The State party argues that, for the same reason, the discontinuation of investigations under section 266 (b) did not preclude a legal action for non-pecuniary damages against his former

employer, under section 26 of the Liability for Damages Act.[4]

4.4 The State party argues that the communication is incompatible with the Convention *ratione materiae*, since the central claim is that the Danish authorities did not interpret and apply section 266 (b) of the Criminal Code correctly. The concrete elements which, according to the petitioner, should have been investigated all relate to the conditions for punishment under section 266 (b), i.e., the place where the statements were made, the number of persons who heard or might have heard Mr. Christensen's statements, etc. in the State party's opinion, the legal assessment by the Chief Constable and the Regional Public Prosecutor of Viborg that the requirements of section 266 (b) were not met in the present case is primarily a matter which relates to interpretation and application of domestic legislation and which the Committee has no competence to review.

4.5 On the basis of the above arguments, the State party concludes that the communication should be declared inadmissible under article 14, paragraphs 1 and 7 (a), of the Convention.

4.6 Subsidiarily and on the merits, the State party submits that the Danish authorities took the petitioner's complaint seriously, as they initiated investigations and interviewed witnesses, as well as the petitioner's former employer, as a result of the complaint. It concludes that the processing and assessment of the complaint by the Chief Constable and the Regional Public Prosecutor therefore fully complies with the State party's obligations under article 2, paragraph 1, and article 6 of the Convention.

4.7 With regard to the requirement that a statement should be made "publicly or with the intention of wider dissemination", the State party admits that grey zones in the delimitation between public and private are unavoidable and argues that it should therefore be for the national authorities to assess whether these requirements have been met in a specific case.

4.8 The State party submits that the two judgements adduced in support of his

---

[2] Section 267 of the Criminal Code reads, in pertinent parts:
"(1) Any person who violates the honour of another [person] by offensive words or conduct, or by making or spreading allegations of an act likely to disparage [that person] in the esteem of his or her fellow citizens, shall be liable to a fine or to imprisonment [...] not exceeding four months.
(2) [...]
(3) [...]."
[3] Section 275 of the Criminal Code reads, in pertinent parts:
"(1) The offences contained in this Part shall be prosecuted at the request of the individual concerned, except for the offences referred to in sections [...] 266 (b).
(2) [...]."

---

[4] Section 26, paragraph 1, of the Liability for Damages Act reads:
"(1) A person who is liable for unlawful violation of another person's freedom, peace, character or person shall pay compensation to the injured party for non-pecuniary damage."

arguments by the petitioner could not be relied upon because, in one case, the judgement contained no specific information on the number of persons present in the news store and, in the other case, the court observed that "many persons must have overheard [...] the incident".

4.9 The State party argues, moreover, that section 266 (b) of the Criminal Code is not the only provision designed to ensure compliance with the State party's obligations under the Convention, since it is supplemented by other provisions, including section 267 of the same Code.

4.10 The State party concludes that, even if the Committee were to declare the communication admissible, it does in any event not disclose a violation of the Convention.

## Comments by the petitioner

5.1 The petitioner submits that section 267 of the Criminal Code, as well as section 26 of the Liability for Damages Act, do not address the issue of racial discrimination and therefore do not provide an effective remedy against acts of racial discrimination, as required by article 2, paragraph 1 (d), and article 6 of the Convention. He claims that the only relevant remedy is section 266 (b) of the Criminal Code, indicating that, in previous cases, it was not held by the Committee that, in order to exhaust domestic remedies, a petitioner should have initiated criminal proceedings under section 267 of the Criminal Code or civil proceedings under section 26 of the Liability for Damages Act.

5.2 As to the requirements of section 266 (b) of the Criminal Code, the petitioner reiterates that Danish courts found violations of that provision in the past even where only one other person apart from the victim(s) had been present during an incident of racial discrimination. He also refers to the Opinion in *Kashif Ahmad* v. *Denmark* (case No. 16/1999, para. 6.1), where the Committee found a violation of article 6 of the Convention on the basis "that the author was insulted in public", since the relevant statements were made "in a school corridor and in the presence of several witnesses".

5.3 Based on the written statement of Mr. Thomassen, the petitioner claims that at least five persons overheard his argument with his employer and that the police failed to

contact the other three colleagues mentioned in that statement.

5.4 The petitioner rejects the State party's argument that the core of his communication is related to the interpretation of domestic legislation and the evaluation of facts and evidence. He argues that the lack of an effective investigation is closely connected to the fact that the Danish authorities concluded that his complaint fell outside the scope of section 266 (b) of the Criminal Code.

## Issues and proceedings before the Committee

6.1 Before considering the substance of a communication, the Committee on the Elimination of Racial Discrimination must, in accordance with rule 91 of its rules of procedure, examine whether or not the communication is admissible.

6.2 The Committee notes that the petitioner brought a complaint under section 266 (b) of the Criminal Code before the police and the Regional Public Prosecutor; and that these authorities, after having interviewed two witnesses and the petitioner's former employer, decided to discontinue criminal proceedings under section 266 (b), as they considered that the requirements of this provision were not satisfied. It has taken note of the State party's argument that, despite the discontinuation of proceedings under section 266 (b) of the Criminal Code, the petitioner could have requested the institution of criminal proceedings against his former employer under the general provision on defamatory statements (sect. 267 of the Criminal Code). The petitioner does not deny the availability of this remedy, but questions its effectiveness in relation to incidents of racial discrimination.

6.3 The Committee observes that the notion of "effective remedy", within the meaning of article 6 of the Convention, is not limited to criminal proceedings based on provisions which specifically, expressly and exclusively penalize acts of racial discrimination. In particular, the Committee does not consider it contrary to articles 2, paragraph 1 (d), and 6 of the Convention if, as in the State party's case, the provisions of criminal law specifically adopted to outlaw acts of racial discrimination are supplemented by a general provision criminalizing defamatory statements which is applicable to racist statements even if they are not covered by specific legislation.

6.4 As to the petitioner's argument that criminal proceedings against his former employer under section 267 would have been without prospect because the authorities had already rejected his complaint under section 266 (b) of the Criminal Code, the Committee notes, on the basis of the material before it, that the requirements for prosecution under section 266 (b) are not identical to those for prosecution under section 267 of the Criminal Code. It therefore does not appear that the Danish authorities' decision to discontinue proceedings under section 266 (b) on the ground of lack of evidence as to whether the employer's statements were made publicly or with the intention of wider dissemination have prejudiced a request by the petitioner to institute criminal proceedings under section 267 (together with sect. 275) of the Criminal Code. The Committee therefore considers that the institution of such proceedings can be regarded as an effective remedy which the petitioner failed to exhaust.

6.5 As to the question of damages, the Committee recalls the State party's argument that the petitioner did not institute civil proceedings against his former employer under section 26 of the Liability for Damages Act and therefore did not exhaust domestic remedies. With regard to the petitioner's arguments that a previous decision of the Eastern High Court held that an incident of racial discrimination does not in itself constitute a violation of the honour and reputation of a person, the Committee considers that mere doubts about the effectiveness of available civil remedies do not absolve a petitioner from pursuing them (see communication No. 19/2000, *Sarwar Seliman Mostafa* v. *Denmark*, decision adopted on 10 August 2001, para. 7.4).

6.6. Accordingly, the Committee considers that, by not exhausting the available domestic remedies, the petitioner has failed to meet the requirements of article 14, paragraph 7 (a), of the Convention.

6.7 The Committee on the Elimination of Racial Discrimination therefore decides:

(a) That the communication is inadmissible;

(b) That this decision shall be communicated to the State party and to the petitioner.

6.8 However, the Committee invites the State party to reconsider its legislation, since the restrictive condition of "broad publicity" or "wider dissemination" required by article 266 (b) of the Danish Criminal Code for the criminalization of racial insults does not appear to be fully in conformity with the requirements of articles 4 and 6 of the Convention.

# Communication No. 28/2003

*Submitted by*: The Documentation and Advisory Centre on Racial Discrimination (represented counsel, Fakhra Mohammad).
*Alleged victim*: The petitioner.
*State party*: Denmark.
*Declared inadmissible:* 26 August 2003.
*Subject matter:* Discriminatory job advertisement; access to effective mechanism of protection; discrimination based on national origin.
*Procedural issues:* Inadmissibility *ratione materiae,* inadmissibility *ratione personae,* status of "victim".
*Substantive issues:* Prohibition of propaganda based on ideas or theories of superiority of one race or group of persons of one colour or ethnic origin, or which attempt to justify or promote racial hatred and discrimination in any form; right to an effective remedy against acts of racial discrimination.
*Articles of the Convention:* 2 (1) (d), 4, 5 and 6.

*Decision on admissibility*

1.1 The petitioner is the Documentation and Advisory Centre on Racial Discrimination, represented by Ms. Fakhra Mohammad, born on 6 May 1960, who is the head of the board of trustees of the Centre. The petitioner alleges violations by Denmark of articles 2, paragraph 1(d), 4, 5 and 6 of the Convention.

1.2 In conformity with article 14, paragraph 6 (a), of the Convention, the Committee transmitted the communication to the State party on 14 April 2003.

*The facts as submitted by the petitioner*

2.1 On 27 January 2002, a private company, "Torben Jensen A/S", published a job advertisement in the Danish newspaper "Jyllands Posten". The advertisement read as follows:

"The construction company BAC SIA seeks Danish foreman who, in cooperation with a Latvian construction expert, will be assigned the general responsibility of renovating and constructing a larger agricultural building approximately 80 kilometres from Riga."

2.2 By letter of 30 January 2002, the petitioner reported the incident to the Chief Constable of the police in Vejle, the district where "Torben Jensen A/S" was located. In the letter, the petitioner alleged a violation by the company of section 5[1] of Act No. 459 of 12 June 1996 on prohibition against discrimination in respect of employment and occupation etc. on the labour market, arguing that the words "Danish foreman" in the advertisement amounted to discrimination on the ground of national or ethnic origin.

2.3 On 5 February 2002, the police interviewed Mr. E.H., accountant of "Torben Jensen A/C". On the basis of this interview, the Chief Constable, by letter of 13 March 2002, informed the petitioner that he had decided to dismiss the complaint:

"In my decision, I have notably given weight to the fact that, based on the police's questioning of Torben Jensen, and, moreover, from reading the advertisement, it is, in my view, quite clear that there is no violation of the said Act. What is sought for the position in Latvia is a Danish resident, and this person could easily be of an ethnicity other than Danish. In the worst case, it is a matter of an unfortunate choice of words, but not of a content which constitutes grounds for further action in this case."

2.4 On 22 March 2002, the petitioner appealed the Chief Constable's decision to the Regional Public Prosecutor of Sønderborg.

---

[1] Section 5 of Act No. 459 of 5 July 1996 reads: "Advertisements may not indicate that a person of a particular race, colour, religion, political opinion, sexual orientation or national, social or ethnic origin is sought or preferred. Nor must it be indicated that a person with the characteristics mentioned in the first clause of this Section is not wanted."

According to the petitioner, it was irrelevant whether the company had actually intended to recruit a Danish resident, as the decisive question under section 5 of Act No. 459 was whether the wording of the job advertisement could be perceived as indicating a preference for a foreman of Danish origin. Since section 5 also criminalizes negligence, this provision would also be violated, if the unintended effect of the advertisement had been to exclude a group defined by one of the criteria enumerated in section 1, paragraph 1,[2] of the same Act from applying for the job. However, the Chief Constable did not appear to have investigated this possibility. Moreover, the petitioner contested that the term "Danish foreman" was supposed to refer to a Danish resident, as such residence could not be regarded a logical requirement for the construction job in Latvia and because it followed from the publication of the advertisement in a Danish newspaper that the group of recipients would essentially be limited to Danish residents in any event.

2.5 By letter of 3 June 2002, the Regional Public Prosecutor of Sønderborg informed the petitioner that he had dismissed the appeal, based on the same reasons as those mentioned in the decision of the Chief Constable.

2.6 On 3 December 2002, "the Documentation and Advisory Centre on Racial Discrimination [represented] by Fakhra Mohammad, head of the board of trustees", submitted the present communication.

*The complaint*

3.1 The petitioner claims that, as the head of the board of trustees, Ms. Fakhra Mohammad "represents the [Documentation and Advisory Centre] when complaints are filed in her name". Although neither Ms. Fakhra Mohammad nor any other person of non-Danish origin applied for the advertised job, she should be considered a victim of the discriminatory advertisement, since it would have been futile for her to apply for the post. Moreover, the petitioner itself should be recognized as having status of victim under

article 14 of the Convention, since it represents "a large group of persons of non-Danish origin discriminated against by the job advertisement in question". In support of this claim, the petitioner states that both the police and the Regional Public Prosecutor have accepted it as a party to domestic proceedings.

3.2 The petitioner claims to have exhausted domestic remedies, as there is no possibility to appeal the decision of the Regional Public Prosecutor of 3 June 2002, and since the case cannot be brought before the Danish courts. Direct legal actions against Torben Jensen A/S would be ineffective, given that the police and the Regional Public Prosecutor both rejected the complaint. Moreover, the Eastern High Court, in a decision of 5 February 1999, held that an incident of racial discrimination does not in itself constitute a violation of the honour and reputation of a person, within the meaning of section 26 of the Act on Civil Liability.

3.3 The petitioner claims that the State party has violated its obligations under articles 4 and 6 of the Convention, as it failed to investigate whether the job advertisement constituted an act of racial discrimination, punishable under section 5 of Act No. 459, and instead admitted the company's explanation that what was meant by "Danish foreman" was a person residing in Denmark. In particular, the State party should have investigated the following questions: (1) whether the person eventually employed was of Danish national/ethnic origin or not; (2) whether the intended meaning of the advertisement should be taken into account; (3) whether the explanation provided by Torben Jensen A/C was logical; (4) whether the publishing of the advertisement constituted indirect discrimination; and (5) whether the publishing of the advertisement was punishable as negligence.

3.4 The petitioner argues that the company's alleged intention to recruit a Danish resident was irrelevant, since the objective meaning of the term "Danish" in the advertisement clearly related to the national/ethnic origin of the person sought. The de facto effect of the advertisement thus was to deprive applicants of non-Danish origin of equal opportunities. Whether this effect was intended or not played no role, since section 5 of Act No. 459 also criminalized negligence. Moreover, it followed from section 1, paragraph 1, of the Act that section 5 also covered indirect discrimination, a modality which the Danish authorities had equally failed to investigate.

---

[2] Section 1, paragraph 1, of Act No. 459 reads: "For the purpose of this Act, the term 'discrimination' means any direct or indirect discrimination on the basis of race, colour, religion, political opinion, sexual orientation or national, social or ethnic origin."

3.5 In addition, the petitioner contests that the term "Danish foreman" was used as a synonym for "Danish resident" by the company, and reiterates the arguments already stated before the Regional Public Prosecutor (see para. 2.4 above).

*The State party's submission on the admissibility and merits of the communication*

4.1 By note verbale of 7 July 2003, the State party made its submissions on the admissibility and, subsidiarily, on the merits of the communication.

4.2 On admissibility, the State party denies that the petitioner has legal standing to submit a communication, under article 14, paragraph 1, of the Convention, as it is a legal entity and not an individual or group of individuals. As such, the petitioner is not in a position to claim that it is the victim of a violation of any of the rights set forth in the Convention. Furthermore, the petitioner failed to present its power of attorney from one or more individuals, claiming to be victims of such a violation, which would authorize it to submit a communication on their behalf. The State party concludes that the communication is inadmissible *ratione personae* under article 14, paragraph 1, of the Convention.

4.3 While conceding that the decision of the Regional Public Prosecutor, acting on appeal cannot be appealed to a higher authority, and that private parties cannot bring charges under section 5 of Act No. 459 before the courts, the State party denies that the petitioner has exhausted available domestic remedies, since such remedies have to be exhausted by the petitioners themselves and not by other organizations or individuals. The fact that the petitioner participated in domestic proceedings by lodging a complaint with the Danish authorities was irrelevant, given that the petitioner, being a legal person, had no victim status under the Convention. The State party concludes that the communication is also inadmissible under article 14, paragraph 7 (a), of the Convention.

4.4 The State party further argues that the determination made by the Chief Constable and the Regional Public Prosecutor that the requirements of section 5 of Act No. 459 were not met in the present case was primarily a matter of interpretation and application of domestic legislation, which the Committee has no competence to review. The communication is therefore also incompatible *ratione materiae* with the Convention.

4.5 Subsidiarily and on the merits, the State party submits that the petitioner has failed to substantiate that the Danish legislation as such was not in conformity with its obligations under article 4 of the Convention. On the contrary, the communication was based on the assumption that the Danish authorities did not apply Act No. 459 correctly.

4.6 The State party argues that, while requiring that an investigation must be carried out with due diligence and expedition and must be sufficient to determine whether or not an incident of racial discrimination has occurred, article 6 of the Convention does not guarantee the initiation, let alone a specific outcome, of such an investigation in all cases reported to the police. If no basis can be found to initiate an investigation, it is not contrary to the Convention to dismiss a complaint. In the present case, the decisions of the Danish authorities were based on sufficient information, namely the interview of the company's accountant by the Police Constable. This was also reflected by the fact that the petitioner did not consider further information necessary to determine that the advertisement was in violation of section 5 of Act No. 459. However, the above question again related to the interpretation and practical application of the Danish legislation, thus falling outside the Committee's competence.

4.7 With regard to the specific questions raised by the petitioner (see para. 3.3 above), the State party argues: (1) that the employment of a person of Danish origin or ethnicity in Denmark cannot in itself be considered to substantiate an allegation of discrimination; (2) that the intention of Torben Jensen A/C was relevant to the interpretation of the wording of the advertisement, while its legal assessment falls outside the traditional field of police investigation; (3) that the question of whether the explanation provided by the company was convincing also is not a matter of traditional police investigation, but rather a matter of assessing critically the information already provided by the police, as well as by the petitioner; that the questions whether the advertisement constituted (4) indirect discrimination or (5) negligence, punishable under section 5 of the Act, was not for the police to investigate, since it related to the application and interpretation of Danish legislation, and can therefore not be reviewed by the Committee.

4.8 Without prejudice to the above arguments, the State party submits that the Chief Constable and the Regional Public Prosecutor of Sønderborg made a correct assessment when they considered that the adjective "Danish" in the advertisement referred to Danish residents, since the nature of the relationship to Denmark required by that wording was not precisely determined. The advertisement was therefore not covered by section 5 of the Act, given that a Danish resident may be of any ethnicity or national origin.

4.9 The State party concludes that article 6 has not been violated, as the petitioner had access to effective remedies, resulting in decisions of the Danish authorities, which were taken on an adequate and informed basis in accordance with the requirements of the Convention.

*Comments by the petitioner*

5.1 By submission of 18 July 2003, the petitioner commented on the State party's observations and extended the claim contained in the communication of 3 December 2002 to the effect that the State party's alleged failure to carry out an effective investigation also amounted to a violation of articles, 5 and 2, paragraph 1 (d), in addition to the initial claim of a violation of articles 4 and 6, of the Convention.

5.2 While conceding that the communication was submitted "by Fakhra Mohammad acting as the head of the board of trustees" of the Documentation and Advisory Centre and therefore "by a legal person", the petitioner contests the State party's conclusion that legal entities cannot file communications, nor claim victim status, under article 14 of the Convention. The petitioner argues that it follows from the *travaux préparatoires* to the Convention that the words "individuals or groups of individuals" in article 14, paragraph 1, should be interpreted broadly so as to be able to include non-governmental organizations among those entitled to bring a complaint before the Committee.

5.3 As to its the status of victim, the petitioner submits that such status cannot, under section 5 of Act No. 459, be restricted to one or more individuals, since that provision generally criminalizes discrimination of non-Danish applicants in job advertisements, thereby protecting everyone of non-Danish

origin against such discrimination. Given the petitioner's specific mandate to assist victims of racial discrimination, the ethnic composition of its board of trustees, as well as its record in representing alleged victims of racial discrimination before the Committee, it should be considered as a victim or as representing an unspecified number of unidentified victims of a violation of section 5 of the Act and, accordingly, of articles 2, 4, 5 and 6 of the Convention. The petitioner concludes that the communication is admissible *ratione personae* under article 14 of the Convention, reiterating that the Chief Constable and the Regional Public Prosecutor recognized it as a party to domestic proceedings (either as a victim or as having a particular interest in the outcome of the case), which was reflected by the fact that its appeal to the Regional Public Prosecutor had not been dismissed on procedural grounds.

5.4 The petitioner submits that it has exhausted all available domestic remedies, in its capacity as petitioner or, respectively, as representative of "a large group of non-identifiable petitioners". The petitioner also argues that the communication is admissible *ratione materiae*, as it does not relate to the legal assessment of the alleged incident, but to the absence of an effective investigation by the Danish authorities, which would have provided an adequate factual basis for such an assessment.

5.5 With regard to the alleged violations of articles 2, 4, 5 and 6 of the Convention, the petitioner similarly bases the claim on the lack of an effective investigation into the matter, rather than on the legal assessment by the Danish authorities. However, it is argued that the Chief Constable would not have reached the conclusion that a Danish resident was sought for the advertised post in Latvia, irrespective of the national or ethnic origin of that person, if he had initiated a formal investigation, rather than merely relying on an informal interview of the accountant of "Torben Jensen A/C", on the report filed by the petitioner and on the wording of the job advertisement. Such an investigation should have clarified who had eventually been recruited for the advertised post, since such clarification would at least have indicated whether an act of discrimination had occurred, and would have provided an adequate basis to determine whether the advertisement constituted indirect discrimination.

*Issues and proceedings before the Committee*

6.1 Before considering the substance of a communication, the Committee on the Elimination of Racial Discrimination must, in accordance with rule 91 of its rules of procedure, examine whether or not the communication is admissible.

6.2 The Committee notes that the communication has been submitted by "the Documentation and Advisory Centre on Racial Discrimination". It further notes that, in its submissions of 18 July 2003, the petitioner clarified that Ms. Fakhra Mohammad, acting as the head of the board of trustees, represented the Documentation and Advisory Centre when initially submitting the communication.

6.3 The Committee takes note of the State party's objection that, as a legal person rather than an individual or a group of individuals, the petitioner is not entitled to submit a communication or to claim victim status under article 14, paragraph 1. It equally notes the petitioner's argument that article 14, paragraph 1, should be interpreted broadly to enable non-governmental organizations to bring a complaint before the Committee, and that it should be considered as a victim of a "violation of articles 2, 4, 5 and 6 of the Convention or, respectively, as representing a large group of unidentified victims", i.e., persons of non-Danish origin who were discriminated against by the job advertisement in question.

6.4 The Committee does not exclude the possibility that a group of persons representing, for example, the interests of a racial or ethnic group, may submit an individual communication, provided that it is able to prove that it has been an alleged victim of a violation of the Convention or that one of its members has been a victim, and if it is able at the same time to provide due authorization to this effect.

6.5 The Committee notes that, according to the petitioner, no member of the board of trustees applied for the job. Moreover, the petitioner has not argued that any of the members of the board, or any other identifiable person whom the petitioner would be authorized to represent, had a genuine interest in, or showed the necessary qualifications for, the vacancy.

6.6 While section 5 of Act No. 459 prohibits discrimination of all persons of non-Danish origin in job advertisements, whether they apply for a vacancy or not, it does not automatically follow that persons not directly and personally affected by such discrimination may claim to be victims of a violation of any of the rights guaranteed in the Convention. Any other conclusion would open the door for popular actions (*actio popularis*) against the relevant legislation of States parties.

6.7 In the absence of any identifiable victims personally affected by the allegedly discriminatory job advertisement, whom the petitioner would be authorized to represent, the Committee concludes that the petitioner has failed to substantiate, for purposes of article 14, paragraph 1, its claim that it constitutes or represents a group of individuals claiming to be the victim of a violation by Denmark of articles 2, paragraph 1 (d), 4, 5 and 6 of the Convention.

7. The Committee on the Elimination of Racial Discrimination therefore decides:

(a) That the communication is inadmissible ratione personae under article 14, paragraph 1, of the Convention.

(b) That this decision shall be communicated to the State party and to the petitioner.

# Communication No. 36/2006*

*Submitted by*: P.S N. (represented by counsel, the Documentation and Advisory Centre on Racial Discrimination).
*Alleged victim*: The petitioner.
*State party*: Denmark.
*Declared inadmissible:* 8 August 2007.
*Subject matter:* Discriminatory statements against Muslims made public by a Member of Parliament; Access to effective mechanism of protection; discrimination based on religious grounds.
*Procedural issues:* Inadmissibility *ratione materiae*.
*Substantive issues:* Right to an effective remedy against acts of racial discrimination; prohibition of disseminating ideas based on racial superiority.
*Articles of the Convention:* 2 (1) (d), 4 (a) and 6.

*See also A.W.R.A.P.* v. *Denmark, communication No. 37/2006, Decision of 8 August 2007.*

## Opinion

1.1 The petitioner is Mr. P.S.N., a Danish citizen born on 11 October 1969 in Pakistan, now residing in Denmark, and a practising Muslim. He alleges a violation by Denmark[1] of articles 2, paragraph 1(d), 4 and 6 of the Convention on the Elimination of All Forms of Racial Discrimination. He is represented by counsel, Miss Line Bøgsted of the Documentary and Advisory Centre on Racial Discrimination (DACoRD).

1.2 In conformity with article 14, paragraph 6 (a), of the Convention, the Committee transmitted the communication to the State party on 23 June 2006.

## Factual background

2.1 In view of the elections of 15 November 2005, Ms. Louise Frevert, Member of Parliament for the Danish People's Party, published on her website statements against immigration and Muslims, under the headline "articles no one dares to publish". These included statements relating to Muslims, such as: "...because they think that we are the ones that should submit to Islam, and they are confirmed in this belief by their preachers and leaders. (...) Whatever happens, they believe that they have a right to rape Danish girls and knock down Danish citizens."

2.2 In the same text, Ms. Frevert mentioned the possibility of deporting young immigrants to Russian prisons, and added:

> "Even this solution is a rather short-term one, however, because when they return again, they will just be even more determined to kill Danes"[2].

[2] The State party provides the context of this statement, by quoting the article: "(...) The law that Islam lays down as the only true law is the law construed on the basis of the words of the Koran and as preached by their preachers during prayers—and the boys have never in their short lives heard any other interpretation. This is the only truth that they know, so no Danish official will ever get a chance of influencing these boys into another direction. As seen by Danish eyes, they are lost to society!
The Danish laws cannot handle these "misguided" young people at all, because they think we are the ones that should submit to Islam, and they are confirmed in this belief every day by their preachers and leaders. The fact that they were born in Denmark and speak Danish does not alter their fundamental attitude—whatever happens, they believe that they have a right to rape Danish girls and cut down Danish citizens indiscriminately. If they are caught and sentenced according to Danish law, it inspires them merely with scorn and contempt—they will just become real martyrs and heroes among their own people, for they have proved that they are the holy warriors who will one day take over the leadership of the ungodly underlings, the Danes. So where is the way forward for Denmark?
We have to consider these young people our opponents at war and not just as disturbed young Danish boys of Muslim background, and opponents

[1] The Convention was ratified by Denmark on 9 December 1971, and the declaration under article 14 made on 11 October 1985.

Another article on the website stated that:

"We can spend billions of Kroner and hours in trying to integrate Muslims into the country, but the result will be what the doctor observes. The cancer spreads without hindrance while we are talking."

2.3 Several of these statements were previously published in a book by Ms. Frevert, under the title "In short—a political statement". In this book, other statements against Muslims read:

"We are hit by our own 'human rights' laws and have to see our culture and governmental system yield to a superior force building on 1000 years of dictatorship, a clerical rule" *(page 36)*.

"The march of events is certainly true. It can be measured. But the Muslim means of achieving the goal of the ongoing third holy war (third Jihad) are secret" *(page 37)*.

2.4 Ms. Frevert later withdrew some of the material from the webpage as a result of the public debate generated by her statements. However, on 30 September 2005, in an interview to the Danish newspaper "Politiken", she upheld the statements. The following extract is from an article entitled "The Danes are overrun":

"(...) (Reporter) *How many are there of those who believe that they have a right to rape Danish girls?*

(Ms. Frevert) I don't know anything about that. It should be seen in consideration of the fact that the Koran says in certain places that you may behave as you like to women in a male chauvinist spirit. It is a

_____

at war must be caught and rendered harmless. Our laws forbid us to kill our opponents officially so we only have the option of filling our prisons with these criminals.
This is an extremely costly solution, and as they will never repent of their acts, they will quickly gain control of the prisons in the same way the outlaw bikers do today. We probably have to think along other lines and, for example, accept a Russian offer of keeping the petty criminals in Russian prisons for DKr 25 per day—that is far cheaper, and their possibilities of influencing their surroundings will be eliminated. Even this solution is a rather short-term one, however, because when they return again, they will just be even more determined to kill Danes. (...)"

rhetorical way of expression relative to the saying of the Koran.

(Reporter) *Are you saying that it is ok according to the Koran to rape Danish girls?*

(Ms. Frevert) I am saying that the Koran allows you to use women as you like.

(Reporter) *How many Danish girls get raped by Muslims?*

(Ms. Frevert) I have no knowledge about that as such, other than that it is very well known that there has been a rape in a toilet by the courthouse. So that is a concrete example. How many I don't know, but you know too from court cases that there have been rapes.

(Reporter) *Yes, but if it more or less appears from the Koran that rape is ok, then one would presumably be able to. bring forth substantially more examples.*

(Ms. Frevert) I am not saying that it is a pattern, I am saying that this is what may happen.

(Reporter) *In the chapter that you have now removed, you wrote that our laws forbid us to kill them. Is that what you would like the most?*

(Ms. Frevert) No, but I am certainly allowed to write it. I am allowed to write exactly whatever suits me. If they rape and kill other people the way they do with suicide bombs, etc.- well, you aren't allowed to do so in our country, are you?"

2.5 On 30 September, 13 October and 1 November 2005, the DACoRD, on the petitioner's behalf, filed three complaints against Ms. Frevert for violations of section 266 (b) of the Danish Criminal code,[3] which prohibits racial statements. In the first complaint, DACoRD claimed that the website statements were directed against a specific group of people (Muslims), that they were taunting and degrading, and that they had a

_____

[3] "**Section 266 (b)**.
(1) Any person who, publicly or with the intention of wider dissemination, makes a statement or imparts other information by which a group of people are threatened, insulted or degraded on account of their race, colour, national or ethnic origin, religion, or sexual inclination shall be liable to a fine or to imprisonment for any term not exceeding two years.
(2) When the sentence is meted out, the fact that the offence is in the nature of propaganda activities shall be considered an aggravating circumstance."

propagandistic character, as they were published on a website directed at a large audience, and at the same time sent to various Danish newspapers for purposes of publication. The DACoRD quoted several decisions of conviction by Danish courts for statements published on websites, which were considered as "dissemination to a wide circle of people". The second complaint related to Ms. Frevert's book, in particular pages 31 to 41, which the petitioner claimed contained threatening, taunting and degrading statements against Muslims. The third complaint related to the article published in the "Politiken". DACoRD claimed that the statements in the article violated section 266 (b) of the Criminal Code and that they confirmed the statements published on the website.

2.6 The first complaint (relating to the website) against Ms. Frevert was rejected by the Copenhagen Police on 10 October 2005, on the ground that there was no reasonable evidence to support that an unlawful act had been committed. In particular, the decision pointed out that it did not appear, with the necessary reasonable prospect for a conviction, that Ms. Frevert had the intent to disseminate the listed quotations, and that it appeared that she was unaware that those statements had been posted on the web. The webmaster (Mr. T.) took entire responsibility for the publication of the statements and was charged with violation of section 266 (b) of the Criminal Code. On 30 December 2005, the Copenhagen Police forwarded the case file to the Helsingør Police for further investigation of the case against him. The case is still under investigation by the Helsingør Police.

2.7 On 13 December 2005, the Regional Public Prosecutor of Copenhagen, Frederiksberg and Tårnby confirmed the decision of the police not to prosecute Ms. Frevert, because she and Mr. T. had concurrently explained their collaboration and that the articles had by mistake been posted unedited on the website. He found that it could not be proved that Ms. Frevert had any knowledge that the articles were put on her website and that she had the necessary intent to disseminate them. This decision cannot be appealed.

2.8 The second complaint (relating to the book) was rejected by the Commissioner of the Copenhagen Police on 18 October 2005, as there was no reasonable evidence to support that an unlawful act had been committed. The decision indicated that the book had been published for the purpose of a political debate and did not contain specific statements which could be covered under the Criminal code section 266 (b). The DACoRD did not appeal the Commissioner's decision.

2.9 The third complaint (relating to the interview) was rejected by the Commissioner of the Copenhagen Police on 9 February 2006, as there was no reasonable evidence to support that an unlawful act had been committed. In reaching this decision, the Commissioner took into consideration the principles of freedom of expression and free debate. He also took into account that the statements were made by a politician in the context of a public debate on the situation of foreigners. He considered that in light of the right of freedom of expression, the statements made by Ms. Frevert were not offensive enough to constitute a violation of section 266 (b) of the Criminal Code.

2.10 On 19 May 2006, the Regional Public Prosecutor confirmed the police's decision not to prosecute Ms. Frevert for the statements in the interview. He considered that the representation of Muslims and second generation immigrants by Ms. Frevert in the interview was not so offensive as to be considered insulting or degrading to Muslims or second-generation immigrants within the meaning of section 266 (b) of the Criminal Code. This decision is final and cannot be appealed.

2.11 The petitioner argues that questions relating to the pursuance by the police of charges against individuals are entirely discretionary, and that there is no possibility to bring the case before Danish courts. Legal actions against Ms. Frevert would not be effective, given that the police and prosecutor have rejected the complaints against her. The petitioner refers to a decision of the Eastern High Court of 5 February 1999, where it was held that an incident of racial discrimination does not in itself imply a violation of the honour and reputation of a person under section 26 of the Act in Civil Liability.[4] The petitioner concludes that he has no further remedies under national law.

2.12 The petitioner indicates that he has not availed himself of any other procedure of international investigation or settlement.

---

[4] See *B.J.* v. *Denmark*, paras. 2.4 to 2.6.

*The complaint*

3.1 The petitioner claims that the decision of the Copenhagen police no to initiate an investigation on the alleged facts, violates articles 2, paragraph 1 (d); 4 (a); and 6 of the Convention, as the documentation presented by the petitioner should have motivated the police to make a thorough investigation of the matter. He contends that there have been no effective means to protect him from racist statements in this case.

3.2 The petitioner further claims that the decisions of the Copenhagen police and the prosecutor to reject his complaints violate article 6 of the Convention. He contends that the Danish authorities did not examine the material in full and did not take his arguments into account.

*State party's observations on the admissibility and merits of the communication*

4.1 On 10 November 2006, the State party made its submissions on the admissibility and merits of the communication. On admissibility, it submits that the claims fall outside the scope of the Convention and that the petitioner failed to establish a prima facie case for purposes of admissibility, as a large number of the various statements comprised by the communication concerns persons of a particular religion and not persons of a particular "race, colour, descent, or national or ethnic origin" within the meaning of article 1 of the Convention. However, the State party acknowledges that it is possible to argue to a certain extent that the statements refer to second-generation immigrants and set up a conflict between "the Danes" and them, thereby falling to some degree within the scope of the Convention.

4.2 The State party further submits that the part of the communication relating to the statements in Ms. Frevert's book is inadmissible under article 14, paragraph 7 (a), of the Convention, as the petitioner has not exhausted all available domestic remedies. When the Commissioner of the Copenhagen Police decided, on 18 October 2005, to discontinue investigation of the case against Ms. Frevert in relation to the publication of her book, the petitioner did not appeal the decision to the Regional Public Prosecutor. Thus, he has failed to exhaust domestic remedies, and the part of the communication concerning the statements in the book should be declared inadmissible.

4.3 On the merits, the State party disputes that there was a violation of articles 2, paragraph 1 (d), 4 and 6 of the Convention. On the claim that the documentation presented to the police should have motivated it to initiate a thorough investigation of the matter, the State party argues that the Danish authorities' evaluation of the petitioner's reports of alleged racial discrimination fully satisfies the requirements of the Convention, even though they did not produce the outcome wanted by the petitioner. The Convention does not guarantee a specific outcome of cases on alleged racially insulting statements, but sets out certain requirements for the authorities' investigation of such alleged statements. The State party argues that these requirements have been satisfied in the case, as the Danish authorities *did* take effective action, by processing and investigating the reports lodged by the petitioner.

*Ms. Frevert's website*

4.4 The State party indicates that under section 749 (2) of the Administration and Justice Act,[5] the police may discontinue an investigation already initiated when there is no basis for continuing the investigation. In criminal proceedings, the prosecutor has the burden of proof that a criminal offence was committed. It is important for the sake of due process that the evidence is of certain strength for the courts to convict an accused. Pursuant to section 96 (2) of the Administration of Justice Act,[6] public prosecutors have a duty to observe the principle of objectiveness. They

---

[5] **"Section 749**.
(1) The police shall dismiss a report lodged if it deems that there is no basis for initiating investigation.
(2) If there is no basis for continuing an investigation already initiated, the police may decide to discontinue the investigation if no charge has been made (...).
(3) If the report is dismissed or the investigation is discontinued, those who may be presumed to have a reasonable interest therein shall be notified. The decision can be appealed to the superior public prosecutor under the rules of Part 10."
[6] **"Section 96**.
(1) It is the duty of the public prosecutors, in cooperation with the police, to prosecute offences according to the rules of this Act.
(2) The public prosecutors shall dispatch any one case at the speed permitted by the nature of the case, and shall thus ensure not only that guilty persons are held responsible, but also that prosecution of innocent persons does not occur."

cannot prosecute a person unless they are of the opinion that the prosecution will lead to conviction with a reasonable prospect of certainty. This principle is designed to protect innocent persons from prosecution.

4.5 The State party is aware that it has a duty to initiate an investigation when complaints related to acts of racial discrimination are filed. An investigation must be carried out with due diligence and expeditiously, and must be sufficient to determine whether or not an act of racial discrimination has occurred.

4.6 The State party points out that upon receipt of the complaint regarding Ms. Frevert's website, the Copenhagen Police initiated an investigation of the case. When interviewed, both Ms. Frevert and Mr. T. stated that the webmaster had created the website and that he had uploaded the relevant material without Ms. Frevert's knowledge. The agreement was that only articles and contributions approved by Ms. Frevert were to be posted on the website. By mistake, 35 articles by Mr. T. were posted on the website in unedited form and without Ms. Frevert's prior approval. When the mistake was discovered, the articles were removed. The webmaster was charged with violation of section 266 (b) of the Criminal Code.

4.7 The State party contends that the police investigated the matter thoroughly. Once it appeared that the articles were posted without Ms. Frevert's knowledge, the public prosecutors rightly assessed that it would not be possible to prove that she had intended a wide dissemination of the statements. Criminal proceedings could therefore not be expected to result in her conviction and the public prosecutors therefore decided not to prosecute her. That the investigation against Mr. T. remains pending shows that the police takes reported acts of racial discrimination seriously and investigates them thoroughly and effectively. The State party argues that the police made a thorough investigation of the matter, that the material was examined in full and that the arguments presented by the DACoRD were taken into consideration, in accordance with article 6 of the Convention. The investigation revealed Ms. Frevert's lack of intent to violate section 266 (b) of the Criminal Code. The fact that the case had another outcome than wished by the petitioner is irrelevant.

*Ms. Frevert's book*

4.8 Under section 749 (1)[7] and section 742 (2)[8] of the Administration and Justice Act, the public prosecutor must assess whether a criminal offence subject to public prosecution was committed. If there is no basis for assuming that a criminal offence has been committed, the public prosecutor has to dismiss the report. The Commissioner of the Copenhagen Police discontinued the investigation concerning the book as it had been published for the purpose of generating a political debate, and as it contained no specific statements that might fall under section 266 (b) of the Criminal Code. In addition, the DACoRD did not mention in its report which statements it considered to fall within the scope of that provision.

4.9 The State party emphasizes that there were no problems of evidence and no need for the police to continue the investigation, as the police was in possession of the book in question, and both Ms. Frevert and Mr. T. were interviewed on this matter. Both stated that the disputed contribution to the book was written by Mr. T., but that this contribution had been edited and approved by Ms. Frevert, who was responsible for the publication of the book. The only question left for the Police Commissioner was whether there were statements in the book that could be considered to fall within the scope of section 266 (b) of the Criminal Code. After a thorough analysis of the book's contents, he considered that the statements were broad and clearly published as part of a political debate in anticipation of the upcoming election. This legal assessment was thorough and adequate, and the public prosecutor's handling of the case satisfied the requirements that can be inferred from article 2, paragraph 1 (d), and article 6 of the Convention.

*Statements made by Ms. Frevert in the newspaper "Politiken" on 30 September 2005*

4.10 The State party recalls that it does not follow from the Convention and the jurisprudence of the Committee that prosecution should be initiated in *all* cases

---

[7] See footnote 5 above.
[8] "Section 742.
(1) Criminal offences must be reported to the police.
(2) The police shall institute investigations upon a report lodged or on its own initiative when it may reasonably be presumed that a criminal offence subject to prosecution has been committed."

reported to the police, in particular if no basis is found for prosecution. In this case, there were no problems of evidence, as the statements were printed in the newspaper as quotations of Ms. Frevert, and therefore there was no need for the police to initiate an investigation to identify the specific contents or the originator of the statements.

4.11 The State party argues that the legal assessment made by the public prosecutors was thorough and adequate. They evaluated the statements in the light of the fact that they were made by a politician in the context of a political debate about religion and immigrants, and balancing the protection of the right to freedom of expression, protection of the freedom of religion and protection against racial discrimination. The statements must be seen in the context in which they were made, namely as contributions to a political debate about religion and immigrants, and without regard as to whether the reader supports Ms. Frevert's viewpoint on these issues. A democratic society has to make room for a debate about such viewpoints, within certain limits. The prosecutors considered that the statements were not so gross that they could be deemed "insulting or degrading" within the meaning of section 266 (b) of the Criminal Code.

4.12 The State party argues that the right to freedom of expression is particularly imperative for an elected representative of the people. She represents her electorate, draws attention to their preoccupations and defends their interests. Accordingly, interferences with the freedom of expression of a Member of Parliament, like Ms. Frevert, call for close scrutiny on the part of public prosecutors. In this case, they interpreted section 266 (b) in the light of the context in which the statements were made and with due consideration of the fundamental principle of the right to freedom of expression for a Member of Parliament. The State party concludes that the public prosecutors' handling of the case satisfies the requirements that can be inferred from article 2, paragraph 1 (d), and article 6 of the Convention.

4.13 The State party concludes that it is not possible to infer an obligation under the Convention to prosecute in situations that have been found not to provide a basis for prosecution. The Administration of Justice Act offers the requisite remedies compatible with the Convention and the relevant authorities have fully met their obligations in this case.

*Petitioner's comments*

5.1 On 29 December 2006, the petitioner commented on the State party's submissions. On the argument that domestic remedies were not exhausted with regards to the complaint about Ms. Frevert's book, it is submitted that the text of the book was also published on her website. The report to the police was meant to cover the whole website, not only the articles under the heading "Articles that nobody dares to publish". When she was interviewed about the website, the police failed to ask her if she was the author of the book, which had been posted as a document on the website. The police apparently based its decision on a very small part of the material placed on the website.

5.2 The petitioner acknowledges that no appeal was filed against the decision of 18 October 2005 of the Copenhagen Police to discontinue the investigation of the case in relation to the book. However, the day before, a complaint was filed against the website, which included the text of the book. Consequently, an appeal of that decision would only have been a duplication of the complaint already sent to the regional prosecutor's office. Therefore, the final decision by the Regional Prosecutor of 13 December 2005 is a final decision both regarding the statements posted on the website and contained in the book. The petitioner therefore considers that he exhausted domestic remedies in respect of all parts of the complaint.

5.3 With respect to the argument that the communication falls outside the scope of the Convention, the petitioner contends that Islamophobia, just like attacks against Jews, has manifested itself as a form of racism in many European countries, including Denmark. After 11 September 2001, attacks against Muslims have intensified in Denmark. Members of the Danish People's Party use hate speech as a tool to stir up hatred against people of Arab and Muslim background. In their view, culture and religion are connected in Islam. The petitioner argues that [the Committee] already concluded that Danish authorities do not ensure an effective implementation of criminal law in relation to hate speech against Muslims and Muslim culture, especially by politicians. He invokes [the Committee]'s 2002 concluding observations on Denmark:[9]

---

[9] CERD/C/60/CO/5 and CERD/C/CO/DEN/17.

["16.] The Committee is concerned about reports of a considerable increase in reported cases of widespread harassment of people of Arab and **Muslim** backgrounds since 11 September 2001. The Committee recommends that the State party monitor this situation carefully, take decisive action to protect the rights of victims and deal with perpetrators, and report on this matter in its next periodic report".

["11.] The Committee, while taking note of the State party's efforts to combat hate crimes, is concerned about the increase in the number of racially motivated offences and in the number of complaints of hate speech. The Committee is also concerned about **hate speech by some politicians in Denmark**. While taking note of the statistical data provided on complaints and prosecutions launched under section 266 (b) of the Criminal Code, the Committee notes the refusal by the Public Prosecutor to initiate court proceedings in some cases, including the case of the publication of **some cartoons associating Islam with terrorism** (arts. 4 (a) and 6)" (emphasis added).

5.4   On the merits, the petitioner refers to the fact that Ms. Frevert was not found responsible for the material on the website. However, in the interview, the journalist quoted the article and asked her "Are you saying that it is ok according to the Koran to rape Danish girls?" She replied: "I am saying that the Koran allows you to use women as you like". The journalist gave her the possibility to disagree, but she stated that "I am certainly allowed to write that. I am allowed to write exactly whatever suits me. If they rape and kill other people the way they do...". The petitioner considers that these statements are insulting and that the Danish Courts should strike the balance between the right to freedom of speech for politicians and the prohibition against hate speech. By not bringing the case to court, the authorities violated articles 2, 4 and 6 of the Convention.

*Issues and proceedings before the Committee*

6.1   Before considering any claims contained in a petition, the Committee on the Elimination of Racial Discrimination must, in accordance with rule 91 of its rules of procedure, decide whether or not it is admissible under the Convention.

6.2   The Committee notes the State party's objection that the petitioner's claims fall outside the scope of the Convention, because the statements in question are directed at persons of a particular religion or religious group, and not at persons of a particular "race, colour, descent, or national or ethnic origin". It also takes note of the petitioner's contention that the statements in question were indeed aimed at persons of Muslim or Arab background. The Committee observes, however, that the impugned statements specifically refer to the Koran, to Islam and to Muslims in general, without any reference whatsoever to any race, colour, descent, or national or ethnic origin. While the elements of the case file do not allow the Committee to analyse and ascertain the intention of the impugned statements, it remains that no specific national or ethnic groups were directly targeted as such by these oral statements as reported and printed. In fact, the Committee notes that the Muslims currently living in the State party are of heterogeneous origin. They originate from at least 15 different countries, are of diverse national and ethnic origins, and consist of non-citizens, and Danish citizens, including Danish converts.

6.3   The Committee recognizes the importance of the interface between race and religion and considers that it would be competent to consider a claim of "double" discrimination on the basis of religion and another ground specifically provided for in article 1 of the Convention, including national or ethnic origin. However, this is not the case in the current petition, which exclusively relates to discrimination on religious grounds. The Committee recalls that the Convention does not cover discrimination based on religion alone, and that Islam is not a religion practised solely by a particular group, which could otherwise be identified by its "race, colour, descent, or national or ethnic origin." The *travaux préparatoires* of the Convention reveal that the Third Committee of the General Assembly rejected the proposal to include racial discrimination and religious intolerance in a single instrument, and decided in the [Convention] to focus exclusively on racial discrimination.[10] It is unquestionable therefore that discrimination based exclusively on religious grounds was not intended to fall within the purview of the Convention.

---

[10] General Assembly resolutions 1779 (XVII), 1780 (XVII) and 1781 (XVII).

6.4 The Committee recalls its prior jurisprudence in *Quereshi* v. *Denmark* that, "a general reference to foreigners does not at present single out a group of persons, contrary to article 1 of the Convention, on the basis of a specific race, ethnicity, colour, descent or national or ethnic origin".[11] Similarly, in this particular case, it considers that the general references to Muslims, do not single out a particular group of persons, contrary to article 1 of the Convention. It, therefore, concludes that the petition falls outside the scope of the Convention and declares it inadmissible *ratione materiae* under article 14, paragraph 1, of the Convention.

6.5 Although the Committee considers that it is not within its competence to examine the present petition, it takes note of the offensive nature of the statements complained of and recalls that freedom of speech carries with it both duties and responsibilities. It takes the opportunity to remind the State party of its concluding observations, following consideration of the State party's reports in 2002 and 2006, in which it had commented and made recommendations upon: (a) the considerable increase in reported cases of widespread harassment of people of Arab and Muslim backgrounds since 11 September 2001; (b) the increase in the number of racially motivated offences; and (c) the increase in the number of complaints of hate speech, including by politicians within the State party.[12] It also encourages the State party to follow up on its recommendations and to provide pertinent information on the above concerns in the context of the Committee's procedure for follow-up to its concluding observations.

7. The Committee on the Elimination of Racial Discrimination therefore decides:

(a) That the communication is inadmissible *ratione materiae* under article 14, paragraph 1, of the Convention;

(b) That this decision shall be communicated to the State party and to the petitioner.

---

[11] See communication No. 33/2003, para. 7.3.

[12] CERD/C/60/CO/5 and CERD/C/DEN/CO/17.

# INDEXES

## Index by article of the Convention

# Subject index

# Author and victim index